The Sounder Few

Yet some there were, among the sounder few
Of those who less presum'd, and better knew,
Who durst assert the juster ancient cause,
And here restor'd wit's fundamental laws.

Alexander Pope, *Essay on Criticism*

The Sounder Few

Essays from the *Hollins Critic*

Edited by R.H.W. Dillard,
George Garrett, and John Rees Moore

University of Georgia Press
Athens

The editors, contributors, and publisher acknowledge permission to quote passages from the following copyrighted material:

The Quarry by Richard Eberhart. Copyright © 1964 by Richard Eberhart. Reprinted by permission of Oxford University Press, Inc.

The Old Glory and *Near the Ocean* by Robert Lowell. Copyright 1965, 1967 by Robert Lowell. Reprinted by permission of Farrar, Straus & Giroux, Inc.

The Collected Poems of Louis MacNeice, edited by E. R. Dodds. Copyright © The Estate of Louis MacNeice 1966. Reprinted by permission of Oxford University Press, Inc.

"Slaughterhouse-Five" by Robert Scholes. © 1969 by The New York Times Company. Reprinted by permission of the author and the publisher.

Library of Congress Catalogue Card Number: 77-129467
International Standard Book Number: 8203-0262-7

The University of Georgia Press, Athens 30601

Printed in the United States of America.

For Louis D. Rubin, Jr.

Special Acknowledgments

These essays are presented in the chronological sequence of their original publication.

The afterwords were written during 1969 and revised so as to be as nearly up to date as possible. Where there are no afterwords it is because there have been no new works published by the author since his work was discussed in the *Critic*. Checklists and biographical notes have been revised and brought up to date.

The original checklists and biographical notes were prepared by Cornelia Magill Whittet, Anne Bowles Bradford, Lucinda Clay Hardwick, Elizabeth Tunstall Collins, Mildred Blair Burns, and Christine Costigan.

Special editorial assistance for this volume was rendered by David R. Huddle, John Carr, and Louise LaValle Simms. The editors are grateful for the assistance of these young writers and especially record a debt of gratitude to Mrs. Faye Ivanhoe who has served as secretary for the *Critic* since the beginning.

JRM, RHWD, GG

Hollins College

Contents

Introduction

The Hollins Critic was conceived not to fulfill a dire need for one more periodical devoted to the literary scene, but as a modest experiment in a new form of literary journalism. Would it work to invite a critic to have his say at fairly generous length—in an essay of between five and six thousand words—about a writer who had done enough to establish his claim on the interest of readers who cared about the state of literature and yet whose reputation was far from settled? The aim would be to look at the writer's work to date and do something more than merely offer a review of his books and something less than deliver a verdict on his "place" in literary history. The readers we hoped for would be knowledgeable about books but not necessarily professionally concerned with literature. We have permitted ourselves a decent latitude in selecting subjects for the essays, sometimes (as in the case of Nabokov, for instance) taking authors whose fame is already great but occasionally introducing relatively unknown writers who seemed to the editors of more than passing interest.

It is true that living and working writers receive considerable attention in the newspapers, magazines, critical journals, and other reviewing media. Yet it is the nature of things that even honored and acknowledged masters must usually receive brisk treatment. Younger writers and writers who are less established are given short shrift and are lucky to get that. For the bestselling writers the machinery of promotion overcomes the limitations of the printing press, and, indeed, extensive promotion can render most criticism irrelevant. But the serious writer is urgently dependent upon critical notice and reception of his work if its very existence is to be known to readers. Meanwhile the major quarterlies and the literary magazines devoted to serious writing have been forced to develop their own awkward habit of survival —the omnibus review dealing with many separate works at once and usually months behind the brute facts, the brief life of a book in the literary marketplace. From the beginning, then, the *Critic* has been the only critical journal in this country which is devoted to a full-length essay review of a recent work by a living author. The difficult choices of what to review are made by the contributing editors themselves, and even though many worthy and important works have not been treated in the *Critic,* the list of those chosen by the contributors is distinguished and various enough to be decently representative of our times.

Besides this central essay in each issue, we have included a brief note on the writer who is the subject of the essay and a checklist of his work, a picture of the author done by our artist, Lewis O. Thompson, and one or more poems. A good deal to fit into a periodical that usually runs twelve pages! The response to our effort has been very encouraging, however. We have the impression that most of our subscribers actually read everything in each issue, an impossible task for a reader when confronted with most of the journals that come his way these days. Many of the writers we have taken up are controversial figures, and our critics have entered into the controversy with zest, but we have gained by not being obliged to deliver instant judgment on new books. And in this anthology from the *Critic* we have asked our contributors to add brief reconsiderations or new thoughts about their essays if they wished to, but we have not allowed them to change one word of the essays themselves. They can, if they want, repent of their original sins but not wipe them out.

The informal afterwords offered with most of the essays included here illustrate another point quite simply. As writers change and grow, so do critics. Criticism is, or should be, alive. So long as it is alive, it is not fixed and frozen, but happening. The afterwords demonstrate this by the example of critics whose chief concern is not with what they have thought and have written, but is with the here and now and with the future. It is in this sense that the critic may justly claim to share something of the energy of creation.

Credit for the conception of the *Critic* belongs to the first editor, Louis D. Rubin, Jr., whose restless mind had been casting about ever since he came to Hollins for a feasible way of expressing his editorial talents and giving the college a distinctive literary organ. In the little over six years of its existence the *Critic* has published essays on more than twenty-five contemporary novelists and poets. We have been encouraged to believe that republishing a selection of these essays in a more permanent form is a worthwhile enterprise. Our gratitude to Hollins College, and especially to President John A. Logan, Jr., who has encouraged the *Critic* from its inception and been unwavering in his support ever since, is a pleasure to acknowledge.

It is the hope of the editors that the *Hollins Critic* will continue to grow and change with and in the times. This collection in book form is a selective backward look at six years, made more present than historical by the afterwords of the critics. But the implicit purpose of presenting the collection is more than a salute to and a record of the recent past. It is also directed towards the future, in sure anticipation of the poetry and fiction which will come to us, each work of art being a new thing in Creation and thus changing everything, from writers known and unknown. Hope is the common currency of the future, but, like faith, it can be spent only in advance, in the present. It is in the present, then, that we offer these essays, hoping that they may lead readers to an increased awareness of some of the riches of our own times, trusting that they may serve as a modest preparation for new works in the days to come.

The Sounder Few

Hard Times and the Noble Savage: J.P. Donleavy's *A Singular Man*

by John Rees Moore

Mr. J.P. Donleavy's new hero for our time is George Smith, the lonely rich man who must disguise himself a thousand ways to save himself from the world and simultaneously assure himself that he is no abstraction but real. "Feel me," his ego seems to cry, "I'm flesh and blood like you. And besides I like to have people feel me. My rod of life can be proved to be extraordinary. Measure it and see. I have nothing to lose but my armor. But every time I take it off I risk a mortal wound." In his second full-length novel, *A Singular Man,* Donleavy has created a madman's world so that his madcap hero may appear sane. Smith's trick is to conform outwardly to the world's (his world's) idea of respectability while all within is turmoil, a chaos of violent alternations between hope and despair. Yet when occasion offers he lets the real Smith peep out, a combination of merry satyr and hurt small boy. Only in moments of physical love does he find blessed relief from the impossible task of steering a proper course between "good and evil."

Evil is letting anyone get the better of you; good is suffering the consequences of evil. Mortality is for those birds who can stand it. George Smith can't.

He invents a life for himself. He is a business executive without a business, but he has an office and a secretary. His "business" correspondence consists of exchanging in an oblique code language veiled threats with a competitor or competitors. At home in Merry Mansions, a kind of black earth-mother, Matilda, looks after his domestic comfort, offering herself as solace when occasion arises. George Smith presents himself to women as an innocent needing care and protection, though he also keeps them guessing. And indeed he turns out to be a wily and resolute seducer, all the more effective because he combines in such unpredictable proportions a cool detachment and a desperate need. He is a "professional" human being who remembers all too well the perils of being an amateur.

In Ireland he had been a member of an old world civilization, however tenuously. And his old brother-in-arms, a certain Bonniface, pursues him to New York. George Smith does not want to meet his old friend; he spends most of the book successfully avoiding his pursuer. Bonniface wants money, of course, but money is only a symbol of something deeper: he wants to drag George Smith back into humanity. For George has become a devotee of death. He is building himself a mausoleum that will cover an acre of ground; and it will not be God's little acre but George Smith's. This project when complete will allow George Smith to "retire"—retire from the human race altogether if he finds that necessary.

Meanwhile George Smith rides around in a limousine equipped with wireless-telephone and bullet-proof glass tinted blue so that he can see out but nobody can see in. On one occasion, abandoning his limousine, he takes a lady for a ride in one of those old horse-drawn cabs that hang around Central Park. He is set upon by a gang of teenagers and escapes only by being tougher and more cunning than they are. George wants to make life a ride in a human-proof limousine; certain necessities require that he get out. He is half way between being a man in society, with a wife and four children—the quintessence of the bourgeois—and being an "angel" who has transcended the embarrassments of flesh and blood. In the end he fails: love for another human being drags him back into involvement in the human race. Not that this is a happy ending. Sally Tomson is killed in a car accident and George Smith is praying for her on the boat which carries her remains to a burial at sea. He has found it impossible to exist half slave and half free, and impossible to exist any other way, either.

To create a singular man is the task the author has set for himself and for his chief character. Mr. Donleavy tries to create a world for his hero that will be recognizable to the reader, yet startling too. The sad and the sweet are magnified, juxtaposed, polarized; then a flash of current lights up the desert that lies between. The landscape revealed is full of ordinary shapes, but the light on their surfaces is harsh and they cast grotesque shadows. The atmosphere is heavy with doom and every contact between people and things is potentially dangerous. At least so it seems to George Smith. Is he alone in wanting to protect his singularity? Everyone he meets conspires to commit him to something outside himself, to make him a party to something he does not want to be part of. We are left to determine whether George Smith is a kind of Everyman fighting for his "democratic right" to safeguard his unique soul in a world determined to wrest it from him, or whether he is a kind of lunatic eccentric who has merely created a world in his own image. These are the alternatives of the book's imaginative logic: George Smith is sane and the world is crazy, or the world is sane and George Smith is crazy.

The hero, though singular enough, fails to keep his singularity intact. Does Mr. Donleavy fail to create in his hero an effectively singular man? His success is peculiarly difficult to judge because he has made George Smith at once so abstract and so eccentric. The humor of the book is original to the point of privacy; the wit is both a method and an evasion. We are never allowed to know enough about George Smith to say whether or not he *has* a soul to call his own. The irony of the book is directed at George Smith as well as at the world; nor do the reader and the author escape. If we play along with the jokes we become hypocritical brothers of the author and are committed, while we are readers anyway, to seeing life as The Big Joke. The most pitiful, horrifying, unjust, cruel, and irrational experiences are grist to the mill; all food for laughter. True, there is a saying about laughing to keep from crying. Better, perhaps, to die laughing than to live crying. At any rate, the author is unwilling to risk descending from farce to comedy, from the antics of clowns (who know) and fools (who don't know) how funny they are to the follies of men who come, even though incompletely, to understand and accept themselves. Mr. Donleavy's humor is a bulwark against the inroads of a too inquiring sense *or* sensibility.

That may be his point, of course. Identification with another, he may be saying, is not only an invasion of the other's singularity, not only an enterprise doomed to failure, but also a contemptible hoax. It is later than you think; we have become a horde of windowless monads performing a dance through space-time according to a Reason whereof we know nothing, not even if it exists. Faith once set in motion a drift which carries us along by inertia; how long we will continue our now aimless cavortings depends on the existence of counter-force which we can neither assume nor predict. But Mr. Donleavy, unlike his French contemporaries, is resolutely unmetaphysical. In fact, he refuses any "explanation"—psychological, ethical, philosophical, or religious.

In another country and more youthful time, Sebastian Dangerfield, hero of Mr. Donleavy's first novel, *The Ginger Man,* romped his despairing way from the married unbliss of a house on Howth rock overlooking Balsacaddoon Bay to the unmarried bliss of a fancy London apartment—at least he is on his way there as *The Ginger Man* ends. Sebastian's problem is that he wants to be both lion and lamb, the roaring playboy of the western world smashing his way to salvation, and an innocent Adam returning to the primeval purity of sinless sexual fulfillment with his Eve. The world is too much with Sebastian; constantly wounded, like his saintly namesake, by the arrows of outrageous fortune, he is always looking for an Irene to bind up his wounds.

Back from the wars to marry an English wife, Sebastian has entered Trinity College in Dublin to study law and support himself, his wife, and his baby on the G.I. Bill. He is living on booze and great expectations. His one-eyed friend Kenneth O'Keefe, a fellow American also on the G.I. Bill, pays a visit while Marion and the child are away with her parents in Scotland. O'Keefe, a classics major from Harvard, obsessed with longings for the pagan days he has read about but never succeeded in experiencing, expounds the travails of his virginity while expertly preparing the chicken Sebastian has procured (along with Cork Gin, Haig and Haig, a whole ham, and cheese) from an innocent Irish shopkeeper so impressed by his gentlemanly accent and appearance that he has eagerly opened an account for Sebastian, to be billed quarterly. Sebastian's motto is live now, pay later, but both he and his one-eyed friend are haunted by visions of failure. Their whole way of living is a preparation for death and takes whatever dignity it has from that fact. The indignity comes from the meanness of spirit they are sometimes reduced to.

In the midst of chaotic squalor Sebastian insists on a certain decorum in the conduct of his life. Marion's complaints about unpaid bills, about his idleness, irresponsibility, and drunkenness drive him to destructive frenzy; he smashes lamps, chairs, dishes; he smashes Marion and is ready to smother his baby with a pillow. His book of etiquette is modeled not on the House Beautiful but on Sporting Life. Sebastian refuses to allow anyone else to substitute his or her idea of him for his own idea of himself: a man in continuous flight from the devils of Chastity (married), Poverty, and Obedience (to all negative commandments, profane and sacred). Nevertheless, he consistently sticks to his blue-blooded code of aristocratic mastery. No one will get the better of *him.* Despite the unjust conditions the world imposes, he will live as a lord, not a slave, of life. For money he will substitute cunning, for security violence, for social stability erotic communion.

Not in a stable, but in a dark, damp coal and turf shed, Sebastian discovers the virgin (?) Mary who may redeem him. He had met her in one of the underground wine cellars where the Dublin *cognoscenti* gather without having to worry about closing time. She had led him to her house. Her mother dead, she takes care of her father and younger brothers. And her father beats her, for no reason at all. But now she is strong enough so that he can no longer really manage her. Yet she lives in terror of him; moreover, she has a strong sense of responsibility for her younger brothers. Faith in her love for Sebastian overcomes all obstacles; she knows he is married but she does not care; she will follow him anywhere and put her life in his hands. As long as they can be free with each other's bodies. He tells her to write to him using another name.

> ". . . I want you to use Percivil Buttermere. The spelling's important. P-E-R-C-I-V-I-L B-U-T-T-E-R-M-E-R-E."
> "This is fun."
> "This, Mary, is a matter of playing who lives the longest."
> "You're sweet. And we will have a room together and you'll do all of it? Will we?"
> "We will."
> "I don't care if we die."
> "Don't say that. Give God ideas. We must discourage that attitude. Just put three bottles in some paper."

And Mary comes through. She sends money (which Sebastian promptly spends) and soon after turns up in London, pleased but almost surprised that Sebastian actually meets her at the station. Everything is as it should be for a couple of weeks and then Mary leaves. Sebastian has brutally asserted his theory that women must realize man is the master of woman. Meanwhile an old friend has come into money and hands it out freely to Sebastian, compensating him for the trick his father has played on him: dying and leaving an annuity of six thousand—to begin twenty years hence when Sebastian is forty-seven. And also meanwhile Mary has landed a movie contract. In a knock-down-drag-out scene Sebastian establishes his right of eminent domain over Mary and then magnanimously confesses his own worthlessness. They are reconciled and Sebastian indulges in a little sentiment.

> "Mary, you're beside me now. And I want to ride on the train to Dublin, along the cliffs and through the tunnels to Bray. When it's raining. You've got tiny ears. . . I'll buy a little mower to take outside to the lawn and give it a fast trim every Friday. Not much of a lawn because I don't want to overdo this exercise. Ten by ten. We'll have a small sitting room with plants one of which will be a rubber plant. And during tea on gray afternoons I want you to read me stories of adventure."
> "Why aren't you like this more often, cuddly and cozy and things?"

Sebastian is not often that way—though more often than Mary realizes—because Sebastian's way and the way of the world are so infrequently, and then only fleetingly, congruent. The verve of the book comes from the bouncy rhythm: Sebastian never comes to rest in a routine; he ascends from one situation and descends with a *pock* into the next. The man with the racket is always in full cry, but this ball has a life of its own and bounces, apparently, wherever it will. The ginger man creates his own game as he goes and stoutly refuses to be anybody's tennis ball. He is successful with women because they sense under his witty bravado and sinister destructiveness a whole-hearted commitment to bodily pleasures—and in spite of his swagger a surprising tact and tenderness in offering himself for their pleasure. Men like him for the daring resourcefulness of his imagination; when he's around it's impossible to feel, no matter how desperate the situation (and most of his friends live lives of noisy desperation), that things are as bad as they seem. Yet the gaiety is always ironic. All their lives are fragmentary, full of uncompleted gestures and unrealized potentialities. The exhilaration of Youth making common cause against the Enemy is offset by the nerve-wracking suspense of waiting for the next blow to fall.

The Ginger Man was first published in Paris in 1955, then in a revised edition the next year in England. This edition came out in hardback in the United States in 1958 and in paperback the following year. In 1963 the complete and unexpurgated edition appeared in paperback in England. An extra chapter in the full version, about Sebastian's horrible experience riding a suburban Dublin train with everyone acting very oddly toward him because he has inadvertently left his fly open, gives fuller motivation to Sebastian's exasperated quarrel with Marion in the next chapter and is hilarious in itself, but it is not a vital omission. In other places fuller explanations of various sexual experiences make clearer what was vague before, but again they do not add anything either very essential or even very shocking—except to those who would find most of the book shocking.

Which brings us to the issue of pornography. If to succeed in writing exciting descriptions of sexual encounters is pornographic, Mr. Donleavy has surely succeeded. But this is a matter of art, not of clinical frankness and accuracy. Mr. Donleavy's art consists of giving the reader a lyrical account of what goes on in the mind of his characters from moment to moment, skillfully alternated with objective comments which place the characters at a little distance. The dialogue is never hot and breathy, but aerated, brisk, restrained, and graceful. It combines exchanges of simple information with sharp and witty reactions of the characters to each other. And yet it is flexible enough to accommodate real tears, sudden insights, panic, tenderness, cynicism, outrage, and a pure, frivolous absurdity. Perhaps the test of a book's value is its ability to convert its chosen raw material into an experience offering the reader a broader, or deeper, sense of possible patterns underlying apparent chaos—and it is better for a novel, at any rate, if this process does not involve dispensing with the chaos. The more disparate and inclusive the original material, the more compelling any genuine design that emerges. That, I should suppose, is the argument for not regarding anything human as automatically excluded from the workshop of art. What the artist does with his material, not the material itself, is what we should judge him by. Not that it is always easy, or even possible, to separate the two completely.

In *The Ginger Man* two images of desire, sex and money, dominate the imagination. Their local habitation is centrally the mind and body of an impoverished graduate student in Dublin who, surely, thinks the thoughts and does the deeds that many have done before him. But not with his style. Like most people Sebastian Dangerfield is frustrated, but his frustration comes almost entirely from outer circumstances, not from inner repression. He enjoys an extraordinary freedom of thought and expression precisely because he can acquit himself of all responsibility for the ridiculous and desperate situation in which he finds himself. This does not mean, however, that he has no code of behavior; only that his code is dictated by the role he has conceived for himself and not any social contract. After a devastating quarrel with his wife Marion, Sebastian muses:

> Things not so bad. Wait and see what happens. Have to take what comes. Good with the bad. Lot in these old sayings. How one can tell lies in times of stress. My God, it's absolutely awful. Be made for the world. But the world was made for me. Here long before I arrived and they spent years getting it ready. Something got mixed up about my assets.

The world is essentially good, and all appearances to the contrary are the result of some frightful mistake at Headquarters. Until they clear this up and assign Sebastian his rightful place as Fortune's Child, he is obliged to act as though the mistake has not been made. *Noblesse oblige.* Sometimes the strain is great; one must take the good with the bad. The unpardonable sin would be to lose one's faith, to doubt whether one belonged to the Elect. And so Sebastian holds the line: he will not be made for the world, for the world was made for him. Thus Sebastian, even when beaten to his knees by fear, always remains in some sense above the battle. He is saving himself for the grand epiphany to come. And in the end he gets money and the girl, and Mary gets her lamb.

Considered thus, the novel sounds (I hope) attractive. The Archbishop of Dublin, quite naturally, judged otherwise when the necessarily watered down version Mr. Donleavy prepared for the stage came fresh from its London triumph to what turned out to be a three-day run at the Gaiety Theatre, home of the big time in Dublin. The play is a clever patchwork of episodes from the novel and shows how naturally stageworthy much of the dialogue is; but it is a much diminished thing (at least in the reading; I have not seen the play). This, of course, is not what bothered the Archbishop and a good many other Dubliners. Mr. Donleavy has described the experience of returning to Dublin with the four-member cast of the play and its director, Philip Wiseman, with a combination of vividness, detachment, and melancholy humor that shows his journalistic talents match his talents as a novelist. He brings us into the city with him and is bound to revive memories in anyone who has spent a winter in Dublin. But what is germane here is the reaction of some Dubliners to his play. That reaction must be seen as belonging to a great Dublin tradition that goes back as far as Yeats's *Countess Kathleen,* but is most famously remembered in connection with plays of Synge and O'Casey. The Irish are peculiarly sensitive to any depiction of Irish womanhood that suggests that Catholic morality, especially in sexual matters, may not provide a complete and valid guide to proper conduct. In his play Mr. Donleavy has a scene in which a certain Miss Frost is thawed into adultery by that vagabond prince and married man, Sebastian Dangerfield. Not only that. It is suggested that Miss Frost might find certain confessors more charitable than others. All this to top off a theatrical evening that had shown a "hero" outraging common decency and flouting good taste almost constantly. It is an old Irish irony that the writers Dublin nourishes are most adept at wounding her. For that matter when it comes to malice (and kindness) your Irishman can simply not be outdone.

Here are excerpts from the newspaper reactions Mr. Donleavy quotes: "The picture of student life on a G.I. grant, an expense of spirit in a waste of gin, is all too true within its squalid limits. . . . Mr. Donleavy almost achieves his ambition of running Dangerfield into a latter-day Hamlet." A generally favorable and civilized, though not always perceptive, review *(Irish Times).* "There is one scene near the end of the second act which is probably the most offensive ever performed on a Dublin stage. . . a travesty is made of everything that stage entertainment is supposed to mean, morals are mocked at and indecency is flaunted. It is all very well to talk of art and freedom of expression in the theatre, but I think we have gone far enough" *(Irish Press).* Another review described Dangerfield as "an American student in post-war Dublin who should never have been allowed out of the U.S. in the first place. He is obviously a mental case" *(Evening Herald).* To sum up: "It is an insult to religion and an outrage to normal feelings of decency" *(Irish Independent).*

Art is obviously dangerous, and never more so than when it suggests a liberation from convention, an attempt to view accepted beliefs from the "outside." But of course the violence of the reaction was a tribute to Mr. Donleavy. If the play had really been as "dull and dreary" as one reviewer said it was, no one would have cared. The Irish take art seriously just as Plato did, though perhaps a little less philosophically. O dreary day when the Irish meekly applaud scandal and outrage, or as the English do, blandly turn bitter gibes at themselves into occasions for complimenting the author. Let us offer the following definition as our final contribution to the continuing seminar on the causes and cure of obscenity: that is obscene which gives us a secret pleasure we dare not share with those less gifted with the virtue of self-control than we are.

I haven't left much space to comment on Mr. Donleavy's other venture into the theatre, *Fairy Tales of New York.* I think this superior to the dramatization of *The Ginger Man* because it is conceived in genuine and original theatrical terms. Each of the four episodes, or acts, shows that pilgrim Cornelius Christian on a stage of his progress to the Heavenly City. Starting in the Slough of Despond, we see Christian arriving in New York with his dead wife in a coffin. She had died on the way to America, and that no-good Christian is suffering an acute attack of agenbite of inwit. Next (in the funniest episode) Christian is applying for a job with a manufacturer of spark plugs. He has perked up considerably, though self-confidence and panic alternate to hilarious effect in his behavior. The third episode takes place in a boxing club. Christian is now known for his sass, but he is reminded of the danger of *hubris* when, agreeing to play a joke by pretending to let an older man knock him out, he finds himself (or rather fails to find himself) laid out like a corpse. The final act shows him in an expensive restaurant with his girl—a childhood sweetheart. He is dressed to kill and is wearing peach shoes; his girl is dressed in her grandmother's wedding dress. The waiters refuse service, he shouts for it, the girl remonstrates, and he exits. She is left to the mercy of two waiters who leave her in no doubt (as they think) that her boy friend is a bounder and a cad. She sits while the table is cleared and taken away. Finally she is left on her knees, weeping, when even the chair is taken away. She refuses all offers of comfort. And she is rewarded. Christian returns, garbed in all the formal splendor of some Eastern potentate. His feet are bare but he has a large sparkling diamond on each toe. The waiters rush forward, the young couple are served a glorious meal with all punctilio, and a waiter brings a satin stool for Christian to rest his feet on. The closing lines:

> GRAVES [the girl] (a hand forward over Christian's head): I'm sorry.
> CHRISTIAN (Christian that forgiver of all minor sins): That's all right. You see (Christian presenting a foot), the colour of this, too, is peach.

Curtain
Applause

This play is a step toward *A Singular Man*. Interest in abstraction and design are growing at the expense of wayward and unpredictable chaos. The fairy tale implicit in *The Ginger Man* has now become explicit. Perhaps the change of milieu meant that Mr. Donleavy would have to become either more realistic or more fantastic as a novelist. In Ireland the two modes blur into each other naturally; at least so it seems in Irish literature. Here they tend to diverge and remain distinct, even when they occur in the same book. *A Singular Man,* in spite of its gaiety, is ultimately a gloomy novel, whereas *The Ginger Man,* in spite of its melancholy, is ultimately a gay novel. As the names indicate, George Smith is a more sober hero than Sebastian Dangerfield. Smith is older and he lives not in Ireland but in America. He has no O'Keefe he can trust and feel superior to. His four children are growing up to despise him. His relations with women are all connected with "business" in some way: his maid and his secretaries. In going from poverty to riches, from Dublin student life to the life of a New York business man, the Donleavy hero—more credit to him—finds life appalling, more unreal, more perplexing than ever.

One can imagine Sebastian Dangerfield as a seedy descendant of Mozart's Don Giovanni: he has some of the creative energy, the daring, the *sprezzatura*, and the laughing contempt for all lawful obstacles that give the Don his vitality. In his way Dangerfield too is both a creator and destroyer of folly. If he cannot achieve the Mozartean harmony of grandeur and intimacy—and he cannot—he nevertheless displays a mind always capable of rising above local pettiness and yet catlike in its alertness to the problems and possibilities of each new situation. Much of the humor depends on this double vision—seeing the short and the long of things simultaneously. George Smith has this ability too, but the long and the short have stretched far apart; it is almost impossible to hold them in one view. And he lacks Sebastian's self-confidence.

Take for example the anecdote of the hat. One Monday George Smith comes into the office wearing a new hat. Miss Tomson thinks it's an improvement; she gives him a little lecture on sartorial good taste. He rushes wildly into his office.

> I locked the door after her. Being bullied by good taste is not exactly my dish. When we get to know each other better, let's see the underwear, Smith. The hat was only to take off in a situation where there was nothing else to do. Chap in the shop said this is what they're wearing. Who are they. Awkward to say I am not them. But the burning words, anything you're trying to be. I took my paper shears and dumbfounded by my own dexterity reduced the hat to pieces and parts. Packaged it neatly. Addressing it elsewhere. And had to let Miss Tomson back in to mail it.

George Smith is always fighting this sort of humiliation. He is a greenhorn constantly being instructed by people. Or threatened. His power consists in his money and the status it gives him, not in himself. His need for love is more desperate than Sebastian's because, in spite of his money, or perhaps because of it, he is poorer in himself. Only when he is out in the country does he become more masterful. The very strength of his physical capacity for love, which amazes and delights the women who discover it, becomes a symbol of his incapacity to cope with all the loveless aspects of the world. And they are the ones that win.

AFTERWORD

Since I wrote my piece, Donleavy has entered on his alliterative phase. *The Saddest Summer of Samuel S, Meet My Maker the Mad Molecule,* and most recently *The Beastly Beatitudes of Balthazar B* have appeared. To watch the dandy dance toward dusty doom of the Donleavy hero is to submit oneself to a style distinguished by a defiance of gravity and a surrender to sentiment. All the Donleavy hero wants is the goodies of life, but he finds himself on an obstacle course devised by the ignoble lords and masters who grant degrees, control the funds, make the laws, and generally have the power over life and death. He must play a game of hide and seek with authority. In *The Ginger Man* lack of money was a great problem, but money is still a problem even when you have plenty of it, as *A Singular Man* and *The Beastly Beatitudes* demonstrate. Love is the other great problem. How is one to enjoy the perfect bliss of intimacy when all the world conspires against love? And at the same time yearns for it. Love depends on trust, but who in the world can be trusted?

Though eager to succeed, the Donleavy hero has an aristocratic disdain for Success. He insists on playing the game his way, even though the prospect of failure makes him giddy. In his aggressive phase, he is willing to employ violence, cunning, and a ruthless energy in the pursuit of his goals; in his passive guise he offers his vulnerability as proof of his goodhearted innocence. He may be wise in the ways of the world, but he is never worldly wise. Even Beefy, the great and good friend of Balthazar B, finds himself foiled by the cruel and witty grandmother who holds the pursestrings—and Beefy is a self-possessed master of the darker secrets of sin. He is grosser than Sebastian Dangerfield, just as Balthazar is more refined.

The once unified hero is now separated into his component parts. Balthazar, happily seduced by a nanny twice his age when he was twelve, never again finds a love so sure and pure. And he is disabled by his need to fill the vacuum the lovely Bella leaves in her wake. He must wait for love to find him, and both his beauty and his money are assurances that it will. But class and money and death itself combine successively to deprive him of the love he was born for. He has all that money can buy. And he is thoroughly disconsolate.

In the twenties Scott Fitzgerald offered the innocent but sophisticated young an image of flaming youth. To live in the high style meant using money while spurning the money-getting process. The fun, while it lasted, depended on the camaraderie of a set of people sharing values that clearly distinguished them from the lesser breeds unable to afford either material or spiritual luxury. In the sixties Donleavy has attracted a considerable "underground" following, especially on campuses in the East. He, too, offers an image of rebellious youth, but the company of the elite is sadly diminished. More single-minded and more embattled in their quest for erotic pleasure, apparently born with the taste of defeat in their mouths, they invent (or their creator does) a style of life for themselves, nervous and lyrical, compounded of tough-minded vulgarity and tender-minded elegance. The glamor of fine clothes, good food, and handsome bodies is still very much in evidence, but the hero is more and more isolated. To dream of the good life in any substantial sense would be a hypocrisy beyond his spiritual means; the best he can manage is a defiant protest on behalf of the single man against the world that would unman him.

ABOUT
J.P. DONLEAVY

"Writing," says Mr. James Patrick Donleavy, "is turning one's worst moments into money." He states that his motives for pursuing a career in writing are "women and money, fame and money, and sometimes, just money all by itself." Mr. Donleavy believes that the greatest tools a writer may possess are "a suicidal and ruthless nerve and empty head."

Born in Brooklyn, New York, in 1926, Mr. Donleavy attended Trinity College, Dublin. His career has been extremely varied: by his own admission, he has been "a prize fighter, a painter and a student of science." He now considers himself a lawyer, having a large number of lawsuits in process simultaneously.

Mr. Donleavy makes his home in France, Ireland, and England, keeping houses in Brooklyn, New York, the Isle of Man, and elsewhere. He is married and has two children.

Mr. Donleavy's formula for remaining a writer is to "live to be forty, still be solvent, and still love your trade."

BOOKS BY
J. P. DONLEAVY

THE GINGER MAN
Paris: Olympia, 1955.
London: Corgi, 1963. (pb)
New York: Dial, 1965.
Toronto: S.J.R. Saunders, 1965.
New York: Dell, 1966. (pb)
Expurgated version:
London: Neville Spearman, 1956.
New York: McDowell, Oblensky, 1958.
New York: Berkley, 1959. (pb)

THE GINGER MAN (play)
New York: Random House, 1961.
as *WHAT THEY DID IN DUBLIN, with THE GINGER MAN*
London: MacGibbon & Kee, 1962.

FAIRY TALES OF NEW YORK
New York: Random House, 1961.
Toronto: Random House, 1961.
Middlesex: Penquin, 1962. (pb)

A SINGULAR MAN
Boston: Little, Brown, 1963.
Toronto: Little, Brown (Canada), 1963.
London: Bodley Head, 1964.
New York: Delacorte, 1967.
New York: Dell, 1967. (pb)
Middlesex: Penguin, 1967. (pb)

MEET MY MAKER THE MAD MOLECULE
Boston: Little, Brown, 1964.
Toronto: Little, Brown (Canada), 1964.
London: Bodley Head, 1965.
New York: Delacorte, 1967.
Middlesex: Penguin, 1967. (pb)
New York: Dell, 1968. (pb)

A SINGULAR MAN (play)
London: Bodley Head, 1965.

THE SADDEST SUMMER OF SAMUEL S
New York: Delacorte, 1966.
Toronto: S.J.R. Saunders, 1966.
London: Eyre & Spottiswoode, 1967.
New York: Dell, 1967. (pb)

THE BEASTLY BEATITUDES OF BALTHAZAR B
New York: Delacorte, 1968.
New York: Dell, 1970. (pb)

John Cheever and the Charms of Innocence: The Craft of *The Wapshot Scandal*

by George Garrett

These stories were no worse than the stories of talking rabbits he had been told as a boy but the talking rabbits had the charms of innocence.

—The Wapshot Scandal

The first thing that should be said and not forgotten is that *The Wapshot Scandal* is a very good novel, an outstanding piece of work and craft by any known standard of judgment, and it is the best book John Cheever has written. Since his earlier and first novel, *The Wapshot Chronicle,* received the National Book Award for 1957, this means that in the world of prizes and awards and in the circles where there is jostling for the laurel wreath of success, a game as shrill and chaotic as Drop-the-Handkerchief, it is a book and Cheever is an author who must be taken quite seriously this season. Already *The Wapshot Scandal* has received very good notices and reviews and, what is more important, these have been in the most prominent and choice spots, as significant as the fire hydrant in front of a fashionable restaurant where only certain shiny limousines with very special license tags are permitted to park. In the front page leading review for the *Tribune* (and other papers) Glenway Wescott, not only an artist himself but an arbiter with charm, influence, and definite opinions, saluted the publication of the book with high praise, seasoned with just a mere *soupçon* of qualification. He found in the book many of the virtues which he at once celebrates and pleads for in *Images of Truth:* clarity, lucidity, decorum, a fine surface of sensuous aesthetic experience supported on the firm rock strata of meaning and implication. He saw it as tragi-comic, a book thus accurately reflecting the ambivalent feelings of a man of feeling in our time. Elizabeth Janeway in the front page review of the *New York Times Book Review* celebrated the book chiefly in terms of anecdotes she just couldn't resist retelling and by pointing out the extremely clever and "deceptive" use of symbol and analogy employed by Cheever to give the haunting resonance of deep meaning and wide implication. The *Washington Post* offered its highest compliment by stating that the cosmic view of the novel, unflinching honesty lifted by the wings of hope and wisdom, was a fine example of the working philosophy of our late president. Most recently

Cheever has received the mixed blessing of a *Time* cover story. It remains to be seen whether or not the celebrated jinx will work.

If there is any justice in this world, *The Wapshot Scandal* is on its way. Whether or not it climbs to a place on the best-seller lists and endures there for a proper interval remains to be seen, is in the hands of Lady Luck and, of course, that vast, faceless, surging, restive mob, the reading public which, like the voting public and the razor-blade-using public nobody really knows for sure and practically everybody mistrusts. *The Wapshot Scandal* may or may not sit in the spotlighted position of the best-seller list, but it does not take a gypsy to predict that the book and its author will be much discussed in the coming months, not only in cocktail parties and reading groups, but also in seminar and classroom. High time too. John Cheever has been producing honorable work for more than twenty years and from the beginning he has always threatened to become "a major writer." Perhaps he has at last earned that title. One thing we can be sure of. He has written a good book in a time when good books are few and far between. And that's a cause for celebration. It is, however, at once a better and a *different* book than his reviewers have allowed, and it is quite good enough to be subjected to the kind of inquisition, the rack of speculation and the thumbscrew of questions without easy answers, which only the strong and the brave should be asked to endure.

> *She loves the fine, the subtle, the non-cliché. . . .* From an advertisement in *The New Yorker.*

John Cheever is a *New Yorker* writer and may be the best of the bunch. Of course, we all know that both the editors and writers for that distinguished magazine would deny and have denied that a *type* exists. Let us understand the reasons for the denial and ignore it. No use pretending Shakespeare didn't write for the Elizabethan stage. Any magazine worth its weight has a character, one which is partly created by editorial standards and equally by the relationship the magazine enjoys with its readers. *The New Yorker* has another power haunting, if not dominating the present—a history long enough already to be called a tradition. We know a good deal about the beginning and the early years of *The New Yorker.* The names—Ross, Thurber, E.B. White, Gus Lobrano, Gibbs, and so many others—are celebrated, have been recorded in many a popular, nostalgic reminiscence and have passed beyond mere household familiarity to stand, aloof but never lonely, bronzelike with a nice patina, in the cluttered museum of public mythology. By now at least two generations of Americans have thumbed through *The New Yorker* with pleasure. Didn't we cut our teeth on the magazine's one major contribution to our culture—the cartoons? Still, a popular magazine is a business. Just as the politician must get himself elected, so a magazine must turn a profit to insure its own self-preservation. We have seen magazines come and go, succeed and fail. *The New Yorker* has not only survived, it has prospered, bloomed. Which means that no matter how adventurous the editorial policy and no matter how well it has been able to adapt itself to the facts of life, change and decay, there is still at heart a basic purpose, that of self-preservation. And thus the preservation of the *status quo* is not just an aim but a duty.

The literary history of *The New Yorker* reflects all these things yet has a general history of its own. And there are a few general things about it which have to be said. One is that over many years *The New Yorker* has been a patron of many writers. More and more steadily than have foundations or colleges or rich old ladies with buzzing hearing aids and ropes of pearls. It is also true that it has specifically patronized the finest second-rate talents of our times. No use arguing. It is simply a fact that none of the acknowledged masters of the art of writing fiction or poetry from the first half of our century has been a regular contributor to the magazine. Maybe this will change, but a literary historian would not bet on it. The remarkable thing is that *The New Yorker* has always maintained a very high level of consistent quality and craftsmanship. Which, of course, is something even, perhaps especially, the masters themselves have not done.

The vintage *New Yorker* story has become a model for the modern short story. Briefly it was the maximum exploration and exploitation of a single dramatically presented incident, more or less strictly observing the unities of time and place and rich in implication, both in depth of characterization and in a larger implied story which had a past and predicated a future. Plot, in the conventional sense, was largely absent, as were the middle class moral dilemmas of slick fiction. In setting the stories were either regional—the East and occasionally the uncorrupted West or the passive and amusing South, or foreign and exotic. Naturally the stories reflected the general moral views of the magazine and its public—reasonably but not ostentatiously well-informed, perhaps a little snobbish, though united against the more common forms of snobbery, more or less liberal politically. It was never, not even in the case of certain religious writers, religious. Its moral fiber, its touchstone was a kind of secular humanism coupled with a gentle intellectual agnosticism. The virtues it honored were all civilized virtues, sedentary, sophisticated and rational, all defended by the curtains (never made of iron) of humor, irony, sensitivity, the skeptical intelligence, and a form of gentility which was *au courant.* Minor figures who entered wearing the white hat signifying a good guy were charming eccentrics, happy-go-lucky losers, cheerful outsiders. Members of the lower classes, those of whom it could be safely said they didn't read *The New Yorker,* and people from other older generations were permitted to display a healthy-minded vulgarity. Those worthy of attention from the class (let's face it—middle) of the readers themselves were usually attractive physically, possessed of charm, and perhaps distinguished by the blessing or burden of a little extra sensitivity and more intelligence than is average. The mortal sins in this universe were, inevitably: vulgarity without the redemption of eccentricity, self-pity, stupidity, hypocrisy, bad manners, complacency, excess of passion, and a lack of good health or physical attractiveness. In short, *New Yorker* fiction was a fiction of manners, and its purpose, classical from tip to toe, was to instruct as it delighted. Nature, of course, was neutral and basically good. It was, however, an idyllic nature, in its own way as formalized and stylish as an 18th Century pastoral. There was a kind of tourist's view of the natural world replete with the names of plants and animals, these, however, always shining like coins or rare stamps in a collector's album. Still essentially progressive, still haunted by the last of the evolutionary analogies, *The New Yorker* viewed the worst excesses of modern civilization with distaste and sometimes with alarm, but never with despair. For, no matter how black the present, how fraught with peril the future or how quaint the past, the fiction and poetry of *The New Yorker* walked forward hand in hand with the advertisements and "The Talk of the Town," always moving toward the vague, but discernible horizon, the glow of which indicated at least the possibility of a Jerusalem of The Good Life somewhere up there among the Delectable Mountains and just beyond the reach of the clean fingernails of the Ideal Reader.

During the Second World War the form of the story began to change. And here we return to John Cheever, who had something to do with changing it.

We are no longer dealing with midnight sailings on three-stacked liners, twelve day crossings, Vuitton trunks and the glittering lobbies of Grand Hotels.
—The Wapshot Scandal

From the beginning with *The Way Some People Live* (1943) and on through the publication of *The Enormous Radio* (1953) the stories of John Cheever in *The New Yorker* (as of this date he has published more than 100 there) have exhibited an independence of form. Perhaps it was inevitable that this would happen now that the "single event" story has been widely anthologized, taught in schools, and is somewhat less than *chic*. Anyway, for whatever reason, the stories of John Cheever and of some others who appear in that magazine, are now most often much less "dramatic," much more free in the survey of time and space. Cheever, for example, characteristically ranges widely in point of view and also in tense, sometimes past, sometimes present, occasionally even future and conditional. There is a much more positive exploitation of the narrator-writer of the story. He appears openly like the chorus of an early Elizabethan play, does his best to establish an intimacy and rapport with his reader, and then cheerfully re-enters from time to time to point out significant objects or to make intelligent comment. Like a cultivated and slightly superior museum guide, the narrator is clever and witty yet always *sympatico* to the reader because of his slight, pleasing smile, his gentle habit of self-deprecation, and his wry, yet knowing shrug. The narrator is up to date in his allusions, his knowledge of the *things* of this world, and can, if necessary, but not without a wink of misgiving, use the latest slang. His own language is exact, always a model of lucidity and decorum, free from the unrefined extravagance of poetic frenzy, yet able from time to time to reach a modest altitude on the slopes of Olympus, far from the sweaty chaos of the laughing white gods, but anyway a place with a view near timberline where a gourmet picnic might be spread.

Cheever has introduced a new freedom in the form. The meaning of this kind of form is fairly clear. It wants to *say more,* not only about persons, places and things, but about what these things mean, what patterns they make. Cheever has, for example, from the beginning blithely and easily introduced the world of dreams into his stories. His characters dream a good deal and they do it matter-of-factly. He has also permitted them to digress, to reminisce, to imagine. And it is one of his special abilities and triumphs that he can lead them (and the reader) step by step credibly from a perfectly "realistic" situation into the areas of farce or nightmare. Perhaps this is what one reviewer meant when he wrote—"It is as if Marquand had suddenly been crossed with Kafka."

Cheever is deeply interested in character and he knows his fictional characters by giving them depth, veils and layers of experience, and the loose ends and untied shoe laces of living, breathing beings. One has only to compare and contrast his treatment of characters with that of

Mary McCarthy. Her people are mannequins, shoved in a store window and stripped naked for the amusement of the reader. It would be obscene if her characters were not wooden. It would be cruel if her characters did not in the end seem to be lifted out of somebody else's book or story she is criticizing. Cheever has a good deal of sympathy for his people and if they sometimes fail, in spite of the latest methods of resuscitation and artificial respiration, to breathe the breath of life, it is apt to be because he becomes impatient, quite naturally, with the extremely difficult demands he has set upon himself.

On the early stories, probably the most intelligent critical remarks come from William Peden in his excellent notes to the anthology *Twenty-Nine Stories* (1960). First Peden makes an important comparison, calling Cheever "an urbane and highly civilized social satirist" like Galsworthy. Peden goes on to say, judiciously: "Few writers have depicted more skillfully than he the loneliness and emptiness of certain segments of contemporary society." And he points out that each and all of the stories have been chiefly concerned with "the corrosive effect of metropolitan life upon essentially decent people who are isolated, defeated, or deprived of their individuality in the vastness of a great city." If you wisely include the proliferating suburbs as a part of the great city and if you weigh Peden's words, that is about the long and the short of it.

But we are talking about Cheever the novelist. Even though both his novels have appeared in bits and pieces, slightly re-edited for formal reasons, as stories in *The New Yorker.* And even though his two most recent collections of stories—*The Housebreaker of Shady Hill* (1958) and *Some People, Places, and Things That Will Not Appear in My Next Novel* (1961)— are so constructed as to qualify as novels if the definition of that form is at last liberated from certain arbitrary restrictions. More and more *all* the parts of Cheever's work are clearly parts of a whole. What he has to say to the world has changed a little as the world has changed. But not so much as one might imagine. And not so much as *The Wapshot Scandal* intends.

One thing needs to be said here and now. Clearly it is more than difficult, it is a *feat,* to be a serious writer and at the same time to share without much questioning not only the standards, but also the whole set of rules and by-laws of a social club as cozy and intimate and proud as *The New Yorker.* It is hard not to end up sounding like a tape recording of clever cocktail party chatter. Yet John Cheever has achieved the delicate balance and done it with the bravado of the tightrope walker in top hat and tails, bottle in hand, who seems to stagger across the dangerous wire. No one can deny that he is a good serious writer. No one can deny the achievement he has already demonstrated. And this would be true if he never wrote another line.

The Wapshot Chronicle appeared in 1957 and won the National Book Award for that year. As in the case of all prizes, it was and will remain debatable whether his first novel was the *best* book of the year, but it was a fine one and it was a cause for jubilation in the circles of those who care. More important than prizes, praise, or blame, he created with economy and dispatch a lively novel which included a town, St. Botolphs, and its people, a family, the Wapshots, from the *Arabella* up to, almost, the present; a variety of characters and events, of anecdotes and parables and fables, and at least two thoroughly memorable and realized characters—Leander and Miss Honora. It was full of humor ranging from bathroom jokes (the Wapshot toilet was haunted and occasionally flushed itself in the middle of the night), to farce (the book *opens* with a runaway horse-drawn float bearing the Women's Club far from a Fourth of July parade), to moments of modern sophisticated comedy involving psychiatrists, crazy castles and the style and tone of Leander Wapshot's journal, one of the happiest devices of the novel. That Leander has sinned grievously and has a truly nightmarish vision of a rutting hell before he drowns himself becomes at least modified by the fact that he is allowed to have the last word in his journal, a word of advice for those who come after him.

> Advice to my sons. . . . Never put whiskey into hot water bottle crossing borders of dry states or counties. Rubber will spoil taste. Never make love with pants on. Beer on whiskey, very risky. Whiskey on beer, never fear. Never eat apples, peaches, pears, etc. while drinking whiskey except long French-style dinners, terminating with fruit. Other viands have mollifying effect. Never sleep in moonlight. Known by scientists to induce madness. Should bed stand beside window on clear night draw shade before retiring. . . . Avoid kneeling in unheated stone churches. Ecclesiastical dampness causes prematurely gray hair. Fear tastes like a rusty knife and do not let her into your house. Courage tastes of blood. Stand up straight. Admire the world. Relish the love of a gentle woman. Trust in the Lord.

In this history of the Wapshots and St. Botolphs Cheever offered a history of the nation, its growth, bloom, and the question of its possible decay and corruption. The tone was tolerantly amused and nostalgic dealing with the past, lyrical about nature and especially about trout fishing in the unspoiled Canadian wilderness, a little sad about the decline and decay of the small town, satirical about the excesses of the urban and suburban revolution and the desperate impersonality, the flight from freedom and responsibility of modern times. A beautiful satirical point of view was offered by sending Young Moses Wapshot to Washington and Young Coverly first to New York and then to a missile site or two, two young rubes against whose bemusement and bafflement the modern urban *milieu* could be measured.

The book is rich in implication, gained by the "tricks" Elizabeth Janeway so admires, the time honored method of story tellers from Homer on of gaining larger implication by allusion, analogy, the echo of an event or a myth. And, as one might expect, these allusions and echoes are chiefly from the wellspring, the pure water of our culture, the classics and the Bible, always used in such a way as to be *functional* decoration. Venus is the reigning deity, yet she is ambiguous, sometimes seen *in bono,* sometimes *in malo.* There are deaths, births, and entrances. It is truly a chronicle, giving the impression of sprawling largesse, weight and size, whereas, in fact, it is not really a long novel. A virtuoso performance.

What does the book say? It says all men are sinners, but it is possible to be good, loving and brave. It says the good old days weren't all that good, but that, indeed, something has happened to the American dream, that it is approaching nightmare. It says that the nightmare is there in the best of us, but it is still possible to hold up your head and "admire the world." For a book with much pathos and misfortune it ends on a positive note of instruction, made palatable by the sweetness of Leander's simplicity and Cheever's irony.

And that could be that. Except that he has chosen to continue the Wapshot history by continuing it into our time. The books are related, but not strictly sequential. Though some of the people appear in both, they are somehow changed and modified by the times. They are not quite the same characters. And the world, even its history, is now different. The tone and style are different. (We miss the vitality of Leander's journal, which only appears once.) Things disintegrate, decay, blur out of focus, fall apart. The relationship is much like that of *The Rainbow* and *Women in Love* or, closer to home, of *The Hamlet* to *The Town.* Which is to say the two books are Cheever's old testament, written of the time of myths, the law and the prophets, and his new testament, beginning now on a Christmas Eve and ending, although on Christmas, with a curious last supper to be followed shortly by the last book of the Bible—the Apocalypse. The sins of *Chronicle* are original sin. *Scandal* moves inexorably toward the the end of the world. This the two books must be taken together; but, as in scriptural exegesis we must not gloss the new law with the old.

The difference between the two can be illustrated by a small thing. Cheever's writing has always been marked by its representative use of the five senses. But in *Chronicle* it is smell, the odors of the world, the flesh and the devil, which predominate. There are great patches and lists of good odors, rich savors. *Scandal* is, by contrast, practically odorless. Most of the odors are bad or sordid and linger to haunt us like ambivalent ghosts. The author-narrator makes this quite explicit, saying that "we leave behind us, in the hotels, motels, guest rooms, meadows and fields where we discharge this much of ourselves, either the scent of goodness or the odor of evil, to influence those who come after us." In another place a character surveys fallen apples: "Paradise must (he thought) have smelled the windfalls." But in contrast to *Chronicle* the predominant sensuous patterns of *Scandal* are all black and white, the presence or the absence of light. "'Light and shadow, light and shadow,' says old Cousin Honora of the music. She would say the same for Chopin, Stravinsky or Thelonious Monk."

> *I want to put on innocence like a bright new dress. I want to feel clean again!*
>
> —*The Wapshot Scandal*

The Wapshot Scandal begins in St. Botolphs and somehow ends there, after following the young sons of Leander, Moses and Coverly, through many misadventures and following Cousin Honora to Rome and back, fleeing an investigator of the Internal Revenue Service, to her death by self-starvation. It is, however, principally concerned with Coverly, Moses' wife Melissa, and Cousin Honora. Moses, the favored and luckier of the two boys, was never fully realized in *Chronicle* and is really no more than a shadow in *Scandal.* Concentrating on these three characters, Cheever keeps the story happily bouncing back and forth, pausing now and then for a wonderfully relevant digression, moving across wide spaces and through patches of time as if waving a passport which reads "freely to pass." Now Cheever is for the most part on his old stamping ground, and Proxmire Manor, where Moses and Melissa exist, is a dead ringer for Shady Hill. The opportunities for satire of the present state of things are manifold and Cheever doesn't miss a trick. It's all there —suburbia, the economy of indebtedness, the religion of the churches, T.V., space exploration, scientists and missiles, drugs and cancer, repairmen, undertakers, drive-in theaters, superhighways, frozen food, computers, "the sumptuary laws," travel, indifferent clerks and airline stewardesses, a daring airlines robbery, Congressional hearings, security clearance and the income tax, homosexuality, advertising slogans, doctors, and the A.M.A., a male beauty contest, blue plastic swimming pools, outdoor barbecues, shabby and unsuccessful adulteries; oh it's all there all right, God's plenty of the outward and visible signs of a time when "standards of self-esteem had advanced to a point where no one was able to dig a hole," a wild, yet terrifying imitation of "a world that seemed to be without laws and prophets."

The full range of humor is there too. The basic slapstick—"Oh, the wind and the rain and to hold in one's arms a willing love! He stepped into a large pile of dog manure." The irony of character, a wounded veteran thinks: "He could have gotten a deferred job at the ore-loading docks in Superior and made a fortune during the war but he didn't learn this until it was too late." The author-narrator's special brand—describing Proxmire Manor as a village which "seemed to have eliminated, through adroit social pressures, the thorny side of human nature."

It is part of the irony and humor of this book that the whole plan of the story is told in capsule in what appears to be an irrelevant digression, the story of a woman, scarcely known by Melissa, whose ruin and downfall began the day the septic tank backed up. Step by step, we follow her into a nightmare of disintegration as, one by one, each of her appliances breaks down and cannot be repaired; she becomes a drunk and an adulteress and ends a suicide. (The book is full of suicides to underline the suicidal inclination of the age.) The pattern of this digression is repeated over and over again. Begin with the credible, typical situation, push it an inch or two into the realm of hilarious farce, then the farce of a sudden becomes dream, and all dreams turn to nightmare. It is typical of Cheever that he backs into his moral plea to the world behind the mask of irony, permitting his mouthpiece to be a decrepit old senator in a Congressional Investigating Committee speaking out to Doctor Cameron, a mad missile scientist:

> "We possess Promethean powers but don't we lack the awe, the humility, that primitive man brought to the sacred fire? Isn't this a time for uncommon awe, supreme humility? If I should have to make some final statement, and I shall very soon for I am nearing the end of my journey, it would be in the nature of a thanksgiving for stout-hearted friends, lovely women, blue skies, the bread and wine of life. Please don't destroy the earth, Dr. Cameron," he sobbed. "Oh, please, please don't destroy the earth."

Yet the earth and the people in it seem inevitably headed for destruction. Even grand old Cousin Honora kills herself. But, like Leander, she leaves a legacy, not a journal but a Christmas dinner to which she has, as always, invited enough strangers to make the magic number twelve. It is Coverly, unlucky and so often defeated, who pulls together, picks up the pieces and keeps the last Christmas dinner in honor of his cousin. He attends a Christmas Eve service performed by a drunken, ineffectual Episcopal priest, and does his duty by staying alone in the Church until the last *amen.* In the morning he collects what is left of the Wapshots and they await the arrival of Honora's eight invited guests. Who turn out to be all inmates of The Hutchins Institute for the Blind, only two of whom are identified, an old testament type muttering the wrath of God on the sinners and a sweet Negress who carries the simple message of love and mercy in a gesture. Of these guests Coverly thinks:

> They seemed to be advocates for those in pain; for the taste of misery as fulsome as rapture, for the losers, the goners, the flops, for those who dream in terms of missed things—planes, trains, boats and opportunities—who see on walking the empty tarmac, the empty waiting room, the water in the empty slip, rank as Love's Tunnel when the ship is sailed; for all those who fear death.

It is a profoundly moving conclusion and as close to an explicit statement of Christian faith as I have seen from a *New Yorker* writer, perilously close to religion. Venus has been ubiquitous in this book, too, but here she is clearly the old Venus *in malo,* whose rewards are folly and degradation, who is the first handmaiden of Dame Fortune who gives all who serve her a spin on the wheel. (If this sounds almost Medieval, it is. There is even a mysterious archer, clad all in red, who fires an arrow at Coverly and, fortunately, misses.) In *Scandal* John Cheever makes a firm and definite distinction between false love (*cupiditas*) and the love that moves the stars (*caritas*). And he ends on the note we are now familiar with, for there is no other song or burden for our times, that "we must love one another or die."

For all these reasons *The Wapshot Scandal* is at once John Cheever's most ambitious work and his finest achievement. Because he is an artist with his own voice and because he has earned the right to speak out in that voice, it is a fine achievement in the art of the novel this year or any year.

> *It seemed incredible to him that his people, his inventive kind, the first to exploit glass store fronts, bright lights and continuous music, should have ever been so backward as to construct a kind of temple that belonged to the*

> *ancient world.* [Johnson, an agent of the Internal Revenue Service, views a classic white-steepled New England church.]
>
> —*The Wapshot Scandal*

Now the quibbling begins. It will be brief. Yet there are a few things to be said—a few. They will not be exactly objective or fair, for ultimately critical judgment cannot be. It may be that if I break the rules and simply state a few personal prejudices and feelings, it will enable the *reader* anyway to judge for himself. First, I am southern and from as far back as any Wapshot. The southern background does make a difference. We have never rejoiced in the civilization Mr. Cheever satirizes. In fact it is none of our own. Deep in our hearts, if not in our heads, we feel, perhaps smugly, that it is the end result of all that grand, hypocritical spirit which erupted in New England and would not rest until it had destroyed ours. We feel New England and Mr. Cheever are getting what they asked for and deserved. Perhaps a little more rational is the notion, which is inevitably entertained by those who have had the historical experience of defeat, that disillusionment is a naive posture. There is an air of human suffering, of its trinity of devils—poverty, disease and ignorance. One must resist the temptation of the inner smile, the inner voice which says—"'Tis new to thee."

People do not live like people in *The New Yorker,* try as they will, and they never will. The insulation of that world is foolish and as forlorn as the storm windows Cheever characters are forever putting up and taking down. There may well be a system of election and damnation, but the elect are not necessarily the charming, the gifted, the beautiful, the eccentric or even the innocent. Nor are they necessarily children, cripples, Negroes or victims. There is no text which says that God cannot look with love upon the stupid, the cruel, the vulgar, the hypocritical and the guilty. It is these who need His love most, and it is these whom we have been commanded to love. And that is most difficult. I am not talking about Salinger's Fat Lady. (There's a Fat Lady seen briefly in *Scandal.*) After much trial and error Salinger's Glass family discovered that it is possible to love the Fat Lady. Cheever has come to that conclusion too. But in truth we are not advised to love the unlovable, we are *commanded to.* You don't get medals or merit badges for obeying orders. It is to the point that in medieval allegories most of the time the devil did not wear red at all. He came in green, camouflaged in the color of faith.

What I am saying is that although this book makes a plea for charity, it does not practice it. Sympathy, yes; compassion, yes, for some characters; and sentimentality is abundant and aplenty. For what is sentimentality but a deep concern for human suffering which disregards the human spirit?

Now a few quibbles in rapid, random order:

(1) *historical—political—social*
Historically the book is very inaccurate precisely because it exists in a vacuum. More obviously in *Chronicle* but also in *Scandal,* both of which intend to deal with the American experience, the *events* of that experience impinge almost not at all upon the characters. It is as if Cheever divided American history into two periods—the Quaint Period, from the *Mayflower* to the middle thirties, and The Vulgar Now, the time of guided missiles and frozen food. Does he really believe that all the Wars and the Depression had *no* influence on the American character? Or is it that "we all know all about that anyway"? Do we really? Have we progressed that far?

(2) *moral—theological*
Have already quibbled once. But we have been told, wisely I believe, by a Pope, that to consider our own age as especially characterized by sin and corruption is a form of spiritual pride and also quite silly. We may be destroyed or destroy ourselves, but it will not be because of our highly developed and high-powered immorality. Morally Cheever appeals to every sane human being. Nobody, even the men at the missile stations, wants to destroy the world or do away with blue skies, trout streams, butterflies, old houses, *The New Yorker,* or even the literary *status quo.* It is not likely, on the other hand, that Cheever's moral message will restrain one maniac from pulling a lever or a trigger.

(3) *literary*
Though an innovator of sorts, Cheever has made a *habit* of his innovations. They are altogether acceptable now and, it seems, that suits him fine. At times his method and virtuosity disguise a kind of carelessness and indifference. The verisimilitude he must start with, no matter how deeply into dream or farce he goes, is not always there just because he is able to hang out a list of *things* and current phrases (like the little flags on used car lots). He drops characters who don't interest him and lets others exist in a realm of two-dimensions and cliché. Well, it is his world, isn't it? And one has to admire his bravado. Still, with all admiration, it

would be a lie not to admit to the feeling that it is very *safe.* The man on the flying trapeze with a good safe net beneath. The lion tamer cutting a caper in a cage full of toothless tigers.

These quibbles don't add up to much. What should one ask of *The Wapshot Scandal?* It is a good book by a good writer, more than good enough and better than we deserve. It is just good enough to be judged against the ideal of greatness. Which may be asking too much.

AFTERWORD

In this country the integrity of *criticism* is seldom questioned openly. The integrity of artists is fair game, but our critics have assumed, as an inevitable perquisite hand in glove with the undeniable power they wield (that power being a self-sufficient pecking order much like the rating systems used by the television networks), that they are above and beyond not only any scrutiny of motive or malice, but also that such consideration is irrelevant. Pragmatically irrelevant.

Who, after all, would care (*dare?*) to question the integrity of a "major" critic? Perhaps another critic; but surely neither the passive "reading public" nor some misrepresented and misinterpreted writer. Our laws, in fact, protect the critic from the normal recourse of any citizen who has been libeled and injured *professionally.* The critic's shield and buckler being "presumed objectivity." But recent years have shown that criticism *de facto* is beyond this sensible limit; which is intended, of course, to protect the single and powerless individual from the power and leverage of the mighty. There must be a dozen prominent critics who have flaunted their disregard of this ancient limitation by announcing openly, before or after the fact, their intention to "get" a given author for one or another extraneous reason.

Nevertheless, even in these times, there must be some form, some quality of integrity which could apply to criticism. It would seem, for the most part, to be a matter of *being.* Criticism of contemporary authors, who are living, growing, changing workers, would seem to preclude the criterion of consistency. The consistency of our critics is most manifest in those whose views and judgments are controlled (openly or covertly) by ideology, political commitment, deep-rooted personal obsessions or problems, ambitions, etc. All of which things serve to eliminate from consistency any sense of... simple honesty.

A roundabout way to begin a brief comment upon the two books John Cheever has produced since *The Wapshot Scandal*—*The Brigadier and the Golf Widow* and, most recently, *Bullet Park*. Roundabout, but circling the point not to avoid it but to come closer to it. For it seems to me that there is still the possibility of some integrity in criticism. An inner integrity, as it were. The duty of the critic being to question himself and his reactions with an inquisitorial intensity, to apply rack and thumbscrew to his own reactions and feelings, to submit himself to trial by ordeal. And then not to render judgment, but to offer opinion. Not to make record, but to tender a report.

The stories of *The Brigadier and the Golf Widow* delighted and surprised me, even as in sum they seemed to give the lie to my particular reservations about the limitations of *The Wapshot Scandal.* Here, together with a deepening and broadening of Cheever's well-known means, was a new sense of technical innovation, an ease and playfulness which seemed sponsored by joy, more compassion *for* character and in, with, and among the human beings in these stories. As in no previous work—except perhaps in the historical recollections, the remembered myths of *The Wapshot Chronicle*—there was a sense of charity, the love without which all the natural creation—blue skies, bright flowers, clear streams, visible stars—which Cheever so passionately celebrates, would be as unnamed and incomplete as the Creation before the breath of God made Adam out of dust. The organization, the arrangement of the stories, decently disguised within the shades and colors of a motley variety, seemed to reinforce this feeling. The final story of the book, "The Queen," taking its narrator all the way down as he seemed to lose all the things most dearly valued in our world—his work, his "honor" in the world, the love of his wife and daughter, and finally the shreds of his secular yearnings and pride which we might call his sanity.

And then and there at the deepest and darkest moment comes the transformation, one as magical and irrefutable as, say, the glorious changes at the end of *Fellini's 8½* or *Juliet of the Spirits;* and, as in both those magnificent examples, an alchemy of the real and the imaginary in which the distinctions between those two worlds are no longer meaningful. So adroitly and simply achieved as the narrator simply *chooses,* all choice being reduced to the essential: "But I awoke at three, feeling terribly sad, and feeling rebelliously that I didn't want to study sadness, madness, melancholy, and despair. I wanted to study triumphs, the rediscoveries of love, all that I know in the world to be decent, radiant, and clear. Then the word love, the impulse to love, welled up in me somewhere above my middle. Love seemed to flow from me in all directions, abundant as water. . . . "

The joyous burden of this story seemed to me as much an achievement for the author as for his narrator-character—credible, infinitely simple, exactly right and admirable.

And therefore my slight reservations about the wholeness of *Scandal* seemed quite foolish, unimportant.

And now we have the next novel *Bullet Park,* prominent, well-promoted, successful, praised by most of the critics who "count." And now my reactions are equally surprised. And I am less delighted. So much less pleased with the technique, tone, and tenor of this new work that I at once looked back to the copyright dates of the individual stories of *Brigadier.* Those stories were published from 1952-

1964. Much that is terrible has happened since then, much that can help explain the almost apocalyptic urgency of this new novel, an urgency obvious in the disregard for the *surface* of the story, its quality of fable. A fable of doom and despair in which the outward and visible events are to be taken no more literally than Aesop's talking foxes and crows. A grotesque comedy, synoptic and gag-ridden, in which the "happy ending" is gratuitous, sarcastic, and essentially negative. In sum a sort of scornful, self-righteous judgment passed upon the particular world (and its particular people) Cheever has chosen to exploit. In a deeper and sadder sense, then, a scornful self-judgment. For, whether he intends it so or not, when an author heaps coals upon the funeral pyres of his imagined world and imaginary people and creatures, it is himself, the maker, who is tried by fury. The savagery, the misanthropy of this work might be (and *has been,* by casual critics) called Swiftian. But Swift's contempt of the world was of a very different order, being firmly based upon faith and hope and, sometimes explicitly, sometimes by assumed implication, charity. Swift's cutting and cauterizing was done in imitation of Christ, the Physician, the aim being to cure and to heal in sure and certain belief that both are possible. *Bullet Park* is richly worked with figures of religious symbolism, but it is the religion of the Old Law, despite its trappings; and the author for all his gritty gags and jokes, comes on (again) as a prophet calling down fire and brimstone on the heads of the "unworthy," wishing none of us well, his only hope, it would seem, to reverse the process of Providence and return Creation to its pristine (and incomplete) beauty before the coming of Adam and Eve. Full of Christian signs and symbols, this story perverts them one by one as the author (who else?) ignores the gospel. There are no glad tidings here.

In that sense *Bullet Park* has considerable value, beyond both its ways and means. It is beautifully representative, as only the work of a good and gifted writer can be; but what it represents is much that is wrong not with the world but with the *view of the world* which our latter-day prophets (no saints) proclaim.

John Cheever has said (in the modern tradition of the literary artist) that he intends no "history of the times," but is a storyteller recapitulating the verities. Which would be well and good, perhaps even true, if he did not so carefully enter into his record all the *things,* all the immediate concerns of the here and now. Indexed, this book would seem to have them all, all the announced and widely-advertised singularities of our day and age—from "the sexual revolution" to a good "guru," from race to mace. Therefore I return to my original questions. Rather, they return, though uninvited, to me.

As a picture of our world and times Cheever's stylized vision is distorted, and wrapped in the enviable transparent materials (*plastic?*) of privilege. He remains a *New Yorker* writer and is increasingly a cartoonist. He remains a representative of the New England moralistic tradition—stern, unyielding, straitlaced, self-righteous. One who can pillory a backslider, duck a eccentric (and sometimes lovable) characteristics of the New England spirit. The curious mixture of profound conservatism on the one hand and the "liberal" spirit which knows what is best and right for others and would impose those qualities upon them. One thinks of Thoreau who loved nature—as he found it by the tranquil shores of Walden Pond. Thoreau who would rather go to jail (for one night) than support the Mexican War, but who likewise was conned by brutal John Brown into believing his kind of killing was inspired and good; and who dutifully contributed money to his cause, causing the death of many who were innocent and, ultimately, the death of Brown himself. And ultimately the evisceration of this nation, not a baptism, but a flood of blood, the stains of which remain to this day. Who, therefore, was instrumental in initiating the very process which manifests itself in the celebrated coke stand at Walden Pond and the kleenex and candy wrappers and polaroid trash left behind by tourists who come, humbly enough, to this shrine.

Cheever's vision in *Bullet Park* might be (and has been) called "dark comedy" were it not that the standards it presupposes, the implied sanity against which the folly of our times is measured, are as absurd and absurdly dangerous as anything upon which the scorn of criticism is focused. The ridicule of human suffering (and he finds most human suffering ridiculous and vulgar) is only explicable because it is so abstract from the author's experience. The enormous fear and confusion of the common citizen today is not in itself *common* and is only foolish to those who have no cause for fear and anxiety. From the high castle of princely privilege the lords and ladies can look down with vaguely tolerant amusement as the tiny peasants have at each other with scythes and rocks and clubs.

It is a comforting position. And why shouldn't it be, coming from safety, being so comfortable?

It would seem from *Bullet Park,* from the fable which outweighs all pretense of storytelling, that the Apocalypse itself would be welcomed at this point as a diversion from *ennui* on one hand and the triumph of vulgarity on the other.

That, of course, is a greater folly than any

John Cheever has chosen to satirize in this new book.

The integrity of criticism is to report one's feelings and reactions as truly as possible, acknowledging that much of the sum of all is likely wrong. And even so, in the case of a good and gifted writer like Cheever, to wish that one *is* wrong and that the proof of the critic's failure will be in the work to come.

For me, *Bullet Park* is a bitter book and so in a literal sense a bitter disappointment. But I can still return to the joyous virtuosity of "The Ocean" where the narrator discovering his own folly ("How stupid I had been!") can imagine seizing a laundry marker to "write luve" on the wall: "I wrote 'luve' on the staircase, 'luve' on the pantry, 'luve' on the oven, the washing machine, and the coffeepot, and when Cora came down in the morning (I would be nowhere around) everywhere she looked she would read 'luve,' 'luve,' 'luve.'"

I would rather listen to that wise fool than to the foolish prophet who would offer us only scathing graffiti and other four-letter words to contemplate were the latter, in their persistent Anglo-Saxon purity, not inadmissible in a little world populous with good-mannered, self-righteous, arrogant pharisees.

ABOUT JOHN CHEEVER

John Cheever has had a long professional writing career, beginning at the age of eighteen when the *New Republic* published his short story, "Expelled," a reminiscence of the life at Thayer Academy in South Braintree, which institution had seen fit to expell him at sixteen.

Born May 27, 1912, in Quincy, Massachusetts. Moved to New York about the time (October 1930) that the *New Republic* published his story. Served in the Army in World War II. Except for a brief teaching stint at Barnard, he has been a fulltime writer ever since the war. Has published extensively in many magazines including *Collier's, Atlantic,* and *The New Yorker.* Of his long association with the latter Granville Hicks has written (*Saturday Review,* September 13, 1958): "For years every discussion of what constitutes a typical *New Yorker* short story has got around to Cheever, the common view being that he is quite representative and yet a good deal better than average."

His stories have been adapted for the stage and for movies, and he has written a number of television scripts.

His honors include a Guggenheim Fellowship, the Benjamin Franklin Magazine Award, the O. Henry Award, the National Institute of Arts and Letters Award in literature, and, in 1958, the National Book Award.

He is married and has three children.

BOOKS BY JOHN CHEEVER

THE WAY SOME PEOPLE LIVE
New York: Random House, 1943.
Toronto: Macmillan, 1943.

THE ENORMOUS RADIO AND OTHER STORIES
New York: Funk & Wagnalls, 1953.
London: Gollancz, 1953.
New York: Harper & Row, 1964. (pb)

THE WAPSHOT CHRONICLE
New York: Harper & Row, 1957.
London: Gollanz, 1959.
New York: Bantam, 1957. (pb)

THE HOUSEBREAKERS OF SHADY HILL AND OTHER STORIES
New York: Harper & Row, 1958.

London: Gollancz, 1959.
New York: Macfadden, 1958. (pb)

SOME PEOPLE, PLACES, AND THINGS THAT WILL NOT APPEAR IN MY NEXT NOVEL
New York: Harper & Row, 1961.
London: Gollancz, 1961.

THE WAPSHOT SCANDAL
New York: Harper & Row, 1964.
London: Gollancz, 1964.

THE BRIGADIER AND THE GOLF WIDOW
New York: Harper & Row, 1964.
Ontario: Longmans, Green, 1964.
London: Gollancz, 1965.

BULLET PARK
New York: Alfred A. Knopf, 1969.
New York: Bantam, 1970. (pb)

LT

The Long Chronicle of Guilt: William Golding's *The Spire*

by Walter Sullivan

Surely no novelist writing today has been so reluctant to take his images from the modern world as William Golding. Even when he starts with the here and now—the recent past or the perhaps not too distant future—he immediately puts his characters beyond the far perimeter, where they can contend with themselves or each other undisturbed by contemporary affairs. Two of his novels (*The Inheritors* and *The Spire*) take place in the past. Two (*Lord of the Flies* and *Pincher Martin*) take place during wartime on remote islands. Only *Free Fall* makes use of the present, and the use it makes is as sparing as Golding can manage. I bring this up, because I know of nothing quite like it in the development of the novel. There have always been the historical novelists: Scott, for example, loved to probe what had gone before, but this is not quite what Golding is up to. Conrad set many of his novels outside Europe, but this too was different from Golding's impulse toward what finally seems to be a kind of other-worldliness. This early in Golding's career, this close to the books he has written, one can only speculate concerning his literary motives. But he is a serious novelist who means to speak to the modern world; and one guess is that in order to say what he has in mind, he must transcend our divisive imagery.

Take, for example, the first and so far most popular of his books, *Lord of the Flies.* As everyone knows by now, this is a story about the depravity of man. It sets out to show that human beings are originally sinful, absolutely and purely so, regardless of all other considerations. Such an assertion may seem simple enough if it is taken as part of one's mythology or as an article of faith, but how is a novelist really to make it stick as a literary theme when most of the world is more than nalf convinced of its falsity? The very people who are charged with teaching it as doctrine deny it again and again in their public and private utterances and in their support of programs which they claim will lead to the elimination of evil and of guilt. The Church of England is committed to a full and complex program of social and economic reform—which is perhaps as it should be—but commitment to the welfare state seems to require a belief in the final efficacy of the welfare state. And such a belief is incompatible with the doctrine of original sin.

Given the temper of the times, the hegemony of the social sciences with their extravagant claims concerning man's behavior, how would a novelist go about showing the natural depravity of a group of young men growing up in London or Paris or Berlin or Chicago? Certainly, they would be naughty: this much we expect even out of television or the comic strips. But immediately every knowledgeable reader—and all readers are that these days—would want to know *why* they were naughty. And the author would have to say why in sociological or psychological terms. Were the boys culturally deprived? Did they come from broken homes? Did their parents drink too much? Were they members of minority groups? Well, my observation has been that if they lived in this world, there would have to be something putting pressure on them. Christian doctrine holds that the only act of pure evil ever performed was that of Satan when he revolted against God: he was free of outside temptation and all social influences. But since this precedes the human condition, the next best thing for the novelist out after original sin is to find some parallel to the story of Adam and Eve; so Golding uses children, for effect and by thematic design, and puts them on an Edenic island.

Or consider *The Inheritors,* which is about the last of the Neanderthals, a somewhat dull, but good and innocent group who fall to some early examples of *homo sapiens.* The fall of the Neanderthals is twofold. It is first moral, this is to say, spiritual; then it is physical. Knowledge becomes guilt. Corruption of the mind leads to annihilation. As can readily be seen, the theme here is an extension of the conventional metaphysics that Golding began to work out in *Lord of the Flies.* The tribe of men who come to conquer the Neanderthals are god-like in a way. Their weapons seem to be magical, their language is sophisticated, they have overcome man's traditional fear—according to Golding—of water. They know and they can do, which makes them exactly like us. As Eric Voegelin points out, we members of this most advanced technological society are the new gnostics. Because like the boys in *Lord of the Flies* we are sinful, our knowledge is our doom. We lie awake at night in mortal fear of our own scientific and mechanical efficiency.

But how portray this in modern terms? It is a commonplace of recent criticism that novelists can no longer write big books in the old sense, because no mind is capable of coming to grips with the threat of the bomb. I have some differences with this view which I will bring up later. But obviously any effort to show the guilt knowledge of man in the dimensions of the present circumstances is one doomed by the complexities of the situation and by the political overtones which the novel would necessarily emit. Our modern sickness is such that a book which attempts to portray it in conventional terms is likely to be more a mirror reflecting our distinctive sinful mannerisms than a statement of the basic, changeless evil which they manifest.

In *Pincher Martin,* the method is much the same. Here, a man fights for his life—and for his soul too, though Martin does not quite understand this—with a God who is anxious to be merciful. Ostensibly, Christopher Martin, a naval officer during World War II, is cast up on a rock in the ocean after his ship has been sunk, and here he strives for survival. The fact is he is already dead. The struggle on the rock is Martin's effort to cling to his earthly shape, his own ego. Once more the theme is a ramification of the doctrine of original sin. We destroy ourselves by clinging to what we are: salvation lies in transcending our own nature. At last, God Himself comes to the rock, a large figure in seaboots, and Golding makes Him believable. This is drama on the highest plane: the importance of the outcome is grave indeed. But how could one cast this situation in terms of the modern city?

Angels appeared in the old morality plays, it is true; Faustus had the devil into his study. But not now. In contemporary society, supernatural intelligences, whether good or bad, are slightly comic figures: no one believes in them any more and obviously the author introduces them for the purpose of having a romp. Only queer ducks like C.S. Lewis and Charles Williams take such things seriously, and they are not, strictly speaking, novelists at all. Even in Graham Greene, when Scobie talks to God, the voice comes from inside the man: God remains invisible.

While Golding was working out the lineaments of his stern metaphysics, he was developing as a craftsman: with each novel he sharpened his tools. This was necessarily the case, because perhaps no writer in history ever chose more difficult fictional material with which to deal. *Lord of the Flies* was a fable, a vehicle to carry a preconceived notion; and the difficulty with this sort of thing is that it must be rigidly controlled from the outside. There can never be any proper interchange between author and characters: there is never any moment when the people break truly free. The boys themselves were forced into symbolic postures. Simon, according to Golding, was a Christ figure. Piggy was the spirit of humanism. Ralph was the ideal of young English manhood, the Coral Island type who would be expected to see things through. To comprehend what disaster lies in wait for even a good novelist who chooses to work this way, one need only look at Faulkner's *A Fable*, where the narrative is dead and flat beyond description and the allegory finally escapes the author's command.

In *Lord of the Flies*, nothing escapes the firm hand of Golding. One of his greatest assets is his ability to make ultimate use of a set of controlling images: the shell, the beast, the signal fire. I think it is because these images are so fiercely symbolic, so totally realized and so complexly conceived that the novel assumes its full stature and its almost universal appeal. The conception of the images is a tribute to Golding's mind. But only a pronounced technical proficiency allowed him to drop the dead pilot almost into the dead center of the novel, to break the shell near the end as a signal of catastrophic dissolution, and ironically to employ the destructive fire as a means of rescue. Golding's eye for detail and his ear for dialogue are superb. Yet a good deal of his strength lies in his succinctness, his refusal to describe or report anything that does not heavily count. Even a simple greeting has significance, as in the final scene of *Lord of the Flies*.

> A naval officer stood on the sand, looking down at Ralph in wary astonishment. On the beach behind him was a cutter, her bows hauled up and held by two ratings. In the sternsheets another rating held a sub-machine gun.
>
> The ululation faltered and died away.
>
> The officer looked at Ralph doubtfully for a moment, then took his hand away from the butt of the revolver.
>
> "Hullo."
>
> Squirming a little, conscious of his filthy appearance, Ralph answered shyly.
>
> "Hullo."
>
> The officer nodded, as if a question had been answered.

And of course one has—an unutterable question concerning Ralph and England, man and civilization, which carries much of the meaning of the book.

The Inheritors and *Pincher Martin* are both technically self-limiting, the first because it centers on innocence, which is a lack of knowledge, a lack of sophistication, an inability to make complicated plans; the second because its main action is confined to the area of a minute island and to the thoughts of one man. Perhaps as a result of these limitations, neither book seems to me as good as *Lord of the Flies*, but both are demonstrations of Golding's virtuosity. He has the ability to focus on a scene with amazing and sometimes agonizing clarity: Lok watching the debaucheries of the new people from the tree top; Pincher Martin struggling through the ocean toward the rock. The images are strong and beautifully organic. The deaths of the Neanderthals—or their disappearances—ring through the book like the strokes of a bell proclaiming doomsday. The divine ice, the water, the living flowers, and the dead animals all signify. In *Pincher Martin,* the ocean is eternal. Life on the rock is so hard as to make that life appear to be not worth clinging to. The images of sinful appetite culminate in the one fat maggot in the buried Chinese box. Always, Golding is the master: he is here, behind the scenes, pulling the strings. But he pulls them so well and so meaningfully that few people object.

Yet, in spite of their virtue, these books appear to be the products of Golding's apprenticeship. In my judgment, *Free Fall* is the initial fruition of his major phase. Here for the first, and so far for the only time, Golding makes use of the ordinary tensions of the modern world. Sammy Mountjoy grows up in a slum, goes to school, learns to paint, takes an interest in politics, fights a war. Where he needs to, Golding sketches in his enveloping background with characteristic precision: a street, a child, a church, a school, a suit of armor in an antique shop, a plane circling high above an airdrome. But as it was in the earlier novels, the main flow of the action is inward. The images are exactly that—images carefully wrought, not mere details used to fill in a backdrop.

In his moral complexity, Mountjoy is an amalgamation of Golding's earlier characterizations. Like the boys in *Lord of the Flies,* he is originally sinful; like the new people in *The Inheritors,* he is guiltily knowing; like Pincher Martin, his attention is centered on himself. But the book is cast as a reminiscence, written after the fact and illuminated by subsequent grace and hard won understanding. His painting, the work of his days at which he has been successful, is treated as being of no great consequence. He is concerned with the business of living, which to him now means the quest to discover at what point he lost his freedom of will. "I have walked by stalls in the market place," he writes in the beginning, "where books, dog-eared and faded from their purple have burst with a white hosanna. . . . I have felt the flake of fire fall, miraculous and pentecostal. . . . Where did I lose my freedom? For once I was free."

Another of Golding's remarkable qualities emerges in this novel: his ability to be at once modern and traditional, to compound existentialism and Freudianism with the old heritage of Christian mystery now passing out of vogue. Mountjoy is looking for self and for meaning, but the "systems," he tells us, "do not fit." His choice is to have what he wants, which is carnal knowledge of the beautiful Beatrice. But the consequences of this relationship, the long seduction, the final consummation, are never clear. Beatrice must end her life in a mental institution. "You probably tipped her over," the psychiatrist tells Sammy. "But perhaps she would have tipped over anyway. Perhaps she would have tipped over a year earlier if you hadn't been there to give her something to think about. You may have given her an extra year of sanity and—whatever you did give her. You may have taken a lifetime of happiness away from her." This division, this uncertainty of specific guilt within the framework of general human depravity, is the fate of man.

"The innocent and the wicked live in one world," Sammy Mountjoy says. "But we are neither the innocent nor the wicked. We are the guilty." He proposed to direct this to Miss Pringle, the deeply committed, the Christian school teacher who was utterly devoid of love. But the "we" takes in most of us—all who populate that vast area between the boundaries marked by demons and saints. For the guilty, there is no final answer, no workable system, no durable explanation. Lost and fragmented, we can only look for mercy, hope for grace.

If one rejects the mundane solutions to human agony, which is to say the authority of the social sciences, and casts humanity in the traditional role of sinful weakness, he must sooner or later make his own particular apology for the ways of God to man. Or put it another way: if Christian history is circumscribed by the paradox of the fortunate fall, by the first and the last Adam, then each man's little personal history is a microcosmic representation of the same progression. Each is the author of his own fall; each may receive the gift of salvation if God so wills and the recipient's heart is not hardened. So goes the abstract formula. In specific cases, things are a little more complicated, for the road to hell is paved with virtuous designs. This is true because man is a creature of pride. We cannot work for the glory of God without working also for the glory of self. We cannot keep the two glories separate and in perspective.

Such is the problem of Father Jocelin, the main character in Golding's *The Spire.* The time is the thirteenth or fourteenth century; the action is the addition of a four hundred foot spire to the Cathedral Church of St. Mary at Salisbury; the complication rises out of the weakness of the basic cathedral structure. The walls lack proper foundation; the columns were never meant to hold additional weight. Jocelin will build in spite of this, feeling that he has an angel at his back encouraging him to the task, believing that the work he does is the work and will of God. Unquestionably, Jocelin follows his own will and builds his own sinful monument. He thanks God that he has remained humble; but he does not object to the project being referred to as "Jocelin's folly," and he takes pleasure in examining the stone gargoyles, images of himself which will stand two hundred feet above the ground for centuries to come.

Jocelin is willing to sacrifice not only himself, but whatever and whoever else the job may require. Expenses mount; the riotous workmen kill a citizen in a tavern fight; one of the builders falls to his death; another is burned with hot lead; Pangall, the caretaker, is persecuted and driven away by the workers; Pangall's wife is seduced by Roger Mason, the master builder, and dies in childbirth; and Mason is himself broken and his career is ruined. But this is a small price to pay for an "apocalypse in stone," Jocelin tries to explain to Mason.

> "The building is a diagram of prayer; and our spire will be a diagram of the highest prayer of all. God revealed it to me in a vision, his unprofitable servant. He chose me. He chooses you, to fill the diagram with glass and iron and stone, since the children of men require a thing to look at. . . . We can neither of us avoid this work. . . . It frightens us and it's unreasonable. But then—since when did God ask the chosen ones to be reasonable?"

Beyond the question of motive, there is another; how is the purity of work to be preserved from the tainted mind that achieves the concept, the unclean hands that lay the stone? To drive this point home, Golding makes it clear that the spire is not only a celebration of piety. It is a phallic symbol. Early in the novel, we are shown a small mock-up of the cathedral, complete with spire.

> The model was like a man lying on his back. The nave was his legs placed together, the transepts on either side were his arms outspread. The choir was his body; and the Lady Chapel, where now the services would be held, was his head. And now also, springing, projecting, bursting, erupting from the heart of the building, there was its crown and majesty, the new spire.

Everything is like this, double-edged, ambiguous: all life, all things man is connected with or tries to do. The workmen are blasphemers and infidels: they sing lewd songs in the nave, knock off on mid-summer's eve to build bonfires, carry mistletoe, pagan talisman against evil, to the heights where they must work. Jocelin, too, they consider a bringer of good fortune when he joins them on the scaffolding: their superstitions are all-inclusive; they will propitiate all gods. In the nave, the main construction of the altar is covered, the candles are extinguished, the floor is besmirched. Sounds of construction disturb the worshippers in the Lady Chapel and finally no services can be held in the cathedral at all. Rains come, soaking beneath the foundations, and from an exploratory excavation in the floor of the nave there rises the putrid stench of the decaying dead.

The living flesh also is decadent. Jocelin's body must be flagellated against his dreams of devils. He loves Pangall's wife as his "daughter in God," but he is acutely conscious of her mortal beauty. Part of the money with which he is building his spire comes from his aunt, who became rich by being whore to the king. Old friendships between priests are ruptured. The materials of construction are recalcitrant. Mason fights a losing battle to save himself from the sin of adultery. Accidents happen. The elements are frequently unfavorable. But the spire climbs.

On the night it is finished, a night of howling storm and darkness, two emissaries arrive from Rome. One brings the nail, purportedly a relic from the true cross, which is to be driven in at the top of the spire to preserve it from evil. The other is the Visitor, come to investigate Jocelin's strange behavior. Unkempt after his long days with the workmen, fearful that the spire will fall before he can affix the nail to it, half out of his mind from the ordeal of construction, Jocelin attempts to answer the Visitor's questions. He does not know how long it has been since he went to confession. He cannot say whether or not the workmen were obscene, blasphemous cutthroats. His mind wanders. There are no words by which he can explain his first vision of the spire, the encouragement he received from his angel, the test his will has undergone in seeing the project to its end. And on this same, terrible night, his aunt too is waiting for him—to say that it was her foul practice which made him dean.

Long ago, on an occasion when she had lain with the king and pleased him, he asked her what she wanted. Having already everything she could need or desire, she mentioned Jocelin, and the king replied, "We shall drop a plum in his mouth." Without the help of the king, Jocelin might never have risen. Without the dalliance of his aunt, he might never have had power to see that the spire was built. All the time he has believed in his own virtue and the purity of his call from God. Now at last he sees himself for what he is.

But how might it have been different? How else, except through the instrumentality of sinful men, can God's work be done? "Nothing will come of nothing," Lear said to Cordelia, and in his petulance, he spoke the truth. Whatever gets accomplished in this imperfect world requires its price. The spire was built, it did stand, but at a cost that cannot be calculated in simple terms of burnt flesh and broken bones. There was the cost to the spirit, the cost perhaps even to the soul. And yet, God is merciful to the last.

The rising spire has one further symbolic value; it signifies the increasing pride of Jocelin—the indispensable will. While the tower of stone endures, the tower of pride must be dismantled. This is the evidence of God's mercy; and the eradication of pride in Jocelin is the denouement of the book. Stripped of his office, physically sick and spiritually exhausted, Jocelin lies in his bed of pain and considers what he has done. He has alienated his friends, brought suffering to those who loved him and to some who didn't. He has disrupted the life of the cathedral. In creating dissensions among those around him, he has brought about death and mortal sin. But Pangall's wife has died fortified by the last sacraments, and Mason's attempt at suicide has failed. This is God's intervention—the care He takes of those who are guilty in the faith. Finally Jocelin, himself, dies with the host on his tongue.

The Spire is an altogether remarkable performance. Golding's talent seems to encompass everything. He has worked at the problem until he knows the human condition by heart. The book is tight and profoundly researched. The spire stands at the center of the action controlling all, putting all into perspective. Every stone that is laid is laid with authority. One gets the feeling that if the actual spire were to tumble, Golding could direct the rebuilding of it piece by piece. The people, the streets, the taverns, the close and the cloisters are all real; and standing on the scaffolding with Jocelin, one gets a sense of acrophobia: you can feel the tower sway.

The only cavil I have to make is a strange one: the novel may be too tightly held together, too firmly under Golding's intellectual control. Golding's mental faculties are fantastic. In the sheer power to think, to mold intellectually, to grasp and keep straight a complex tapestry of profound ideas, he is certainly better than Dickens and probably better than Tolstoy. Both of these older novelists are guilty of lapses sometimes, and they occasionally leave rough edges unsmoothed. But what their work abounds in—the sense of life as it is lived, the big and little joys, the small and great heartbreaks—is what *The Spire* and Golding's work in general seem to lack. One feels the need of a little more warmth, a little more temperament perhaps and a little less brain.

If, however, Golding comes off not so well when compared to the masters of the last century, he is, in my judgment, clearly the best of his time. No English novelist who has come into prominence since the end of the war can approach him. Amis may be funnier, Murdoch may be more lively and sophisticated, Sillitoe may address himself more directly to the society from which he sprang. But beside Golding all other post-war English novelists seem to participate in a certain sameness. Concerned as they are with sex and politics and various manifestations of existentialism, they work around the periphery of man's nature and his relation to the universe. They nag at the small assumptions that man used to take for granted. They proclaim for the salvation of the flesh and the pleasures thereof. Golding, a man of the spirit, stands firmly in the middle of an older tradition and diligently works against the present grain.

I referred earlier in this essay to the contention, often met with in recent criticism, that the awful threat of the bomb has deprived us of the possibility of the big novel. No one's mind, it is claimed, can come totally to grips with the shadow under which we live. This may be true, but I view this aspect of our decline not as a first cause, but as a symptom: or worse, an excuse by means of which we avoid facing up to the failures and fragmentations of our age. Certainly it is a good thing to seek for disarmament, to strive for social justice, to work for the eradication of evils and inequities in the world. But no effect can proceed to accomplishment simply on its own. Life is of a piece no matter how we try to divide and fracture it. Action must be based on principle and the materialistic principle will not do.

In speaking of how he came to write *Lord of the Flies,* Golding said that before the second world war he believed in the efficacy of human effort. He shared the view that the world's problems could all be solved by a greater number of competent psychiatrists and bigger and better programs to clear the slums. The war with its everyday cruelties, its constant exhibitions of man's essential nature caused him to change his opinion. He came to see that man is evil. And because he is evil, his actions must be made within the framework of some metaphysic. Otherwise, there is no propritiation for his guilt. And no hope of success.

For England, during her time of fruitfulness, the metaphysical frame has been the Christian religion. And in England, as elsewhere, innumerable atrocities have been perpetrated in the name of Christ. The Roman Catholics burned Cranmer. The Anglicans hanged and disembowled Edmund Campion. In the sixteen-forties, the Puritans desecrated the tombs and the altars in the cathedrals, killed the king, disbanded Parliament, and paved the way for the hegemony of the Whigs. Thus religion was subordinated to the ownership of property: God was captured by the materialists, from whom He has not escaped. It is small wonder then that in these days of fear and suffering, we look to our own devices for relief.

But whatever man does to distort his relationship to the metaphysical reality, the moral law of the universe continues to operate. As Dorothy Sayers pointed out, the natural law is as real as the physical law: it is not an *a priori* concoction; it is a codification based on fact. We are free to deny the law of gravity, but we must suffer the consequences if we do so. It is equally perilous to deny the inherent sinfulness and continuing guilt of all mankind. A profound understanding of this truth underlies the work of William Golding. At the end of *Free Fall,* Sammy Mountjoy considers Nick Shales, the charitable atheist, and Rowena Pringle, the uncharitable Christian, and the worlds they represent.

> All day long the trains run on rails. Eclipses are predictable. Penicillin cures pneumonia and the atom splits to order. All day long, year in, year out, the daylight explanation drives back the mystery and reveals a reality usable, understandable and detached. The scalpel and the microscope fail, the oscilloscope moves closer to behaviour. The gorgeous dance is self-contained, then, does not need the music which in my mad moments I have heard. Nick's universe is real.
>
> All day long action is weighed in the balance and found not opportune nor fortunate or ill-advised, but good or evil. For this mode which we must call the spirit breathes through the universe and does not touch it; touches only the dark things, held prisoner, incommunicado, touches, judges, sentences and passes on.
>
> Her world was real, both worlds are real. There is no bridge.

The two systems operate side by side and each generates its own necessity. Even in the old days of building cathedrals, in the old good and bad time when there was in the western world perhaps as much unity of feeling and philosophy as there has ever been, the two necessities had to be and could not be met. This complication is put in more secular terms in the work of Conrad: man conceives of himself as better than he is; he is doomed to attempt what he cannot possibly do. In Golding, God's and the angel's demand for a spire does not obviate the architectural realities of stress and strain. Nor does a high purpose wash away the guilt assumed in its execution. As *The Spire*—and all of Golding's work—seems clearly to say, the beginning of hope lies in the recognition of our mortal limitation.

And the fact that the spire continues to stand is the proof of grace.

AFTERWORD

Concerning William Golding I want not so much to modify my essay as to extend it in terms of Golding's more recent work. Since *The Spire* he has published *The Pyramid,* a trilogy of novellas which center on the same character—Oliver Clever—and share a common locale—the small English town of Stilbourne, near Salisbury—but which are otherwise separate variations on Golding's usual theme. The first of the three narratives deals with Oliver's pursuit of the body of Evie Babbacombe, which is old stuff for Golding—he gives us the same kind of thing in *Free Fall* —but here the material is handled with a new finesse.

The son of a chemist, Oliver is a bright boy soon to leave for Oxford. Evie is the town policeman's daughter and secretary to the physician whose office adjoins Oliver's father's shop. In the pre-World War II atmosphere of Stilbourne, class lines are drawn with considerable rigidity: there can be no question of marriage in either Oliver's mind or in Evie's; and each of them is driven by his own demon. Oliver's need is the yearning of the flesh, simple and intense: Evie's sorrow is corporal too, the result of too many demands having been made upon her body. The relationship and the people—both the main characters and those who fill out the periphery—are done with great skill: the action is enclosed by sweet and hopeless ambiguities: and the shock of the ending is made credible by the clear understatement of the prose.

The second novella is the shortest and the poorest of the three. In giving a satirical account of the efforts of the Stilbourne Opera Society, Golding is poaching on territory better left to Anthony Burgess or Kingsley Amis, and though the narrative is funny in places, it is generally thin. Even the ending, which attempts to be pure Golding—man is savagely flawed, sin is everywhere—fails because the vehicle is not strong enough to carry the weight of Golding's conviction. But in the third story, Golding is back on the track, telling of Miss Dawlish, the music teacher who is already hopelessly an old maid when Henry Williams comes into her life. Henry arrives to drive Miss Dawlish's students to their examinations, he returns to sell her an automobile and later to bring his wife and son to live in the dark old house Miss Dawlish's father has left her. Her case is absolutely bleak. "Music is Heaven," her domineering father had said and so she tries to tell herself, but the words echo in the centers of her loneliness. Miss Dawlish and Mrs. Williams quarrel and fall out: the affable Henry brings them together again: over and over the cycle is repeated. Henry prospers. Miss Dawlish finally grows old and dies, but not before she has made a bonfire of the music that was supposed to have been the wellspring of her life.

The Pyramid reads half-way as if it were offered as an answer to Golding's critics. At one time or another almost all of us have complained that Golding's main strength as an artist—his ability to create fables and thus to outline the human condition in the boldest possible terms—is also the source of his major weakness as a novelist. To some greater or less degree his earlier work seems to have been damaged by the intellectual quality that pervades it, the scaffolding that is never quite disguised. That he can write otherwise, Golding makes evident in *The Pyramid.* It is worth pointing out that he has forsaken the quality of high invention that informs his previous novels and set to work on some of the oldest stuff in English or any other kind of fiction. Our narrative literature is filled with lovers such as Oliver and Evie and vulnerable old maids such as Miss Dawlish. Golding makes the characters in *The Pyramid* human in a way that few of his characters have been human before. One gets the feeling that he let them live their own lives: he allowed them to talk back to him.

I find the result immensely satisfying, but not totally so. Like the coach who sees his own play fall short of the goal line, I have what I asked for from Golding, but it is still not enough. To be the novelist that I continue to think and hope he can be, he will have to pool his virtues, combine his talent for building the big story with the new gentleness and perception and ease that he demonstrates in his newest book. His works so far seem to be the supporting titles of a really first-rate writer. All that is now required is the one masterpiece, the effort in which all the powers are brought to bear and all the plans are nursed through to fruition. For Golding, who started late, the time would seem to be getting short. Yet, he is not much, if any, older now than Cervantes was when he wrote *Don Quixote*, and Golding's vision still appears to be growing. He continues to see new aspects of our common misery and he becomes more technically proficient with every book that he writes. I persist in my belief that he is the best of his generation in England. If we are lucky, he may be even better yet.

ABOUT WILLIAM GOLDING

William Golding's father was one of a long line of schoolmasters. His mother was an active suffragette. Born in 1911 in the province of Cornwall, Golding attended Oxford where he read science for two years before discovering his aptitude for English. Having cultivated an interest in Anglo-Saxon, he lists *The Battle of Malden* as a major influence on his work.

After his graduation, he became a social worker while also directing, acting, and writing for small British theatrical companies.

Golding describes World War II as a turning point in his life. "I began to see what people were capable of doing," he said in an interview in the *New York Post* of December 17, 1963. He saw much action during the war, witnessing both the sinking of the *Bismarck* and D-Day at Normandy.

After the war, he returned to his teaching position at Bishop Wordsworth's School at Salisbury, Wiltshire. His first published novel, *Lord of the Flies,* received little notice and soon went out of print, only to be reissued in paperback in 1959 when it achieved great popularity on college campuses. In 1955 Golding became a fellow of the Royal Society of Literature.

"In all my books," he says, "I have suggested a shape in the universe that may, as it were, account for things. The greatest pleasure is not—say—sex or geometry. It is just understanding. And if you can get people to understand their humanity—well, that's the job of the writer."

BOOKS BY WILLIAM GOLDING

POEMS
- London: Macmillan, 1934. (pb)
- Toronto: Macmillan, Canada, 1934. (pb)
- New York: Macmillan, 1935. (pb)

LORD OF THE FLIES
- London: Faber & Faber, 1954.
- New York: Coward-McCann, 1955.
- New York: Putnam, 1959. (pb)
- Middlesex: Penguin, 1960. (pb)
- New York: Coward-McCann, 1962.
- London: Faber & Faber, 1962. (pb)
- London: Faber & Faber, 1963. (pb; illus.)

THE INHERITORS
- London: Faber & Faber, 1955.

London: Faber & Faber, 1961. (pb)
New York: Harcourt, Brace & World, 1962.
New York: Harcourt, Brace & World, 1963. (pb)
New York: Pocket Books, 1963. (pb)

PINCHER MARTIN
London: Faber & Faber, 1956.
London: Faber & Faber, 1961. (pb)
New York: Putnam, 1962. (pb)
New York: Berkley, 1963. (pb)
as THE TWO LIVES OF CHRISTOPHER MARTIN
New York: Harcourt, Brace & World, 1957.

SOMETIME, NEVER
Three tales of the imagination by William Golding, John Wyndham, and Mervyn Peake.
London: Eyre & Spottiswoode, 1956.
New York: Ballantine, 1957. (bds & pb)

THE BRASS BUTTERFLY
London: Faber & Faber, 1958.

FREE FALL
London: Faber & Faber, 1959.
New York: Harcourt, Brace & World, 1960.
London: Faber & Faber, 1961. (pb)
New York: Harcourt, Brace & World, 1962. (pb)
New York: Pocket Books, 1967. (pb)

THE SPIRE
London: Faber & Faber, 1964.
New York: Harcourt, Brace & World, 1964.
New York: Harcourt, Brace & World, 1965. (pb)
New York: Pocket Books, 1966. (pb)

THE HOT GATES
London: Faber & Faber, 1965.
New York: Harcourt, Brace & World, 1966.

New York: Harcourt, Brace & World, 1966. (pb)
New York: Pocket Books, 1968. (pb)

THE PYRAMID
London: Faber & Faber, 1967.
New York: Harcourt, Brace & World, 1967.
New York: Harcourt, Brace & World, 1968.
New York: Harcourt, Brace & World, 1969. (pb)

LT.

Hunting a Master Image: The Poetry of Richard Eberhart

by Daniel Hoffman

What comes after a poet's *Collected Poems?* Richard Eberhart adds to his thirty years' work in *The Quarry,* his thirteenth book and one of his best. Despite the increasing honor that has come to this long career and the appreciative comment of, among others, Selden Rodman, A. Alvarez, and Philip Booth, Eberhart's place in American poetry still seems to need definition. To the editors of the recent *Poems in Progress* and the earlier Rinehart textbook, *Fifteen Modern American Poets,* he appears as the oldest among the promising. But while Eberhart's work is still in progress, his promise has been fulfilled and the shape of his career thus far can be seen. He belongs to no popular movement; neither his virtues nor his faults are shared by his peers, and his peers are few. A stubborn individualist who has been true to his own gifts regardless of what contemporaries were writing or what others thought the times demanded, he early found a vein of ecstatic revelation whose felicities none other has approached. Yet *The Quarry* confirms what was already evident in *Collected Poems* (1960); there's a new suppleness and gravity in Eberhart's recent verse and the range of experience and expression in his best work is increasing.

Once, a decade ago, I tried to make a case for Eberhart among Dylan Thomas' more ardent disciples, citing one of my favorites among his irreplaceable poems. "Ah, but that's the trouble—if he could only live at the pitch that is *near* madness! Great poetry comes from *madness,* the real thing." There isn't much you can do with some people, not even to show them that Thomas wasn't mad, or that Eberhart in his own way is equally a daemonic man, or that "near madness" is far preferable to madness whether real or feigned, as a source of poetry. For if reason wholly abdicates its place in the imagination, what results is a partial, lessened thing: the *Grand Guignol* of compulsive confession without relevance beyond the self, or that "invention without discovery"—a clam playing the accordian—which Wallace Stevens recognized as the "essential fault" of surrealism. Why not a poetic in which reason merges with the preconscious, making unexampled leaps and spurts between one word or thing or feeling and another; it may be a mere filament, the one thread by which the self can emerge from its labyrinthine mysteries, but it must be always there, a part of the whole, an irreducible minimum if need be when intuition, the obliging and unpredictable revelatory force, blows over the embers of feelings or the ashes of thought. The wildness of fire caught in the intensity of a focussed beam: in Eberhart, the contrary claims of intuition and intellect, of heart and head, are united at the center of poetry.

Yet Eberhart usually thinks of himself as a wholly intuitive poet. In the Christian Gauss lectures he gave at Princeton in 1955, Eberhart divided poems into works of Psyche and works of the Will, a distinction he mentions in the preface to his *Collected Plays* and intermittently in reviews but has not developed discursively with systematic force. One thinks of the cleavage between Muse Poetry and Apollonian verse argued by that rigorous polemicist Robert Graves. While Eberhart is too modest to make an exclusive claim for one sort of poem only, it is unmistakable that what he calls "Psyche poems" are more valuable to him than are the many-versioned splendors arrived at by arduous craft. He comes out unabashedly for "an old-fashioned notion, the idea of poetry as a matter of inspiration." In a recent interview with Denis Donoghue (*Shenandoah,* Summer 1964), Eberhart observes:

> It has been true of me almost from the start that in a sense a poem is a gift of the gods. . . it is something beyond rationality, the fire of it is a potent force which is given to you and in which the personality is held in abeyance, and the personality is a vehicle for the utterance of the poem. Some of my best poems. . . have been given in this way and they have been emitted in a high state of consciousness and control and one has not had to change a word or maybe only a word or two.

With consciousness, or Will, in a state of suspension, the bequest of Psyche does seem a gift of the gods; discipline over words, experience, metaphor, and rhythm is instinct with expression itself. But this phenomenon is not unique; all poets know it, and all exegetes who have rummaged through manuscripts with an awareness of the process revealed can acknowledge in others a fact they cannot emulate in practice. It bespeaks the mastery of a style in which the principles of organization have been fused with the heat of imaginative manipulation. Such a fusion is possible only after one has possession of his *donnée,* a stance toward life, an attitude toward experience revealed in linguistic resources, in a personal rhythm and control of sound perhaps anterior to the meanings of individual words.

An early poem (from *Song and Idea,* 1942) suggests Eberhart's personal strategies with language and with experience. From it a range of accomplishment extending through *The Quarry* may readily be inferred:

> I walked out to the graveyard to see the dead
> The iron gates were locked, I couldn't get in,
> A golden pheasant on the dark fir boughs
> Looked with fearful method at the sunset,
>
> Said I, Sir bird, wink no more at me
> I have had enough of my dark eye-smarting,
> I cannot adore you, nor do I praise you,
> But assign you to the rafters of Montaigne.
>
> Who talks with the Absolute salutes a Shadow.
> Who seeks himself shall lose himself;
> And the golden pheasants are no help
> And action must be learned from love of man.

The locked gate and the inexplicable exotic bird evoke a trance-like atmosphere, intensified by the lack of punctuation at the ends of lines one and five, as though the mind's power to distinguish units of thought were in suspension. The only action in the poem is completed in line one; the rest is an extended address to the presence who bars the speaker from whatever end he sought. Why did he wish to see the dead? Perhaps the pheasant is itself their answer to his unasked question. He does learn, at the end, that "golden pheasants are no help," for like the Absolute they prove Shadows and are "assign[ed]to the rafters of Montaigne."

A golden bird upon the gates of death: whether, like Yeats's "artifice of eternity," or like Stevens' peacocks among the hemlocks, menacing man with the cry of darkness, an abstraction still. And therefore the surprising invocation of Montaigne is just. "The rafters of Montaigne" may recall some passage in the *Essays* I can't place; I trust these rafters are in the attic to which "Montaigne in his tower," that most empirical humanist invoked in "The Groundhog," would indeed consign an Absolute, a Shadow. Like him, Eberhart in this poem rejects Spirit without reality.

The diction of the poem is in a style Montaigne would praise. He wrote, in *Of the Education of Children* (I quote Donald Frame's translation),

> The speech I love is a simple, natural speech, the same on paper as in the mouth; a speech succulent and sinewy, brief and compressed, not so much dainty and well-combed as vehement and brisk; rather difficult than boring, remote from affectation, irregular, disconnected and bold; each bit making a body in itself.

Among the sinewy boldness of this speech are such resonant phrases as "fearful method," "Sir bird" who "winks," and "my dark eye-smarting." These words carry the mystery, neither the pheasant's method nor his fear being disclosed, the "wink" suggesting both impassivity and guile, the "dark eye-smarting" perhaps the grief that led the speaker to the gate—or is it his blinking attempt to stare down the pheasant's golden winking eye? Notwithstanding the clarification of the last stanza, even to address the Absolute is to give homage ("Sir bird"). The paraphrase of Matthew 16:25 implies that loss of self is necessary—and will come, even in the attempt to achieve its opposite, self-discovery, which must have been what led the speaker to this place of the dead. Yet what he finds there is "no help," for "action must be learned from love of man." The action of the poem, then, is a withdrawal and return, for we are sent back blinking from the gates of death to the world of living, to the world of love.

These lines seem an epitome of vintage Eberhart. Their humane conclusion is reaffirmed in the "moral answer" demanded by "battalions of mankind" in "If I could only live at the pitch that is near madness" and in the compassion of the war poems and of "The human being is a lonely creature." The resolution of this poem, like that of "In a hard intellectual light," evokes intuitive wisdom, piercing the action of the baffled will. As in these other poems, the form resembles those songs of Blake's in which the argument by an unexpected reversal of its own logic comes to a conclusion as inevitable as it was unforeseen.

The thrust of Eberhart's imagination usually starts in a like direction, moving from a commonplace reality toward a confrontation with its essence, but not always veering away. This is the way the feelings travel in "The Soul longs to return whence it came," another poem of a journey to the graveside. At first we are given such prosaic details as that he has left the engine running in his car. But from the naturalistic fact the soul bursts past the locked gates in this poem, and in an ecstasy of realization arrives at the destination it had not known it was seeking,

> saying, saying
> Mother, Great being, O Source of Life
> To whom in wisdom we return,
> Accept this humble servant evermore.

More frequently the imagination's journey begins in the contemplation of a particular object, often a living creature. In his most famous poem, "The Groundhog," one creature's death becomes all death, a memorable emblem of frangible mortality. Eberhart often seems akin to Emerson and Dickinson in his unmediated confrontations of spiritual energy. While his every sense delights in the natural world for its own sake, Nature is usually luminous, a paradigm of the Oversoul. Such poems as "The Book of Nature" bespeak a Wordsworthian pantheism. Eberhart celebrates also a radiance in the created world with a purity of perception that recalls Traherne:

> Go to the shine that's on a tree
> When dawn has laved with liquid light
> With luminous light the nighted tree
> And take that glory without fright.

What's celebrated in a more recent poem, "Sea-Hawk," is not song or felicity but the fierce unchanging nature which seems "To make the mind exult. . . . A blaze of grandeur, permanence of the impersonal." Another of the late *Collected Poems* praises a humbler grandeur yet a similar one, a primordial nature in man:

> Dark, gray men at work,
> Impersonal as pines and sky,
> I watch the heavy scene,
> The slow, mute progress
> Of torso, arm, leg and rake
> As seeing a dark core
> And sombre purpose of life,
> Primitive simplicity,
> Dignity beyond speech,
> My mute salutation,
> Time-deepened love
> To clam diggers,
> The diggers of sea worms.

Ever since Wordsworth met the leech gatherer, poets have praised simpler men who toiled without speech. Better than any I know, this poem confers upon them the dignity discovered in their gestures.

In *Stewards of Excellence,* Alvarez speaks of Eberhart's "lust for system." Indeed it is his need to wrench assurances of meaning from the accidents of life that make poetry necessary for him. The world however is not always a perpetual revelation, and Eberhart has sometimes failed through too much trying. Either he makes too conscious a reading of a

Significance into a fact of nature, or he tries too hard to find what may not in fact be there. His faults are allegory and a kind of pawky abstract diction no one else would think of putting into poems. It is true that he has been all too prodigal of his talent and uncritical of its exercise; even in this latest book he does not balk at rhyming "poetry" with "immortality" or at telling us that "Individuation is the way to the universal." Diction so studded with inkhorn terms has no discernible relation to any norms of spoken usage. Yet despite his lust for systems and his tendency to grab at large abstractions to supply them, Eberhart is essentially—like Montaigne—empirical, knowing in the end that his imagination must makes its way without one. There is a new note in *The Quarry,* not of skepticism, but of a willingness to take the world with its disasters, and outlast them through compassion if not beat them down by an immediate affirmation. Eberhart has been praised as a religious poet by Philip Booth, yet in his interview with Donoghue he seems a bit reluctant to think of himself primarily in Christian terms. Natural piety indeed is his, a deep religious emotion that comes not from systematic doctrines or a theological conception of the world. It is rather a testimony of the senses. I think compassion is for Eberhart as natural as the other precious five.

Confronting the realm of Nature, where man is but an observer and a celebrant, in *The Quarry* as in his earlier books Eberhart can praise what he sees from his rugged peninsula on the Maine coast: in one case, three eagles

> in unison and swift flight,
> As if purpose were absolute,
> They flew passionate, inexorable
> And wheeled from my sight.

But among human lives such absolute purpose is lacking, or it is secreted behind the appearances of random catastrophes. In "Flux" he searches a summer's losses for evidence of such a purpose, but "There is a somber, imponderable fate. / Enigma rules, and the heart has no certainty." Again, in "The Master Image,"

> The years were a glimpse of something undefined.
> They obscured as much as they revealed. Tined
> Hay tossed up. Why a girl died in a day.
> Would a master image spring in the heart,

> The elusive and incredible mystery?
> Molasses and water for the hot hay-pitchers.
> A broken-down hearse seeks the harsh rocks.
> The changing people cannot see the centuries.

The Quarry continues Eberhart's perceptions of the harmonies of nature, the disharmonies of man, and the capacity of the imagination to impose nature's resolutions upon human disorder by the discovery of spiritual unities in meditation of the chances of life. Thought—that is poetry, the poetic process—frees the individual from the seeming chaos that surrounds him, from the dualisms between which he cannot wisely choose, and makes possible to his understanding the possession of all truths simultaneously.

Eberhart's themes are restatements in individual and contemporary terms of traditional Romantic dispositions toward experience. His gritty acknowledgments of physical reality are joined with an insistence upon the reality of spirit, and it is this which few of his contemporaries can so directly experience or make us believe. This must be why Kenneth Rexroth, reviewing *Great Praises,* called Eberhart "the most profound poet of his time." His mind, his style, with its *enjambement* of abstractions amid colloquialism, suggest his kinship to Emerson. So does his enterprise:

> I had enjoined the battle of being
> In harshness of inner seeing
> . . . .
> And in true sensuality
> Discover the nativity
> And history
> Of the soul among its immortalities.

At some point we ask of a poet's work, Who's in this world he has imagined for us? How much experience, how various, shared by whom? The Romantic Ego answers, "I am here, among the Primal Forces. I look into my heart, I carry mankind in my side. All fate is my destiny," We may not find this an ingratiating answer, unless that ego has a humility we might not think to require of a dramatic poet who flashed a Punch and Judy show of masks and characters before us. He who speaks always as "I" runs the risk of the Lawgiver among the Philistines, or of the naif Apostle to the doctors of an agnostic philosophy. Until recently Eberhart had run these risks with such temerity one thought there were no other kinds of poems for him to write. His early poems held scarcely any mention of politics, the Depression, breadlines, Hitler, FDR, liberal hopes; their *persona* was not given us in a society, or often in specific relationships to others. In the war poems in *Burr Oaks* reality includes not only the non-mechanical world but is increasingly societal. Then, in the early 1950s, he began experimentally to write plays. In these, new concerns become his subjects and a new clipped rhetoric appears. He has said of his plays, "The motives are the same as those for lyric poètry; they come from a basic split in the soul and a need to create, to compensate, to make a whole world. There is a desire for expansion, for a larger canvas." Although he never solved certain formal problems—all his plays are plays within plays, our attention divided between the fates of the characters and the problems of their authors—in their most effective scenes Eberhart did extend his imaginative world. In *The Visionary Farms,* his most successful play, he presents a sardonic fable of cupidity and deceit as intrinsic to the success of a business empire, success itself begetting and requiring a crooked ethic against which no decency can prevail. A man of individual virtue is undone by the self-interest of his employer whose business had been made bigger and better through the chicanery of another employee they both had trusted. As Denis Donoghue observed in *The Third Voice,* if "the satire is based not so much on derision as on solicitude," the characters and actions are yet simplified and distorted. "Motives are so attenuated that they are indistinguishable from the movements of a machine." This simplicity requires a direct, colloquial diction, a conversational line.

Now, in *The Quarry,* he has assimilated into his verse some of the gains from his playwriting. A group of new poems unlike any of his lyrics and different from the plays whose brisk rhetoric they yet resemble, presents characters quite unlike the Reader of the Spirit who usually speaks in Eberhart's style. If there be distortion through simplification, these characters yet give the illusion of personalities fully revealed:

My death was arranged by special plans in Heaven
And only occasioned comment by ten persons in Adams, Massachusetts,
The best thing ever said about me
Was that I was deft at specifying trump.
I was killed by my father
And married to my mother
But born too early to know what happened to me.
And as I was an only child
I erected selfishness into a personal religion.

This "New England Bachelor" is recognizably akin to other last Puritans, but the abrupt movement of his thought and the wry humor of its juxtapositions convey the character's individuality and the style's. As was true of his other themes, Eberhart touches on such matter as Frost might have used but stamps it as his own. There are a half-dozen such sketches in *The Quarry.* Next to the genteel sobriety of the bachelor is "A Maine Roustabout"—"It's an old gut forced with whiskey keeps me going." Others give us a beloved spinster dying at ninety, and a neurotic widow going mad. No conclusions drawn, no morals derived: these poems are completely given to presentation. They show a gift for dramatic monologue unanticipated in *Collected Poems,* and a new objectivity.

Eberhart was nineteen years old when Eliot published *The Waste Land.* After a Minnesota boyhood and graduation from Dartmouth he studied at Cambridge University (Empson was his classmate) and began to publish verse in England when Auden and Spender were rocking the boat of the Fisher King with their poetry of pylons and revolution. In America, despite the thirties, the dialectic of our poetry proved a little different: the great debate, still unresolved, between versions of Classicism and forms of Romanticism. Eliot made himself the representative classicist; his most influential antagonist—of whom he never took any notice— has made him stand for enslavement to Tradition and the Iamb. Dr. Williams for his part tendentiously proposed the Romantic ways to Freedom and the American Identity. In *The Quarry* Eberhart acknowledges this conflict in an affectionate poem that makes shrewd comments on his friend's polemics:

> With gusto to toss the classics out, and with them
> The sonnet, you live yet in a classic Now,
> Pretend to advance order in your plain music
>
> And even preach that Form (you call it measure
> Or idiom) is all, albeit your form would mate
> The sprawling forms, inchoate, of our civilization.

No less than Williams, Eberhart is both a Romantic and a typically American poet. But no need for him to chuck out the sonnet or the classics. One of his finest poems is the sonnet "Am I My Brother's Keeper?" in which he takes a line from Keats and invokes Socrates while meditating on a murder in New Hampshire. Yet no one with an ear for tongues would take this, or any of Eberhart's other successes, to be in any lingo but American and his own. His characteristically impure diction runs all the risks I've mentioned, but when it works, the abstract language of judgment and qualification really qualifies and judges the simpler terms of presentation, the collision between them vibrant with surprises, "the profound caught in plain air."

In his forms Eberhart is partly improvisatory but not, as Williams demanded, absolutely so. His rhythm is an individual modification of traditional stress patterns, and his best work frequently makes a slantwise, offhand use of minimal forms. With a simple stanzaic pattern of quatrains or triplets, using off rhyme, interior rhyme, or no rhyme, Eberhart makes the shape of the feelings dominate the form of the poem, and the images break into consciousness from the nature of the things they embody. He takes over a simple hand-me-down and, tinkering with it, gets somehow something identifiably his own:

> Alas! Any place will do.
> There is no poetical place,
> America continues its practices.
>
> Final toughness of the word,
> The word bawling imperfections,
> Its paradox to be heard.

This is his personal idiom, and the passage suggests its source. Curiously congruent with his urgent moral sense and his natural piety is an equal reverence for what Stevens called "the gaiety of language." These motives couple and beget poems that use the "words" described in *Great Praises,*

> Durable with the fate of things
> When I had lived enough.
>
> Then I had a total myth
> Sounding on an eternal shore.
> It was the world-memory alone
> When I was dead and gone.

These affirmations suggest both Cassirer's notion of language as itself conceptual of meaning and of myth, and the psychic mythography of Jung, who discovers our "total myth" in "the world-memory" where all experience is hoarded. Eberhart would probably hold both views without distress. However his theory of language may eventually be described, the language he uses is resonant with energies plumbed from psychological depths, and the movement of his poems is strong with the strength of ancient dispensations of our feelings.

As he has grown older—he is now sixty—Richard Eberhart has "lived enough" for his words indeed to be "durable with the fate of things" while they reveal "the harshness of inner seeing." There is about Eberhart's vision now a "primitive simplicity" such as he discerned in the labor of the clam diggers, "seeing a dark core / And sombre purpose of life." Like "The Kite," our minds "fly, secreted, dark / Riding on the winds of chance," and the adventure of the flight suggests that God is within the capricious wind. Here is another unexpected congruency, a Santayanan joy in the imaginative power conjoined with, not substituted for, the Deity of conventional belief. Although Eberhart's views seem to resemble Santayana's formative ideality, I think he remains true to the Emersonian strain in the rest of his thought. The Over-Soul may be a Platonic Absolute, indeed a Shadow, but it does exist; and we learn from love of man and "The Book of Nature" what resembles it.

Perhaps Eberhart's Quarry is not only the granite rock of reality into which he digs, but at the same time a truth as alive as a creature which he hunts. His poem "The Master Image" ends with a buck leaping over a chasm, yet even this does not seem sufficiently to subsume all other images any more than the stag crashing from the lake served so in Frost's poem, "The Most of It." *The Quarry* begins and ends with Eberhart's most ambitious recent efforts to find such a master image. In the long opening poem, occasional gusts lift the detailed actuality of manoeuvering a large navy target kite into the upper air of higher truths. But the wind turns out to be "an Abstract God," and the intermittent delight of sailing does not in the end inform actions beyond itself. Perhaps the difficulty is that the master image eludes him still, and to give kite-sailing such a burden in a twelve-page poem seems as much an act of Will as the bequest of Psyche. The mastery of experience may reveal itself not in that single image which would satisfy his lust for system but in the action of the mind itself, a rhythm by which our natures discover our deepest selves. This is what I think Eberhart discovers in his two concluding "Meditations." These poems accept the complexities that "The Kite" tried to sail above and, with the spare clarity of a morality play, enclose them within a double affirmation of belief in God and in the resolving power of the imagination. "Meditation One" starts where Eberhart had indeed begun thirty years ago, at the graveside in "The soul longs to return whence it came," but this time that is but a beginning, not a destination:

> We begin with the belief in a great mother,
> The motherwater and the ancient, grand indestructibility
> Of birth-thrust, and in this mystery remaining alive. . . .

he spans our attempt to live through time in the knowledge of oncoming death—

> Then where shall we go? And to whom apply?
> Who but to God the anchor of man's vanity. . . .

At the end he enjoins us to "Give the Devil his due, praise God for invented Heaven, / And hold to the end every last thing in view."

The second meditation defines style, not as an aesthetic end so much as "Aeschylean right-mindedness,"

> the perfection of a point of view
> Nowise absolute, but held in a balance of opposites
>
> So that for a moment the passage of time is stopped
> And man is enhanced in a height of harmony. . . .

Style thus makes possible that completion of the self by which we may live among our mortalities:

> Hoping the improbable advent of unity
> Will triumph over the mocking dualisms. . . .
>
> As whether to fly out, and shout with the government,
> Or, silent as a crab, burrow in the sands of solitude. . . .
>
> Whether to accept the brotherhood of the many
> Or live for the talents and the truths of the few.
>
> So should style amplify and refine man's poise,
> Be an instrument as lucid as the best of his knowing.

Such lucidity is not likely to be in fashion nowadays, especially among those who would deny new grist to the relentless mills of *The Explicator.* The psychology current in what Donald Hall has, perhaps pretentiously, labeled "a new kind of imagination" in American verse is of course that of a familiar kind of imagination in French poetry. Like René Char and Reverdy, among others, the new poets rely not upon logical connectives but on the more tactile movement from image to image for the release of meaning in their verse. This accords well with Whitman's and Williams' examples, and there is much joy for the reader in the latest forays of these Romantic forces against the Instant Classicism which the New Critics have left behind. Eberhart has had nothing to do with this seeming new direction. Although his meditations seem didactic, what is it they preach or teach but submission to a movement of feeling inscrutable to the formulations of thought? Perhaps he gets near where the others are going by hewing his own way, as he always has. At "the best of his knowing," Eberhart touches primal simplicities, sombre truths, and possible joys. If we judge him by his best it seems likely that a score or more of his poems will prove indestructible. More than this we have no right to desire, yet in the vigor of maturity his imagination is still adding to their number and variety.

AFTERWORD

Richard Eberhart has brought out two books since *The Quarry.* One, a collection of sonnets written some thirty years ago, is pretty far from the style of the later tough-minded lyrics which in my view comprise this poet's lasting work. His other recent book, however, *Shifts of Being* (1968), adds several rigorous poems to that number by which his verse will continue to claim our admiration.

Shifts of Being is a typical Eberhart performance. One of the astonishing things about this poet is his consistent and unbelievable unevenness. Nobody of comparable reputation has written half as many bad poems, nor has, it would seem, so little capacity for strict self-criticism. Every Eberhart book forces the reader to choose up sides between its duds and its marvels. In *Shifts of Being,* especially in the first thirty pages or so, he seems determined to show how little he has learned from his forty years of authorship, for his failures (as they seem to me) are all flawed by the same flaws: poems clogged with abstractions; poems self-indulgent in their diction, alternately refulgently romantic and pretentiously polysyllabic; poems rhyming to excess, with many of the rhyme-sounds weary and clichés. One quatrain may suffice to illustrate some of these qualities:

> My brains are slipping in the fields of Eros.
> My contamination of the absolute
> Intrigues me with the confrontation of imperfection
> In which I veer from the cradle to the grave.

Such writing fails for being the product of the straining will. Eberhart, as I have noted, is, by his own terminology, a poet of the psyche. There seems no perceptible connection between his willful awkwardness and purposed abstraction on the one hand, and the clarity of vision and diction with which he speaks in his best poems.

Not that it's likely to do any good, but I'd say to him, after reading *Shifts of Being,* "Dick, give up rhyme forever, don't ever write a poem on purpose, simply go about your life, teaching the Dartmouth boys, taking trips abroad, spending summers in the rugged splendor of the Maine coast, with your pencil ready until the mysterious gift falls on you from the skies. Let the muse speak in her own perspicuous accents, not to be invoked by murky philosophizing or by efforts to wring the beautiful from the concatenation of multisyllabic sounds." I'd say this—I'd presume on long acquaintance to say this—yet as the words leave me I know them to be futile.

For why should Eberhart heed my advice any more than he has taken the counsel of other friends, reviewers, or critics over the years? And besides, how do I know that he doesn't *need* to write verses that seem to me mere mouthings of gibberish in order to awaken or provoke his muse to speak in the clearer accents of true knowledge and delight? Long ago Eberhart must have recognized that his outflow would likely always be a mixture of tones, dictions, and styles, and decided that his readers would have to take him in the large and let each choose according to his taste. He once told me that hardly ever did favorable reviewers of any of his books praise the *same* poem. It may be thought that a poet nonetheless should be able to identify his own best work. But that would require this poet to become another sort of poet. I guess his seeming indiscriminateness is somehow intrinsic to his virtues. Although he's now a professor of English like the rest of us, like most of his reviewers and critics and so many of his readers and fellow-bards, Eberhart is not really at all an academic writer or thinker. He is cast in a different mold from poet-critics like Tate and Ransom and Jarrell.

My own taste makes me flip through and forget those poems I find too sweetly musical or sentimental, too forcedly transcendental. Instead of those leapings of the will toward the empyrean, I read and re-read the tough Eberhart poems that honestly confront actuality and somehow, by a power they embody but do not define, succeed in wresting from experience an intimation of sublimity. Poems in *Shifts of Being* which I think so succeed include "Shy?," "The Immortal Type," "The Wild Swans of Inverane," "Thoor Ballylee," "Lions Copulating," "A Wedding on Cape Rosier," and "Outwitting the Trees." In some of these Eberhart uses the simple quatrain which seemed his undoing in other poems earlier in the book; in these successes he usually eschews rhyme, saving himself from surrendering sense to sound. The results are likely to be surprising.

In others of these poems Eberhart writes in a longer line, similar to that used in *The Quarry* in the poems whose movement, approaching that of seemingly ordinary speech, appears to have been influenced by his playwriting:

> Today there is another marriage
> Of the very young by the side of the sea.
> The caterer is so pleasant he seems one of the
> guests.
> The parents are divorced but the yachting young
> Take communion along with their vows. . . .

What could be more natural-seeming than this verse movement, so deceptively like conversation yet structured by its own inevitable rhythm? So the poem goes on, meditating about the meaning of marriage, of this marriage, with nothing in it an anticipation of the concluding lines:

Father Emerson puts out the candles.
His father knew Emily Dickinson.

It takes such a short time to get married,
We noticed no change in the tide.

Poems in *Shifts of Being* reflect Eberhart's travels, to Europe one year, another to Africa. His two poems from Ireland make an interesting pair. In "The Wild Swans of Inverane" he echoes, inevitably, Yeat's "The Wild Swans at Coole," using the inevitable image for his own primordial affirmations:

Seven wild swans descending out of the heavens,
Out of myth, sacrifice, out of ancient ecstasy
Settling with rough vigor on turbulent waters
In magical union of reality and dream. . . .

But in "Thoor Ballylee" Eberhart is quite his own man:

I read The Tower in 1928.
Great. I moved and thrilled then.

I had only youth's experience.
Sense of all savage riches. . . .

The Tower I saw in 1965. . . .

The view from the top was half closed in,
Had been open and had been free.

But what drew the soul down small
All around was the little rill

For the great symbol of water, thin above pebbles
Unable to utter the mildest trebles,

A lazy stream with no drinking cup,
Dried up, almost gone out, quit.

Thus, his artifice of eternity,
Not free, square, too short, squat. . . .

The true tower of course is Yeats's own artifice, not the ungainly structure maintained as a tourist stop by the good ladies of the Kiltartan Historical Society. Eberhart's artifices are, like Yeats's, in his own best poems. As he edges toward the latter side of middle age he has begun to look intently not only on what passes immediately before his eyes but backward over the inexorably vanished past. Memory is looming larger for this poet of hitherto immediate perceptions, and his retrospective poems specifically invoke Plato as a consolation for the ravages of time and the limits of mortality. One such poem is "The Immortal Type":

> I cannot admit to the roughage of time
> When I am told that her time is over, and ruthless
> Death takes her into corruption.
> I refuse to believe in death: death, be truthless!
>
> Yet I approach her loss as a symbol and gall of all
> Who fall from life. My mind now admits death.
> My being sees everywhere naked disaster,
> Yet my spirit clings to Plato to her last breath.
>
> From me this last breath of her an eternal vision
> Flows into my eyes with radiant acclaim.
> Through me the vision flowers, and to you
> I pass its subtle, invisible, and nameless name.

When this metaphysical vein of contemplation is occassioned by a particular experience and articulated in language as clear as the realization it embodies, Eberhart writes at his characteristic best, in love of life and fear of loss and hope of holding something against destruction.

Another of these latest poems is almost a restatement of his early knocking on the gates of mortality in "The Soul longs to return" and "I walked out in the graveyard to see the dead." This time, in "The Ides of March," the action is similar—the poet, again in his car, approaches a graveyard in New England, but now by accident, not design; and he ends not with the mystical affirmation of immortality as in the earlier poems, but with questionings. For now, he says, "I wondered what I signified":

> The car bore on through the countryside,
> Plunging in the meshes of society,
> We were going to meet our friends in the world,
> In the next connection of belief and delight. . . .

Unexpectedly he comes upon the graveyard, where

> It is that glance of the eternal judgment
> Of the silence of the manifold gravestones
> Frightens me as we seize in love and belief
> The love not to ask what is our ultimate end.

Eberhart's most engaging quality is not the wisdom he so frequently seeks but the sense of wonder he can so successfully communicate, as much through his questions as in any answers to them. He has a magnificently simple and unforgettable poem in *Shifts of Being* called "Lions Copulating," an unexpected by-blow from his State Department inspection tour of Peace Corps projects in Africa. (What strange duties our poets perform for the state, and what strange rewards they are given!) This time Eberhart was given an unusual *donnée,* as his landrover closed in on a pair of lions, somewhere in Kenya:

> I pressed so hard on my 8 mm. color film
> I almost lost this gigantic naturalism
> Trying to preserve it for my friends and astoundees. . . .

The poem beautifully describes the expressionless union of the king of beasts "Prodding in and out of the great female" as if he "had to put up with his baser nature." I commend this poem to the reader's enjoyment, and to all prospective anthologists. And I value it, too, as a perhaps unintentional clue to the difficulties and rewards of reading the rest of Eberhart's work. When he presses too hard on his 8 mm. color film he nearly loses his "gigantic naturalism." But when the excitement in his poetry is both relaxed and controlled, as it often is, then what unexpected shots are preserved for his friends and astoundees!

ABOUT RICHARD EBERHART

Richard Eberhart has managed to combine successfully two strikingly disparate careers. He is a poet and lecturer as well as vice-president and member of the board of trustees of a large manufacturing firm. On the subject of the poet's duality, he says, "A poet has to be two persons, more than two. He has to have superior energies, enough for the world as it is, in which he does not believe, and an abundance for the world of becoming, which he makes real" (*Twentieth Century Authors,* First Supplement, p. 297).

Eberhart received his A.B. degree from Dartmouth College, his B.A. and M.A. degrees from Cambridge University. In 1930 he served for a time as the private tutor to the son of King Prajadhipok of Siam. From 1933 to 1941 he taught English at Saint Mark's School in Southborough, Massachusetts.

In 1950 he helped in the founding of the Poets' Theater in Cambridge, Massachusetts, and served as its first president. The same year he was awarded the Harriet Monroe Memorial

Prize by *Poetry* magazine. In 1951 he received the Shelley Memorial Award from the Poetry Society of America. Dartmouth College awarded him its honorary LL.D degree in 1954, and the next year he received a National Institute of Arts and Letters grant.

"Perhaps the reader may discover me in my poetry," he says, "for that is where I have tried to discover myself. . . . Poetry is a maneuvering of ideas, a spectacular pleasure, achievement and mastery of intractable material, no less than an attempt to move the world, to order the chaos of man, insofar as one is able. Love, harmony, order; poise, precision, new worlds."

BOOKS BY RICHARD EBERHART

A BRAVERY OF EARTH
New York: Jonathan Cape and Harrison Smith, 1930.
London: Jonathan Cape, 1930.

READING THE SPIRIT
London: Chatto & Windus, 1936.
New York: Oxford, 1937.
Toronto: Macmillan, 1937.

SONG AND IDEA
London: Chatto & Windus, 1940.
New York: Oxford, 1942.

POEMS, NEW AND SELECTED
New York: New Directions, 1944. (bds & pb)

WAR AND THE POET (edited with Selden Rodman)
New York: Devin-Adair, 1945.

BURR OAKS
New York: Oxford, 1947.
Toronto: Oxford, 1947.
London: Chatto & Windus, 1947.

BROTHERHOOD OF MEN
Pawlet, Vt.: Banyan Press, 1949.

AN HERB BASKET
Cummington, Mass.: Cummington Press, 1950.

SELECTED POEMS
New York: Oxford, 1951.
Toronto: Clark, Irwin, 1951.
London: Chatto & Windus, 1951.

UNDERCLIFF: POEMS 1946-1953
New York: Oxford, 1953.
Toronto: Clarke, Irwin, 1953.
London: Chatto & Windus, 1953.

GREAT PRAISES
New York: Oxford, 1957.
Toronto: Clarke, Irwin, 1957.
London: Chatto & Windus, 1957.

COLLECTED POEMS 1930-1960
New York: Oxford, 1960.
London: Chatto & Windus, 1960.

COLLECTED VERSE PLAYS
Chapel Hill: University of North Carolina, 1962. (regular and signed, limited edition)

THE QUARRY
New York: Oxford, 1964.
London: Chatto & Windus, 1964.

SELECTED POEMS 1930-1965
New York: New Directions, 1966. (pb)

THIRTY ONE SONNETS
New York: Eakins, 1967.

SHIFTS OF BEING
New York: Oxford, 1968.
London: Chatto & Windus, 1968.

That Old Triangle: A Memory of Brendan Behan

by Benedict Kiely

In the end of all, the hostage, Leslie Williams, rose from the dead in full view of the audience and mocked the bells of hell that go ting-a-ling-a-ling, and in cheery parody of Saint Paul, asked the grave where was its victory, and death where was its sting-a-ling-a-ling. The victory and the sting are in the sore truth that the bold Brendan, quiet for the first time since he yelled as a newborn babe, has drawn the Glasnevin coverlet over his head and is no longer to be found raising the roof or entertaining the customers in any one of the many places of public resort that lie between the two White Horses: the one in Greenwich Village and the one that Michael O'Connell keeps on Burgh Quay by the River Liffey.

He was, as we say in Ireland, much missed at his own funeral, for he was always one to bury the dead with sympathy but with a spirit that mocked at mortality, and he would have appreciated the verbal slip that made one graveside speaker say that he had had the privilege of being interred with Brendan. He meant interned: and while the dead man in his time had had his reservations about the joys of internment he would, of a surety, have preferred them to the *nox perpetua* of the grave. Dying as a "lark," he often said, had no attractions for him. It was a lonely business and he was, even to the detriment of his work and health, the most gregarious of men. The one thing he found most wearisome in prison was to be locked alone in his cell: "There were noises of key-jangling and door-banging. I hoped they would open my door. Even if they were distributing nothing better than kicks or thumps, I'd prefer not to be left out in my cold shroud of solitude. Fighting is better than loneliness."

Even in prison, where he spent eight years of his short life, he did his best to beat off loneliness, and so much of the best of what he really wrote—not talked about into a tape-recorder when he was sick —is that very odd thing, a shout of laughter from the cell. The name of the prison in North Dublin City, where his play *The Quare Fellow* was played out to its end in a hanging, was ironic enough to please him: Mountjoy, for yet further irony abbreviated into The Joy. An ale brewed in that part, his own part, of Dublin was called by the same name as the prison, and an enticing advertisement displayed at one end of Russell Street where he was born, and visible every Sunday to the followers of games in Croke Park which had, once, its Black and Tan Bloody Sunday, said: "Joy Be with You in the Morning."

Song erupts from the punishment cells as the curtain rises on *The Quare Fellow,* a song that Behan adapted from a cruder original by another prisoner:

> A hungry feeling came o'er me stealing
> And the mice were squealing in my prison cell,
> And that old triangle
> Went jingle jangle,
> Along the banks of the Royal Canal.

He understood and could make laughter out of the old lag's perverted pride in his record between stone walls and iron bars. One old prisoner says to a novice: "Meself and that man sitting there, we done time before you came up. In Kilmainham, and that's where you never were. First fourteen days without a mattress, skilly three times a day. None of your sitting out in the yard like nowadays. I got my toe amputated by one of the old lags so I could get into hospital for a feed." Warden Regan says to a prisoner who boasts that he has been in English prisons: "There's the national inferiority complex for you. Our own Irish cat o' nine tails and the batons of the warders loaded with lead from Carrickmines aren't good enough for him. He has to go Dartmooring and Parkhursting it. It's a wonder you didn't go further when you were at it, to Sing Sing or Devil's Island."

His temperament, a comical sight more than that of Lovelace, made light of prison, because prison was familiar to his rebel family and his Irish blood and, in prison as outside it, he had a passion for making mockery of authority. He looked, for instance, in *Borstal Boy* at the Governor of Walton Prison, England, and saw a "desiccated old-looking man, in tweed clothes and wearing a cap, as befitted his rank of Englishman, and looking as if he'd ride a horse if he had one. He spoke with some effort and if you did not hear what he was saying you'd have thought from his tone, and the sympathetic, loving and adoring looks of the screw, P.O., and Chief that he was stating some new philosophical truth to save the suffering world from error."

Dunlavin, the greatest of all his old lags—called, by the wild comic spirit that made Behan laugh even at those patriotic things that were dearest to him, by the name of a Wicklow village famed in the heroism of the Rebellion of 1798—expresses his disgust at having to live cell-by-cell with a sex criminal: "Dirty beast! I won't have an hour's luck for the rest of me six months." Those who are alive, even though they lie in jail, must accommodate themselves to the conditions of living, and Behan took his durance vile as a priceless part of his experience and all the time intended to use his prison memories when he turned to writing. Once when I complained to him that if things were as they once were the rising cost of living in Dublin would land me in jail for debt he said, with affected horror: "Don't take from me the one advantage I have in this hard-backed book business."

His best hard-backed book, superbly done as the scattered, dictated notebooks were not done, was, too, in the oddest way, a continuation of the considerable library written by Irishmen in English prisons or on the run from English law: Doheny, Davitt, Kickham, Tom Clarke, Darrell Figgis, *et al.* Through his mother's brother, Peader Cearnaigh, who wrote the song, by no means his best, that was to become the Irish national anthem, Behan was very much part of all that. But no accused patriot adding to that holy scripture "Speeches from the Dock"—a paper-backed national piety once a bestseller in Ireland—could have permitted himself the humour, the mockery, the bad language of Behan; and the resonant Carlylean voice of John Mitchell, of Young Ireland in 1848, orating rather than writing his classical "Jail Journal," finds an uproarious *reductio ad absurdum* in *Borstal Boy.*

The Joy, then, was a fine and quiet place compared with The Bog (the long term Portlaoise Prison in the flat Irish Midlands) and had, because of a kindly governor whose blackthorn stick Behan borrowed and never returned, the name of being easy: easy, that is, until matters went as far as hanging. Then the laughter sourly dies in the cell, and the prisoner called Neighbour tells how once for two bottles of stout he took the hood off "the fellow was after being topped" and how he wouldn't do it a second time for a bottle of whiskey for the "head was all twisted and his face black, but the two eyes were the worst; like a rabbit's; it was fear that had done it."

Brendan was in The Joy, not for politics as was his wont, but, like the bold Thady Quill, for "batin' the police," when the last man to be hanged in the Republic of Ireland went to the drop. With two warders he and the condemned man made a four for handball. He drank the condemned man's daily bottles of stout because the crime for which the unfortunate fellow was doomed to suffer had been done under the influence of that beverage and he could no longer be convinced that

Guinness was good for him. When the pitiful wretch asked Brendan if hanging hurt, Brendan assured him, with his own special type of kindness, that he didn't think so but then he had never been through it himself nor had he talked with anyone who had. He was in prison for politics when the original of the Quare Fellow was hanged: a pork-butcher who had murdered his brother and fileted the corpse so skilfully that nothing was ever found. It was one of Behan's more lurid jokes that the murderer had sold his brother as fresh pork to the Jesuit Fathers in Tullabeg. That Brendan Behan, like Lord Byron, woke up to find himself famous overnight, right in the middle of the English debate on capital punishment, was in no small measure due to that hanging; and that was the only good turn hanging ever did him or anybody else. For decent people are as interested in hangings nowadays as they were on the night before Larry was stretched—in public; and think of all the long years during which Tyburn was London's greatest theatrical draw, a popular open-air theatre.

The famous drunken appearance on BBC television came to the aid of the hangman in the popularization of Brendan Behan, and that was the only good turn drink ever did him. Now that I've raised the question, and since it must be answered, let me say how grossly by the lower-class London papers the drunken legend was exaggerated. It was no news at all that an Irishman should be sober and working. Yet while Brendan did not invite such publicity he did nothing by word or deed to squelch it: he went on a long ways further than Samuel Johnson in believing that to be talked about, well or ill, drunk or sober, was the best way for a writer to bring in "the Readies": meaning dollars and pounds. It is the way of the vile world, but Henry James, and others, would have demurred. It is customary and correct to lament the drinking and the waste, as my friends, Irving Wardle, the London critic, and Francis MacManus, the Dublin novelist, have done, but it is also a wonder that so much writing was done in such a short time, not because of the impediment of drink but because Brendan never had any regularly developed habits of work, and being, as I said, the most gregarious of men, he craved company, which in Dublin frequently leads to drink unless you care to join the Legion of Mary or the Pioneer Total Abstinence Association which neither he, myself, nor any of our friends in Dublin ever showed any fanatical signs of doing. The mornings I have been aroused at six or seven to find Brendan smiling at the foot of my bed with the bright idea that we could start the day well in the early bars in the fruit markets or on the docks! There's a sweet story that once when, following his first trade, he was painting a ceiling in the Land Commission office in Merrion Street, and had his head out the window for air and looking at the people, James Sleator, the painter, passed and invited him round the corner for a "tincture," and Brendan went and never came back, leaving the ceiling half-painted and his kit for anyone who cared to collect it. He painted the flat of the poet, Patrick Kavanagh, for free but, for laughs, did it, in the poet's absence, a complete and total sable. He had an odd sense of humour. He was also, we must remember, in his final years a sick man with a sickness that craved the sweet heat of drink and that the drink only aggravated.

He was, first and before all, a Dubliner from that restricted area of North Dublin City to which true Dubliners confine the high title of the Northside. The rest of the North City is suburbia inhabited by provincials. After that he was an Irishman and a member of the underground Irish Republican Army at its most troublesome period since the bloodshed and burning ceased in 1923. He was, by his own definition: "a bad Catholic" or, as Irish euphemism has it, a "lapsed" or "non-practicing" Catholic.

His I.R.A. activities brought him at an absurdly early age to an English prison and a Borstal institution, gave him the makings of his best book, which either as autobiography or as part of the literature of penology has established itself as a classic, and inspired him for various reasons with a healthy respect and a liking for the English people. Although his first feeling, after two months studying and experiencing the brutalities of the warders in Walton Jail, was that he was most anxious for a truce with the British, that not only was everything he had ever read or heard about them in history true but that "they were bigger and crueler bastards" than he had taken them for because "with tyrants all over Europe I had begun to think that maybe they weren't the worst after all but, by Jesus, now I knew they were, and I was not defiant of them but frightened." But later acquaintance with kindlier types—they included sadly enough a decent Borstal chap called Neville Heath later to be renowned, although Behan with splendid restraint does not say so nor fully name him, as the sadistic murderer of two women—made him modify his opinion, and he allows himself that deliberately exquisite understatement: "The British are very nationalistic." He was, too, always glad and grateful that London Town gave him his first and best welcome as a playwright and that once when on the way through England from Ireland to France he was arrested under a deportation order the British authorities deported him not back to Ireland but onwards to France, paying his fare—a humorous and decent people.

For all previous sharp statements about the neighbours he made amends in the character of Leslie Williams, the hostage, also a voice from a prison, an ordinary young English boy caught fatally and wonderingly in a situation he cannot hope to understand. Teresa, that sweet young country girl, so lovably played by Celia Salkeld, an orphan as the hostage is, tells him that Monsewer the old mad owner of the house in which he is held, is an English nobleman: "he went to college with your king."

SOLDIER: [i.e. Leslie]: We ain't got one.
TERESA: Maybe he's dead now, but you had one one time, didn't you?
SOLDIER: We got a duke now. He plays tiddly winks.
TERESA: Anyway, he [i.e. Monsewer] left your lot and came over here and fought for Ireland.
SOLDIER: Why, was somebody doing something to Ireland?
TERESA: Wasn't England, for hundreds of years?
SOLDIER: That was donkey's years ago. Everybody was doing something to someone in those days.

Caitlin Ni Houlihan and John Bull have never spoken so simply, so comically nor so wisely to each other as in that passage. And mad Monsewer was, indeed, English, the son of a bishop, and had gone to "all the biggest colleges in England and slept in one room with the King of England's son" until one day because his mother was Irish he discovered he was an Irishman, or an Anglo-Irishman, which in Behan's misleading definition was "a Protestant with a horse." Anglo-Irishmen only work at "riding horses, drinking whisky and reading double-meaning books in Irish at Trinity College." To become Irish, Monsewer took it "easy at first, wore a kilt, played Gaelic football on Blackheath. . . took a correspondence course in the Irish language. And when the Rising took place he acted like a true Irish hero." But when he lays down his bagpipes and raises his voice in song, as all Behan's people, including himself, were forever ready to do, his father's blood proves living and strong:

In our dreams we see old Harrow,
And we hear the crow's loud caw
At the flower show our big marrow
Takes the prize from Evelyn Waugh.
Cups of tea or some dry sherry,
Vintage cars, these simple things,
So, let's drink up and be merry,
Oh, the Captains and the Kings.

Monsewer has a dual, lunatic significance: the house he owns and in which the young hostage is held and accidentally killed by his rescuers is, as Pat the caretaker says, a "noble old house" that had housed so many heroes and is, in the end, "turned into a knocking shop." It is also romantic, idealistic Ireland fallen on sordid, materialistic days, and that a madman of that most romantic people, the English, should in his imagination, lead the last Irish Rebellion, playing the pipes and making heroines out of dacent whores, would seem to be a fair chapter of our national story. But the house is more than heroic Ireland down in the dumps; it is the world in a mess and God gone off his rocker: the very first stage direction says: "the real owner isn't right in the head." Monsewer, in fact, is one of Behan's visions of God, and as he parades, salutes, plays the pipes and sings of tea and toast and muffin rings, the old ladies with stern faces and the captains and the kings, he falls into line with images of the Divinity that appear elsewhere in the plays and prose.

The ministers of religion, because of Brendan's experience with prison chaplains who had to tell him that as a member of the I.R.A. he was excommunicated, seldom come well out of his story. Yet God is, nevertheless, not to be judged by the deficiencies of his servants; and Dunlavin, satirizing the Higher Civil Servants talking big in the back snugs of pubs in Merrion Row, defends the Almighty against their patronization: "Educated drinking, you know. Even a bit of chat about God at an odd time, so as you'd think God was in another department, but not long off the Bog, and they was doing Him a good turn to be talking well about Him." The same turn of phrase, almost, recurs in "The Hostage" when Meg attacks the canting and quite impossible Mr. Mulleady. In a good cause Brendan was never afraid of repeating himself.

The cynical Meg may say that "pound notes is the best religion in the world" even though the "chokey bloke" in *Borstal Boy* points out that some men are so miserably constituted that they "couldn't be 'appy no matter where they were. If they was in the Ritz Hotel with a million nicker and Rita Hayworth they'd find some bloody thing to moan about." God could sometimes be faltering, as Monsewer was, in his judgments of people, for Ratface, the altar server in prison, looked like "a real cup-of-tea Englishman with a mind the width of his back garden that'd skin a black man, providing he'd get another to hold him, and send the skin 'ome to mum, but Our Lord would be as well pleased with him, if he was in the state of grace, as He'd be with St. Stanislaus Kostka, the boy Prince of Poland, and race or nationality did not enter into the matter, either one way or another." Regardless, the Maker of All Things had compensatory qualities. Following in a mob the course of the Saviour's Passion around the Stations of the Cross in the prison chapel, the prisoners were enabled, in a passage that is pure Hogarth, to fuse and mingle and exchange cigarettes and even fragments of food. The crooked greyhound men taking the doped dog to the races in one of the best sketches in *Brendan Behan's Island* were respectfully pious enough to warn Brendan that it wasn't a lucky thing to mock religion and they going out to "do a stroke." If the law that excommunicated the I.R.A. had not existed and Brendan had been allowed to go to confession he would have missed the sight of one of the nastiest of the warders slipping and falling and floundering in a snowdrift, and shaking his fists in anger and falling and floundering again while the prisoners from their cell windows roared with laughter. Brendan sat down again at his table and, in the terms of an old Gaelic proverb, thanked God and His Blessed Mother for all that: "God never closed one door but He opens another, and if He takes away with His right hand, He gives it back with His left, and more besides." Pressed down and flowing over in fact; and we are back with God as Monsewer, a decent fellow, not quite in control of things. Whose actions even when He doesn't plan too well frequently turn out for the best. Even the "lapsed" Catholic comes out in defence of the Old Faith when he tells Hannen Swaffer, the columnist who has just announced that he is a spiritualist, that Catholicism keeps a better type of ghost.

Borrowing a sentence from the lingo of his beloved Dublin streets, he was fond of saying that every cripple had his own way of walking. It is also true that every writer has his own way of writing, and I have already pointed out how wonderful it was that so much good writing came out of Brendan's gregariousness and chronic restlessness. His great kindly spirit had to express itself in every possible way, and what was writing—it if didn't go on too long—but another form of movement. *Borstal Boy, The Quare Fellow, The Hostage* and the better portions of the notebooks or sketchbooks are the considerable achievement that he has left us, although one stage direction in *The Hostage,* reading, "what happens next is not very clear," would seem to indicate that Behan threw his hat (he never wore one) at the whole business of writing and said: "Joan Littlewood, the dacent girl, will look after that and—the Begrudgers." Reading your own works, he argued in his sad book on New York, was a sort of mental incest but, as a rule, it is better at least to write them; and to the New Yorkers who have been disappointed in what he had to say about their stupendous city, which as cities go he loved next to Dublin, I keep saying that the book was not so much written as spoken by a sick and weary man into a tape recorder.

Yet even in the tired ramblings-on of a man who was so close to the grave, there is flash after flash of the spirit that made him the most entertaining companion I have known or am ever likely to know. One night in Michael O'Connell's White Horse when sick with laughter at his antics—(1) Toulouse-Lautrec, by walking up and down the floor on his knees, (2) the Poor Old Woman, Mother Ireland, with the tail of his jacket over his head for a shawl, (3) an aspiring Irish politician mouthing every platitude ever heard from an Irish platform and borrowing a few from the pulpit, (4) Sex in the Abbey Theatre, for which there are no words but only mime and the mimic is now forever motionless—I remember thinking that if he ever got a wider audience he'd make a fortune. I can't claim much credit for the prophecy: it came easy. My sadness is that this great kind comic man held the stage only for such a brief time. We have left, as I say, the plays, including the one-act "The Big House," effective on radio but a dead loss on the stage, the autobiography, and what was good in the notebooks. To come, there may be yet another piece of dictated autobiography, and the play *Richard's Cork Leg* which, borrowing a title from a very irritated James Joyce, was to be the meeting of all Ireland around the grave of Honor Bright, an unfortunate whore done to death by gunshot on the Dublin mountains forty or so years ago. *The Scarperer* we may dismiss, forgiving as well as we can the person who wrote the publisher's blurb to say that Behan having accomplished this and that, now turned to the novel and made it his own: the sort of praise that can only damage a writer's reputation. But for a delightful brotherly sidelight on the ways of the wonderful Behan family and on the lovable father and mother, Stephen and Kathleen, Dominic Behan's *Teems of Times and Happy Returns* is valuable.

Brendan had a happy boyish belief that you could find a good man everywhere and, being a friendly man, he liked meeting people and being always, in some ways, a boy he liked talking about the important people he had met. He liked being invited to the inauguration of President Kennedy. Who, politics apart, wouldn't have? He liked talking about the late Gilbert Harding, who was a fine man, and about Oona Guinness, who is a great lady, and about John Betjeman who is, anyway, a sort of Irish institution. I detect an ironic flicker of the eyelids, even if by then they were very tired eyelids, when he says: "As Hemingway once remarked to a friend of mine." He was vain and proud of his success and eternally talkative. But he was not so much a name-dropper as a friend naming friends, and Princess Margaret and Rosie Redmond, the Dublin whore, were all equally to him just people.

Rosie Redmond we will remember from Sean O'Casey's *The Plough and the Stars,* and I feel that Brendan and certainly his father, Stephen, knew stories about her that even O'Casey had not heard. This is not the place to tell them, yet the mention of her fair name brings me by a most "commodious vicus of recirculation back to Howth Castle and Environs," to the "fort of the Dane, garrison of the Saxon, Augustan capital of a Gaelic nation," to the city built around the body of the fallen Finnegan and the more catastrophically fallen giant: Haveth Childers Everywhere.

A city, he said, was a place where you were least likely to get "a bit of a wild sheep," and the test of a city was the ease with which you could see and talk to other people, and New York was the friendliest city he knew. But Dublin was his own town, not the middleclass Dublin that John Mitchell had found a city of bellowing slaves and genteel Dastards, and that Pearse said had to atone in blood for the guilt of Robert Emmet's execution, but the Dublin of the fighting poor who were led by Larkin in 1913 and the Dublin with the everlasting memory of the Post Office in flames. It was the Dublin, too, that the prisoners, Neighbour and Dunlavin, fondly dream over in *The Quare Fellow.* Meena La Bloom belonged to it, who, with Dunlavin's help, gave many's the Mickey Finn to a sailor; and May Oblong who debagged the Irish M.P. on his way to Westminster to vote for Home Rule, and locked him in her room, and neither for the love of her country or his would liberate him until he slipped a fiver under the door; and the patriotic plumber of Dolphin's Barn that swore to let his hair grow 'til Ireland was free; and Lottie L'Estrange that had got up for pushing the soldier into Spencer Dock. They belong in Joyce's Nighttown and on the shadowy streets that Liam O'Flaherty wrote about in "The Informer."

Behan's Dublin, too, as the plays show, was as much or more that of Boucicault and the old Queen's Theatre Variety as it was of the Abbey Theatre, except when O'Casey was in possession of the Abbey Stage. And his Dublin was my Dublin from 1937 onwards, and with warm brotherliness he once told me that I was one of the few country——he knew who had enough in him to make a Dublin jackeen. From an early age he had what he called a "pathological horror" of country people, because to a Dublin child the symbols and exercisers of authority, teachers and civic guards, all came from the country, the provinces, and the jungle began where the Dublin tram tracks came to an end. But his heart was too big for one city to contain, and it opened out to Ireland, the Aran Islands, London, Paris, New York; although to the end he had his reservations about Toronto and Berlin—as they had about him.

He would have died and almost did die for Ireland, but he was sharply conscious of the delirium of the brave in the Robert Emmet pose of the dying hero. It was fine to feel like Cuchullain guarding the Gap of Ulster, his enemies ringed round him, his back supported by a tree, calling on "the gods of death and grandeur to hold him up until his last blood flowed." But if the only spectators were two Walton jailers, Mr. Whitbread and Mr. Holmes, clearly Private Compton and Private Carr in later life, and if Mr. Holmes was methodically beating you up, then the hot glow went out of the heroism. You could be mangled in an English prison and who would "give a fish's tit about you over here. At home, it would be all right if you were to get the credit for it. . . . But the mangling would have to be gone through first." He was brave from boyhood to death, but there were no false heroics about him and he felt that between mangling and martyrdom there should be some satisfactory, poetic and preferably unpainful relationship.

Like Peter Wanderwide—and how Behan would have mocked at me for quoting Belloc—he had Ireland "in his dubious eyes." In Irish and English its ballads and classical folksongs were ready to his lips, and when he wasn't deliberately roaring his head off he could sing. At penal work, digging on the Borstal farm, his fork uncovered from English soil a golden apple "as hard and as fresh as the day it fell there," and biting it surreptitiously and feeling the juice sharp on his tongue he thought of Blind Raftery, the poet, and of the spring coming, after the feast of Brigid, to the wide plains of Mayo. But in the swift switch of humour that was characteristic of him he would admit that digging was an activity he wouldn't pick for pleasure and would tell how his father, Stephen, during a Dublin strike brought him out to help farm an acre of land on ground, at Glasnevin, once associated with Dean Swift. Stephen dug for a bit "with great function," talked about the land, how his ancestors came from it, how healthy it was, and how if they kept at the digging they might uncover relics of Swift or Vanessa or Stella or Mrs. Delaney. But next day, bored, he got a countryman to dig the plot in exchange for Stephen's doing the countryman's strike picket-duty. That is a touching, endearing picture of father and son—two rare comedians.

But Brendan was grateful for the golden apple and the good weather. He was always grateful and pious in good weather, and the day he found the apple was the sort of day that "you'd know Christ died for you." A bloody good job, he thought, that he was born in rainy Ireland and not in the South of France or Miami Beach where he'd have been so grateful and holy for the sunshine that Saint Paul of the Cross would have only been trotting after him: "skull and crossbones and all."

As a great swimmer, next to the sunshine he loved the sea: the eastern sea at the Forty Foot, the swimming pool famed in "Ulysses"; the laughter of the western Galway sea which, according to Louis MacNeice, juggled with spars and bones irresponsibly. Brendan did not view it so sombrely. On the Aran islands, and 'long the Connemara shore, and in Glenties in Donegal with the Boyles and the Harveys, he claimed he could forget all the cruel things of this world. He wrote so pleasantly of the night, after the licensed hours, in the pub in Ballyferriter in Kerry, in the Southwest, when the Civic Guards obligingly sent word that they were going to raid so that the customers could withdraw a little up the mountain slope, taking supplies with them, and drink in peace until the raid was over: "It was a lovely starlit night and warm, too; and one of my most cherished recollections is of sitting out there on the side of Mount Brandon, looking at the mountain opposite called the Three Sisters framed against the clear moonlit sky and the quiet shimmering Atlantic, a pint of the creamiest Guinness in my hand as I conversed in quiet Irish with a couple of local farmers."

That was a happy Irishman at home in Ireland. Mount Brandon, as he said with proprietary pride, was called after his patron saint, Brendan the Navigator, who, the legend says, reached the New World before either Norsemen or Columbus and who left to all who came after him the promise of the Isle of the Blest that all mariners might one day find.

"And that," as Brendan said when he finished his sketchbook about the island of Ireland, "is the end of my story and all I'm going to tell you and thanks for coming along."

ABOUT BRENDAN BEHAN

Born in Dublin, Ireland, in 1923, Brendan Behan became a part of a long family tradition of Irish patriotism. His uncle, Peader Cearnaigh, wrote "Soldier's Song," which later became the Irish national anthem. The family also had long had an interest in drama; many of Behan's relatives became involved with the work of the Abbey Theater in its early years and P. J. Bourke, another of Behan's uncles, owned his own theater in Dublin.

Since the age of nine Behan had been a member of Fianna Eireann, the Republican "Boy Scouts." In 1939 he took the next logical step and joined the Irish Republican Army. In this year, at the age of sixteen, he was sent to blow up the ship *King George V.* On this mission he was arrested and charged with illegal possession of explosives. After spending two months in a Liverpool jail, he was sent to Borstal, a reform school. On his release in 1942 he was almost immediately arrested again and sentenced to four years for attempted murder by a Dublin military court. Freed again in 1946 under general amnesty, he was arrested twice more and finally deported from the country in 1952.

Between the years of 1951 and 1956 Brendan Behan worked as a free-lance journalist, submitting articles and poetry to journals in England, France, and Ireland. In February of 1955 he married Beatrice ffrench-Salkeld.

His career as a playwright began in 1956 with the opening of *The Quare Fellow* in Dublin and London. Its American production at Circle-in-the-Square Theater in New York was directed by Jose Quintero.

Written in two weeks while Behan was in the Balearic Island reporting for a Spanish newspaper, *The Hostage* became a hit in 1958 under the direction of Joan Littlewood.

After a long illness Behan died in 1964 at the age of forty-one.

BOOKS BY BRENDAN BEHAN

THE QUARE FELLOW
London: Methuen, 1956.
Toronto: Ryerson, 1957.
New York: Grove, 1957. (limited and regular edition)
New York: Grove, 1957. (pb)
London: Methuen, 1960. (pb)

THE HOSTAGE
London: Methuen, 1958.
London: Methuen, 1959. (pb)
New York: Grove, 1959.
New York: Grove, 1959. (pb)
London: Methuen, 1962. (revised)

BORSTAL BOY
London: Hutchinson, 1958.
New York: Knopf, 1959.
London: Corgi, 1960. (pb)
New York: Avon Book Div., Hearst Corp., 1964.

BRENDAN BEHAN'S ISLAND: AN IRISH SKETCHBOOK
London: Hutchinson, 1962.
New York: Geis, 1962.

HOLD YOUR HOUR AND HAVE ANOTHER
London: Hutchinson, 1963.
Boston: Little, Brown, 1964.
London: Corgi, 1965. (pb)

BRENDAN BEHAN'S NEW YORK
New York: Geis, 1964.

THE SCARPERER
Garden City: Doubleday, 1964.
London: Hutchinson, 1964.

THE QUARE FELLOW & THE HOSTAGE
New York: Grove, 1965. (pb)

MOVING OUT & A GARDEN PARTY (ed. by
Robert Hogan)
California: Proscenium, 1967.

CONFESSIONS OF AN IRISH REBEL
New York: Geis, 1966.
London: Hutchinson, 1966.

LT

Flannery O'Connor, Sin, and Grace: *Everything That Rises Must Converge*

by Walter Sullivan

The stories in *Everything That Rises Must Converge* are the last fruits of Flannery O'Connor's particular genius; and though one or two of them display an uncertainty that must have been the result of her deteriorating health, they are for the most part successful extensions of her earlier fiction. God-ridden and violent—six of the nine end in something like mayhem—they work their own small counter-reformation in a faithless world. Flannery O'Connor's limitations were numerous and her range was narrow: she repeated herself frequently and she ignored an impressively large spectrum of human experience. But what she did well, she did with exquisite competence: her ear for dialogue, her eye for human gestures were as good as anybody's ever were: and her vision was as clear and direct and as annoyingly precious as that of an Old Testament prophet or one of the more irascible Christian saints.

Her concern was solely with the vulgarities of this world and the perfections of the other—perfections that had to be taken on faith, for the postulations and descriptions of them in her work are at best somewhat tawdry. She wrote of man separated from the true source of his being, lost, he thinks and often hopes, to God; and of a God whose habits are strange beyond knowing, but Who gets His way in the end. That she was a Southerner and wrote about the South may have been a fortunate coincidence. The South furnished her the kind of flagrant images her theme and her style demanded, and Southern dialogue augmented and perhaps even sharpened her wit. But the South as locale and source was quite peripheral. She once wrote Robert Fitzgerald, "I would like to go to California for about two minutes to further these researches [into the ways of the vulgar]. . . . Did you see that picture of Roy Rogers' horse attending a church service in Pasadena?" Had she been born in Brooklyn or Los Angeles, the surface agonies of her work would have been altered: perhaps they would have been weakened: but the essential delineations of her fiction, the mythic impulse itself would, I believe, have been essentially unchanged.

As a novelist she was not successful. She could never fill a book-length canvas: the colors thinned out, the relationships weakened, the images became, before the denouement, rigid and brittle. The weakness obviously was not in her theme, which was big enough to fill the world, powerful enough to shape some of the greatest of all literary careers in the past, and in our own time those of Eliot and Mauriac and Graham Greene and William Golding. What went wrong was technical. Flannery O'Connor used to be fond of saying that the way she wrote a story was "to follow the scent like an old hound dog." At first glance one might conclude that her novels were written with too little forethought. *Wise Blood* is full of loose ends: the theme dribbles away through the holes in the structure. According to Fitzgerald, the idea for having Hazel Motes blind himself came to O'Connor when, stuck at the crucial point in her manuscript, she read *Oedipus* for the first time. Then the earlier parts of the novel had to be reworked to prepare for the ending.

But a lot of novels get written and rewritten this way. And some novels of real power have ends as loose as that left by Enoch Emery who is last seen disappearing into the night in his ape's suit. Except for Haze all the characters fade off—Hawkes and Sabbath and Hoover Shoates. The landlady fills the void in the last chapter. But what Motes means to do, and what O'Connor meant for us to understand concerning what he does, seem clear enough. Driven by the Christ he cannot escape from, the "ragged figure" who "moves from tree to tree in the back of his mind," and motions "him to turn around and come off into the dark where he was not sure of his footing," he murders his double, the false prophet of his own false religion and therefore kills that part of himself. Then by blinding himself, he exhibits the strength of belief that Hawkes was unable to muster: he redeems Hawkes' failure and turns his vision totally inward away from this world, toward the Christ who exists in the inner darkness.

A better case can be made for *The Violent Bear It Away.* The beginning is extraordinarily powerful: the old man dies at the breakfast table, the boy abandons the partially dug grave, gets drunk, and burns the house down. The lines of the conflict are clearly drawn between the scientific attitude—which is to say, the new gnosticism—of Rayber and the gift of Christian grace which Tarwater has not been able to escape. That Tarwater is a reluctant vessel enhances the drama of the novel: he does the work of God in spite of himself and a part of the resolution of the story is in his understanding of his role and his acceptance of it. Having been abused by a homosexual, he has a vision of a burning bush, and a message comes to him: GO WARN THE CHILDREN OF GOD OF THE TERRIBLE SPEED OF MERCY. And in the final scene he is moving toward the darkened city where the "children of God" lie sleeping.

The characters here are fewer than in *Wise Blood,* which is in itself a kind of virtue: every novelist needs to learn what he can do without. The plot is rounded off neatly. The old man has been buried by some Negroes. The feeble-minded child has been baptized and drowned. The prophet's will has been done: Rayber is defeated. The scent has been true and truly followed and all ought to be well, but the novel remains, for me at least, unsatisfactory. The difficulty does not lie in faulty concept or structure: the scenes balance out nicely and the pace is sure. The trouble, I think, is with the characters: brilliantly drawn and fascinating and symbolically significant as they are, they will not hold up through a long piece of fiction. They are too thin, in the final analysis, and too much alike.

Yet the characters, the clothes they wear, the gestures they make, the lines they speak, the thoughts they think are what make Flannery O'Connor's work so magnificently vivid and so totally memorable. The dialogue ranges from the outrageous to the absolutely predictable, the latter done so well that it never fails to delight. For example, in "The Life You Save May Be Your Own," Mr. Shiftlet says, "There's one of these here doctors in Atlanta that's taken a knife and cut the human heart—the human heart. . . out of a man's chest and held it in his hand. . . and studied it like it was a day old chicken, and lady. . . he don't know no more about it than you or me."

Or take this passage from "The Displaced Person":

> "They came from over the water," Mrs. Shortley said with a wave of her arm. "They're what is called Displaced Persons."
>
> "Displaced Persons," he said. "Well now, I declare. What do that mean?"
>
> "It means they ain't where they were born at and there's nowhere for them to go—like if you was run out of here and wouldn't nobody have you."
>
> "It seems like they here, though," the old man said in a reflective voice. "If they here, they somewhere."
>
> "Sho is," the other agreed. "They here."
>
> The illogic of Negro thinking always irked Mrs. Shortley. "They ain't where they belong to be at," she said.

Again, in "The Life You Save," Shiftlet offers the old woman a stick of chewing gum, "but she only raised her upper lip to indicate she had no teeth." In *The Violent Bear It Away* Tarwater makes a face suitable for an idiot to fool the truant officer, the old man lies down in his coffin to try it out—his fat stomach protrudes over the top—and the wire to Rayber's hearing aid characterizes the quality of his intelligence. All this is very fine, supported as it is with O'Connor's keen sense of the world in its various aspects: the buildings and sidewalks and trolley cars of the city, the fields and trees and clouds—many clouds—and barns and houses and pigs and cows and peacocks. Her people function richly as images and frequently they evolve into symbols.

In "A Good Man is Hard to Find" the Misfit represents the plight of man from the beginning of Christian history to the modern age, and he sets forth the dilemma with such blunt clarity that it cannot be misread. Jesus was truly God or he was not: between being God and not being God there is no middle ground. If He were, then He must be followed. If He were not, then all men are free to work out their own destinies and the terms of their own happiness for themselves. The Misfit is aware of his own helplessness. Life is a mystery to him: the ways of fate are inscrutable: he denies flatly that he is a good man, and he expects neither human charity nor the mercy of God. He knows only that he does not know, and his awareness is the beginning of all wisdom, the first step toward faith.

It is an awareness that the grandmother and the other characters in the story do not share. "You're a good man!" she says to Red Sammy Butts, owner of the roadside restaurant, and he readily agrees. But he is not: nor is she a good woman: nor are Bailey or his wife or his children good. Their belief in their own virtue is a sign of their moral blindness. In pride they have separated themselves from God, putting their trust in modern technology: in paved roads and automobiles (Red Sammy gave two men credit because they were driving a Chrysler); in advertising messages along the highway and tapdancing lessons for children and in motels and pampered cats. "A Good Man is Hard to Find" makes clear—as does *Wise Blood*—that the characters in Flannery O'Connor's work may not be distinguished as good or bad, or as guilty or innocent. All are guilty; all are evil. The distinctions are between those who know of God's mercy and those who do not, between those who think they can save themselves, either for this life or for the next, and those who are driven, in spite of their own failings, to do God's purpose. In the general retreat from piety, man and the conditions under which he lives have been perverted.

It was Flannery O'Connor's contention that the strange characters who populate her world are essentially no different from you and me. That they are drawn more extravagantly, she would admit, but she claimed that this was necessary because of our depravity: for the morally blind, the message of redemption must be writ large. This is not to say that she conceived of her art as a didactic enterprise: but rather that like all writers of all persuasions, she wrote out of her own ontological view which remained orthodox and Catholic, while the society in which she lived and for which she wrote became more profane and more heretical every day. She could no sooner have stopped writing about God than Camus could have ceased being an existentialist. She was committed and she had to shout to be heard.

But in writing, as in all other human endeavors, one pays his money and makes his choice. He gives up something to get something, and to get the outrageously drawn, spiritually tormented character, it is necessary to sacrifice the subtlety that long fiction demands. Complex characterization is the *sine qua non* of the novel: the characters must not only have epiphanies: they must change and develop in terms of what they have done and seen. It was the nature of Flannery O'Connor's fictional vision that discovery on the part of her people was all. When one has witnessed the flaming bush or the tongues of fire or the descending dove, the change is final and absolute and whatever happens thereafter is anticlimax. This is why the characters in O'Connor's novels fade and become static and often bore us with their sameness before we are done with the book. But fulfilling their proper roles—that is of revelation, discovery—in the short stories, they are not boring and they do what they were conceived to do.

In the society which is defined by the grandmother and the Misfit, the central conflict is between those who are driven by God and those who believe in their own self-sufficiency. This idea was put forth in *Wise Blood,* but the struggle took place too much inside the mind of Motes, and O'Connor's efforts at finding images for her values were not entirely successful. In the heavily ironic "Good Country People," the conflict is between two of the godless. Hulga, the Ph.D. in philosophy, is deprived of her wooden leg by Pointer, the Bible salesman, when she will not submit to his advances. But more than this, she is robbed forever of her belief in the final efficacy of the rational process. This issue is fully joined, as I indicated earlier, in *The Violent Bear It Away:* Rayber believes in the social sciences, their theories, their statistics. To him all mysticism is superstition, nothing is finally unexplainable, and man is the product of his environment. That the latter may not be quite true is made clear from the outset by the presence of Rayber's idiot son. But Rayber sees Bishop as the kind of mistake of nature that will ultimately be eradicated in the course of scientific advancement. All things will sooner or later be subject to the control of man. Tarwater, the unwilling instrument of grace, represents the super-rational quality of the Christian impulse. Determined not to do what his uncle, the prophet, had set for him to do, he does so anyway. Every step he takes away from the task of baptising Bishop takes him closer to that very act. All his bad temper, his country cunning and his determination to be and to act to suit himself avail no more than Rayber's educated scheming. God snatches whom He will and sets His will in motion.

One of the most successful stories in *Everything That Rises,* and in my judgment one of the best pieces Flannery O'Connor ever wrote, is a shorter and somewhat more realistic reworking of *The Violent Bear It Away.* The characters in "The Lame Shall Enter First" are three: Sheppard, city recreational director and volunteer counselor at the reformatory; Norton, his son who still grieves over the death of his mother; and Rufus Johnson, a fourteen-year-old, Bible-reading criminal with a club foot. Like Rayber, Sheppard knows the answers to everything. When he discovers, during his ministrations at the reformatory, that Rufus has an I.Q. of 140, he determines to rehabilitate him, hard nut that he is. "Where there was intelligence, anything was possible." Immediately on seeing the boy, Sheppard discovers the source of Rufus' delinquency: "The case was clear to Sheppard instantly. His mischief was compensation for the foot."

To know everything is to be able to solve everything, and therefore Sheppard sets out to rearrange life for the mutual benefit of Rufus and Norton, who, being an only child, is selfish and needs to learn to share. Reluctantly, Rufus comes to live with Sheppard, but he does nothing to make himself pleasant. Where Sheppard is kind, Rufus is surly. He betrays Sheppard's trust in many ways, the most important of which is by corrupting Norton. He disputes Sheppard's claim that when one is dead he is simply gone, that the entry into the grave is final. Rufus knows himself to be evil, and if he does not repent he will go to hell, but the good go to heaven and everybody—including Norton's mother—goes somewhere.

Sheppard points out that a belief in God or Satan is incompatible with the "space age," and in order to turn the minds of the boys from superstition to healthy reality, he installs a telescope at the attic window. Sheppard tells the boys to look at the moon: they may go there someday: they may become astronauts. But Rufus is more interested in what will happen to the soul after death, and Norton thinks what he sees in the sky is his mother. Norton kills himself in the end, preferring death to life—or rather preferring the life to come that he has learned about from Rufus to the drab logical existence he has lived with Sheppard. The victory here belongs to Rufus, who is lame and evil and conscious of both. He takes pride in his club foot, not because it explains his character or causes him to be forgiven his trespasses, but because it represents to him something of the burden of being human, the lameness of soul, the weight of sinfulness that we all must endure.

In spite of its typical O'Connor grimness, "The Lame Shall Enter First" comes to a more optimistic conclusion than does *The Violent Bear It Away.* Sheppard has his epiphany. When Johnson has finally been carried off to the police station, Sheppard reflects that he has nothing to reproach himself with. "I did more for him [Johnson] than I did for my own child."

> Slowly his face drained of color. It became almost grey beneath the white halo of his hair. The sentence echoed in his mind, each syllable like a dull blow. His mouth twisted and he closed his eyes against the revelation. Norton's face rose before him, empty, forlorn, his left eye listing almost imperceptibly toward the outer rim as if it could not bear a full view of grief. His heart constricted with a repulsion for himself so clear and intense that he gasped for breath. He had stuffed his own emptiness with good works like a glutton. He had ignored his own child to feed his vision of himself. He saw the clear-eyed Devil, the sounder of hearts, leering at him from the eyes of Johnson. His image of himself shrivelled until everything was black before him. He sat there paralyzed, aghast.

Jacques Maritain says, in *Art and Scholasticism,* "A reign of the heart which is not first of all a reign of truth, a revival of Christianity which is not first of all theological, disguises suicide as love." This is to say, in a more complex and sophisticated fashion, that the road to hell is paved with good intentions. And who in Flannery O'Connor's work is without his good intentions? Only those who are conscious of their own evil. Only those who are driven by the grace of God. Julian in the title story of *Everything That Rises* is charity itself in his view toward the world at large; but his mother, in whose house he lives, is the object of his scorn and hatred. He despises her for her stupidity which is real and for her narrowness: she is against integration. On the bus Julian sits beside Negroes and makes conversation with them, not because he loves his fellow man, but to annoy his mother. Later, she patronizingly offers a penny to a little Negro boy, is knocked down by the boy's mother, and

Julian is delighted. But like Sheppard, he too in the end is forced to see his own guilt.

Once more, in the same volume, the same theme is introduced in "The Enduring Chill." The story opens with Asbury's return from New York where he has been living and trying to write, to his mother's farm in Georgia where he thinks he will die. He has come because illness has forced him to come, and he has in his possession the only piece of writing he was ever able successfully to finish: a long statement of his grievances, an indictment blaming his mother for all his failures, his weaknesses, his unfulfilled desires: he holds her accountable for every miserable thing that has ever happened to him. The source of his present misery, however, is his previous disobedience of one of her rules for conduct in the dairy. Earlier he was home to do research on a play he was writing about "The Negro." To get close to his subject matter, he worked in the dairy with his mother's hired men, and here to prove his solidarity with the other race, he suggested that they all drink milk together. The Negroes would not, but Asbury did, and now he has undulant fever.

The end of "The Enduring Chill" and the end of life as Asbury has heretofore led it are marked by the descent of the Holy Ghost, the sign of God's mercy. But until this point all of Asbury's affection for mankind has been as vague and directionless in his mind as are the outlines of the lecture on Zen Buddhism he attended in New York. Negroes for him are not human beings, but "The Negro," and he shows a kindness to those on the farm that he may learn more about them for the advancement of his own projects. He abhors his mother and his sister, the priest and the doctor who try to help him. But God snatches him away. Of such is our hope.

Of the nineteen stories by Flannery O'Connor so far published—I am told that at least one has not yet been printed—nine end in the violent deaths of one or more persons. Three others end in or present near the end physical assaults that result in a greater or less degree of bodily injury. Of the remaining seven, one ends in arson, another in the theft of a wooden leg, another in car theft and wife abandonment. The other four leave their characters considerably shaken but in reasonable case. Each of the novels contains a murder and taken together, they portray a wide range of lesser offenses, including sexual immorality, ordinary and otherwise, voyeurism, mummy-stealing, self-mutilation, assault with a deadly weapon, moonshining, vandalism, and police brutality. All this, performed by characters who are for the most part neither bright nor beautiful, is the stuff of Flannery O'Connor's comic view.

Her apparent preoccupation with death and violence, her laughter at the bloated and sinful ignorance of mankind informed her continuing argument with the majority view. Believing as she did in a hereafter, she did not think, as most of us do, that death is the worst thing that can happen to a human being. I do not mean that she held life cheap, but rather that she saw it in its grandest perspective. Nor did she conceive of earthly happiness and comfort as the ends of man. The old lady in "The Comforts of Home" brings a whore into the house with her own son because she believes that nobody deserves punishment. This is the other kind of sentimental, self-serving charity, the obverse of that practiced by Sheppard and Asbury. Both kinds result from a misunderstanding of ultimate truth. But so much of even the apparent worst of O'Connor is funny, because, as Kierkegaard made clear, under the omniscience of God, the position of all men is ironic: measured against eternity, the world is but a dream.

In her work the strain of hope is strong. "Revelation" stands not necessarily as the best story she ever wrote, but as a kind of final statement, a rounding off of her fiction taken as a whole. O'Connor's version of the ship of mankind is a doctor's office and here sits Mrs. Turpin surrounded by the various types of humanity: the old and the young, the white and, briefly, the black, the educated and the uneducated, trash and aristocrat and good country people. Mrs. Turpin's thoughts are mostly on differences—on how, if Jesus had asked her to choose, she would have come to earth as a Negro of the right sort before she would have come as a trashy white person. The conversation is of human distinctions and of the race question, and from the beginning a silent girl with a bad complexion and a Wellesley degree regards her with loathing from behind a book. Finally, while Mrs. Turpin is in the act of thanking Jesus for making her who she is and putting her where she is, the girl attacks her and calls her an old wart hog from hell.

Mrs. Turpin's satisfaction with herself is broken: for her the scuffle in the doctor's office has shaken the scheme of things: her concept of herself and her relationships with both God and man have been called into question. She has a vision at the end.

> She saw the streak as a vast swinging bridge extended upward from the earth through a field of living fire. Upon it a vast horde of souls were rumbling toward heaven. There were whole companies of white trash, clean for the first time in their lives, and bands of black niggers in white robes, and battalions of freaks and lunatics shouting and clapping and leaping like frogs. And bringing up the end of the procession was a tribe of people whom she recognized at once as those who, like herself and Claud, had always had a little of everything and the God-given wit to use it right. . . .

> They were marching behind the others with great dignity, accountable as they had always been for good order and common sense and respectable behaviour. They alone were on key. Yet she could see by their shocked and altered faces that even their virtues were being burned away.

So no one escapes the need for grace: even the virtues of this world, being worldly, are corrupt. But it is easy to guess what Mrs. Turpin sees. Passing before her is that gallery of rogues and lunatics who are the *personae* of Flannery O'Connor's work—all of them loved from the beginning, and all of them saved now by God's mercy, terrible and sure.

AFTERWORD

In an introduction to a re-issue of *Wise Blood,* Flannery O'Connor noted that her novel had reached the age of ten and that it was still alive. After one-third that length of time, I feel that my essay on Miss O'Connor retains most of whatever life it ever had, and there are not many of my judgments of her work that I would want to change. I do think, however, that a little more might profitably be said concerning the southern quality in her writing and her sense of herself as a southern writer. I said that in her work "the South as locale and source was quite peripheral," which was, as I well knew at the time, a denial of her own views of the impulses that informed her fiction.

In speeches and interviews, particularly those given in the early phases of her career, she claimed to regard her southernness and her Roman Catholicism as equal forces in the shaping of her art. From the church came the general metaphysical principles that were her themes, from the South the specific images that were her dramatic vehicles. She sometimes referred to these two traditions as the theological and the biblical, and if one were not so absolutely certain that such a notion would have offended her profoundly, the amalgamation of Faith and country that she achieved might be cast as a dialectic with the syntheses being the sense of the Holy in fiction which was one of the values she was attempting to achieve. Or if this is going too far, then take her on a technical and a more mundane level. "When one Southern character speaks," she said, "regardless of his station in life, an echo of all Southern life is heard. This keeps Southern literature social, keeps it from being a literature of purely private experience." This was of particular importance to Flannery O'Connor. For talented as she was, she had difficulty with the larger images: her failure, if she failed at all, sprang from her inability to develop the larger contexts of her work.

And the fiction itself attests the importance of the southern element. I do not know which of Flannery O'Connor's stories I consider her finest, but "The Displaced Person" is a splendid accomplishment, and here the Protestant South and Roman Catholicism, that foreign religion, are held in a terrible balance that results at last in characteristically violent death. Mr. Guizac, the Pole, who represents theology, the unvitiated Faith, is triumphant at the end, dying as he does, fortified by the last sacraments. But the story is heavily dependent on the Shortleys, the Negroes, Mrs. McIntyre and Mrs. McIntyre's farm, the fields and woods, the barns and the animals. Mr. Guizac does seem in a way to be an abstraction. He is kept at a distance, largely separated from the reader to the end of the story: his humanity is less intense than that of the other, more familiar figures. On the other hand, the southern scene, the southern people are concrete, but they are deformed by the failure of their fragmented theology. Only the priest who participates fully in both traditions is whole: it is he who sees the Christ in man and recognizes the transcendent in the beauty of the peacocks. It is clear that without the southern element neither the priest as Miss O'Connor drew him nor the story could exist.

And the same can be said, though perhaps to a lesser extent, of *Wise Blood* and of all the stories in *A Good Man is Hard to Find.* They are more dependent on the southern scene and southern imagery than I was inclined to admit in my essay. But what I wish to do here is to modify my original position, not to recant it. It seems to me that with *The Violent Bear it Away* and increasingly with the stories in *Everything That Rises Must Converge,* Miss O'Connor's work became less southern, less dependent on the South as locale and more concerned with her quarrel against the modern world and its prevailing temper which she took to be destructively gnostic. More and more, the catalytic elements in her fiction were intellectual and moral aberrations from beyond the South: Asbury's Zen Buddhism in "The Enduring Chill"; the Wellesley student in "Revelation"; the procrustean psychological theory that infects both Rayber in *The Violent Bear it Away* and Sheppard in "The Lame Shall Enter First." Even the indigenous figures in such stories as "Greenleaf" and "Everything That Rises" are only titularly southern: separated from all tradition, they participate as fully as any northerner or Frenchman in the destructive self-sufficiency of our age.

Calculating, as we must, from the dates that her works were published, the turn in Flannery O'Connor's career came in 1955. After that time there were no more strictly southern stories such as "A Good Man is Hard to Find" and "The Artificial Nigger" and "The Life You Save May be Your Own." That Miss O'Connor's career should have entered a second phase is a tribute to her range as a writer, a testament to her deepening wisdom and increasing technical proficiency. But it is interesting also to note how rapidly the country and her section of it were changing during the fifteen years between 1949 when Flannery O'Connor began to publish and 1964 when she died. One of the final measures of her genius, the aspect of her talent that never failed her was her eye for the cheap and the obscene and the spurious, no matter under what guises they presented themselves, no matter where or under whose auspices they occurred. She saw the tragic polarization of our contemporary agonies and she displayed them for us as they sadly developed, but in her own style, drawn larger than they were, made more absurd. It was of this achievement that I was thinking when I gave short shrift to the southern qualities in her work.

Finally, four years are not long in which to mature a critical judgment. But for me at least, her fiction retains the pristine delineations of its beauty: her voice has lost none of its originality: she seems quite likely to endure.

Mystery and Manners is a collection of Flannery O'Connor's criticism, essays and occasional pieces, selected and edited by Sally and Robert Fitzgerald. The title is from a speech Miss O'Connor made to a group of college writers. "There are two qualities that make fiction," she said. "One is the sense of mystery and the other is the sense of manners." In her own work the mystery was provided by the Christian faith which she practiced; the manners evolved from the Southern milieu in which she lived and about which she wrote. The writings in this collection are mainly about the amalgamation of these two elements that were for her in every way inseparable, the interwoven threads that were the total fabric of her life.

Concerning what she had to say about the craft of fiction there can be no argument. She began and ended with those basic principles which are known to even the worst writers and which are to be found even in the most fatuous books. She quotes Conrad and James, she points to examples in Flaubert, she tells us that fiction is action directly rendered and that all good writing begins with an appeal to the senses. Here she is on the safest sort of ground, but she puts forth her case in such concrete terms and with such absolute clarity that the old lives and becomes new once again: she makes us see more perfectly what we have encountered a thousand times before.

And so it is when she is writing about the South as source for fiction. She reminds us that we lost the war, that we read the Bible, that we know a grotesque when one appears. "We in the South," she writes, "live in a society that is rich in contradiction, rich in irony, rich in contrast, and particularly rich in its speech." We all know this, and we know how these elements have shaped the work of Faulkner and Warren and Welty and Cormac McCarthy and Madison Jones. At first glance one might think that O'Connor's outrageous characters and situations are the most southern of all—the method of the southern grotesque pushed to its logical conclusion. But she will not allow this. The vision informs the work, she tells us, and her vision is out of Bethlehem, by way of Rome.

She said, "I shall have to speak, without apology, of the Church, even when the Church is absent; of Christ, even when Christ is not recognized." This necessity, on the simplest level, explains why she wrote the way she did. Exaggeration was her manner of making the blind see and the deaf hear. But her belief did more than affect her style—even when the term is used in the broadest sense. Stories, as Flannery O'Connor liked to point out, do say something, have to say something since they are concerned with the stuff of life. The vision, which is the complex of beliefs held by the writer, selects and gives final shape to the material: it informs and in every way qualifies the writer's world.

Since Flannery O'Connor believed in the communion of saints and the life to come, she could not be much concerned with the limitations of mundane existence. It was, I think, her sense of the transitory and preparatory nature of mortal life that made her as tough as she was in her own work and in her comments about writing in general. She could admire the gentleness in other artists; she could be amused that Henry James had worked out a rigmarole for turning the untalented aside without hurting their feelings. But for her, writing was a vocation in the strictly religious sense, life was lived solely to prepare one's "death in Christ," and so her sharp honesty spared no one: not old ladies in California, not student non-writers, least of all herself.

The last piece that the Fitzgeralds print is in many ways unliterary, and yet it seems to draw together most completely all the elements that shaped Flannery O'Connor's art. It is an introduction to a memoir, written by nuns, of a girl who lived for twelve years and died of cancer. Miss O'Connor helped the sisters with their manuscript and found in the child that she never knew an image that could contain and organize as much of her own sense of life and work as she would ever draw together in the pages of a single essay. Thus "A Memoir of Mary Ann" establishes the true dimensions of the O'Connor scandal. What I mean by this the following passage perhaps will show.

> One of the tendencies of our age is to use the suffering of children to discredit the goodness of God, and once you have discredited his goodness, you are done with him. The Alymers whom Hawthorne saw as a menace have multiplied. Busy cutting down human imperfection, they are making headway also on the raw material of good. Ivan Karamazov cannot believe, as long as one child is in torment; Camus' hero cannot accept the divinity of Christ, because of the massacre of the innocents. In this popular piety, we mark our gain in sensibility and our loss in vision. If other ages felt less, they saw more, even though they saw with the blank, prophetical, unsentimental eye of acceptance, which is to say of faith. In the absence of this faith now, we govern by tenderness. It is a tenderness which, long since cut off from the person of Christ, is wrapped in

> theory. When tenderness is detached from the source of tenderness, its logical outcome is terror. It ends in forced-labor camps and in the fumes of the gas chamber.

This is a kind of new iconoclasm that will test the tolerance of the modern intellectual community. The question is not whether any significant number will agree with her, but how many will listen without anger or even grudgingly allow her to have her say. The danger of our not listening seriously is twofold: having loved her blindly and perhaps too well, we may now turn against her; or worse, we may ignore the sources she claims for her vision and interpret her works and her life not as she has explained them, but according to what we think they should have meant and been. This, I think, would be the larger scandal which would impoverish us all.

ABOUT FLANNERY O'CONNOR

Flannery O'Connor was born in 1925 in Savannah, Georgia. She received her B.A. from Georgia State College for Women and was awarded an M.F.A. in creative writing from the State University of Iowa in 1947.

Miss O'Connor's first short story was published in 1946 in the *Kenyon Review.* From that time on, she published regularly in the *Partisan Review,* the *Sewanee Review,* and *Harper's Bazaar,* among others. In the O. Henry Awards of 1955 she placed second with "A Circle of Fire." In 1957 she took the first prize with "Greenleaf." She became a Kenyon Review Fellow in 1954 in creative writing, and in 1957 she was awarded a grant from the National Academy of Arts and Letters.

Granville Hicks, editor of *The Living Novel: A Symposium* (Macmillan, 1957), included

Flannery O'Connor's essay, "The Fiction Writer and His Country." In this essay she spoke of the stereotype of the Southern writer, "an image of Gothic monstrosities and the idea of a preoccupation with everything deformed and grotesque. Most of us are considered. . . to be unhappy combinations of Poe and Erskine Caldwell." But, she said in an interview granted to Harvey Breit for the *New York Times Book Review,* "my people could come from anywhere, but naturally, since I know the South, they speak with a Southern accent."

BOOKS BY FLANNERY O'CONNOR

WISE BLOOD
New York: Harcourt, Brace, 1952.
Toronto: McLeod, 1952.
New York: New American Library, 1953. (pb)
London: Spearman, Neville, 1955.
Toronto: Burns & MacEachern, 1955.
New York: Farrar, Straus & Cudahy, 1962.
Toronto: Ambassador, 1962.
London: Faber & Faber, 1968.

A GOOD MAN IS HARD TO FIND
New York: Harcourt, Brace, 1955.
New York: New American Library, 1956. (pb)
London: Faber & Faber, 1968.
As: THE ARTIFICIAL NIGGER AND OTHER TALES
London: Spearman, Neville, 1957.

THE VIOLENT BEAR IT AWAY
New York: Farrar, Straus & Cudahy, 1960.
London: Longmans, Green, 1960.
Toronto: Ambassador, 1960.
New York: New American Library, 1963. (pb)

THREE: WISE BLOOD, A GOOD MAN IS HARD TO FIND, & THE VIOLENT BEAR IT AWAY
New York: New American Library, 1964. (pb)

EVERYTHING THAT RISES MUST CONVERGE
New York: Farrar, Straus & Cudahy, 1965.
Toronto: Ambassador, 1965.
New York: Noonday, 1966. (pb)
London: Faber & Faber, 1966.
New York: New American Library, 1967. (pb)

MYSTERY AND MANNERS (ed. by Sally and Robert Fitzgerald)
New York: Farrar, Straus & Giroux, 1969.
New York: Noonday, 1970. (pb)

An Embarrassment of Riches: Baldwin's *Going to Meet the Man*

by John Rees Moore

James Baldwin's most valuable quality as a writer is authenticity. In his new collection of stories, *Going to Meet the Man*, we can trace in little the testing out of experience that is writ large in the novels. The first two stories, "The Rockpile" and "The Outing," take us back to Baldwin's memorable first novel, *Go Tell It On the Mountain*, dealing as they do with young John (the hero of the novel) and his attempt to discover in what ways he belongs and doesn't belong to his family. The scene in which Roy, John's younger brother and the father's favorite, is the center of family tensions as he lies savagely wounded in the forehead as the result of a gang fight is brought to life in the novel with all the painful freshness of a physical blow. In "The Rockpile" both the racial implications and the violent family antagonisms are much less fully developed, and the story is far less powerful than the corresponding episode in the novel.

A trip up the Hudson to Bear Mountain is the setting for the annual outing of "the saints" in the second story reminiscent of *Go Tell*, though it has no real analogue in the novel. John and Roy, on the brink of adolescence, and their hated and feared father are all in this story, too; in it John makes the unnerving discovery that David, the slightly older friend to whom he has entrusted the love nobody else wants from him, is growing away from him as he develops an interest in girls. John is left with a feeling of panicky loneliness. The story has a richer potential than Baldwin is able to realize fully within the limits he has imposed upon himself, but the characters and situations are sharply evoked. These stories, like the novel, are close to the marrow of personal experience.

By contrast "The Man Child" is a *made up* horror story. Two men have gone through the war together; one has land and wife and son—the other, at thirty-four, has nothing but his dog. His love-hate for his relatively successful and only friend leads the failure to kill his friend's little boy. It cannot be denied that this chilling story is unforgettable, and the flow of feeling among the four characters is projected with subtlety and skill. Nevertheless, it is *too* well made to carry conviction. One is left with an unpleasant sensation of the author's self-indulgence, not with a sense of tragic inevitability.

Baldwin is a very conscious artist in all his fiction. Represented experience must have a meaning. And he applies all his skill and intelligence to making sure that the shock and pain of this meaning will not be lost on the reader. His people are lonely, frustrated, fearful, often angry, and above all lovelorn. They reach out for the security of love like a drowning swimmer trying to grab a spar from the wreckage to keep himself afloat in the wide, wide ocean. Most of them have a vision of a better land, a better life, but their moments of happiness are always precarious and the surrender to love costs not less than catastrophe. As soon as they are old enough to have a sense of themselves becoming adults (if they live that long), his children, at least the gifted ones, must construct a strategy for finding and then trying to maintain their identities. In expressing the strain and suffering of a person trying to be true to himself and to others Baldwin almost always gives us, often powerfully, a sense of authenticity. But when his imagination is overwhelmed by fantasies of sadism or masochism, the objective reality of his art blurs and the result is bizarre, repellent, and unconvincing. The difficulty is that the territory Baldwin is exploring *does* lie between blatant social fact and nightmare. Besides, he writes on controversial subjects about which "everybody" has strong opinions and, even more to the point, deep-rooted feelings. To Baldwin the distinction between bad dreams and waking horror, or the attempt to make the distinction (even though some of his characters worry about this very thing), may well seem academic. Nevertheless, he knows that for the artist the truth that is stranger than fiction has no place there. At least not in his kind of fiction.

Childhood is frequently important in the five later stories of *Going to Meet the Man*, but the focus is on adult problems, and we don't see these problems from a child's standpoint as we do in the first three. "You are full of nightmares," says Harriet to her worried young husband, who has become a famous musician during his twelve-year stay in Europe. He has just made a film in Paris and is on the point of leaving for America with his wife and sister and seven-year-old son. He is a Negro from Alabama; his wife is Swedish. By leaving America he was able to establish a life of his own; otherwise he could not have entered his own life.

> For everyone's life begins on a level where races, armies, and churches stop. And yet everyone's life is always shaped by races, churches, and armies;

> races, churches, armies menace, and have taken, many lives. If Harriet had been born in America, it would have taken her a long time, perhaps forever, to look on me as a man like other men; if I had met her in America, I would never have been able to look on her as a woman like all other women. The habits of public rage and power would have blinded our eyes. We would never have been able to love each other. And Paul would never have been born.

And because it saved his life, he loves Paris. He remembers his three-month trip to America when his mother died eight years ago. And how glad he was to get back to Paris. In the film he has just made he played the part of Chico, a half-breed troubadour who, hating his father and mother, flees from Martinique to descend "into the underworld of Paris, where he dies." At first he tried to base his characterization on the Algerians he had known in the city, but the famous director, Vidal, shows him that his performance is not truthful; it becomes truthful when he keeps in the bottom of his mind all the possible fates in store for his son Paul. Nightmares in art ring true when they are based on nightmares in life. "This Morning, This Evening, So Soon" exhibits one of Baldwin's recurring themes: the dread of the exile *returning* home. And yet, ironically, a bad thing happens the last night in Paris, of a kind that would be unlikely in New York. The narrator and Vidal have met some young American Negro college students and gone to a Spanish night spot where Boona, an Arab from Tunis who once befriended the narrator, joins them. He apparently steals ten dollars from one of the girls. Amid protestations of trust on both sides, the mistrust is a glaring fact. The Arab is in a worse position than they are (in Paris)—lonelier, poorer, more *unknown.*

In contrast to the "blessed" life possible in Paris for a Negro, "Previous Condition" assures us of the purgatorial necessities of the poor but emancipated Negro in New York who has white friends and a white girl, but is never sure that he may not return home at night to find himself forced out of his lodgings. The hatred of the young unemployed actor for *some* whites poisons the liking he wants to have for others. Nor is Baldwin unaware of the difficulties this situation creates for the whites. But a still harder and more poignant problem confronts the hero of "Sonny's Blues" when he discovers his younger brother has been arrested as a heroin addict. His first reaction is not to get involved: let Sonny sink or swim, even if he is a kid brother. As usual in a Baldwin story, we are brought to an understanding of a present crisis by an exploration of the past. Just before he was married, the older brother learned from his mother how his father, who had always seemed such a tough and independent man, would have collapsed after an accident in which *his* brother had been killed by some drunken white boys who ran over him, if the mother hadn't supported him by being there—"to see his tears." His mother had only smiled when her eldest son had said he wouldn't let anything happen to Sonny. "You may not be able to stop nothing from happening. But you got to let him know you's *there*." After his release, Sonny comes to live with his brother and sister-in-law. And one day Sonny talks about what taking the drug, what music, what life, has meant to him, even while he is telling his brother that there is no way he can tell him these things. It is beautifully done. But the climax of the story comes when Sonny takes his brother to his "kingdom" in Greenwich Village and succeeds in saying through the music he creates what he could never say in words. This, I should say, is the most unequivocally successful story in the book.

Love, the poets tell us, is what makes the world go round. Modern novelists show us varieties of sexual experience, often with the suggestion that "love" is a neurotic disorder that can only interfere with our pleasure and ruin our mental health. In Baldwin's work lovers carry the additional burden of racial consciousness, of revolt against social convention, of a guilt that self-righteousness cannot absolve them from. Yet the very obstacles that make love all but impossible for them give it a peculiar preciousness. Most of them do believe in love with a primitive intensity that civilization cannot destroy, though it often destroys *them* for so believing. Ruth in "Come Out the Wilderness" is a country girl who has come to the big city to find love and fortune. She is living in Greenwich Village with a young artist, Paul. She is black and he is white. And she knows that the end of their affair is approaching, that Paul will soon leave her. The insurance company she works for in midtown Manhattan has recently hired Negroes; she finds herself "in an atmosphere so positively electric with interracial good will that no one ever dreamed of telling the truth about anything." Ruth thinks of her parents who, though they have labored all their lives in the South, would not have a penny for burial clothes if they should drop dead tomorrow, and of her older brother, almost thirty, still unmarried, "drinking and living off the woman he murdered with his love-making." She wishes she had never left home and never met Paul. She is called into the inner office of Mr. Davis, the only other Negro employee, who tells her she is to be his secretary if she will take the job; he is choosing her not for any racial reason but because she seems the most sensible girl available. She does not really find him attractive but is touched by his humanity. Her love for Paul is "like a toothache," but love ought to be something else, "a means of being released from guilt and terror." Paul would never be able to give her this release. And yet because of Paul she is ashamed and unable to give herself to Mr. Davis. After work, as she sits by herself in a bar, unable to reach Paul by phone and finding the thought of going home to wait for him intolerable, she catches sight of a young fellow whom she finally recognizes as a rising actor. He is pale and fair and boyish and he reminds her of other men she has known—in spite of his coming fame she sees in his face and head that he is "lost." She has seen that look on many, including Paul. And she thinks, "The sons of the masters were roaming the world, looking for arms to hold them. And the arms that might have held them—could not forgive." She stumbles out into the rain, not knowing where to go or where she is going. Her capacity for love combined with her need to use it is her undoing. But here we do feel a potentially "happy" ending withheld. Mr. Davis is an undeniable comfort to have in the background.

In "Going To Meet the Man," the last story in the collection, no such comfort is in sight. Sex, violence, history, the Negro and the South are brought together in a shocker as up to date as tomorrow's newspaper. A deputy sheriff, in bed with his wife, is dismayed to find himself impotent. He tells how he has beaten up a young Negro leader who refused to order his followers to disperse and stop their singing. He remembers a night long ago, riding in a car, sleepy, between his father and his mother. They were one of a long caravan of cars coming back from a lynching. Like a Fourth of July picnic, white men, women, and children had gathered to witness the last rites of a Negro who had, apparently knocked down a white woman. The boy Jesse was terrified by what he saw—and the burning, castrating, and dismemberment are described in meticulous detail. The boy notices the faces of the watchers as he is perched on his father's shoulders. His mother's "eyes were very bright, her mouth was open: she was more beautiful than he had ever seen her, and more strange. He began to feel a joy he had never felt before." He wishes he were the man with the knife approaching the hanging, naked black body. And when it is over, Jesse feels a great love for his father. "He felt that his father had carried him through a mighty test, had revealed to him a great secret which would be the key to his life forever." Reliving it all, the deputy feels his manhood return to him, and he takes his wife with triumphant violence. With sardonic irony, Baldwin leaves his little fable to speak for itself. It is a tale of outrage and grief and yet of the greatest possible ambivalence, like a ritual at once sacred and obscene.

II

The trouble with Richard Wright's *Native Son*, Baldwin has written, is that it presents a dangerous myth of the Negro at the expense of reality. Bigger Thomas is isolated, he has no vital relationship with his own people nor with anyone else; at the end of the book we know no more about him than we did at the beginning. And by making this ignoble savage a symbol of the Negro problem and the focus for social protest, Wright has both glamorized and falsified the grayer and grimmer fact of what it means to be a Negro in America. In spite of his keen awareness of the dilemma, Baldwin himself has not always been able to avoid the same pitfall. Small wonder, either, since he believes the general American fear of experience means that most Americans live largely in a fictitious world of their own devising. If so, the world of myth *is* the world of fact. But Baldwin has never made the mistake of leaving his characters unaccounted for: we always know the people and places and experiences that have shaped them.

From his first novel, *Go Tell It On The Mountain*, to "Going to Meet the Man," he shows people caught in crisis who *must* understand their past if they are to go forward. To put it extremely: they must either grow or die; they cannot stand still. *Go Tell* is the story of fourteen-year-old John's conversion. The boy is struggling to escape the hateful domination of his father. He is both in search of a father and in search of a way to "kill" his father. And he is terrified at the discovery of his own "sinful" sexuality. Like many another son, he makes the decision: "He would not be like his father, or his father's father. He would have another life." He fears that hatred of his father has hardened his heart against the Lord.

In the second part of the novel we get the background that helps us understand John's father and mother and aunt (and hence John himself). Aunt Florence left home in the South, had a disastrous marriage, found out that her brother Gabriel had had a bastard child and allowed the mother to die alone and deserted. Now she is an old woman come to Harlem to die in an unfurnished room. She hates John's father and sympathizes with the boy. So far Gabriel has appeared in a very unattractive light, but now we see things from his point of view. After a night spent with a whore, he experienced at twenty-one the "conversion" his mother had always hoped for him. He began to preach and married Deborah, severe and sexless after the rape she had suffered in girlhood, but a pillar of strength to Gabriel. He tried to keep secret from her a nine-day affair which resulted in a son, but she guessed his secret when she discovered he had stolen her savings. For years she said nothing of this to him. His sense of sin only increases Gabriel's determination to be a man of God. "One day God would give him a sign, and the darkness would all be finished—one day God would raise him, who had suffered him to fall so low."

Then we are back with John trying to pray. Why are their lives so troubled if God's power is so great? He imagines God reconciling him with his earthly father. "Then he and his father would be equals in the sight, and the sound, and the love of God. Then his father could not beat him any more, or despise him any more, or mock him any more—he, John, the Lord's annointed. He could speak to his father then as men spoke to one another—as sons spoke to their fathers, not in trembling but in sweet confidence, not in hatred but in love. His father could not cast him out, whom God had gathered in." And yet he does not *want* to love his father; he wants to cherish his hatred.

Next we learn that Elizabeth, the boy's mother, had loved but never married a young man who had killed himself after being falsely accused of a robbery and beaten up by the cops. She was left with her child John (whose father died never knowing she was pregnant). So Gabriel is not really John's father. In the third part of the novel—and an extraordinary, almost surrealist piece it is—John has the sensation of being torn to pieces by a morally ambiguous power overwhelming and terrifying in its intensity. While he is writhing on the floor in church, a voice commands him to "rise from that filthy floor if he did not want to become like all other niggers." He imagines a knife in his father's hand descending on him. Finally a voice says, "Go through, go through," and a sweetness fills his soul. He is not reconciled with his father, but he has found a weapon for competing with him. Never again will he be a helpless victim.

Baldwin's portrait of the artist as an adolescent differs from other such portraits in the strenuousness of its commitment to the necessity of rebirth by ordeal. John's initiation into selfhood has a curious fatality, partly the product of John's will, partly something deeper in himself that he doesn't understand, partly a communal ritual binding him to the whole of his racial past. It is one of the book's achievements that individual psychology and social history fuse into a single, indivisible unity.

In *Giovanni's Room* Baldwin moves on to try something entirely different. Here the two main characters are experimentally, so to speak, uprooted and isolated from their pasts. David is about to go home to America and his friend Giovanni is about to be guillotined. Hella, the girl David might have married, has just left him, and he is alone with a memory he will never be able to expunge. Through flashbacks we learn of the inferno he has lived through. (The motto or legend of the book is

Whitman's "I am the man, I suffered, I was there.") This novel, really a novella, seems strongly influenced by French example—we think of Gide and Camus.

As David thinks back over what brought him and Hella together, he decides it was the security they gave each other against too frightening freedom. They were American innocents in Paris. David had left a meaningless existence in America to "find himself" in France. His mother had died when he was five, but her memory had dominated the little family group of his father, his father's sister, and himself. The boy despised his weak and drunken father and hated his aunt. His second year in Paris he met Giovanni; Hella had gone to Spain and David was "free" to form any attachment he chose. Giovanni was working in a bar of dubious character; when David realized what was beginning to happen he had an impulse to rush out and find a girl—any girl. But instead he goes home to Giovanni's room. Standing in a room in Southern France, on the eve of his departure, he remembers the joy and amazement at the beginning of his days with Giovanni, and the anguish and fear never far underneath. Giovanni's room, ugly and poor and always in great disorder, became a symbol of their intolerable relationship, the disorder being a "matter of punishment and grief." The yellow light hanging in the center of the room is emblematic of "a diseased and undefinable sex" at the center of Giovanni's life. While Giovanni is at work, David spends his time in various ways, but "no matter what I was doing, another me sat in my belly, absolutely cold with terror over the question of my life." Giovanni knows that David is going to leave him, that his girl is coming back from Spain. Thinking back, "I understood why Giovanni had wanted me and had brought me to his last retreat. I was to destroy this room and give to Giovanni a new and better life. This life could only be my own, which, in order to transform Giovanni's, must first become a part of Giovanni's room." But David wants children, unquestioned manhood, a woman who can be the steady ground for his life. He thinks by an effort of his will he can be himself again. When Hella gets back from Spain, David does not return to Giovanni's room for several days. Giovanni begins to lose his grip on life and sinks to the lower depths of sexual and human degradation; finally he murders the *patron* of the bar where he used to work. The case becomes a national scandal. David is struck with terrible remorse and grief; Hella can do nothing to assuage it. When they go to the south of France, David finds his love for her changing to hate. "Much has been written of love, turning to hatred, of the heart growing cold with the death of love. It is a remarkable process. It is far more terrible than anything I have ever read about, more terrible than anything I will be able to say." Hella finally realized the hopelessness of the situation when she pursues David to a bar in Nice where she discovers him with a sailor. She leaves for home. As he stares naked into the mirror in his room, David sees in his mind's eye the last moments of Giovanni's life. He too must pack up and go home, a sadder and wiser man than he came.

The sense of disaster that pervades this story and the high degree of symbolic concentration do not prevent Baldwin from giving us a vivid rendition of the sights and sounds and people of a Paris convincingly real. Once and for all he proves (among other things) that he does not need to be writing about some aspect of the Negro "question" to be writing truly and well. Some of the detail in the book is unconvincing (for instance, that Giovanni should have left his wife in Italy because of the death of their child), and Hella is a rather elusive characterization, but if the ability to evoke pity and terror is a sign of tragic power, it cannot be denied that Baldwin displays this power.

After these two relatively small-scale novels it was inevitable (and right) that Baldwin should try a "big" novel. *Another Country* combines the themes found in his previous work and adds new ones. Negro-white relationships, homosexuality, the conflict of older and younger generations, marital and extra-marital quandaries, the dangers of success and unsuccess, the terrors of innocence and the remorse of experience are all brought to life in this richly orchestrated problem novel in many brilliantly-executed scenes. But the book suffers from its ambition. It is as though Baldwin were trying to cram everything he knows and thinks between two covers. And there is no ballast of normality to keep the boat from rocking; every situation is extreme or rapidly becomes so. Previously Baldwin was very successful at maintaining the proper esthetic distance from the experience he was putting into artistic order; here his touch is uncertain and the tone is sometimes unpleasantly close to hysteria. Yet this effect, we are convinced, comes at least partly from Baldwin's determination to write with greater honesty than ever before, to get nearer the quick of experience.

Rufus Scott, a young Negro jazz musician, dominates the book, although he commits suicide by jumping off the George Washington Bridge quite early in the novel. A victim of guilt and circumstances, he is a cause of guilt in others. Forced by a compulsion he partly understands but cannot control, he has driven Leona, a poor white Southern girl whom he lived with and whose main fault was loving him too voraciously, literally to madness. In the process he cut himself off from friends and family, and his suicide is a challenge to them to examine their own consciences. How have they failed him? And does their failure imply a fault more in the stars than in themselves? Vivaldo, a poor and struggling (and unsuccessful) young novelist, was Rufus' best friend. He could have insisted on keeping Rufus with him on their last evening together. His love for Ida, Rufus' beautiful sister, is doomed from the start not only because he is white and she is black but because the memory of Rufus comes between them. Ida wants her revenge on the world for her brother's death and is determined to be as hard as necessary to get it. Yet she loves Vivaldo for himself and for something precious he represents for her in the world. Vivaldo is insanely jealous but is determined not to abuse his rights over her. She has an affair with Ellis, a rich show business promoter who can further her musical career. When his worst fears are confirmed, Vivaldo is both destroyed and purged; yet there is a chance their love will survive this loss of innocence and be all the stronger for it. The discovery scene between Ida and Vivaldo is one of the best in the book.

Love and power are fatally intertwined in Baldwin's scheme of things. Soul-shattering recognition scenes are counterpointed against scenes of hectic sexual bliss and revulsion. Getting ahead in the world seems to demand the death of love. As a student Vivaldo had almost revered Richard and had thought of Richard and Cass as being an ideal couple. But when Richard writes a successful novel Vivaldo is contemptuous of it, and Cass finds herself steadily drifting away from her husband. To stay on top you have to convince yourself that fraudulence is genuine. In her despair Cass turns to Eric, a homosexual who fled Alabama and made a life for himself in France. There he discovered Yves, a young Frenchman off the streets of Paris, and began to get some reputation as an actor. The description of their relationship is tender and convincing, and (significantly) the most "normal" in the book. Eric has come home to America to take an important role in a play; Yves is to follow later. At one time Eric too had loved Rufus and been humiliated by him, just as Leona was. Now that Eric is home he is equally scared of succeeding and of failing; he doesn't know whether he can stand America; and he worries about what will happen to him and Yves when the young Frenchman arrives. And he is frightened to see what a few years in age have done to Richard and Cass and Vivaldo, the friends he left behind. Eric is an appealing and well developed characterization, but the episode in which he and Vivaldo spend the night together has an absurdity greater than Baldwin intended. At least they don't have to worry about the color problem.

If love and power are intertwined, so too are the moving and the grotesque. There is very little dead writing in this long novel—Baldwin has suffered it all and it is impossible not to respect that suffering and the range and knowledge he commands. Among the impressive pieces of writing are the description of the rapport between Ida and her audience the first time she sings in public and the account of the French movie in which Eric has a bit part. Baldwin can be superb on music and the movies. Much of the dialogue is witty, intense, and true. But the people in this novel are asked to *represent* so much! Baldwin doesn't *tell* us to take Rufus as a symbol of Negro hopelessness in a white world—most Negroes aren't jazz drummers—but we find it almost impossible to think of Rufus except in terms of his plight. Are we meant to ask ourselves what stops all Negroes (unless they're Uncle Toms, anyway) from jumping off Washington Bridge? (Perhaps that's a fair question). On the other hand, the structure of this novel proves Baldwin's intellectual power—if proof were needed. Oddly, there is something almost cold about the skill with which he manipulates his harrowing material. And though the characters are mirrors held up to his own ideas, they seem real, too. Sometimes, however, the book reads like an address to white liberals assuring them with anguish and contempt that there is Another Country in New York of which they know, and at bottom can know, nothing.

At this stage in his career it is evident Baldwin is out for the championship. If his novels give the impression that life is over at thirty-five, this will no doubt change with time. He has brains, talent, and a conviction of what art should do: make us change our lives. The unwary reader might get the impression from *Another Country* that sex is the only alternative to a solution of the world's problems. Or perhaps the only solution there is. But Baldwin does not make this mistake. His endeavor is to show us—even to the point of hallucination—that the public life and the private life are an indivisible whole, that sanity cannot exist half slave and half free.

John Rees Moore

AFTERWORD

Practically every one of his critics has commented on the two faces of James Baldwin. As an essayist he is given full marks for his passionate and lucid analysis of the "race problem," but as a novelist his very ability to handle ideas is considered a deficit. His fictions seem devised to illustrate a text. After his first, highly-praised novel, *Go Tell It on the Mountain,* his novels have had a very mixed reception. The sensationalism of his themes, the inflated rhetoric, the overcharged relationships of his characters, the over-simplification of moral issues have all been scored by his detractors as vulgarizations or falsifications of the experience he is trying to present. One difficulty here is that very few of his critics have first-hand knowledge of Baldwin's terrain, including this one. This does not mean, of course, that they have no right to judge his books. After all, not many of us know Dostoevsky's Russia or Kafka's Prague or, for that matter, Shakespeare's England, but when has that been a bar to entering the worlds of their imagination? But we are too close to Baldwin to take him in the same way, even if he deserved it. He speaks "our" language and we think we understand him—and what we understand seems lacking in the subtlety and depth we expect of a major novelist. His vision does not convince us of its authority.

Why? The reasons are hard to untangle. Great writers, including Faulkner, have been accused of all the faults mentioned above—melodrama and excess—without the damage being fatal to their reputations. But Baldwin's reputation as a writer of fiction, to judge by reviews of his most recent novel, *Tell Me How Long the Train's Been Gone,* is in a steep decline. He has been dismissed, for instance, as a writer whose use of stereotyped situations and phony style put him on the level of the purveyors of standardized entertainment to the readers of the *Ladies Home Journal.* What is offensive is that he is dealing with potentially great themes in a way intended to be taken seriously and reducing them to tired abstractions. Is he in too great a hurry to make his points? Or are his critics in too great a hurry to oppose his abstractions with a set of their own? If a reader would like to see Baldwin present a convincingly normal relationship between two people for once, whereas Baldwin is insisting that a so-called normal relationship is impossible in the world he knows, are reader and writer at hopeless cross-purposes? We can say, it is up to the artist to convince us by his art that we stand to gain more than we lose by submitting ourselves to his view of things. But he might reply, you are so pre-conditioned to resist my view of things that you will not permit my art to work on you—and anyway your opinion makes no difference to me; I must do the work I have to do. Let's hope Baldwin *does* feel that way. There is plenty of honorable precedent. And then he can get on with his work. In the long run the truer he makes his work the more likely he is to receive the justice he wants. In the meantime he must write in the light of the truth as he sees it.

ABOUT JAMES BALDWIN

At the age of fourteen, James Baldwin became a Holy Roller preacher at the Fireside Baptist Church in Harlem. His evangelical career, however, met its end in 1943 with the death of his father, also a minister. The oldest of nine children, Baldwin found himself head of the household and chief provider for his family at the age of nineteen. Working in a defense plant in Belle Meade, New Jersey, he found himself caught in the "racial tensions generated by shifts in population to meet the demands of the World War II labor market" (*Current Biography,* 1964). Therefore, together with the realization of his desire to write came the knowledge that he would have to leave home to pursue his talents.

In 1945 he received a Eugene F. Saxton Memorial Trust Award, through the efforts of Richard Wright and because of the literary promise displayed in the then unfinished *Go Tell It On The Mountain.* Receiving a Rosenwald Fellowship in 1948, he went to Paris where he completed *Go Tell It On The Mountain, Notes of a Native Son,* and *Giovanni's Room.*

Baldwin has now returned to New York, the city of his birth, where he has continued an active and impressive career. In 1964 he was appointed a member of the National Institute of Arts and Letters.

Through his writing and lectures Baldwin has become an ardent spokesman for the Civil Rights Movement.

BOOKS BY JAMES BALDWIN

GO TELL IT ON THE MOUNTAIN

New York: Knopf, 1953.
Toronto: McClelland & Stewart, 1953.
London: Michael Joseph, 1954.
New York: Grosset & Dunlap, 1961. (pb)
Toronto: McLeod, 1961. (pb)
New York: Dial, 1963.
New York: New American Library, 1954. (pb)
New York: Dell, 1964. (pb)
London: Longmans, 1967. (ed. by E. N. Obiechina)

NOTES OF A NATIVE SON

Boston: Beacon, 1955.
Boston: Beacon, 1957. (pb)
Toronto: S. J. Reginald Saunders, 1955.

London: Mayflower, 1958. (pb)
Gloucester, Mass.: Peter Smith, 1961.
New York: Bantam (pb)
New York: Dial, 1963.

GIOVANNI'S ROOM
New York: Dial, 1956.
London: Michael Joseph, 1957.
Toronto: Longmans Canada, 1957.
New York: Apollo, 1962. (pb)
New York: Dell (pb)

NOBODY KNOWS MY NAME
New York: Dial, 1961.
Toronto: S. J. Reginald Saunders, 1961.
London: Michael Joseph, 1963.
New York: Dell (pb)

ANOTHER COUNTRY
New York: Dial, 1962.
Toronto: S. J. Reginald Saunders, 1962.
London: Michael Joseph, 1963.
New York: Dell, 1963. (pb)

THE FIRE NEXT TIME
New York: Dial, 1963.
London: Michael Joseph, 1963.
Toronto: S. J. Reginald Saunders, 1963.
New York: Dell, 1964. (pb)
Toronto: S. J. Reginald Saunders, 1964. (pb)
London: Hutchinson, 1967. (pb)

BLUES FOR MISTER CHARLIE: A PLAY
New York: Dial, 1964.
London: Michael Joseph, 1965.
New York: Dell, 1965. (pb)

NOTHING PERSONAL (photography by Richard Avedon)
New York: Atheneum, 1964.
Middlesex: Penguin, 1964.
New York: Dell, 1965. (pb)

GOING TO MEET THE MAN
New York: Dial, 1965.

London: Michael Joseph, 1965.
New York: Dell, 1966.

TELL ME HOW LONG THE TRAIN'S BEEN GONE
New York: Dial, 1968.

AMEN CORNER
New York: Dial, 1968.

Not Text, But Texture: The Novels of Vladimir Nabokov

by R.H.W. Dillard

Art is never simple. . . . Because, of course, art at its greatest is fantastically deceitful and complex.

—*Vladimir Nabokov, Playboy,* January 1964.

The occasion for these pages is the publication of a newly-translated and revised version of Vladimir Nabokov's Russian novel, *Despair* (*Otchayanie,* originally published in Berlin in 1936). To approach Nabokov's novels with anything less than complete humility is not only an act of arrogance but of foolishness, for if the novelist's art, as Nabokov suggested in his autobiographical memoir, *Speak, Memory,* is to compose elaborate and significant puzzles in which "the real clash is not between the characters but between the author and the world," too often even his most dedicated and enthusiastic critics lose the game disastrously and are left red-faced and gasping for breath. I should, then, prefer to make of this piece something more and perhaps less than a review—a celebration of the master's latest gift and a grateful appreciation of his plexed artistry and combinational delights.

Nabokov's position in literary life is unique: he has no double in recorded literary history. He is, with Boris Pasternak, one of the two greatest Russian novelists of his time, and he is, with William Faulkner, one of the two great American novelists of that same time. He is, in fact, his own double—at once the two greatest living novelists, himself the mirror of his own reflection. And his novels are genuinely Russian and as genuinely American—*The Gift* is, to my knowledge, the best modern Russian novel in both manner and matter, and *Pale Fire* is, to my mind, one of the best novels in English to have been written in this century.

There are eight novels and a novella in Russian and five novels in English, and these fourteen volumes, for all their being in two languages and the products of two literatures, are of a piece, forming together a real canon, a multi-mirrored labyrinth of reflecting and repeating dreams and nightmares, disasters and delights. Speakers and voices may vary from volume to volume, but the maker's hand is consistently firm as the hallmarks of his steady and continuing vision remain clear and sharp from first to last. He is clearly and always the maker of these books, the serious and deceptive artist with whom we must play the game.

The central figure of Nabokov's novels is the artist, the man of sensitivity and imagination. Hero and dragon alike dream the creative dream and either shape that dream into immutable art or are destroyed by it in a mutable world—Fyodor Godunov-Cherdyntsev and John Shade on the one hand; Aleksandr Luzhin and Hermann, the doomed writer of *Despair,* on the other.

Hermann, the son of a Russian-speaking German father and a pure Russian mother, lives in Berlin; his business is chocolate. He is a man without a proper identity, neither at home in Germany nor an exile from lost Russia; he is, in many respects, an invisible man, yearning to create himself in a world that pays him no attention. This novel is the account of his one artistic act, a crime, the discovery and murder of his secret self in order to create himself anew.

The plot line is deceptively clear. Hermann meets a tramp, Felix Wohlfahrt, who, when his features are relaxed, is clearly his double. He plots to murder Felix after switching clothes and identities with him in order to collect the insurance and begin a new life. He weaves a skein of involved lies around himself which deceive only his wife Lydia. He kills Felix and escapes, but he is trapped by his own invisibility, for Felix is immediately identified and Hermann is tracked down and cornered by the police. Hermann as much as Felix is the victim of his deeds; his work of art is not the crime he hoped it would be, but rather the comic record of his failure, the novel which he could only produce by the destruction of himself.

Hermann's doom is the result of his "hypertrophied imagination" which leads him away from the world around him and betrays him to a Dostoevskian romanticism. The novel is a parody of Dostoevski, of "old Dusty's great book, *Crime and Slime.* Sorry: *Schuld und Sühne* (German edition)." It is the story of a Raskolnikov who feels no guilt and finds no expiation, who is simply a murderer and a madman, the victim of artistic dreams failed by a lack of creative imagination. Or rather, an imagination without connections in reality: Felix is Hermann's double only to Hermann, whose plot is an artistic construct only to himself. He learns too late that although life may copy art, art must be formed from life, must be (to use Poe's terms) the product of "multiform combinations of the things and thoughts of Time" but in tune with the patterns which a whimsical and implacable fate has already woven into those things. Man's freedom is involved in finding and fulfilling his destiny rather than changing it. The final irony of Hermann's story is that he creates *Despair,* his one successful work, not as a work of art but as a defense of his failure.

> I have nothing to blame myself for. Mistakes—pseudo mistakes—have been imposed upon me retrospectively by my critics when they jumped to the groundless conclusion that my very idea was radically wrong, thereupon picking out those trifling discrepancies, which I myself am aware of and which have no importance whatever in the sum of an artist's success. I maintain that in the planning and execution of the whole thing the limit of skill was attained; that its perfect finish was, in a sense, inevitable; that all came together, regardless of my will, by means of creative intuition. And so, in order to obtain recognition, to justify and save the offspring of my brain, to explain to the world all the depth of my masterpiece, did I devise the writing of the present tale.

Hermann convinces no one of his crime and convinces no reader of its artistic value, no more than the narrator of "The Tell-Tale Heart," can convince anyone of his sanity. His novel gives us the opposite understanding. He is a man doomed to fall for flying too near the sun (his car is appropriately an Icarus) for he acted from groundless imagination and exceeded the limitations of human action. Nabokov, in a *Playboy* interview, said that "The artist should *know* the given world" else his art will be no more than "the crank's message in the market place." Hermann fails as an artist and as a man, a human being, because he is a fool. The novel ends appropriately on All Fool's day as Hermann tries to convince the crowd come to see his arrest that he is in truth an actor in a film, that he wants "a clean getaway." But reality is waiting for him, the gallows at the end of the signposts he saw but could not understand. His crime is a crank's message to the world; the novel resulting from that clumsy crime is, however, a fine and rich novel, a visionary artist's message to us and to the world.

The Russian novel is traditionally a product of Russian fatalism; the world of Russian literature is one in which a coincidence is a controlled event and in which the creative freedom of man is involved in the discovery of the pattern of his destiny rather than forming that future himself out of a chaos of possibility. Pasternak's *Doctor Zhivago,* for example, is an elaborate and consciously artificial scheme of fateful coincidence, and all of Nabokov's novels are concerned with the awesome complexity and beauty of fate's designs in life. The elaborate constructions of an artist, whether they be of words, sounds, colors, shapes, or moves on a chessboard, are, then, in varying degree harmonious with the larger designs played out in reality; the artist makes his own world in small, plays God and fate to his characters, and gives us in that game a share in the divine, an understanding of ourselves and our position in the world of living and continually transforming figures and of the order of and beyond that world. Nabokov's witty, elaborate and artificial novels are, then, designed to give us a taste of reality that palates trained to a material world guided only by natural laws or the long-term interests of Providence find strange and "unrealistic." They are, however, entirely realistic, given the context of Nabokov's understanding of the orderly, if somewhat whimsical, nature of fate.

The heroes of three of his Russian novels offer illustrations of the range of human experience, success and failure, possible within Nabokov's world: Aleksandr Luzhin, Cincinnatus C., and Fyodor Godunov-Cherdyntsev. All three are men of artistic and imaginative temperament, but one is defeated by his imagination and fate, one escapes his apparent doom by learning the form of his own destiny, and one gains that perfect and active fusion of imagination and fate which gives birth to real art.

Aleksandr Ivanovich Luzhin is the hero of *The Defense,* which was originally published in Russian in 1930 as *Zashchita Luzhina (The Luzhin Defense).* He is a chess grandmaster, an artist as involved in the pattern and rhythms of chess as a musician is to those of music, involved deeply and totally with the "exquisite, invisible chess forces." Unlike Hermann he is a true artist, sensitive to the patterns of the game, his art, and its "forces in their original purity." He is, however, like Hermann in a fatal way, for his imagination functions apart from reality and is, thus, out of harmony with the richer creative force of life. He plays blind in exhibitions in which, cut off from the real and materially eventful world by the blindfold, he feels himself to be "in a celestial dimension, where his tools were incorporeal qualities." Tarrasch's dictum, that "chess, like love, like music, has the power to make men happy," does not apply to Luzhin, for so deeply involved is he in his art that his perception of reality is distorted. Chess becomes for him the real world, and the human world, especially that of love and simple human relationships, seems a dream, pleasant and desirable but fragile to the disruptive and destructive influence of "reality," of chess.

In his genius and his devotion to his art, he goes mad and, with his wife's help, tries to escape his own destructive mania by avoiding chess and living in his "dream" of life. But, life itself has become for him a vast, carefully patterned game played against fate itself; the defense of the title is the chess defense he attempts to construct against his invincible opponent and his own corrupt imagination. That defense is, of course, doomed to failure, for Luzhin, like Hermann, designs in madness and is blind to life. His love is directed only to chess, and apart from life, all love and all devotion is fatal. His defense proves erroneous, and the error has been foreseen by his opponent.

> The key was found. The aim of the attack was plain. By an implacable repetition of moves it was leading once more to that same position which would destroy the dream of life. Devastation, horror, madness.

As he had done once before when playing the Italian champion Turati, Luzhin cannot avoid defeat and is only able to halt the match, "to stop the clock of life, to suspend the game for good, to freeze" and thus lose the match and his life. His suicide is his surrender; it dooms him to an eternity designed by his own imaginative failure, an eternity of "dark and pale squares. . . obligingly and inexorably spread out before him." His defeat is eternal, and, to the world of the living and the loving, there is "no Aleksandr Ivanovich."

Luzhin is, then, like Hermann, a victim of his own imagination, for the imagination is totally destructive when, for whatever reason, it is out of tune with the movements of reality. Cincinnatus C. is also a victim of a distorted view of things, but one who discovers the truth and brings himself into tune and into life. The hero of *Invitation to a Beheading* (which was originally written in 1935 and published in Russian as *Priglashenie na kazn'* in 1938), he is the sole prisoner in an enormous fortress, condemned to death according to the law for an unstated crime, accepting his condition with no understanding of it at all. The beginning of the novel is Cincinnatus' first realization that his death is imminent, and Nabokov equates his life with a work of art, a novel, on the second page:

> So we are nearing the end. The right-hand, still untasted part of the novel, which, during our delectable reading, we would lightly feel, mechanically testing whether there were still plenty left (and our fingers were always gladdened by the placid, faithful thickness) has suddenly, for no reason at all, become quite meager: a few minutes of quick reading, already downhill, and—O horrible!

But *Invitation to a Beheading* has 211 pages to go, and Cincinnatus' life is not so near its end either, for he has yet to separate hard fact from fancy, to find the reality in a confusing and confused world of sham. His jailers and tormentors blend and blur, seem separate entities at times and at others to be a few men awkwardly acting dual roles. The prison cell in which he resides seems often a bad stage set, designed and constructed by madmen. Everything becomes deceptive, as Cincinnatus' identity and that of the narrator, the maker of the book and the world, begin to be involved, and together they believe in the deceptions and "infect them with truth." On the day of his execution, Cincinnatus finds his strength, survives his ordeal, and separates himself from his past, his condemned self, and his death. The world of his imprisonment and despair is truly a bad stage set, and he moves out of it, purged of his despair, sure in his own destiny and in harmony with the new and proper end of the novel, which is really an opening into life beyond illusion.

> A spinning wind was picking up and whirling: dust, rags, chips of painted woods, bits of gilded plaster, pasteboard bricks, posters; an arid gloom fleeted; and amidst the dust, and the falling things, and the flapping scenery, Cincinnatus made his way in that direction where, to judge by the voices, stood beings akin to him.

Cincinnatus masters his imagination, and by that artistic feat fulfills himself and finds both his destiny and the direction of reality. He is, then, an artist-hero, and *Invitation to a Beheading* points the way to a fuller account of the artistic life and Nabokov's finest Russian novel, *The Gift* (in Russian, *Dar*) is the story of Fyodor Godunov-Cherdyntsev's growth to artistic maturity, to the beginning of his freedom and fulfillment.

"The most enchanting things in art and nature," says Fyodor, the young poet-hero, "are based on deception," and his understanding of nature and art is a major source of his eventual success. The novel itself is an elaborate and misleading puzzle, partaking of that ultimately enlightening deception of art itself, a deception designed to reveal the world as a pattern of fate quite as involved and intricately arranged as the cleverest of literary artifacts. Like the poems of Wallace Stevens, it is about art and an artist, and because of the relationship of art and reality, it is about life and the world.

The narrator is Fyodor's imagination, that part of him which is writing the novel over the three and a half years of its happening, so that the end of the novel is Fyodor's conscious decision to write the novel that his imagination has just completed. The gift, then, is both Fyodor's artistic gift and the novel itself, a gift to him from his imagination. The plot is as involved with the history of Russian literature as it is with the characters' lives, for Fyodor's growth parallels the development of Russian literary art. The first chapter concerns Fyodor's youthful poems, the juvenilia of literature; the second is romantic in the tone of Pushkin; the third is grotesque and darkly comic in the manner of Gogol; the fourth is Fyodor's brilliantly witty biography of N.G. Chernyshevsky, the nineteenth century novelist most revered by Marx and Lenin; and the fifth marks Fyodor's attaining an artistic stature of his own (in a style distinctly Nabokov's own). The events of Fyodor's life are appropriate to each style, and the remarkably rich "parodies" are as practically enlightening as they are delightful in their own right.

The novel is audaciously conceived and executed; Fyodor's life is both comic and significant, at once a moving story and a literary fable. He is a real artist, human, fallible and fully alive, while the subject of his biography, Chernyshevsky, comes to represent the man who fails art and whom life fails. The novel is what Fyodor dreams of writing, "a classical novel, with 'types,' love, fate, conversations. . . and with descriptions of nature."

The Gift closes with a last admonitory twist of fate, a joke that heightens Fyodor's sense of joyous success as much as it continues to teach him at a time when he thinks he has all the keys to his destiny. At its end, it opens out, as do the other novels, and is no summing up but an awakening, even though it is Nabokov's farewell to his Russian literary career. Nabokov, like Fyodor, was, after those eight novels and assorted shorter works, at a new beginning. He stated his themes and developed his forms in Europe and in Russian, and he was to reach his full maturity and artistic stature in America and in English.

Nabokov has written and published five novels in English: one written in Paris in 1938, *The Real Life of Sebastian Knight* (1941), and four written in America, *Bend Sinister* (1947), *Lolita* (Paris, 1955; New York, 1958), *Pnin* (1957), and *Pale Fire* (1962). Although he will always be at heart a Russian, he stated in an afterword to *Lolita* that he is "trying to be an American writer" and in the *Playboy* interview that since in America his "weight went up from my usual 140 to a monumental and cheerful 200. . . . I am one-third American—good American flesh keeping me warm and safe." His latest novels, like his flesh itself, are Russian and American, and the three most recent ones form an American trilogy in which he is able, in the New World, to bring together all of the themes and images of his Old World art into a new substance which is that of supreme artistic achievement.

The lives of his heroes and the clarity of his vision combine more successfully than ever before, and John Shade, the American poet in *Pale Fire,* understands more fully than any of his Russian heroes the total involvement of life and art and, thus, the nature of being itself:

> But all at once it dawned on me that *this*
> Was the real point, the contrapuntal theme;

> Just this: not text, but texture; not the dream
> But topsy-turvical coincidence,
> Not flimsy nonsense, but a web of sense.
> Yes! It sufficed that I in life could find
> Some kind of link-and-bobolink, some kind
> Of correlated pattern in the game,
> Plexed artistry, and something of the same
> Pleasure in it as they who played it found.

Not text, but texture in life and art is what matters; the reflection is as significant as the object; the mirror set up to life catches the reflections in other mirrors as well as "reality" itself; art is not didactic, but it is the key to truth; life, like art, may be seen through and solved with imagination and spirit; we can find the land where dwell beings akin to us.

Humbert Humbert, like Hermann, is an artist who attempts to create his dreams in life, the pawn trying to shape the movement of the game. Also like Hermann, he fails, but he learns as he fails and the account of his failure, *Lolita,* is a conscious and beautiful work of art. Nabokov himself notes the difference between the two in the preface to *Despair:*

> Hermann and Humbert are alike only in the sense that two dragons painted by the same artist at different periods of his life resemble each other. Both are neurotic scoundrels, yet there is a green lane in Paradise where Humbert is permitted to wander at dusk once a year; but Hell shall never parole Hermann.

Humbert earns his reward by a realization of his guilt at the end of the novel when he hears the distant melody of children at play and knows that "the hopelessly poignant thing was not Lolita's absence from my side, but the absence of her voice from that concord." His penance is performed in the fifty-six days during which he writes *Lolita* and gives their lives the permanence of "durable pigments, prophetic sonnets, the refuge of art." His dream can only be real in artificiality, in the artifice of art; but that reality is a truer one than that of the psychologists who read *Lolita* as a case history, Dr. Blanche Schwarzmann (white blackman) and John Ray, Jr. (J.R., Jr.) who are self-cancelling, mirrors set up only to other mirrors.

Humbert's final artistic triumph is purchased, however, with the destruction of himself. Throughout the novel, he dwindles away, from the vital, darkly handsome hero of Part One to his disappearance as H.H. at the end of Part Two; even the name Humbert Humbert, behind which he hides by his own choice, is self-cancelling.

The novel is the account of Humbert's attempt to recreate the dream of his past (his lost Annabel Leigh) in the present (young Dolores Haze, Lo, Lola, Dolly, nymphet Lolita). The scene is America, land of impermanence and change, dream and illusion, and the presiding influence from whom Nabokov absorbs the essential American substance is Edgar Allan Poe. *Lolita* is "Ligeia" made new, as Nabokov brings the Poe tradition home to America where it was born and belongs. Like a Poe character, Humbert is mad and sees his madness too late, a victim of illusions who can speak poetry only out of his own disaster. It is the story of a love that fails because it is real too late; the seducer is seduced as is his seducer; villain becomes avenging hero, and dream is broken on painful mortality's back. As Humbert becomes unreal, an artifact with "long agate claws," his love becomes real, and the object of his love, at first a selfish and unreal dream, becomes painfully real, doomed to die by giving birth to a stillborn girl on Christmas day in Gray Star, "a settlement in the remotest Northwest." And the whole complex pattern, illusion as well as reality, is presided over by "precious fate, that synchronizing phantom."

The novel is a shimmer of errors, a labyrinth of mirrors, in which Humbert loses himself and Lolita, but out of that confusion of fact and dream, he fashions *Lolita*, his confession and penance, his plea for mercy ("Imagine me; I shall not exist if you do not imagine me. . . . "), and his transmutation of suffering into beauty, of a "tangle of thorns" into the eternity of "aurochs and angels." If I seem to have slighted the novel's comedy and sexuality, I have done so consciously, for they are widely enough known and are really but a part of the texture of the whole; Humbert is the artist-hero, not as successful as Fyodor, but no failure doomed to his own despair as were Luzhin and Hermann. He marks a fusion of victim and hero, loser and winner, and *Lolita* is a richer and subtler novel for that fusion.

Pnin is a quiet and gently comic interlude between the involved magnificence of its predecessor and *Pale Fire.* Its images and themes are often those of *Lolita,* and its central character and his dream of exile are in *Pale Fire,* although separately.

Professor Timofey Pnin is an exiled Russian scholar, reduced to teaching at levels far beneath his capabilities, an object of laughter and ridicule in a land where he is neither understood nor able to understand. His life is a comic tissue of mistakes which confirm his belief that the "history of man is a history of pain," but it is also presided over by a benevolent fate which smooths away his confusions and enables him to love and live in an alien world, far from his lost home.

> He did not believe in an autocratic God. He did believe, dimly, in a democracy of ghosts. The souls of the dead, perhaps, formed committees, and these, in continuous session, attended to the destinies of the quick.

Pnin is neither the artist-hero nor the mad artist failure; he is a man of intelligence and feeling, sentiment and nostalgia, harmless but easily harmed, lost in a land far from home, from beings of his own kind. But he also partakes of the spirit of life, is able to love and, of all Nabokov's characters, is perhaps the easiest to love. At the end of the novel, he moves through ridicule and beyond it, comically and bravely, "up the shining road, which one could make out narrowing to a thread of gold in the soft mist where hill after hill made beauty of distance, and where there was simply no saying what miracle might happen."

Pnin is subject to "one of those dreams that still haunt Russian fugitives, even when a third of a century has elapsed since their escape from the Bolsheviks," a dream that he is a deposed king, forced to flee from his country and live disguised and unknown in a foreign land. He shares that dream with Dr. Charles Kinbote, a colleague at Wordsmith College, who may really be an American scholar named Botkin, but who thinks he is "Charles II Xavier Vseslav, last king of Zembla, surnamed the beloved." It is Kinbote's edition, with an introduction, notes and index, of John Shade's last long poem, "Pale Fire," which is Nabokov's most recent novel, *Pale Fire.* Mary McCarthy first pointed out that Kinbote was Botkin and that the novel could be read as a kind of detective story in which the false clues of Botkin's dreams of Zemblan glory could be eliminated and the truth revealed. John Rodenbeck expanded and corrected her understanding by showing that Charles the Beloved and Kinbote are quite as real as Botkin and Shade, and that Kinbote's invented identity is a necessary balance, antithesis and counterpart, to Shade's own reality which is also of fact and fiction, figure and shadow. Rather than repeat their arguments, I shall merely try to indicate far too briefly how both Shade and Kinbote are artist-heroes and how both find the truth of things—one by reflection and discovery, the other by imagination and invention.

Shade's poem, a long, personal meditation on his life in which he arrives at a pleasurable understanding of life's plexed artistry, speaks clearly for itself. His conclusions are tentative (as the poem is circular), but they are the products of a joyous new awakening.

> I feel I understand
> Existence, or at least a minute part
> Of my existence, only through my art,

> In terms of combinational delight;
> And if my private universe scans right,
> So does the verse of galaxies divine
> Which I suspect is an iambic line.

Kinbote's commentary, the bulk of the novel, is a mad interrelating of his own fantasies into the texture of Shade's poem. The poem stands by itself, but read with Kinbote's notes it takes on an entirely new richness and credibility, for they are texturally right, are appropriate both to Shade's art (romantic where his is classical, but as carefully detailed and constructed) and to his universe. Kinbote gives Shade a hero's death, and, at the end of his labors, mad and alone, even as he knows his own doom and destiny, he has joined Shade in an artistic combination worthy of eternity.

Into the index Nabokov wove an active example of John Shade's favorite word game, Word Golf. In the note to line 819, we are told that Kinbote moved from *lass* to *male* in four strokes; in the index, "lass" refers us to "mass, mars, mare" which in turn refers us to "male"—a game, Kinbote's game, complete in four. This is a playful detail, an indication of Kinbote's vanity, but it is also something more. If we were to consider the entire book as a game of Word Golf, moving from its first word, *pale,* to its last, *land,* we can complete the game in three: *pale, pane, lane, land.* If this is the book in essence, then it can be read meaningfully. Watch my hands carefully, for this is artificial, but no trick.

Pale: A reference to our confused world of "reality," the world described by Shakespeare in *Timon of Athens* (IV, iii, 443-449) in which the moon steals "her pale fire. . . from the sun" and "Each thing's a thief," a world of illusion and deception, the earthly pale separate from but reflecting eternity dimly.

Pane: The pane of glass in which may be reflected the world around us, but also through which we may see another world beyond us, destructive to us if we believe the reflections to be true ("the waxwing slain / By the false azure in the windowpane"), related to pain, but also the medium of art, the mirror by which we can merge interior and exterior, time and eternity, put the furniture on the lawn, catch the rays of the sun, and perhaps see through to beauty and another reality; Hourglass (Our Glass) Lake in which Charlotte Haze drowned, the ice through which Hazel Shade plunged, the glittering ice land of Zembla, and the medium of reflection by which John Shade glimpsed eternity.

Lane: The road to a new reality found through reflection and art; Franklin Knight Lane, American lawyer and statesman, who wrote on the eve of his death following an operation:

> And if I had passed into that other land, whom would I have sought?. . . Aristotle!—Ah, there would be a man to talk with! What satisfaction to see him take, like reins from beneath his fingers, the long ribbon of man's life and trace it through the mystifying maze of all the wonderful adventure. . . . The crooked made straight. The Daedalian plan simplified by a look from above—smeared out as it were by the splotch of some master thumb that made the whole involuted, boggling thing one beautiful straight line.

Land: The other land, the land of light, recovered Zembla, both Pope's Zembla ("An Essay on Man," II, 221-224) and his orderly world (263-270) where we can see "the blind beggar dance, the cripple sing, / the sot a hero, lunatic a king," and "Supremely blest, the poet in his Muse," Poe's Arnheim, recovered Eden, Pnin's divine committee room and the land where dwell beings akin to us, our true selves, what we are through and beyond illusion.

This is but one of a multiplicity of approaches to *Pale Fire,* and all of those ways are rewarding, for it is, as Mary McCarthy said, "one of the very great works of art of this century." In it Nabokov reconciles past, present, and future and finds the lost homeland, the world of light and innocence in an eternity growing from ourselves even as it gives the pattern of our destinies. Hermann and Fyodor are reconciled here, for genius and madness are akin and in this novel are drawn into creative action together—the one understanding reality and the other dreaming a parallel reality. It is at once an artistic masterpiece and the fullest flowering and synthesis of Nabokov's long devotion to art and to life.

AFTERWORD

There are now books about Nabokov: L.S. Dembo's excellent anthology of critical pieces by various hands with its full bibliography (*Nabokov: The Man and His Work*), Andrew Field's important if over-eager *Nabokov: His Life in Art,* Page Stegner's unfortunate *Escape Into Aesthetics: The Art of Vladimir Nabokov* and his Viking portable *Nabokov's Congeries,* and Carl R. Proffer's *Keys to Lolita.* All of these books are interesting; none of them fortunately is "definitive." Carl R. Proffer, for example, seeks the allusions and examines the style of *Lolita* thoroughly and well (although he did not find, among other things, Claire Quilty lurking in Aubrey Beardsley's "The Ballad of a Barber"); he enjoys the game, plays it well, but is embarrassed by it, makes no attempt to get at the significance of the novel's shimmering and enormously allusive texture. He does his task with scholarly competence; he avoids kinbotic reading of self onto the page. But he leaves it to the reader to construct the important conclusion to be drawn from his efforts, to understand how completely *Lolita* is about the essential relationship between life and art, between the unstable world of daily variety and the serenely stable one of art, Henry James's "dim underworld of fiction, the great glazed tank of art [where] strange silent subjects float."

And there are more critical books to come, among them a promised study by Alfred Appel, Jr., which promises much light, his annotated *Lolita,* and a special *festschrift* issue of *Tri-Quarterly* honoring Nabokov's seventieth birthday.

More importantly, Nabokov has published several books: a revised and expanded *Speak, Memory;* a collection of four stories, *Nabokov's Quartet;* and two new novels, *King, Queen, Knave* (a translation and recreation of his second Russian novel, *Korol', Dama, Valet,*

1928) and *Ada,* his acrobatic and wondrous new novel in English.

If *Despair* is a version of *Crime and Punishment* as *Lolita* is of "Ligeia," then *King, Queen, Knave* is a version of the popular romantic triangle novel, say Dreiser's *An American Tragedy.* It takes its coloring from such diverse sources as a nursery rhyme, *Madame Bovary,* fairy tales, Russian Gulch, and *Candida.* And, of course, it is a uniquely Nabokovian fairy tale, set in bourgeois pre-depression Germany but, as always, concerned with the human eye and heart and with the artistic forms and meanings of the world.

The novel is about spiritual myopia and is a comedy of vice and folly. Its characters live in a world ruled by the God of Chance, Cazelty, or Sluch, simply because they haven't the vision and the imagination to see or dream the true order of their lives. They are mere playing cards in the hands of their creator (who makes several appearances to them as Vivian Badlook, Blavdak Vinomori, and the "remarkably handsome man in an old-fashioned dinner jacket" who visits the later chapters of the book with his wife), but they are so self-absorbed that, unlike John Shade, they are unable to see the "correlated pattern in the game," much less that there is any game at all. They feel a discontent with the pointlessness of their lives and with their bondage to Cazelty, but they cannot see that they are sharing a hand with a wild joker and death the spade in a comic game as serious and meaningful as life can ever be. They find, then, none "of the same / Pleasure in it as they who played it found."

The novel is very much true to the rich duplicities of Nabokov's other novels, both Russian and English: to be able to see clearly beyond the self and to be able to see the plexed artistry of the pattern in which one lives and sees is to be able to take real pleasure in the moment and to live truly; to be able to see only the self through the dark glasses of petty passions blinds one to truth and dooms one to the hell of failed dreams and painful disappointment. Think on the one hand of John Shade, Cincinnatus C., and Fyodor Godunov-Cherdyntsev, and on the other of Hermann, Humbert, and Luzhin.

In an interview with Alfred Appel, Jr., Nabokov admits to having "good eyes," but Franz Bubendorf, the young lover and knave of *King, Queen, Knave,* is hopelessly myopic and possesses "those eyes, those eyes, poorly disguised by glasses, restless eyes, tragic eyes, ruthless and helpless, of an impure greenish shade with inflamed blood vessels around the iris." Franz is the nephew of Kurt Dreyer, the owner of the Dandy Department Store in Berlin, and he becomes the lover of Dreyer's wife, Martha. Both Franz and Martha are hopeless romantics of a totally unimaginative sort; they dream the cliché, as Franz wanders from blurred fact to blind error throughout the novel, always seeking the sexual Sodom and Gomorrah of his adolescent dreams and finding only a hectic and sordid affair with his aunt. Martha rejects her jolly husband's sexual advances for a dream in which "Three lecherous Arabs were haggling over her with a bronze-torsoed handsome slaver." And she finds only bumbling Franz who can offer her only his dull village memories and the opportunity to cheapen and debase herself. Both are not at home in the physical world, but neither has the imaginative capacity to escape it or transform it. Martha becomes as much a knave as Franz, and both share a fool's adventure.

Dreyer, the cuckolded king, is able all along to see better than either his wife or his nephew. He is inquisitive and possessed of a sense of humor (which both Franz and Martha sadly lack), but his very geniality blinds him and renders him incapable of final action. He sees the world innocently and happily as a "dog pleading to be played with" where "every day, every instant all this around me laughs, gleams, begs to be looked at, to be loved." And he strives to play with the world within his limitations: he is trying to learn English (but only to be able to read Galsworthy), is struggling appropriately with Shaw's *Candida* and his dictionary, and is involved with an inventor of automannequins—lifesize, mobile models for use in his department store and perhaps more interesting places. He is also capable of remembering the past and its moments of love. His enthusiasm for the world causes him, however, to see it too simply; he has a sense of Eden but not of its necessary serpent. He is not an artist designing a life, for, like Humbert, he seeks the permanent in the moving and mutable world instead of in the memory and imagination whose weavings do partake of immortality. His blindness allows Martha and Franz their adulterous deception and plunges Dreyer into the undeserved grief which he feels at Martha's death. But *King, Queen, Knave* is a comedy, and Nabokov, the artist and sole designer of Dreyer's life, sets things in comic order and brings the tale round to its proper end.

Martha and Franz eventually come upon the idea of murdering Dreyer, but because of Franz's inability to see the present and Martha's to remember a past, both are totally incapable of shaping the present into a future. All they succeed in doing is killing Dreyer's dog Tom, a clear-eyed animal (akin perhaps to Peeping Tom), a grand lively beast by whom both Martha and Franz are disgusted. But Tom lives again in Martha's dying words just as the life she never really participated in continues with little notice of her absence save the grief of her betrayed husband and the hysterical joy of her freed young lover.

Franz, near the end of the novel, oppressed by Martha's domination, unable to dance, watches two foreigners dance by, Nabokov and his wife:

> The girl had a delicately painted mouth and tender grey-blue eyes, and her fiancé or husband, slender, elegantly balding, contemptuous of every thing on earth but her, was looking at her with pride; and Franz felt envious of that unusual pair, so envious that his oppression, one is sorry to say, grew even more bitter, and the music stopped. They walked past him. They were speaking loudly. They were speaking a totally incomprehensible language.

Unlike Cincinnatus C. who understood the voices of the beings akin to him, Franz cannot understand what he hears. Perhaps it is simply the language of genuine love that he finds incomprehensible, for he has been kept from love by callowness and lust as Martha has by greed and egoism. Perhaps Dreyer does not understand either, but he struggles on with his dictionary. He may often be more jester than king, but he is more king than his knavish nephew, more royal than his incurably bourgeois wife.

Enricht, Franz's landlord and secretly Menetek-El-Pharsin the Conjurer, thinks he dreams the world, but is observed once looking at his own behind in a mirror. Lost in the world of Cazelty, his upside-down and backwards vista may well be the proper view of things, the only apt handwriting on the wall, but from without, the reader, Nabokov's partner in the game, sees truly and sees the comic rightness of it all. The eye and heart can only together be alive and true, clearly and warmly; blind lust and vulgar greed lead only to comic and deadly despair.

The queen is dead in her avarice; the knave is free in his blindness; the king is swollen-eyed with grief. And the author of the tale, the "happy foreigner hastening to the beach with his tanned, pale-haired, lovely companion," has dealt us a royal hand in a game well worth the playing.

Ada or Ardor, a family chronicle is more than a comedy of vain folly, although the characters are as much and wholly Nabokov's, living in his dreams, his imaginings, his combinational art, and his book. Many critics have already noted the novel's closeness to Nabokov, the parallels between Ardis and his boyhood home, between the events of the novel and certain events of his life. Memory is, of course, always the source of art, of its inspiration in the moment and of the materials with which it must be brought to life. The past, according to Van Veen, the narrator of *Ada,* is in one view "a coherent reconstruction of elapsed events," and "what we are aware of as 'Present' is the constant building up of the Past, its smoothly and relentlessly rising level." "How meager!" he adds, "How magic!" Past and present are, then, products of consciousness, coherent only insofar as one is able to reconstruct or recombine the sensations and memories available to the mind.

Edgar Allan Poe, speaking of the nature of originality in art in "Peter Snook," said that "There is no greater mistake than the supposition that a true originality is a matter of impulse or inspiration. To originate, is carefully, patiently, and understandingly to combine." To Nabokov, as I think it was to Poe, to live truly is consciously to be able to engage the facts of the moment, which is too an accumulation of remembered moments, imaginatively and creatively, to recombine them into a coherent construction "carefully, patiently, and understandingly." The artist in his art does that vital task for all of us capable of joining him in it. The game of art is, then, the most significant of all games, of all actions, for it is the type of living truly, the rich evidence of conscious being.

Fiction, according to the narrator of Nabokov's story "Time and Ebb," requires imagination, and truth requires memory. In *Ada,* as in all great novels, imagination, and memory work in harmony to produce a work that is fiction and truth, no mere "autobiographical" novel and no mere work of fancy, but what Wallace Stevens called "a supreme fiction." And remember how Stevens ended his "Notes Toward a Supreme Fiction":

> How simply the fictive hero becomes the real;
> How gladly with proper words the soldier dies,
> If he must, or lives on the bread of faithful speech.

Ada is a novel about time and immortality, lust and love, hell and heaven, the past and the present, the fictive and the real. It begins and ends as a family chronicle, a *Buddenbrooks* or a *Forsyte Saga,* novels which (to use Nabokov's summary of *Ada* at the end of the novel) move "at a spanking pace" and in which a young woman's "tragic destiny" may constitute "one of the highlights of this delightful book." But it is, of course, "much, much more." Van Veen says that his aim was "to compose a kind of novella in the form of a treatise on the Texture of Time, an investigation of its veily substance, with illustrative metaphors gradually increasing, very gradually building up a logical love story, going from past to present, blossoming as a concrete story, and just as gradually reversing analogies and disintegrating again into bland abstraction." Ada wonders "if the attempt to discover these things is worth the stained glass," but *Ada* follows a similar course, moving from banal family history to a living story (a supreme fiction) and returning to the banal plot summary of its conclusion. Most of the reviewers have lingered over the bright edenic gardens of Ardis and the youthful ardor of Van and Ada, but the whole rising and falling pattern is there and necessarily there. The novel does give one a sense of the texture of time, of the living moment that is all of the moments which have preceded it; it offers its reader the opportunity to share the intensity of Van's perception when he hears Ada's voice on the telephone in Switzerland: "That telephone voice, by resurrecting the past and linking it up with the present, with the darkening slate-blue mountains beyond the lake, with the spangles of the sun wake dancing through the poplar, formed the centerpiece in his deepest perception of tangible time, the glittering 'now' that was the only reality of Time's texture."

Impossible to summarize, the novel is the story of Van Veen and his love for his cousin (really his sister), Ada Veen. The story takes place on Anti-Terra, a science-fiction parallel earth (a device common enough to be standard practice, for example, in the super-heroic comic books of the National Comics group in which the two planets are referred to as Earth One and Earth Two). History moves along roughly parallel to our history, but out of phase (Anti-Terra is ahead of Terra). The Anti-Terrans are aware of Terra by means of madmen, visionaries, and artists, and there is, in fact, a belief that Terra is heaven (literally heaven on earth). But Anti-Terra is also an opposite to earth in some way; it is Demonia, perhaps a hell on earth. (Ada means, among other things, *of hell* in Russian, but it also contains a *yes.*) Certainly the characters of the novel are sinners, and, as

Matthew Hodgart has pointed out, Lord Byron may be the guiding spirit of this novel as much as Poe is of *Lolita.* Van and Ada are incestuous lovers. Van and dark-haired Ada tease their sister (half-sister, cousin), blond and light Lucette, to death. Van and his father, Demon Veen, have a way of killing or crippling those who get in their way. Even Van and Ada's love is as much ardor as love, and Van admits late in the novel and in his life that "sensuality is the best breeding broth of fatal error."

If Ardis, Ada's family estate, is an Eden, the demon and the serpent are already there: the fatal flaw is as much a part of Anti-Terran paradise as it was in the earthly garden. What begins as youthful and innocent ardor, children tumbling together in sexual joy in every corner, every glade, every eave, becomes with the passage of time befouled; Van begins to speak of sex in terms of dirt (he remembers a black girl student he had "fondled and fouled"; he curses "nature for having planted a gnarled tree bursting with vile sap within a man's crotch"; he even feels "his lust sharpened by the shame").

"One can even surmise," Van says in the last "straight" sentence of the novel, "that if our time-racked, flat-lying couple ever intended to die they would die, as it were, *into* the finished book, into Eden or Hades, into the prose of the book or the poetry of its blurb." And in the last paragraph of that appended blurb, guided by many similarities between this novel and Nabokov's story "The Vane Sisters," one can find Ada and perhaps a Russian guitar laced among "a doe at gaze in the ancestral park." Is she in the Hades of her name and the blurb, or is that ancestral garden truly a recovered Eden? The answer is not difficult to discover. John Shade is invoked in this novel, and the titles of Nabokov's stories and novels are woven throughout. The answer is the same answer that has been there all along, recreated, recombined, but partaking of the same truth.

When Van is most depressed by the evil of his life and his world, by the failure of his dreams and the impenetrability of the "veil of time... the flesh of space," by the fact of death, he maintains his hope for reasons that he cannot name:

> He wondered what really kept him alive on terrible Anti-Terra, with Terra a myth and all art a game, when nothing mattered any more... and whence, from what deep well of hope, did he still scoop up a shivering star, when everything had an edge of agony and despair, when another man was in every bedroom with Ada.

He realizes that "on *this* planet Lucettes are doomed," but he realizes, too, that for all the lust and all the evil, his love is real, his life is real, the moment is real, and his art may be a game but it is the only path to immortality. Van may be sterile, and he and Ada may be the last of their line, but he nevertheless gains John Shade's faith in the moving present with no need of the promised future, in the creative and living mind with no need for absolute certainties. Terra, we know, is no myth, nor is it a heaven. It is a fallen world like its opposite, and a living world. Ardis may become a home for Blind Blacks, but it lives in *Ada* as paradise and hell, in the past and in the present at once. The mind holds time even as the flesh surrenders to it. Humbert Humbert finds a certain expiation in the making of *Lolita*; Van finds the texture of time and the only immortality he can know in Van's book, in *Ada*. And Van's book is truly Nabokov's.

Van does what Humbert does, what Fyodor Godunov-Cherdyntsev does, what Cincinnatus C. does, what Kinbote wished Shade to do for him and what Shade did for himself; he untangles the knot of death and immortality with the keen slice of harmonious memory and imagination. The world is Eden and Hell at once; the serpent and the garden are one as life and death are one. And the conscious and perceptive mind can still scoop up a shivering star in the darkness of unknowing. *Ada* is a reassertion of human value and the value of the game of art, of the works of man with all their necessary flaws.

And *Ada,* as Wallace Stevens insisted a supreme fiction must, gives pleasure. It is, like *Lolita* and *Pale Fire,* comic and tragic at once. It has what Nabokov calls "human humidity," and it is constructed with his usual wit and dazzling artifice. It is, for example, an *Anna Karenina* in reverse; it parodies Mann and Flaubert and Proust, even as it uses them for serious departures. It finds its sources in an enormous variety of unusual places: Nabokov's stories (especially "Time and Ebb," "Lance," and "The Vane Sisters"), science fiction, the history of art, the history of the novel, Chateaubriand and Tolstoi, Byron, Poe, Borges, even Konrad Lorenz's promiscuous greylag goose Ada. The novel is a treasure box of delights, the opening of which is a pleasure not only to those "exegetical critics" for whom Nabokov's detractors claim the novel was written, but for anyone who enjoys the elaborate webs of "combinational delight." And *Ada* is as well a novel which, to use Poe's words, attains "a portion of that Loveliness whose very elements, perhaps, appertain to eternity alone."

Since Page Stegner and Andrew Field have tangled on the question of whether Shade created Kinbote (Field) or Kinbote created Shade (Stegner), I should like to add here a note on line 1000 of "Pale Fire." Certainly Field's position is the more tenable of the two. In fact, about the only critic I know of who adheres to

Stegner's position is the fictional Maurice Stonecock in the only really unfavorable review I have yet seen of *Ada* (except for a certain poetaster's tasteless remarks in *The New Yorker*), but I fear that the entire question blurs the centrally important fact that Nabokov created both Shade and Kinbote, that they are both equally "real," and that they are both elements of a remarkably balanced and meaningful novel which is concerned directly with the nature of art and its relation to fact and truth. Field, Stegner, and Stonecock are all in grave danger of falling into what Nabokov calls "the old-fashioned, naïve, and musty method of human-interest criticism that consists of removing the characters from an author's imaginary world to the imaginary, but generally far less plausible, world of the critic who then proceeds to examine these displaced characters as if they were 'real people.' "

I hold to my earlier statement that "both Shade and Kinbote are artist-heroes," that "both find the truth of things—one by reflection and discovery, the other by imagination and invention." Both are also figures of the elements of the whole artist. According to the scheme of "Time and Ebb" again, Kinbote's imagination and warped memory create the fiction for the truth of Shade's imaginative memory. Mad imagination and sane memory and reflection are the necessary elements of true fiction. But to hold to this reading and expect it to answer all of the questions of the novel is to belittle the novel and to limit one's own freedom as a responsive reader of the novel. The question of the missing line 1000 of John Shade's poem "Pale Fire" requires another approach.

The novel is neither a tragedy nor a comedy: it is at once both and something more. Shade's serious poem, a meditation on death, is a true comedy that creates a renewal of order that is Shakespearean in magnitude and vitality; Kinbote's comic notes lead to a tragedy of lost dreams and failed perception, a surrender to the past and the fatal order of despair. The novel, a compound of poem and notes, of comedy and tragedy, is one of the richest and truest works of art of this or any other century, a weave of fact and fancy which gives the truth beyond saying in a texture of which surface and substance, style and content, are one. For Nabokov as it was for Poe, the work of art is an emblem for and indication of cosmological and ontological truth; it is as untranslatable as the universe itself, and it strives to be as beautiful and harmonious.

John Shade's poem is in ryhming couplets and has 999 lines. The last line does not have a rhyming partner, and it leaves the poem suspended with a suggestion of being unfinished. Kinbote, the American poet's mad Russian editor, says that, since the last word of line 999 is *lane,* the first line of the poem ("I was the shadow of the waxwing slain") was intended by Shade to be also line 1000, thereby bringing the poem full circle and back to its initial musings on shadow and reality. This reading is a plausible one, one which I accepted for some time. But I shouldn't have. Kinbote's circle (and its attendant despair) is too easy; like all the rest of his annotations, it Europeanizes Shade's American poem.

Gertrude Stein's definition, in "The Gradual Making of The Making of Americans," of what it is that is specifically American is useful here. "Think," she says, "of anything, of cowboys, of movies, of detective stories, of anybody who goes anywhere or stays at home and is an American and you will realize that it is something strictly American to conceive a space that is filled with moving, a space of time that is filled always filled with moving." Certainly motion, the harmonic and necessary union of destruction and creation, is at the center of the American consciousness, and American art has, since Poe, Emerson, and Melville, been concerned with a union of opposites, the moment of creative harmony when spirit is freed within necessity to action and being. The autobiographical or inside narrative examines the self for fact in the making, the moment and act of creation. As W.R. Robinson has put it (in the *Hollins Critic* for February 1968), the American imagination "bears witness to and exemplifies creation, the individuating process whereby, having gathered its powers at the source, purified of whatever would weigh it down, whether matter, guilt, or egotism, the imagination leaps free." John Shade's "Pale Fire" is a poem in that tradition, like Wordsworth's *The Prelude* in its iambic regularity but more like Whitman and Thoreau in its vigor and humor, its celebration of the world and its exemplification of that world's harmony and lively form in its own "combinational delight." The poem's last line is line 999, for while the poet's life continues, his poem should remain open-ended, suspended into the growing moment. If his death does write the last line, that line should still not be the first.

In *Speak, Memory,* Nabokov says that "The spiral is a spiritualized circle. In the spiral form, the circle, uncoiled, unwound, has ceased to be vicious; it has been set free." In the poem Shade lightly mentions "spiral types of space," and finally comes to terms with life and its spiral form (of space and time), a life of play and motion, matter and spirit, of meaningful change. Kinbote reads the poem as a circle because he is reading himself, because he is European, exiled and held by the past, because, like

Luzhin and Hermann or one of Poe's victims of time, he is trapped in a viciously circular fate, doomed to the locked room of his own static fantasy and dreaming despair by his madness and his inability to thrive in a world of motion and change. No wonder that he tries to make the poet a tragic hero in his world, for Shade is a true hero in *his* world, the active world, mutable and baffling and alive. No wonder that the poem ends with *lane,* for it is both Whitman's open road to an indeterminate but true future and Franklin Lane's dream of Aristotle. Kinbote gives Shade a hero's death, shielding a king from an assassin's bullet, but more importantly Shade made in his poem and of his life a hero's life, one of motion and creation in a country where there need be no kings for heroism.

Pale Fire is, then, both American and European (like the Anti-Terran country of Van and Ada), both comic and tragic, alive and filled with change and time and also touched with the serene sense of repose of the finest works of art. And like all of Nabokov's novels, it is far richer than any critic can suggest. Perhaps because of that, I should close as I began, with a statement of my complete humility before Nabokov's art using the kinbotic words of Samuel Johnson's note to his edition of *Timon of Athens:* "In this Tragedy are many passages perplexed, obscure, and probably corrupt, which I have endeavored to rectify or explain with due diligence; but having only one copy, cannot promise myself that my endeavors will be much applauded."

ABOUT VLADIMIR NABOKOV

Vladimir Nabokov was born April 32, 1899, in St. Petersburg to Vladimir Dmitrievich and Helene Rukavishnikov Nabokov, one of three boys and two girls.

He has listed among his ancestors in "Conclusive Evidence" (*Harper's,* 1951) "the first caveman who painted a mammoth... a medieval Russified Tartar prince... ; a long line of German barons; an obscure Crusader... ; a well-known composer... ; boyars, landowners, military men; a... rich Siberian merchant;... the first president of the Russian Imperial Academy of Medicine (my mother's maternal grandfather);... a State Minister of Justice (my father's father)."

Nabokov's father was a liberal Anglophile and one of the founders of the Constitutional Democratic Party, member of the first Duma (Imperial Parliament), and co-editor of the only liberal newspaper in St. Petersburg. His father was in the liberal revolution of March 1917 but opposed the Bolshevik's October Revolution; he was killed in Berlin in 1922 at a meeting of emigrés by a monarchist assassin whose bullet was meant to hit the scholar and statesman Paul Miliukov.

Nabokov learned English before he could read Russian and began to write at thirteen. His first poems were printed privately in his native city when he was fifteen. A second volume, also containing poems by V. Balaslov, was published in 1917.

Nabokov stood to inherit the equivalent of $2,000,000, but had to go into exile (without the cash) after the October Revolution.

He entered Cambridge, taking a B.A. in Russian and French literature from Trinity College in 1922.

The years after graduation were extremely fruitful: *Gorny put'* (*Heavenly Way,* 1923); *Grozd'* (*The Grape,* 1923); *Mashen 'ka* (*Mary,* 1926); *Korol', Dama, Valet (King, Queen, Knave,* 1928); *Vozrashchenie Chorba* (*Chorb's Return,* 1928); *Podvia* (*The Great Reed,* 1932);

Kamera Obskura, 1932 (*Camera Obscura,* London, C.J. Long, 1936); *Laughter in the Dark,* New York, Bobbs-Merrill, 1938; *Otchayanie,* 1936 (*Despair,* London, C.J. Long, 1937); and *Soglyadatay* (*The Spy,* 1938), all novels in Russian, plus the following plays: *Smert'* (*Death,* 1923); *Dedushka* (*Grandfather,* 1923); *Polyus* (*The Pole,* 1924); *Tragedia Gospodina Morna* (*Tragedy of the Morn,* 1925); *Cheloveh in SSR* (*Man from the USSR,* 1927); *Sobytiya* (*The Event,* 1938) and *Isobroteniye Val'sa* (*The Waltz Invention,* 1938).

He came to the U.S. in 1940 to teach at Stanford. He had declined several invitations in the thirties to return to the USSR and became a U.S. citizen in 1945. He taught only a summer at Stanford, settling at Wellesley from 1941 to 1948. From 1949 to 1959 he was professor of Russian literature at Cornell.

Long a student of lepidopterology, he was a research fellow in entomology at the Museum of Comparative Zoology at Harvard University from 1942 to 1948. He has discovered several species and subspecies, including Nabokov's wood nymph and contributed a paper, "The Neartic Members of the Genus Lycairdes Hubner" to the *Bulletin of the Museum of Comparative Zoology* in 1949.

In 1943 and in 1952 Nabokov held Guggenheim fellowships in creative writing and in 1951 received the American Academy of Arts and Letters Award. He was nominated for the International Publishers' Prize in 1964 and has received Brandeis University's gold medal for literature.

He now lives in Montreux, Switzerland, with his wife, Vera Slonim Nabokov, whom he married in 1925. His son, Dmitri, who is an opera singer, sometimes acts as his translator. His wife serves as his secretary and literary agent.

BOOKS BY VLADIMIR NABOKOV

CAMERA OBSCURA (trans. by W. Roy)
London: John Long, 1936.
London: John Long, 1938.
As LAUGHTER IN THE DARK (trans. & revised by V. Nabokov)
New York: Bobbs-Merrill, 1938.
Toronto: McClelland & Stewart, 1938.
New York: New Directions, 1960.
London: Weidenfeld & Nicolson, 1960.
New York: Berkley, 1967. (pb)

DESPAIR (trans. by V. Nabokov)
London: John Long, 1937.
London: John Long, 1939.
New York: Putnam, 1966. (revised)
London: Weidenfeld & Nicolson, 1966.

THE REAL LIFE OF SEBASTIAN KNIGHT
New York: New Directions, 1941.
London: Nicolson & Watson, 1945.
New York: New Directions, 1959.
London: Weidenfeld & Nicolson, 1960.
Middlesex: Penguin, n.d. (pb)

NIKOLAI GOGOL
New York: New Directions, 1944.
London: Editions Poetry London, 1947.
New York: New Directions, 1959. (pb)

NINE STORIES (trans. by V. Nabokov)
New York: New Directions, 1947.

BEND SINISTER
New York: Holt, 1947.
Toronto: Oxford, 1947.
London: Weidenfeld & Nicolson, 1960.
New York: McClelland, 1960.

NEARCTIC MEMBERS OF THE GENUS LYCAEIDES HUBNER
Cambridge, Mass.: Museum of Comparative Zoology, 1949. (pb)

CONCLUSIVE EVIDENCE
New York: Harper, 1951.

Toronto: Musson, 1951.
As SPEAK, MEMORY: A MEMOIR
London: Gollancz, 1951.
New York: Grosset & Dunlap, 1960. (pb)

LOLITA
Paris: Olympia, 1955.
New York: Putnam, 1958.
Toronto: Longmans, Green, 1958.
London: Weidenfeld & Nicolson, 1959.
New York: Crest, 1960. (pb)
New York: Berkley, 1967. (pb)

PNIN
New York: Doubleday, 1957.
London: Heinemann, 1957.
New York: Avon, 1959. (pb)
New York: Atheneum, 1964. (pb)

NABOKOV'S DOZEN
New York: Doubleday, 1958.
Toronto: Doubleday, Canada, 1958.
London: Heinemann, 1959.
As SPRING IN FIALTA
New York: Popular Library, 1959.

INVITATION TO A BEHEADING (trans. by Dmitri Nabokov)
New York: Putnam, 1959.
London: Weidenfeld & Nicolson, 1960.
Toronto: Longmans, Green, 1960.
New York: Capricorn, 1965. (pb)

POEMS
New York: Doubleday, 1959.
Toronto: Doubleday, Canada, 1959.
London: Weidenfeld & Nicolson, 1961.

PALE FIRE
New York: Putnam, 1962.
London: Weidenfeld & Nicolson, 1962.
New York: Lancer, 1963. (pb)
New York: Berkley, 1968. (pb)

THE GIFT (trans. by M. Scammell & V. Nabokov)
New York: Putnam, 1963.

Toronto: Longmans, Green, 1963.
London: Weidenfeld & Nicolson, 1963.
New York: Popular Library, 1966. (pb)

THE DEFENSE
New York: Putnam, 1964.
London: Weidenfeld & Nicolson, 1964.
New York: Popular Library, 1967. (pb)

NOTES ON PROSODY
Princeton, N.J.: Princeton, 1964.
Princeton, N.J.: Princeton, 1970. (pb)
London: Routledge & Kegan Paul, 1965.

THE EYE (trans. by D. Nabokov)
New York: Phaedra, 1965.
New York: Pocket books, 1966. (pb)

THE WALTZ INVENTION (trans. by D. Nabokov)
New York: Phaedra, 1966.
New York: Pocket Books, 1967. (pb)

SPEAK, MEMORY: AN AUTOBIOGRAPHY REVISITED
New York: Putnam, 1966.
London: Weidenfeld & Nicolson, 1967.
New York: Popular Library, 1967. (pb)

NABOKOV'S QUARTET (three of the four stories trans. by D. Nabokov)
New York: Phaedra, 1966.
London: Weidenfeld & Nicolson, 1967.

KING, QUEEN, KNAVE (trans. by D. Nabokov)
New York: McGraw-Hill, 1968.
London: Weidenfeld & Nicolson, 1968.
New York: Crest, 1969.

NABOKOV'S CONGERIES (ed. by Page Stegner)
New York: Viking, 1968.

ADA
New York: McGraw-Hill, 1969.
New York: Fawcett, 1970. (pb)
MARY (trans. by Michael Glenny and V. Nabokov)
New York: McGraw-Hill, 1970.

"Mithridates, he died old": Black Humor and Kurt Vonnegut, Jr.

by Robert Scholes

It seems obvious now that the best young novelists in this country are nearly all connected in some way with the literary movement that has been called "Black Humor." Barth, Donleavy, Friedman, Hawkes, Heller, Purdy, Pynchon, Southern, and Vonnegut have all been stamped with this dark label at one time or another, and, various as the writings of these men actually are, their works differ from those of the previous generation in a manner special enough to justify some common terminology and some consideration of what their work, collectively, implies about the current literary situation. The term Black Humor is probably too clumsy to be of much use to criticism, but before discarding it we should do well to milk it of such value as it may have in helping us to understand this new fiction and to adjust to it. We can begin with a view from the inside:

> They say it is a critic's phrase, Black Humor, and that whatever it is, you can count on it to fizzle after a bit. . . . I think they may be wrong on that . . . count. I have a hunch Black Humor has probably always been around, always will. . . .

The quotation is from Bruce Jay Friedman's shrewd and engaging foreword to an anthology, *Black Humor,* that he edited for Bantam Books in 1965. The anthology itself is worth looking at, as it includes work by a number of exciting writers including Mr. Friedman himself. But it is not a really successful book, this anthology, mainly because some of the best black humorists tend to use larger forms than the short story, building effects over many pages. Selections from Barth's *Sot-Weed Factor* and Heller's *Catch-22,* for example, hardly begin to work in this format.

But I don't mean to review Mr. Friedman's anthology here. I mention it because I want to use his definition as a point of departure for some theorizing of my own. Friedman suggests that we have a kind of Black Humor movement in contemporary writing because events Out There in the contemporary world are so absurd that the response of the Black Humorist is the most appropriate one possible. But he also suggests, in the lines just quoted, that Black Humor is not merely a modern fad but a continuing mode of literary activity. He doesn't say how this apparent contradiction is to be resolved, however, and this is where I want to begin. I think he is right on both counts. Black Humor is a modern movement but also a development in a continuing tradition.

Most of the literary kinds and modes are with us all the time, but in every era some are very alive and others quite dormant. If we consider literature as a way of looking at the world, for every age certain modes serve better than others to bring things into focus, to align the ideals of the age with actuality. In a historical perspective Black Humor seems allied with those periodic waves of rationality which have rolled through Western culture with continually increasing vigor for over two thousand years. The intellectual comedy of Aristophanes, the flourishing satire of imperial Rome, the humanistic allegories and anatomies of the later Middle Ages, the picaresque narratives of the renaissance, the metaphysical poems and satires of the seventeenth century, and the great satiric fictions of the age of reason—all these are ancestors of modern Black Humor. Of course, an illustrious pedigree does not guarantee the worth of any individual offspring. Nevertheless, since understanding and evaluation depend hopelessly on recognition of kind, pedigree is where we must begin. This is especially important in the case of the so-called Black Humorists for two important reasons. First, because their immediate point of departure has been the novel, a form which we view with certain realistic expectations. And second, because nearly two centuries of literature dominated by romantic notions of value lie between the modern Black Humorists and such immediate ancestors as Swift and Voltaire.

Developments in current fiction are very closely analogous to the poetic revolution of a generation or so back, when the rediscovery of the metaphysical poets helped spark a revival of witty, cerebral verse. Current interest in Rabelais, Cervantes, Aleman, Grimmelshausen, Swift, Smollett, and Voltaire is a part of the general drift of fiction into more violent and more intellectual channels. The sensibility and compassion which characterized the great novels of the nineteenth century are being supplanted by the wit and intellectual vigor of Black Humor. Walpole's epigram about life being tragic for those who feel and comic for those who think is a gross oversimplification, no doubt, but it is useful to us in describing such a massive change in literary climate as the one we are considering here. Such changes, like variations in the weather, are not things one can do much to alter. The question is how to adjust to them.

In the case we are concerned with, the question, like most literary questions, becomes one of how to read. What expectations should we bring to this new writing? What benefit can we hope to derive from it? To put it crudely, what's in it for us? I think there is a lot in it for us. It is our literature, speaking to us most immediately. If it seems out of focus, perhaps we must change our lenses to see it clearly. First of all, we must discard the notion that these works are "novels" as novels have been written. They are different from their immediate predecessors. Here the pedigree of Black Humor will help. It is surely better to think of Voltaire and Swift when reading Vonnegut and Barth than to think of Hemingway and Fitzgerald. But we must not take the pedigree in too simple-minded a fashion either. If we say, "O yes, satire" or "O yes, picaresque" we may go just as wrong as if we expect another realistic novel. Though these works are offshoots of a family tree we recognize, they are a new mutation, a separate branch with its own special characteristics and qualities. To define the special attributes of this new branch is surely the critic's business. But it is a hard business. Hard because the writers are a mixed group, really, differing in temperament, intellect, and experience, and because they themselves are experimenting with this new uncrystallized mode of writing, often trying new things from book to book. A writer like John Hawkes seems almost to obliterate his humor with his blackness, while Bruce Jay Friedman makes just the opposite emphasis. How can we unite such disparity other than by mere verbal trickery or sleight-of-word?

I am hedging here, warning the reader to take my attempt to define a revolution in progress as having all the tentativeness necessarily involved in such an attempt. But despite the difficulty, I think enough can be said to justify the project. I see Black Humor as crucially different from its satiric and picaresque ancestors. It is generally more playful and more carefully constructed than either of the earlier forms. It is more certain esthetically and less certain ethically than its ancestors. These shifts in balance result in the special tone that the phrase "Black Humor" so inadequately attempts to capture. The spirit of playfulness and the care for form characteristic of the best Black Humorists operate so as to turn the materials of satire and protest into comedy. And this is not a mere modern trick, a wayward eccentricity. These writers reflect quite properly their heritage from the esthetic movement of the nineteenth century and the ethical relativism of the twentieth. They have some faith in art but they reject all ethical absolutes. Especially, they reject the traditional satirists's faith in the efficacy of satire as a reforming instrument. They have a more subtle faith in the humanizing value of laughter. Whatever changes they hope to work in their readers are the admittedly evanescent changes inspired by art, which need to be continually renewed, rather than the dramatic renunciations of vice and folly postulated by traditional satire.

The special tone of Black Humor, often derived from presenting the materials of satire in a comic perspective, is perfectly illustrated in a passage from Vonnegut's *Cat's Cradle.* The narrator in this passage is interviewing the son of a Schweitzer-type jungle doctor on a small Caribbean island:

> "Well, aren't you at all tempted to do with your life what your father's done with his?"
>
> Young Castle smiled wanly, avoiding a direct answer. "He's a funny person, Father is," he said, "I think you'll like him."
>
> "I expect to. There aren't many people who've been as unselfish as he has."
>
> "One time," said Castle, "when I was about fifteen, there was a mutiny near here on a Greek ship bound from Hong Kong to Havana with a load of wicker furniture. The mutineers got control of the ship, didn't know how to run her, and smashed her up on the rocks near 'Papa' Monzano's castle. Everybody drowned but the rats. The rats and the wicker furniture came ashore."
>
> That seemed to be the end of the story, but I couldn't be sure. "So?"
>
> "So some people got free furniture and some people got bubonic plague. At Father's hospital, we had fourteen hundred deaths inside of ten days. Have you ever seen anyone die of bubonic plague?"
>
> "That unhappiness has not been mine."
>
> "The lymph glands in the groin and the armpits swell to the size of grapefruit."
>
> "I can well believe it."
>
> "After death, the body turns black—coals to Newcastle in the case of San Lorenzo. When the plague was having everything its own way, the House of Hope and Mercy in the Jungle looked like Auschwitz or Buchenwald. We had stacks of dead so deep and wide that a bulldozer actually stalled trying to shove them toward a common grave. Father worked without sleep for days, worked not only without sleep but without saving many lives, either."
>
> [*After an interruption*]
>
> "Well, finish your story anyway."
>
> "Where was I?"
>
> "The bubonic plague. The bulldozer was stalled by corpses."

> "Oh, yes. Anyway, one sleepless night I stayed up with Father while he worked. It was all we could to to find a live patient to treat. In bed after bed after bed we found dead people."
>
> "And Father started giggling," Castle continued.
>
> "He couldn't stop. He walked out into the night with his flashlight. He was still giggling. He was making the flashlight beam dance over all the dead people stacked outside. He put his hand on my head, and do you know what that marvelous man said to me?" asked Castle.
>
> "Nope."
>
> " 'Son,' my father said to me, 'someday this will all be yours.' "

In the passage an excess of the horrible is faced and defeated by the only friend reason can rely on in such cases: laughter. The whole episode is a comic parable of our times. Progress, that favorite prey of satirists from Swift and Voltaire onward, means that some people get free furniture and some get the plague. Some get Biarritz and some get Auschwitz. Some get cured of cancer by radiation; others get radiation sickness. But the spuriousness of progress is not seen here with the *saeva indignatio* of the satirist. Progress is seen not as a conspiracy but as a joke. The Black Humorist is not concerned with what to do about life but with how to take it. In this respect Black Humor has certain affinities with some existentialist attitudes, roughly distinguishable in terms of the difference between seeing the universe as absurd and seeing it as ridiculous—a joke. The absurd universe is a pretty dismal affair. The best, in fact, that Camus found to offer humanity as a response to the human condition was "scorn." In "The Myth of Sisyphus" he told us that "there is no fate that cannot be surmounted by scorn." The Black Humorists offer us something better than scorn. They offer us laughter. The scorn of Sisyphus leads finally to resignation. "He, too, concludes that all is well." Beneath the hide of this scornful hero beats the heart of Dr. Pangloss after all. Vonnegut's fictional prophet Bokonon suggests a better posture for man on the mountaintop than that of Camus' Sisyphus, who simply starts down again to pick up his burden. At the end of *Cat's Cradle,* with the world nearly all frozen, Bokonon gives one of his last disciples a bit of advice:

> If I were a younger man, I would write a history of human stupidity; and I would climb to the top of Mount McCabe and lie down on my back with my history for a pillow; and I would take from the ground some of the blue-white poison that makes statues of men; and I would make a statue of myself, lying on my back, grinning horribly, and thumbing my nose at You Know Who.

What man must learn is neither scorn nor resignation, say the Black Humorists, but how to take a joke. How should one take a joke? The best response is neither acquiescence nor bitterness. It is first of all a matter of perception. One must "get" the joke. Then one must demonstrate this awareness by playing one's role in the joke in such a way as to turn the humor back on the joker or cause it to diffuse itself harmlessly on the whole group which has participated in the process of the joke. Even at the punch line of apocalypse, feeble man can respond with the gesture prescribed by Bokonon, suggesting an amused, tolerant defiance. Of course, a joke implies a Joker, as Gloucester observed amid the cosmic tomfoolery of *King Lear:* "They kill us for their sport." But I do not think the Black Humorists mean to present us with a new Deity, crowned with a cap and bells in place of thorns. No more than Paul Tillich do they wish to "bring in God as a *deus ex machina*" to fill the great hole in the modern cosmos. To see the human situation as a cosmic joke, one need not assume a Joker.

Some accidents are so like jokes that the two are indistinguishable. Moreover, it is possible to conceive of all human history as part of a master plan without thinking of the Planner in quite the traditional way. In an early science fiction novel, now temporarily out of print, Kurt Vonnegut developed such a view. In *Sirens of Titan* he presented a cosmos in which the whole of human history has been arranged by intervention from outer space in order to provide a traveller from a distant galaxy with a small spare part necessary for his craft to continue its voyage to the other side of the universe. Such purposefulness to entirely extrahuman ends is indeed a cosmic joke, but is not intended as such by those superior beings who have manipulated earthly life for their own ends. This novel suggests that the joke is on us every time we attribute purpose or meaning that suits us to things which are either accidental or possessed of purpose and meaning quite different from those we would supply. And it doesn't matter which of these mistakes we make.

Samuel Johnson, whose *Rasselas* is a rather solemn ancestor of *Cat's Cradle,* picked on just this aspect of the vanity of human wishes in one of his finest works—an *Idler* paper so black and humorous that Johnson later suppressed it. In this essay Johnson presented a dialogue between a mother vulture and her children, in which the wise old bird, looking down at a scene of human carnage from a recent European battle, tells her young that men do this at regular intervals as part of a divine plan which has shaped the best of all possible worlds—for vultures. In presenting this view of life as a joke on all those who think this is the best of all possible worlds for men, Johnson is very close to his modern descendants. For the joke is the key to this modern mode. To see life as joke is to see it as having a form which makes it tolerable. And to make a joke about life is to find a correspondence between the forms life takes and the forms we would like to take. In laughing at the darkest aspects of life we domesticate them, we face them in human solidarity, and we strengthen ourselves to endure what we must endure.

Of all the things that men endure, war must be one of the worst. Certainly a war brings the contrast between human ideals and human actions to the highest possible degree of visibility. In time of war the drums, the rituals, the rhetoric all collaborate to suppress reason and its ally laughter, to prevent any rational scrutiny of such an irrational process. But satirists and picaresque novelists have subjected these phenomena to their fierce scrutiny nonetheless. Grimmelshausen's *Simplicissimus* is an honored ancestor of Céline's *Journey to the End of Night*, and the king of Brobdingnag's pronouncement of European history still reverberates in our ears with an eerie relevance to modern conditions. The Black Humorists of today, of course, have found the fields of Mars as fertile as ever. *Catch-22* and *Dr. Strangelove* are among the triumphs of modern comic fiction. Thus it should not surprise us to find that two of Kurt Vonnegut, Jr.'s strongest performances also deal with modern war: one with World War II, and one with the scientific discovery of an ultimate weapon.

Cat's Cradle and *Mother Night* will be the subjects of the rest of this discussion, but before getting directly into them I want to back-track a little in order to consider Vonnegut's career as a writer. It is an unusual one, and I expect that most of my readers will be unaware of it—in fact I am assuming that the name Vonnegut will be an unfamiliar one to many who read these words. But I certainly don't consider him my "discovery." Awareness of his work is growing in much the same way as awareness of Joseph Heller and John Barth grew before they received much official acclaim. The brief chronicle of Mr. Vonnegut's writing history I am about to set forth indicates plainly that recognition of him as an important American writer is all but accomplished already.

After *Player Piano* (1952) his next three books were published directly in paperback without ever appearing between boards. They were *The Sirens of Titan* (1959), *Canary in a Cat House* (a collection of short fiction written during the fifties), and *Mother Night* (1961). His second appearance in hard covers was in *Cat's Cradle* (1964) which drew high praise from Graham Greene and a number of other critics. This was followed by *God Bless You, Mr. Rosewater* (1965), of which Nelson Algren wrote, "The novel happens to be excellent. It explores the problem of how to love people who are of no use with such fantastic humor that we at first do not realize that it is ominous." Then in 1966 Holt, Rinehart and Winston reprinted *Player Piano* (a mildly futuristic vision of the U.S.A. as a technocracy) in hard covers, and Harper and Row did the same with *Mother Night.* Now a New York producer has contracted to stage a musical version of *Cat's Cradle* and Peter Sellers is filming *Mr. Rosewater.* A new volume of short fiction is planned by Harper and Row. And Dell will bring back *The Sirens of Titan* in paper this year. As of December all five of Vonnegut's novels will be in print, and a new novel should be ready soon. This brief history suggests, I trust, a movement already well under way and a literary success of the best sort, dependent on the continuing interest of readers rather than any persuasion from reviewers.

From the riches listed above I have selected two for discussion here: *Cat's Cradle,* which is headed for Broadway; and *Mother Night,* the most recent novel to appear in hard covers. They also happen to be the two I like best.

Cat's Cradle explores contemporary aspects of the old collision between science and religion. The book is dominated by two characters who are offstage for the most part (and I wonder how much they will be brought on for the musical version of the book): a brilliant scientist, "Nobel prize physicist Felix Hoenikker," is presented as a child-like innocent who is finally as amoral as only an innocent child can be. He is a "father" of the atomic bomb (rather more of a father to it than to his three children) and he finally develops a much more potent device—*ice-nine*—which can (and does) freeze all the liquid on this watery globe. One of his children tells the narrator this anecdote about him:

> For instance, do you know the story about Father on the day they first tested a bomb out at Alamagordo? After the thing went off, after it was a sure thing that America could wipe out a city with just one bomb, a scientist turned to Father and said, "Science has now known sin." And do you know what Father said? He said, "What is sin?"

This anecdote parallels that told of the jungle doctor by his son, which I quoted in the first part of this discussion. The contrast between the aware humanity of the one and the terrible innocence of the other is pointed up by the parallel structure of the anecdotes. The doctor, however, is a minor figure, almost eclipsed by the major opposition between the sinless scientist and the distinctly fallen religious prophet, Bokonon.

As the scientist finds the truth that kills, the prophet looks for a saving lie. On the title page of the first of the *Books of Bokonon,* the Bible of this new religion, is the abrupt warning: "Don't be a fool! Close this book at once! It is nothing but *foma*!" *Foma* are lies. Bokonon, a Negro from Tobago in the Caribbean, has invented a religion for the island of San Lorenzo (where he arrived, a castaway, after considerable experience of the world). His "Bible" includes some parable-like anecdotes, some epigrams, and many psalm-like Calypsos, such as this one:

I wanted all things
To seem to make some sense,
So we all could be happy, yes,
Instead of tense.
And I made up lies
So that they all fit nice,
And I made this sad world
A par-a-dise.

The epigraph of Vonnegut's book reads this way:

Nothing in this book is true.
"Live by the *foma*[1] that make you brave and kind and healthy and happy"

—*The Books of Bokonon.* I:5

The author's disclaimer is partly a parody of the usual "any resemblance to actual persons. . . " hedge against libel suits. But it is also a way of encircling Bokononism and making *Cat's Cradle* a repository of religious untruth itself. The very confrontation in the book between Science and Religion is aimed at developing the "cruel paradox" that lies at the center of Bokononist thought as it lies at the center of our world: "the heartbreaking necessity of lying about reality, and the heartbreaking impossibility of lying about it."

The ideas I have been sketching out in a brief and clumsy way here are only the string for Vonnegut's cat's cradle. The life of the book is in its movement, the turns of plot, of character, and of phrase which give it vitality. Vonnegut's prose has the same virtues as his characterization and plotting. It is deceptively simple, suggestive of the ordinary, but capable of startling and illuminating twists and turns. He uses the rhetorical potential of the short sentence and short paragraph better than any-

1 harmless untruths

one now writing, often getting a rich comic or dramatic effect by isolating a single sentence in a separate paragraph or excerpting a phrase from context for a bizarre chapter-heading. The apparent simplicity and ordinariness of his writing masks its efficient power, so that we are often startled when Vonnegut pounces on a tired platitude or cliché like a benevolent mongoose and shakes new life into it: "Son. . . someday this will all be yours." Yes, yes.

Despite his mastery of the prose medium and a sense of the ridiculous which is always on duty, Vonnegut never abandons himself to relentless verbal cleverness of the Peter DeVries sort. Sometimes we may wrongly suspect him of this kind of self-indulgence, as in the opening sentence of *Cat's Cradle*—"Call me Jonah"—which seems like a gratuitous though delightful parody of the opening of Moby Dick, until we realize that by invoking Jonah and his whale, along with the biblical leviathan, Vonnegut is preparing us for a story on the Job theme, with the anti-Joblike conclusion provided by Bokonon's advice to the narrator on the proper posture for death in response to the plague of *ice-nine* (quoted in part I).

Vonnegut's prose always serves his vision and helps to make narrative structures of that vision. This process is illustrated nicely by a longish passage from the introduction he wrote in 1966 for the new edition of *Mother Night.* In it he speaks of his actual experience as a prisoner of war in Dresden, in prose which has the lucidity of the best journalism enriched with poetic resources of a born story-teller. (One falls naturally into the word "speaks" in discussing this prose, which gives a strong sense of a voice behind the words.)

> There were about a hundred of us in our particular work group, and we were put out as contract labor to a factory that was making a vitamin-enriched malt syrup for pregnant women. It tasted like thin honey laced with hickory smoke. It was good. I wish I had some right now. And the city was lovely, highly ornamented, like Paris, and untouched by war. It was supposedly an "open" city, not to be attacked since there were no troop concentrations or war industries there.
>
> But high explosives were dropped on Dresden by American and British planes on the night of February 13, 1945, just about twenty-one years ago, as I now write. There were no particular targets for the bombs. The hope was that they would create a lot of kindling and drive firemen underground.
>
> And then hundreds of thousands of tiny incendiaries were scattered over the kindling, like seeds on freshly turned loam. More bombs were dropped to keep firemen in their holes, and all the little fires grew, joined one an-

> other, became one apocalyptic flame. Hey presto: fire storm. It was the largest massacre in European history, by the way. And so what?
>
> We didn't get to see the fire storm. We were in a cool meatlocker under a slaughterhouse with our six guards and ranks and ranks of dressed cadavers of cattle, pigs, horses, and sheep. We heard the bombs walking around up there. Now and then there would be a gentle shower of calcimine. If we had gone above to take a look, we would have been turned into artifacts characteristic of fire storms; seeming pieces of charred firewood two or three feet long—ridiculously small human beings or jumbo fried grasshoppers, if you will.
>
> The malt syrup factory was gone. Everything was gone but the cellars where 135,000 Hansels and Gretels had been baked like gingerbread men. So we were put to work as corpse miners, breaking into shelters, bringing bodies out. And I got to see many German types of all ages as death had found them, usually with valuables in their laps. Sometimes relatives would come to watch us dig. They were interesting, too.
>
> So much for Nazis and me.
>
> If I'd been born in Germany, I suppose I would have *been* a Nazi, bopping Jews and gypsies and Poles around, leaving boots sticking out of snowbanks, warming myself with my secretly virtuous insides. So it goes.

The admission at the end of this passage suggests one reason why Vonnegut and other Black Humorists write the way they do. They would like to prevent us from "warming ourselves with our secretly virtuous insides" while we condone the freezing of others. And as long as we persist in firebombing other human beings they would like to blow our cool for us. Comically but relentlessly they seek to make us thoughtful—in all the senses of that most sensible word.

Mother Night is the autobiography of a fictional hero/criminal of World War II, Howard W. Campbell, Jr. This Campbell is a hero or criminal depending on how one looks at him. He is an American who stayed in Germany during the war to broadcast for the Nazis a special line of virulent antisemitism and other hateful stuff: a Nazi hero, an American traitor. But in his broadcasts he was secretly sending back coded messages for American intelligence: an American hero, a Nazi traitor. The novel begins with Campbell in prison—"a nice new jail in old Jerusalem"—awaiting trial along with Adolph Eichmann. As Campbell unravels his life story we begin to find out how he got there and to worry about what will happen to him. These affairs are managed very skilfully. With perfect aplomb Vonnegut juggles three distinct time schemes: the present, the past of the war period, and the past of the postwar period; and three distinct settings: Israel, Germany, and New York. The effect of this juggling is superbly controlled. It operates not so as to call attention to the juggler himself but so as to combine the narrative suspense involved in resolving these actions with a moral and intellectual suspense generated by them. From *what* and *how* we progress to *why* and *why not*—but without ceasing to care about *what* and *how*. I am not going to give away the lines of narrative development here. The reader deserves the pleasure of experiencing them first hand, without warning. But I will give away one of the morals because Vonnegut himself mentions it in the first paragraph of his new introduction:

> This is the only story of mine whose moral I know. I don't think it is a marvelous moral; I simply happen to know what it is: We are what we pretend to be, so we must be careful about what we pretend to be.

In Vonnegut, as in his contemporaries, we do not find the rhetoric of moral certainty, which has generally been a distinguishing characteristic of the satirical tradition. The writers of modern dark comedy do not seek the superior position of the traditional moralists. Nor do they point to other times and customs as repositories of moral values, or to any traditional system as The Law. Even in essaying to abstract a moral from his own book, Vonnegut makes no special claim for its virtues, or his. The book itself must be the test. Our experience of it must be satisfying and healthy. If this is so, then it may nourish our consciences without requiring reduction to a formula. My feeling is that, far from manifesting sickness (as some critics seem to feel it does), Black Humor is a sign of life and health.

Vonnegut, in his fiction, is doing what the most serious writers always do. He is helping, in Joyce's phrase, "to create the conscience of the race." What race? Human, certainly, not American or German or any other abstraction from humanity. We read this kind of writer, then, to keep our humanity in shape, to exercise our consciences and keep them vigorous, free, and growing. In these times, especially, this kind of literary diet is necessary. Accustomed to the dark and dangerous in this benign literary form, we may hope to continue functioning as we penetrate the moral smog and pollution growing around us. We may not, as William Faulkner suggested in an optimistic moment, "prevail." We may not even "endure." But we can hope to continue a little way. As that underrated Black Poet A.E. Housman put it:

> There was a king reigned in the East:
> There, when kings will sit to feast,
> They get their fill before they think
> With poisoned meat and poisoned drink.

He gathered all that springs to birth
From the many-venomed earth;
First a little, thence to more,
He sampled all her killing store;
And easy, smiling, seasoned sound,
Sate the king when healths went round.
They put arsenic in his meat
And stared aghast to watch him eat;
They poured strychnine in his cup
And shook to see him drink it up:
They shook, they stared as white's their shirt:
Them it was their poison hurt.
—I tell the tale that I heard told.
Mithridates, he died old.

If you look for a prescription of Vonnegut at your local apothecary's, you should find it on a shelf not too far from Voltaire.

AFTERWORD

I really have too much to say to do it in an afterword. I was able to tighten up the argument of my piece some when I revised it for inclusion as a chapter in a book, but I did not solve the one problem which has continued to nag me: I simply did not do Vonnegut justice. Partly because I was somewhat in the position of introducing a writer who was likely to be unfamiliar to most of my audience, and partly because I hadn't gone over all of his work carefully enough, I was not in a position to do it real justice. It seems to me now that I was too guarded, that I did not emphasize the unique qualities of his work that give it value and should make it a permanent part of our literature. Now I do not have time or space to do this thoroughly, but I want to promise (myself, if no one else) to try at least once more to spell out the nature of his special achievement.

In all of Vonnegut's work I value the vigor and range of attitudes he brings to bear on modern life. He is not, like Barth, say, so much a player with concepts of philosophy. He is rather a player with attitudes *toward* ideas drawn from science and philosophy. The prefatory disclaimer to his brilliant science-fiction novel *The Sirens of Titan* is a case in point. The prose, like all his prose, is lucid and direct:

> All persons, places, and events in this book are real. Certain speeches and thoughts are necessarily constructions by the author. No names have been changed to protect the innocent, since God Almighty protects the innocent as a matter of Heavenly routine.

This begins as a parodic inversion of the traditional disclaimer, often a lie, that any resemblance to actuality is purely coincidence. But as the preface to a story about space travel, it acquires an extra irony. Vonnegut is reminding us that even those works which coyly pretend to be real by protesting their fictional qualities too much are actually unreal also. All fictions are equally real and unreal, he is saying, whether or not they are realistic. From this point he moves on to parody another realistic caper, the Dragnet gambit—names changed to protect the innocent. And here jolts us by cleverly shifting the target of his parody before we are aware of it. Just as we think we "get" the parody of realism, he moves on to a parody of the beatitudes of religious orthodoxy. It is pious to say that His eye is on the sparrow, or that the innocent are blessed. But what is it to say that the innocent are looked after "as a matter of Heavenly routine." This suggests that God has no choice in the matter. As an impious Frenchman once observed in claiming that his forgiveness by God was assured: *C'est son métier.* Vonnegut suggests here a Heavenly bureaucracy which will protect the innocent automatically. But he surely implies that we know the innocent are not always protected, that this beatific bureaucracy operates inefficiently, if at all. These four sentences establish a web of ironies, in which we are caught and laughed into thought. Vonnegut's deft parody makes us come out of hiding and declare ourselves emotionally on complex issues like the "realness" of fiction and the "benevolence" of a divinity conceived in the image of our liberal, protective society. Vonnegut's wit is a superb instrument, of world class. We are lucky to have it working on us.

Kurt Vonnegut speaks with the voice of the "silent generation," and his quiet words explain the quiescence of his contemporaries. This is especially true of his sixth novel, *Slaughterhouse Five,* in which he looks back—or tries to look back—at his wartime experience. In the first chapter he tells us how for over twenty years he has been trying to re-create a single event, the bombing of Dresden by American and British pilots. Vonnegut had an unusual perspective on that event. Safe, as a prisoner of war in a deep cellar under the stockyards, he emerged to find 135,000 German civilians smoldering around him. Dresden had been an open city. We closed it. We. We Anglo-Saxons, as the recent ruler of France likes to term us.

For twenty years Vonnegut has been trying to do fictional justice to that historical event. Now he has finished, and he calls his book a failure. Speaking of the Biblical destruction of Sodom and Gomorrah (like Dresden, subjected to a fire-storm), Vonnegut writes:

> "Those were vile people in both those cities, as is well known. The world is better off without them.
>
> "And Lot's wife, of course, was told not to look back where all those people and their homes had been. But she looked back. I'm certainly not going to do it any more.
>
> "I've finished my war book now. The next one I write is going to be fun.
>
> "This one is a failure, and had to be, since it was written by a pillar of salt."

The connection between that Biblical act of God and the destruction of Dresden is not accidental. Vonnegut's book is subtitled "The Children's Crusade." The point is a simple one, but it should serve to illustrate just where the gap opens between the "silent generation" and the present group of childish crusaders who are so vocal in preparing for a Holy Revolution. The cruelest deeds are done in the best causes. It is as simple as that. The best writers of our time have been telling us with all their imaginative power that our problems are not in our institutions but in ourselves.

Violence is not only (as Stokely Carmichael

put it) "as American as apple pie." It is as human as men. We like to hurt folks, and we especially like to hurt them in a good cause. We judge our pleasure by their pain. The thing that offends me equally in former secretary of state Dean Rusk and his most vicious critics is their unshakable certainty that they are right. A leader that certain of his cause will readily send a bunch of kids off to rescue his Holy Land. His rectitude will justify any crimes. Revolution, war, crusades—these are all ways of justifying human cruelty.

It may seem as if I have drifted away from considering Vonnegut's book. But I haven't. This is what his book keeps whispering in its quietest voice: Be kind. Don't hurt. Death is coming for all of us anyway, and it is better to be Lot's wife looking back through salty eyes than the Deity that destroyed those cities of the plain in order to save them.

Far from being a "failure," *Slaughterhouse Five* is an extraordinary success. It is a book we need to read, and to reread. It has the same virtues as Vonnegut's best previous work. It is funny, compassionate, and wise. The humor in Vonnegut's fiction is what enables us to contemplate the horror that he finds in contemporary existence. It does not disguise the awful things perceived; it merely strengthens and comforts us to the point where such perception is bearable. Comedy can look into depths which tragedy dares not acknowledge. The comic is the only mode which can allow itself to contemplate absurdity. That is why so many of our best writers are, like Vonnegut, what Hugh Kenner would call "Stoic Comedians."

Vonnegut's comic prose reduces large areas of experience to the dimensions of a laboratory slide. Consider how much of human nature and the nature of war he has managed to encompass in this brief paragraph:

> Billy... saw in his memory... poor old Edgar Derby in front of a firing squad in the ruins of Dresden. There were only four men in that squad. Billy had heard that one man in each squad was customarily given a rifle loaded with a blank cartridge. Billy didn't think there would be a blank cartridge issued in a squad that small, in a war that old.

The simple-minded thought processes of Billy Pilgrim are reflected in those ultra-simple sentences. But the wisdom and verbal skill of the author shaped the final, telling phrases: "in a squad that small, in a war that old."

That deceptively simple prose is equally effective when focused on peacetime American life. In speaking of Billy's mother (who acquired an "extremely gruesome crucifix" in a Santa Fe gift shop) Vonnegut says, "Like so many Americans, she was trying to construct a life that made sense from things she found in gift shops." The pathos of human beings enmeshed in the relentless triviality of contemporary American culture has never been more adequately expressed.

Serious critics have shown some reluctance to acknowledge that Vonnegut is among the best writers of his generation. He is, I suspect, both too funny and too intelligible for many, who confuse muddled earnestness with profundity. Vonnegut is not confused. He sees all too clearly. That also is the problem of the central character of *Slaughterhouse Five,* Billy Pilgrim, an optometrist from Ilium, N.Y. Billy sees into the fourth dimension and travels, or says he does, to the planet Tralfamadore, in a distant galaxy. Only Billy's time-warped perspective could do justice to the cosmic absurdity of his life, which is Vonnegut's life and our lives. Billy's wartime capture and imprisonment, his ordinary middle-class life in America, and his visionary space-time travelling are reference points by which we can begin to recognize where we are.

The truth of Vonnegut's vision requires its fiction. That is what justifies his activity as a novelist and all imaginative writing, ancient and modern. Art, as Picasso has said, is a lie that makes us realize the truth. Kurt Vonnegut, Jr., is a true artist.

ABOUT KURT VONNEGUT, JR.

Americans love success stories, especially those involving a long term of hard labor and obscurity, followed by the poetic justice of "discovery" and then—a happy ending. Once possible enough to be credible in the arts, these are now vanishing from the literary scene. The "late blooming" writer is as rare as the unicorn. Yet Kurt Vonnegut's story, rare as it is, would seem to prove the exception to the rule. After years of work and struggle he and his works have finally been "discovered" by critics and the public. And at a time when it is not too late to benefit both the artist and his new audience.

Vonnegut was born November 11, 1922, in Indianapolis. He attended Cornell, Carnegie Tech., and the University of Chicago, and served in the U.S. Army in World War II as a scout for combat intelligence. Wounded and captured during the chaos of the Battle of the Bulge, he spent five months in Dresden as a prisoner of war where he, together with the inhabitants of that city, went through what has been called the worst air raid in history—the Dresden fire bombing.

Since the war he has held a number of jobs to support himself and his family, his wife and three children of his own and three adopted nephews, while writing. He worked for the Chicago City News Bureau, as a public relations officer for General Electric, and he has done some teaching, most recently at the University of Iowa. Since 1950 his home base has been at West Barnstable on Cape Cod.

He has written for television and published both fiction and non-fiction in publications such as the *Saturday Evening Post, McCall's, Cosmopolitan, Ladies' Home Journal, Playboy, Life,* and *Esquire.*

Perhaps his earliest formal recognition was the Indiana Author of the Year Award which he received in 1954 for *Cat's Cradle.*

In addition to his writing he paints, carves wood, and makes welded sculpture.

BOOKS BY KURT VONNEGUT, JR.

PLAYER PIANO
New York: Scribner's, 1952.
Toronto: S.J. Reginald Saunders, 1952.
London: Macmillan, 1953.
New York: Bantam, 1953. (pb)
New York: Holt, Rinehart & Winston, 1966.
New York: Avon Book Div., Hearst Corp., 1967. (pb)

THE SIRENS OF TITAN
New York: Dell, 1959. (pb)
Boston: Houghton, Mifflin, 1961.
London: Gollancz, 1962.
Toronto: Thomas Allen, 1962.
New York: Dell, 1967.
London: Hodder & Stoughton, 1967.

CANARY IN A CAT HOUSE
New York: Fawcett, 1961. (pb)

MOTHER NIGHT
New York: Fawcett, 1961. (pb)
New York: Harper & Row, 1966.
London: Jonathan Cape, 1968.

CAT'S CRADLE
New York: Holt, Rinehart & Winston, 1963.
London: Gollancz, 1963.

New York: Dell, 1964. (pb)
Toronto: S.J. Reginald Saunders, 1964. (pb)

GOD BLESS YOU, MR. ROSEWATER; OR, PEARLS BEFORE SWINE
New York: Holt, Rinehart & Winston, 1965.
Toronto: Holt, Rinehart & Winston of Canada, 1965.
London: Jonathan Cape, 1965.
New York: Dell, 1966. (pb)
New York: Dell, 1968. (pb)

WELCOME TO THE MONKEY HOUSE
New York: Delacorte, 1968.
New York: Dell, 1970. (pb)

SLAUGHTERHOUSE FIVE
New York: Delacorte, 1969.
New York: Delta, 1970. (pb)

Ripeness Was Not All: John Barth's *Giles Goat-Boy*

by Benedict Kiely

There is a possibility that John Barth, of Maryland by the Choptank River, may yet turn out to be that English gentleman-adventurer, Sir Charles P. Snow, who has at least, as is so far known, two faces. Barth's identity is mysterious. A fellow scholar of his in New Tammany College has told me that Barth might at one time have been bearded and that the instrument could have been the Irish or the Albanian pipes. His family tree up to and down from him is as involved as the banyan: Cervantes and Swift do there appear, and Ovid and Apuleius, Sophocles, the eye-surgeon, and Sigmund Freud, a veterinary doctor among the goats, and Sterne from Clonmel with his squiggle and his blank page and his mottled page, and Samuel Butler the First with his broken rhymes, and Rabelais with his surfeit and spew and his neck of the goose, delicately applied. Adam and Eve, of course, are there who were the John Dowlands of us all, "whose sinful song all humankind must sing willy-nilly and die for't." There is something of Newton on whom, to make the obvious obvious, the apple fell, and something of Henry More and Plato and, by disobedience and contradiction, something of Descartes. Was there ever a son that didn't disown his father? There is something of all the learned men who in their wisdom compiled the Encyclopaedia Tammanica from Aardvark to Zymurgy and transcribed all history from the days of savage Croaker, the killer ape of Darkest Frumentius, whose secrets are still being sifted from burning shale and sand, down to the late Kanzler of Siegfrieder College who was the killer ape in *gloria excelsis,* and to the Ultimate Computer, WESCAC, who could be Europa's bull or Leda's swan or Jahweh or the Life Force or the Holy Ghost or the lover that came unseen, but blessedly felt, to swive by night a witless girl by the name of Psyche; and could also be the voice of the fire, the Red Angel of destruction.

His two eldest boys, Jacob (Jake) Horner in *End of the Road* and Todd Andrews in *The Floating Opera* were almost enzygotics, or identical twins, in whom fingerprints may often be similar in pattern although the coincident sequence of papillary ridge characteristics have never been found to agree even in uniovular twins. That fascinating piece of information, which I pass on gratis to everybody from here to Scotland Yard, I came upon once when writing a short story which involved, whether I liked it or not, three sets of twins. Having thus acquired an introduction to and an interest in the subject I am all the more prepared to stand in awe and reverence before Barth on twins in *The Sot-Weed Factor* in which book, if to call it a book in any way suffices, Ebenezer Cooke, Virgin, and Poet and Laureate of Maryland, has a twin sister, Anna, to whom it were but trifling to say that he is closely attached.

To Ebenezer then, the protean Henry Burlingame, protean as Bray, the Grand-Tutor or the Prince of Darkness is to be in *Giles Goat-Boy,* discourses at large on the mysteries of twinship or twinity: on the Heavenly Twins, the Sons of Thunder, the Dioscuri, the Boanerges, the twin principles of male and female, mortal and divine, good and evil, light and darkness, on the twin circles of sun and moon, the twin-leaved mistletoe "whose twin white berries betoken the celestial semen," on the two eggs laid by Leda and on the nipples of the bride of Solomon, "on the spectacles of Love and Knowledge, the testicles of maleness, the staring eyes of God," on the several letters of the alphabet sacred to twins and on their several symbolisms. All this to show the poet how deeply in the marrow of man runs the fear and reverence of twins, alike yet opposite. Continuing, Burlingame talks of TAUES and TAOUIS, the twins of Sarapeum at Memphis, and the sisters, TATHAUTIS and TAEBIS, the ibis wardens of Thebes, of Yama and Yami in India, Ahriman and Ormuz in Persia, Huz and Buz in the ancient myths of the Hebrews, as also of Hupfim and Mupfim, Gog and Magog, Esau and Jacob (an odd pair), Cain and Abel and perhaps—and this is vital all the way to the elevation or destruction of Harold Bray at the Maxicaust on New Tammany Campus—perhaps even Lucifer and Michael.

The old Edessans of Mesopotamia, Burlingame lightly adds, "who erst had worshipped Monim and Aziz were wont to regard e'en Jesus and Judas as hatched from a single egg." Then there are Set and Horus, Castor and Pollux, Romulus and Remus, Saints Crispin and Crispian, Florus and Laurus, even Saints Jude and Thomas, "inasmuch as *Thomas* means a 'twin' " and Quetzalcoatl and Tezcatlipoca and, among the naked Indians of the north, Tuskeha and Tawiskara. And many others too numerous here to mention, name piled on name, learned reference on reference until Burlingame, who comes and goes and changes shape as he or Barth pleases, professes his love, even to the willingness to swive, not for Ebenezer alone or Anna alone but for both together, and in a moment of typically eloquent ecstasy proclaims himself the Suitor of Totality, Embracer of Contradictories, Husband to all Creation, the Cosmic Lover. Henry More and Isaac Newton are but his pimps and he cries out: "I have known my great Bride part by splendrous part, and I have made love to her *disjecta membra,* her sundry brilliant pieces; but I crave the Whole—the tenon in the mortise, the jointure of polarities, the seamless universe—whereof you twain are token, *in coito*! I have no parentage to give me place and aim in Nature's order: very well—I am outside Her, and shall be Her lord and spouse."

His aim, and the aim, it could be, of Barth in the two later enormous torrential novels, is to swive life steadily and swive it whole. Marlowe's or Goethe's or the world's Faustus could at his most overweening moments desire no better than that. Sir Epicure Mammon was, by comparison, a paltry specialist who probably didn't even care what was lodged in his cavities and Milton's Satan was a dismal sulk-in-the-corner who, like Dr. Pavlov, never got over the time he fell down the stairs and landed on his head. Pavlov, as we all know, spent the rest of his life torturing dogs.

Burlingame, the Shape-Changer, is Barth's supreme angelic creation and even if there is more than a suspicion that he is a fallen angel he has the good grace never to be morose or begrudging about it. The very physical defect that he shares with his brothers, Billy Rumbly and Charley Matassin, sullen new-caught creatures half devil and half child, may be an angelic quality, for although the angels of God may have desired the daughters of men, the angels looking through golden bars at the lady Helen of Troy, it is not known that they left behind them any long-tailed families as living memorials to that moment of distraction.

Burlingame's sometime pupil, Ebenezer Cooke, is the questing soul and it is in the order of things that the soul should have as tutor an angel, good or bad, or one of each kind if it is possible to find in Barth's choirs an angel of unmixed quality. Ebenezer is the poet, as Billy Bocksfuss or Giles Goat-Boy is hero and prophet and messiah, the poet in the picaresque as Giles is the prophet in the Gothic, the poet, let me say, lost, stumbling and astray in an unkindly world where men may steal the Kingdom into which he expects to come and make of it a den of thieves and harlots and may steal even his title to poetry, his identity. Ebenezer is, sure enough, a suffering Christ-like figure condemned to fall like Adam, and not seven or three but seven-and-seventy and three-and-thirty times, to sorrow over the sorrows of London's harlot daughter, the much-loving Joan Toast Magdalen, to lie with the swine and hear buggery discussed in a piggery, to find shat the philosophers, savants in the temple and sceptred strangers from the east, all shat syllogisms that had neither stench nor stain; nor had they any cure, no not even Henry More's eternal spissitude, for beshotten breeches. Ebenezer is the dangerous light of innocence that shineth in darkness only to blind the eyes of others and set them tumbling arsey-turvey.

In the belly of WESCAC, the Ultimate Computer and Final Effect, Giles Goat-Boy, in the embrace of the ever-warm, ever loving Anastasia, who rose from the foam with no conch to cover her and who later had much trouble from a demonaical Smith by the name of Stoker, found an end to that desire and pursuit of the Whole. Later Giles is to find himself largely alone among and denied by men, with none to pity and few to care, or give credit to his message. Ripeness was not all.

But it is as far to the belly of WESCAC, as it is to Abram's bosom, from the twin-predicaments, each one a significant *ménage à trois,* of Jake Horner and Todd Andrews. Whole worlds lie between, space being obedient to the boundless piece which oped in Mexico and closed in Greece. There are so many fireworks displays of odd but not irrelevant knowledge out of which many instructive booklets could be compiled: Barth on hudibrastics and the nature of rhyme, Barth on ships and the sea, Barth on the disposition and breeding of goats, Barth on colonial history and on the Swiftian electioneering customs of the Ahatchwhoop Indians, Barth on the sort of notebook a poet should choose and use, Barth on terms of abuse in English and eke in French, Barth on the world of the gambler and all its ramifications, Barth on American history (in the person of Peter Greene) from Huckleberry Finn to Bob Dylan by way of the Fords, Vanderbilts, Rockefellers, and others, Barth on the relationship of valet to gentleman and their respective places in society, particularly when the gentleman be also a poet. There is Barth on the Fortunate Isles and how men over the centuries have sought them, with what results may be discovered in a prose poem by Ernest Dowson; Barth on the sorts of heroes and Grand Tutors, and their natures; Barth on the typical graduate and, by comic implication, on Newman's idea of his world's idea of a gentleman; Barth on the one way, in philosophy, to raise a cow; Barth on the Infinite Divisor and the static halfway-house between Tick and Tock, on the chicken and the egg and which came first, with perhaps an appendix on that mystic Phasian bird whose path of flight was a gyre of ever-diminishing concentric circles; Barth on hagiography and the familiar symbols of the saints. All the time in these Alpine ascents towards knowledge he has "that certain nose for relevance which sets apart the thinker from the crank."

E'en and always the fable takes erudition in its seven league stride.

Barth's hagiography, for instance, has continuing high comic and dramatic purpose in the oaths of Richard Sowter, lawyer, physician and minister of the gospel, of Maryland, who can swear by the sparrow of Saint Dominic, the bubbling blood of Januarius, the saw of Simon, the organ of Cecelia, the kneebones of Saint Rosalie, the tanyard of Saint Sever, the wig of Saint Louis, by Saint Huldrick's crablice and the hollow purse of Giles, by Peter's fingers and the eyeteeth of Appolonia, by the wick-dipper of Lucy and the eyeglasses of Fridoline, the gout of Saint Wolfgang, the psalms of Kentigern, the crozier of Wulstan, the hound-bitch of Saint Roque. Against highhandedness on the part of public servants he can invoke Saints Hyginus and Polycarpus, although it is not mere carping, but true fervor, to record here that a more effective invocation, every saint to his or her own corner of the ring, would have been to the bees of Saint Gobnait.

People meet, the mountains never, the Gaelic proverb says, and Barth is splendidly ready to accept life in his novels, certainly in the two long later novels, as a shameless marvellous dramatist "that daily plots coincidences e'en Chaucer would not dare and ventures complications too knotty for Boccacce." His people meet and part and meet again and alter shapes, and he may yet bring the mountains together and cause them to fall on his people and cover them up—for a while. The Ultimate Computer, WESCAC, has the power to EAT. All this restless movement of people and changing of masks, not only face-masks but body-and-spirit-masks, all this muscular hay-forking of erudition, is as knit-together as the action in one of those lewd postcards in which everybody is doing something to somebody else and having, simultaneously—if that's the word, something done to him or her: as if the pattern of life were one endless swive as, indeed, it would fundamentally seem to be. "How does one write a novel?" Todd Andrews asks of himself in the opening pages of *The Floating Opera* where he tries to begin to set down the story of the day, and all that led up to it, when he decided to do away with himself and then didn't. "I mean how can anybody possibly stick to the story, if he's at all sensitive to the significance of things?" And later he laments: "I think that to understand any one thing entirely, no matter how minute it is, requires the understanding of every other thing in the world. That's why I throw up my hands sometimes at the simplest things . . . ."

With his faulty ticker, his chronic infection of the prostate, first detected at the age of twenty-four, embarrassingly early for prostates or rather, for those who have them, his clubbed fingers, his memory of how in the mud of war he had first almost made love to and then bayoneted a

German sergeant, his memory of how he had found his father hanging, Todd Andrews has more reasons for being dismayed than that driving neccessity of understanding everything in the world. But his teeth are sound, he is never constipated, his vision and digestion are perfect and, although not oversexed, at times indeed almost impotent, he is not unpleased, perhaps he is even mildly delighted when a rich husband, an eskimo at heart, and his fine bouncing wife decide to adopt him as their own personal serpent into their own peculiar igloo in Eden. They all do their best in a peculiarly American way to articulate and define. In the old-fashioned European eternal triangle, customarily, though, made up of one man and two women, there was no such compulsion for everybody to tell everybody everything including, God help us, the truth: a Puritan Caliban.

Todd wears his masks to (literally) hide his Damocletian heart but finds in the end that the heart, behind the worn counter of the foul rag-and-bone shop, is master, that the heart and not the will has dictated the shapes and colors of the masks. He does not do away with himself because, for one thing, he is interrupted just as the gas is beginning to work and because if there is no reason for living neither is there, by scrupulous deduction, any reason for putting an end to life. But there are also, although he barely admits it, things worth living for or, at least, coming to terms with: like say the stench of the crabhouses (an odour not sought out by many) when it steams up from the small mountains of red carapaces and other non-edible parts of the crab thrown out in the sun by the pickers. That stench, he says, is: "like many another thing, it can be lived with." He speaks of it in a style that points to Barth's relationship, possibly by way of the hungry Ahatchwhoops, with Flann O'Brien who, it will be recalled, had two other names: "Olfactory pleasures being no more absolute than any other kinds of pleasures, one would do well to outgrow conventional odour judgments, for a vast number of worthwhile smells await the unbiased nose. It is a meager standard that will call perverse that seeker of wisdom who, his toenails picked, must sniff his fingers in secret joy."

Todd Andrews can live with the odor of the castoff fragments of deceased salt sea crabs. He must also enquire into his father's story, from umbilical cord to the belt with which he hanged himself. There, then, is the chief reason for living: to try to understand every other thing in the world.

"The same life," Jake Horner holds in *End of the Road* when he was deep in mythotherapy, or therapy by the conscious adoption of personalities, with that strange dark doctor who murders Eve by abortion and vanishes in the end just as Burlingame and Bray are to do . . . . "The same life lends itself to any number of stories—parallel, concentric, mutually habitant, or what you will." In a somewhat similar fashion Flann O'Brien's Oblomovistic student, in *At Swim-Two-Birds,* lying abed and picking the fluff out of his navel with a pencil, holds that: "A good book may have three openings entirely dissimilar and inter-related only in the prescience of the author, or for that matter one hundred times as many endings."

Jake once has a nightmare in which a weather-announcer tells him that on the day following the announcement there will be no weather. He reflects when awake that, by analogy, there are also days that have no moods. Those days without moods are mainly fair, for the "profundity and limited duration" of the moods keep him from self-destruction, and he can always escape from them, Oblomovwise, by going to bed when things get too awful. He does not say whether or not he went to bed to sleep. Perhaps like the Hermit of Greater Canby (or was it Lesser or Little Canby?) he just felt "safer in bed." He does say that: "This deliberate termination of day was itself a kind of suicide. . . . My moods were little men and when I killed them they stayed completely dead." But the days without moods are more dangerous, and on one such day, like Frank O'Connor's Corkman in the story "The Man Who Stopped," he finds himself forced to a halt in "what passes for the grand concourse of the Pennsylvania railroad station in Baltimore." He says that he ran out of motives as a car runs out of gas, that there was no reason to go to Crestline, Ohio, or Dayton, Ohio, or Cincinnati, Ohio, or Lima, Ohio, no reason to go anywhere or do anything: "My eyes, as the German classicist Winckelmann said inaccurately of the eyes of the Greek statues, were sightless, gazing on eternity, fixed on ultimacy, and when that is the case there is no reason to do anything—even to change the focus of one's eyes. Which is, perhaps, why the statues stand still."

At that moment since the devil finds work for idle hands to do—and who could have been more idle than Jake, that "fugitive from a medieval bestiary" was then?—there enters that rare doctor with his talk of therapies: deceitful talk but of an unstinted Barthian profusion: Nutritional Therapy, Medicinal Therapy, Surgical Therapy, Dynamic Therapy, Informational Therapy, Conversational Therapy, Sexual Therapy, Devotional Therapy, Occupational Therapy and Pre-occupational Therapy, Virtue and Vice Therapy, Theotherapy and Atheotherapy, Mythotherapy, Philosophical Therapy, Scriptotherapy. No man ever talked more of healing who, to our knowledge, accomplishes only hurt. Or was he no more than a dark shadow conjured up by mortal men inflicting torture on each other?

Like Jake's moods, both Jake and Todd are little men. Todd does not kill himself and the woman and her husband go off to Italy. Jake and the husband and the doctor between them manage to kill the woman, and Jake goes off to nowhere in particular, there still being no reason for going anywhere. Between the world of Jake and Todd and that of Ebenezer Cooke there is a great gulf fixed, as between the merely interesting and the stupendous. The mood has changed. Fair sits the wind for Maryland or anywhere in the world we feel like going. Henceforward there will be no days, hardly even minutes, without moods. Ebenezer Cooke as a college student does lament to his sister about the shortness of life, saying that it were an easy matter to choose a calling had one all time to live in: fifty years a barristèr, fifty a clergyman, fifty a soldier, fifty a thief, fifty a judge, and so on. All roads are fine roads, all trade, crafts, and professions wondrous. It is true that he laments his inability to choose one against all the others, but only because all are wonderful to him and he is "dizzy with the beauty of the possible," not depressed by the undesirability of the available, and being so gifted by the gods the world is made to whirl under his feet from wonder to wonder. In such all-loving, all-embracing, all-swiving, all-conquering moods great quests are undertaken and the sounding furrow smitten, and great books written; and Ebenezer and Giles undertake the significant quests for harmony and poetry and the Kingdom on earth, for truth and her brother falsehood, for the womb from which all life springs armed and wingèd, or defenseless or gimping or proxèd to the eyebrows.

In two great books John Barth has written down their findings by the way; and in a comparatively short space of time, too, for he is, it is reported, a mere youth of thirty-six although, by another report, he is as old as blind Gynander who came with ill news to about-to-be-blinded Taliped Decanus who discovered that it was a first-class trauma: "To be told you've humped your momma / And to further hear you've murthered dear old Daddy." He (Barth) could also, by a third report, be as ageless as the Living Sakhyan from Outer T'ang College a sceptreless and bald stranger from the East, who sat wordless and moveless, and deliberately unseeing, by the River of New Tammany College when Anastasia, lovely fleshly bride of the devil, raised her knees to the assault and "unimaginable tup" of Savage Croaker from Darkest Frumentius.

It would be no more than classroom capers to talk of how John Barth has used and what he has done to the picaresque and the gothic or to make a list of the resounding names of those in whose company he now walks worthily. It is sheer joy to read him, now and then aloud, and to fill eyes, mouth, and ears with his words. Those dealers in polite conversation who, knowing that good talk has gone, talk of odds and ends, will be forever in his debt for his restoration to common usage of that verb, gracile as a silver birch, delicately and delightfully suggestive as the whispering aspen: To Swive. The word is, so to speak, a major character in the linkèd adventures of Ebenezer Cooke; and that All-American boy of All the Ages, Peter Greene, uses it again to Giles and Maximilian of the Goat Barns as they all journey (Zarathustra having come down from the mountain) towards New Tammany College, and by using it draws the comment from Max that it is a "fine old verb whose desuetude in all but a few back-campus areas was much to be deplored as it left the language with no term for *service* that was not obscene, clinical, legalistic, ironic, euphemistic or periphrastic." In keeping with the restoration and repetition of a word so delicate, the simple joys of coupling can with equal delicacy, even with tenderness, be pondered upon by Giles when in his innocent, goatish boyhood, Adam on all fours, he oversees a human couple playing at Beism in the bushes: "A mere coupling of this to that, the business of a minute, but which lent zest to any idle pass or chance encounter; among strangers a courtesy, toward guests a welcome, between friends a bond. A meal's best dessert; a tale's best close. What hello more cordial, bye-bye more sweet? What gentler good-day or soothinger good-night?" Fair Daphnis challenging his mate could have put it no better.

That lyricism of Barth has, it may be said in passing, the body in it for an interesting anthology. I think, offhand, of two passages. There is Ebenezer on board ship and meditating on the entire wailing legend of the raped, of Philomela, of Lucretia, of the Sabine Virgins and the daughters of Troy, of the football on the stair or on the path behind, of those most lyrical stars that had looked down on the "numberless wars of men, the sack of nations, and the countless love assaults in field and alley." There is Giles examining and describing Anastasia, Seeing Through Her Ladyship, her nostrils which were not quite a pair, the girth of her forehead which was fifty-nine centimeters, the maximum arch of her eyebrows which was half a centimeter although she could elevate them by three times that amount, and on and on through the most intimate and loving details, for he must realise fully what he holds and calls Anastasia, body and spirit: "a slender bagful of meaty pipes and pouches, grown upon with hairs, soaked through with juices, strung up on jointed sticks, the whole thing pulsing, squirting, bubbling, flexing, combusting, and respiring in my arms; doomed soon enough to decompose into its elements, yet afflicted in the brief meanwhile with mad imaginings, so that not content to jelly through the night and meld, ingest, divide, it troubled its sleep with dreams of *passèdness,* of *love*. . . . "

How all that sets one dreaming of Herrick's mistress and her liquefactions. How interestingly Barth's beautiful hymn to the body, and to the divine discontent of the something unseen that moves the body, compares with that investigation into parts of his belovèd, carried out or at least described in his Amoretti by a certain Edmund Spénser who did well in real estate and married well into the Boyles but who tragically never gave a proper care to his fire insurance. In the Barthian lyric an honest-to-God goat has taken over from Colin Clout. If you have ever studied the centripetal arrangement of a goatherd when the goats belly down to rest you will realize that, to goats, God is a goat.

The sombre Father Alphonsus Rodriguez of the Society of Jesus, of Spain, and of the Spiritual Treatises—no man to draw on himself the pope's reproof for worldliness—advises us in his Treatise on Humility to consider, towards the acquiring of that virtue, our bodies as bags of dung. A weak argument, surely, for if it applies to me then it applies also to the pope and the president, the king, the kaiser, the cardinal, it did apply to the lady Helen and does now to the latest and loveliest starlet. Everyone of us is as bad and therefore as good, or as good and therefore as bad as the other: which is the vision of Giles daring the revolting and beautiful truth about the body, as Todd Andrews dared and learned to live with the stench of the castoff fragments of salt sea crabs decayed by the sun, as Giles and Ebenezer and Burlingame and Maximilian of the Goatbarns, aye even stern Stoker from the Powerhouse, answer for themselves the question that Prufrock asked himself, and dare to dare the universe.

History is one of those African waterholes at which "the most various beasts may drink side-by-side with equal nourishment." The poet is permitted to wonder whether history is a progress, a drama, a retrogression, a cycle, an undulation, a vortex, a right or left-handed spiral, a mere continuum, or if, indeed, the bird of time is not that bird, "called Ouida," that travels toward self-extinction along those ever-diminishing concentric circles.

It was a daring thing for John Barth to dare to write another gospel (the eighth, if we count the Thomasian Apocryphal and Joseph Smith's and Dale Carnegie's) and to cast all history, e'en from the West Campus Cattlebarns of pre-history down to the Thirty-seven Remusian Chancellory and onwards to the hydrogen bomb and the votomatic machine, all our memories of the past, our problems in the present, or hopes and fears for the future, into the image and likeness and lingo of an American college-campus. It was a cunning thing of him to dare (or a daring thing of him to cun) by ever so slight a twisting and distorting of known names, to offer us a searing slanting vision, a new illumination. His success has been startling, and already I see the interpreters, toiling and chanting like the pilgrims in "Tannhäuser," filing after him on the Road of Interpretation. Is our culture really that "recentest fair fungus in Time's hourglass"? How does Eierkopf in his tower, attended by his black brutal slave, relate to Milton's Platonist? What were the true origins of the Ag-Hill Goat Boy and how exactly did WESCAC, the machine, become a father? Has the Rough Beast, his hour come round at last, turned out to be a computer? The Bonifacists of Siegfrieder College we all know, and the Moishians, and Amaterasu College and how it was EATen by Electroencephalic Amplification and Transmission, the destructive force of WESCAC. But discussion on the true powers of WESCAC, on the WESCACUS MALINOCTIS and the Cum Laude Project could fill so many dissertations that if placed end to end they would stretch back from Marshall McLuhan to the Founder's Pomological Test Grove. Long appendices may be written on the parallels between the Petting Party in the Powerhouse and the marriage feast of Cana and/or the feast of Bricriú, and/or the sensual supping in the Satyricon, and/or Finnegan's Wake (with the apostrophe), and/or the Night Before Larry Was Stretched; on the influence of Fritz Lang on the planners of the Campus, or of Addison's Vision of Mirzah; on the connection between the Music of the Spheres and that organic harmony which is a soundwave given off by the sex organs. Why and how did the Cacafile eat the Scroll and is this prefigured in the Patmosian LSD (*Laws Semper Deo*) vision of John the Apostle? Was Bray at any moment Barabbas, or was mad impulsive Leonid any relation to Trotsky, or how stood Maximilian on Relativity? Is the answer truly that the answer is that there is no problem?

Since language is very much the matter of Barth's books, his language, in any discussion of him, may become infectious and, to the point of craziness, a cult language. Men may yet talk Barthian (my own preference would be for Middle as against Late Barthian), and since men are what they are (Founder Pass Them) all that may do them a campus of good.

There is a lot more to be said about Barth, for Barth is Big, Barth is a Broth of a Boy. But space is not here obedient. Regretfully I restore to the security of my cacafiles eighteen rolls of scroll, carefully written as scrolls invariably are, of my not-answers to problems that are not. A lot more will be said about him when that great game of searching for identities, parallels and academic spirit-levels gets going; and when Giles exchanges his sheet or his goatskin for a paper jacket those students hordes that swept eastwards almost to lose themselves in the mere Midlands and West Country of Bumpers Squire Tolkien will reassemble and reorganize and mayhap vanish forever in the vast savannahs and forests and Serbonian bogs of Captain Choptank Barth.

As for me, I rest for the moment with one question: whither away now, oh rare John Giles Ebenezer Barth of Maryland? We have had the rarest picaresque and the rarest Gothic. Could we have a Barthian cosy Victorian in the style say of *Cranford* and on the theme of the Tichborne Claimant?

And to combine Barthianism and Behanism: Swive the Begrudgers.

AFTERWORD

Since this essay was written there has been one volume from John Barth: a collection of short pieces under the title "Lost in the Funhouse," published by Doubleday. It caused considerable concern to a reviewer in *Life* magazine, a rare enough place, indeed, to find a reviewer, particularly a reviewer of John Barth.

This reviewer, Webster Schott by name, took the view that Mr. Barth was too big for his boots, and that the boots were pinching, and that the *Funhouse* collection was a grinding bore, and that Barth had emptied himself in *Giles Goat-Boy* and *The Sot-Weed Factor* and two other novels—quite a lot of emptying, by the way—and that: "The only thing left to write about is how John Barth can't find anything to write about." One could also say that Yeats failed to make a poem out of "The Circus Animals' Desertion."

To give the reviewer a better chance to speak for himself: "If Barth's unfunny autistic parodies of Greek classics, fictive essays on the impossibility of writing fiction, sloppy discourses on how he might write a story if he were going to write one, and various other jejune examinations of the Barth novel truly represent the fiction of the future, then it's ashcan literature awaiting us."

The trouble is that this decent reviewer has never really been with Barth, never really liked him, and if you don't like a writer there's a danger that you won't understand him when he's serious and must, by the very nature of your own gloomy misunderstanding, abominate him when he's sportive. Barth in these short pieces is very frequently at his best, absolutely at his best in that most unautistic (if it's a word) parody of the story of Menelaus. But that Helen should run the risk of going the way Pocahontas went in *The Sot-Weed Factor* must aggravate the morose, who can never see that such gigantic jokes can contain a universal truth.

In "Ambrose His Mark" and "Water-Message" Barth indulges himself in an idyllic simplicity that might go far to console those who fear that the fiction of the future may be beyond them. The prefatory note, less than a page, by the author is mainly what in this book would startle those who wish to be startled and who are unaware of the comical and interesting games that people are playing with machines on the campus of the University of New York State at Buffalo—and elsewhere. The sub-title of the book is: *Fiction for print, tape, live voice.* Mr. Barth may be at fault in too easily assuming when he talks about one piece being "intended for monophonic authorial recording, either disc or tape" and another for "monophonic tape and visible but silent author," that everybody is familiar with these games. The easily-perplexed might wonder if the disc and tape, and the author, came with the book. Yet what are these games, after all, but a legitimate extension of story-telling to be heard, or read out loud, which has been going on for a long time and which in these days, when other noises threaten to drown out the human voice divine, is having a sort of renewal or revival?

By the way, this afterword of mine goes very well to the tin whistle.

The genuine Barthian, or the percipient reader, God bless him or her or in-between, can get out of this book, for instance, in those "fictive essays on the impossibility of writing fiction," an illuminating consideration of a writer's, any writer's, problems. It loses nothing by being neither solemn nor sourfaced.

The long tails and streamlined heads, the thousands drowning, the question of why we swim and whither in that strange piece "Night-Sea Journey" add up to a sound if sombre reflection on man's lot, and Barth displays again his "passionate virtuosity" in making things shockingly clear by oblique description.

His rare and copious equipment of knowledge, on vines and bees and twins and all, displays itself. He comes up with a fearful and ordinary truth in the tale of the twins, Cheng and Eng. He can stop when he likes, and take the reader with him, to make mad discoveries by a whimsical examination of his own technique.

The collection has its own reverberating unity that makes it stand up with his other works and relates it to all of them.

ABOUT JOHN BARTH

John Barth commented on the deluge of literary criticism which has descended upon him by saying "It was nice being underground. . . . One wants attention until it's paid and then wishes it weren't. When everybody starts understanding and approving of you, you feel terribly uncomfortable."

Barth originally intended to become a jazz musician. He attended the Julliard School of Music, where he studied orchestration. However, his interests changed and he received his BA and MA degrees in English from Johns Hopkins and went on to become a professor at Pennsylvania State College. In 1965 he received a research grant from the University of New York and, later, a grant from the National Institute of Arts and Letters.

Born in Maryland in 1930, Barth's literary career has remained closely connected to the state. His first work, which is still unpublished, is set in the Dorchester marshes on the Chesapeake Bay. He refers to this first effort as "a long and gloomy novel about libidinous cretin." In 1954 he submitted the first fifty of a projected one hundred short stories about Dorchester county; however, they proved to be too Rabelaisian for publication.

Commenting on recent trends in American

literature, Barth states that "there is a movement away from realism toward plot, a new sort of contrivance and inventiveness not seen in American fiction since the time of Hawthorne."

BOOKS BY JOHN BARTH

THE FLOATING OPERA
New York: Appleton-Century-Crofts, 1956.
Toronto: S.J. Reginald Saunders, 1956.
New York: Avon Book Div., Hearst Corp., 1965. (pb)
New York: Doubleday, 1967. (rev. ed.)
London: Martin, Secker & Warburg, 1968.

END OF THE ROAD
New York: Doubleday, 1958.
Toronto: Doubleday, Canada, 1958.
London: Secker & Warburg, 1962.
New York: Avon Book Div., Hearst Corp., 1965. (pb)
New York: Doubleday, 1967. (rev. ed.)

THE SOT-WEED FACTOR
New York: Doubleday, 1960.
Toronto: Doubleday, Canada, 1960.
London: Secker & Warburg, 1961.
New York: Grosset & Dunlap, 1964. (pb)
Toronto: McLeod, 1964. (pb)
New York: Grosset & Dunlap, 1966. (rev. ed., pb)

GILES GOAT-BOY; OR, THE REVISED NEW SYLLABUS
New York: Doubleday, 1966.
London: Secker & Warburg, 1967.
Greenwich, Conn.: Fawcett World Library, 1967. (pb)

LOST IN THE FUNHOUSE
New York: Doubleday, 1968.
New York: Grosset & Dunlap, 1969. (pb)
New York: Bantam, 1969. (pb)

The Greatness and Horror of Empire: Robert Lowell's *Near the Ocean*

by Daniel Hoffman

Since Robert Lowell is the most ambitious as well as the most skilled and talented poet of his generation, each of his books is an occasion for reassessing the latest turning of his course. Lowell's career has been a series of violent actions and apparent reversals, both in life and in letters. Among his contradictions, the coherent pattern running through the whole has not always been easy to see. Indeed, his work since *Life Studies* seems to spray out in all directions—translations from some twenty European poets, a version of Racine's *Phèdre,* dramatic adaptations of tales by Hawthorne and Melville, the forthcoming versions of Aeschylus, and two further books of poems. Lowell's gifts are great; as Henry James says an artist must, he has "a grasping imagination." He has written violent and powerful poetry with the deepest historical sense of any in the past quarter-century. His historical imagination is embodied in personal experience, for Lowell is the chief actor in the drama of his own work. And that drama has been moved by potent themes—rebellion against family and inherited pieties; the force of his conversion to the Catholic church, conscientious objection in wartime, treatment in a mental hospital; unbearable crises in relationships with parents, with the government, with history, with God.

Near the Ocean, his latest book, is both a synthesis of some of Lowell's constant themes and yet a new departure in his style. He is clearly mediating between the harsh formality of his earlier work and the contrary position, exhibited in *Life Studies* and *For the Union Dead,* of writing a determinedly anti-rhetorical, anti-metrical, prose-textured verse that chose the virtues of immediacy rather than those of tradition. The new work is a return to formality, but toward a formality that seems the very structure of naturalness. Yet its style, like its themes, has been long prepared for. Lowell has moved beyond the metrical repudiations he felt necessary in *Life Studies,* but he retains the conversational rhythm, the syntax of "ordinary" speech, in short the liberation from a constrained formality which the poems in that book made possible. It may be felt that he is now writing at a lower pitch of intensity than his earlier work has made us expect from him; if this is so, it makes possible a broader range of feeling and a less fractious, though not less tragic, view of experience. Never one to be reconciled with what is, Lowell has earned a hard-won tolerance of our world; the brunt of life, though still almost unbearable, compels us no longer toward apocalypse, but toward a tragic acceptance of our nature. Apocalypse awaits us still, but at a distance—as in the last stanza from the first poem in his new book:

> Pity the planet, all joy gone
> from this sweet volcanic cone;
> peace to our children when they fall
> in small war on the heels of small
> war—until the end of time
> to police the earth, a ghost
> orbiting forever lost
> in our monotonous sublime.

The longest piece of work in *Near the Ocean* is a translation of Juvenal's tenth satire, "The Vanity of Human Wishes." There is also a beautiful rendering of the Brunetto Latini canto from Dante. These are truly, as Lowell says, "as faithful as I am able or dare or can bear to be." And there are freer versions from Horace, Góngora, and Quevedo, as well as half a dozen original poems. "The theme that connects my translations is Rome, the greatness and horror of her Empire. . . . How one jumps from Rome to the America of my own poems is something of a mystery to me." Not at all to the reader. What weekly journalist has not proposed that America is the grotesque creation of social energies—and the lack of cultural restraints—somehow like those that made the Rome of Juvenal, or Suetonius, or Gibbon? In Lowell's work, however, this commonplace—and indeed perhaps misleading—parallel gains the force of a dramatic image, one which must be considered among the other governing images of his recent work.

Among American poets of this century, as every reader knows, there are two main lines of descent: one from Eliot and Ransom, another from Pound and Williams. With great executive intelligence Lowell first mastered one tradition; then, wrenching himself out of it, he chose what were for him the needed aspects of the other. His latest work is built on the accumulated gains of his experiments. His conquest of these traditions is of course not only stylistic, but is deeply involved with his sense of history and of contemporaneity. He has said,

> The kind of poet I am was largely determined by the fact that I grew up in the heyday of the New Criticism, with Eliot's magical scrutiny of the text as a critical example. From the beginning I was preoccupied with technique, fascinated by the past, and tempted by other languages. It is hard for me to imagine a poet not interested in the classics. The task is to get something new into old forms, even at the risk of breaking them.

These convictions establish some of the terms within which his early verse wrestled with its violent subjects. There is exultant energy in the fierce poems of *Lord Weary's Castle,* but those in *Mills of the Kavanaghs,* despite some remarkable passages, seem written in a style too burdened by involution and artifice. After that book there was a long, strained period of silence. Later, Lowell could look back and say, "Everything I did was grand, ungrammatical, and had a timeless hackneyed quality. All this was ended by reading Williams."

His praise of Williams (*Hudson Review,* Winter 1961-1962) is a beautiful tribute. In trying to come to terms with this autochthonous poet so unlike the poet he himself had been, Lowell is driven back to his own beginnings, to a preliterate, wholly natural experience. He sees "An image of a white house with a blotch on it," and wishes he could hold this image "closely and honestly enough" to recognize in its "stabbing detail" the "universal that belonged to this detail and nowhere else." Some such way of going directly to the meaning of things epitomizes Williams' method to Lowell. He is distressed that

> Williams enters me, but I cannot enter him. . . . It's as if no poet except Williams had really seen America or heard its language. . . . When I say that I cannot enter him I am almost saying that I cannot enter America.

What Lowell chiefly values in Williams, then, is his directness of treatment, the accuracy of his language, his grabbing hold of real and proximate life. "A drastic experimental art is now expected and demanded. The scene is dense with the dirt and power of industrial society." In Williams' style Lowell values the thrust, the "quick changes of tone, atmosphere and speed. This makes him dangerous and difficult to imitate." The results of this new enthusiasm are of course evident in *Life Studies.* Somewhere in Stevens' "Adagia" is the apothegm: "A new style, a new subject." In Lowell's case, a new style, a new treatment of subject. The shedding of myth, of historical parallel, of the grand style and rhyme and the formality of the great tradition are all accompaniments of Lowell's shedding also the fervors of his conversion: "Much against my will / I left the City of God where it belongs." For Lowell, who had to make such great repudiations to achieve them, the poems in *Life Studies* were a daring extension of technique and of subject. "Afterwards," he told A. Alvarez, "having done it, I did not have the same necessity." Leaving the field of confessional free verse to his imitators, Lowell once more moved on. But where?

No eight years' silence now. Instead a burst of new poems and the conquest of a new form, the stage play. Lowell moved with seeming ease from dramatic monologue to drama, writing a version of Racine's *Phèdre* effective on the stage, and, in *The Old Glory*, a palpable hit. As for *Imitations*, the poems there have puzzled or annoyed as many readers as they have pleased, torn as those readers are between acknowledging their power and lamenting their violence to the originals.

Each of these works has been widely reviewed, some controversially so. It may remain to be said that all of Lowell's versions in verse and on stage are significant in terms of his own work. If we retrace the ground he has travelled and made his own, we can see how *Imitations* was his exploration of modern Europe. *Phaedra* became for him a prototype of the tragic greatness with which the classical world bore sufferings like those we ourselves cannot escape. And in *The Old Glory* the interpretations of the American past he found already latent in Hawthorne and in Melville provided a means for re-creating that past, for making it illuminate the present. Just as his translations have been attacked for howlers, so has his *Phaedra* for distorting Racine, his *Old Glory* for truncating its sources. I too have some misgivings about the violence he has introduced into these adaptations. But before we judge Lowell's transformations, it is essential to understand what uses he has actually made of these familiar works.

Behind the images of modern Europe stand the poets from Dante and Villon to Pasternak and Voznesenskii who have given Europe tongue. Without their vision and their images neither their contemporaries nor we would know what to feel in the flux of history. In his *Imitations* Lowell has set out not merely to learn from or acknowledge the existence of these poets and their traditions; he has undertaken to master those traditions, as he interprets them. This means to make their work a part of his own imagination and to make his imagination a part of it in turn. The way in to these traditions (or any other) for a poet is not, as for the critic, linguist, historian, or nonprofessional reader, primarily through scholarship and literary history. The way in is through translation. This is how a poet can put his imagination directly in touch with that of each of his spiritual forebears in other languages. As he struggles with their vision, their style, their problems, they become his doppelgängers in their times, and he theirs in our time. Had they not existed—as Baudelaire said of Poe—he would have had to invent them. But luckily they are there, and their existence in other times and cultures gives them an historical actuality far more valuable than the autonomy that any invented characters would have to possess. This is true for Lowell's subjects, no matter how far he may deviate from the letter of their texts.

His deviations raise the question of the right relation between the translator and the original author. Is the original poem a text devoutly to be transcribed into one's own tongue, or is it a suggestion or a theme, to be mastered in an idiom of one's own—to submit to the original, or to overcome it? There must be re-creation successfully to do either; if fidelity be required, to which, the letter or the spirit? Such questions are suggested by *Imitations,* but they were raised—and fairly answered—as far back as in *Lord Weary's Castle.* In a prefatory note to that book Lowell wrote, "When I used the word *after* below the title of a poem, what follows is not a translation but an imitation which should be read as though it were an original English poem." Lowell has always used his originals not as texts but as subjects, and his "imitations" are cadenzi upon themes those originals suggest. This is indeed an Ezratic view of a translator's propriety. Unlike Pound's versions from Provençe and Cathay, however, Lowell's are not from exotic dialects at the earth's ends. He imitates the masterpieces of Western literature. Revising these takes nerve. The first line of *Imitations* announces the method and tone of Lowell's revisions: starting with Homer, he invites the Muse to sing—not Achilles' rage or wrath, but his "mania."

If we accede to Lowell's request and read *Imitations* as "a whole, a single volume," written "in live English" as though the poets "were writing their poems now and in America," the book appears no longer a bundle of garbled, Gothic mistranslations, but a single work comparable in intention to aspects of *The Waste Land* and *The Cantos. Imitations* is a long fragmented poem of the self, struggling in its engagements with history. Its principal themes are the soul's initiation into experience; its coming to knowledge of love, of war, of death; its endurance of the fall of man and the fall of empires; and above all, the self-sustaining energy of the creative man who, like Baudelaire, can triumph over the bitter knowledge that "Infatuation, sadism, lust, avarice possess our souls. . . " because even his self-disgust can be made into the materials of his art. These of course are the themes of Lowell's less "imitative" poems also. It is not surprising that, although *Imitations* ranges from works by Homer to Pasternak, the most potent and central pages are those by the outcast

Villon and the symbolists Baudelaire and Rimbaud. In their work particularly does the poet become the hero of man's journey through time, his passage from the illusions of innocence and freedom into the knowledge of his subjection to history and to his own corruption.

The affinities between his "imitations" and Lowell's poems of the same period are clear. The Paris of "The Swan"—indeed the way the swan image is managed—suggests the Boston and the aquarium and photograph of "For the Union Dead," and the Rimbaud selections obviously parallel the autobiographical poems in *Life Studies.* Lowell's style in *Imitations* has the same nervous energy, broken meters, and sudden stabs of imagistic power as in his own verse. Indeed, it is his style that binds together these versions, an unmistakable voice that readily leaps across temporal and linguistic distances. He has linked together only the most daimonic voices from the past, here heightened, made even more exacerbated by the dark side of their natures intensified through his own. Lowell's version of the tradition which he and we inherit tells us by inference that, because we are the captives of our time, we cannot really inherit everything that the past actually was, not all that it meant to itself. Our exigencies blot out the past's humane balance, its ability to entertain the comic side of destiny. This is perhaps too exacerbated a view of our situation, what Cyril Connolly meant when, in another connection, he called Lowell Caliban to Auden's Prospero.

Lowell's preoccupations with lust, violence, and psychological imbalance have, in the view of some readers, marred also his verse translation of Racine's *Phèdre.* Samuel Solomon, for one, writing in the October 1966 *London Magazine,* complains of Lowell's "promiscuous infidelity" to the text. "He is forever letting lust erupt and shame be erased. Indeed, he has failed to perceive the wood of sanity and remorse, which breathes like the balm of reconciliation through the play, for the trees of lust that he has allowed wantonly to shoot up. . . . " We can, by struggling through Solomon's mixed metaphors, find his meaning; he quotes passages from Racine and then from Lowell, proving that the latter's *Phaedra* contains interpolated allusions linking Phaedra to Pasiphae and the bull. It turns out that Solomon is a rival translator—his own paraphrases of Racine in his article are not more graceful than his prose. Prepossessed by Racine's original, he must have found irrelevant Lowell's prefatory remarks, "Racine quite alters and to my mind even surpasses his wonderful original. . . . His poetry is great because of the justness of its rhythm and logic, and the glory of its hard electric rage. I have translated as a poet, and tried to give my lines a certain dignity, speed, and flare." Lowell takes Racine's liberty with Euripides as warrant for his own alterations of *Phèdre.* In his preface, discussing the heroine's character, Racine wrote,

> Phaedra is neither completely guilty not completely innocent. She is involved, because of her fate and because of the wrath of the gods, in an illegitimate passion, which horrifies her more than anyone else. She bends all her efforts to overcome it: she would rather die than avow it to anyone; and when she is compelled to reveal it, she speaks of it with a confusion which makes it quite clear that her crime is more a punishment of the gods than an act of her will.

It is true that Lowell has drawn a weaker, more carnal queen. The role of the gods is severely truncated and Phaedra is much more the victim of her own nature. The gods in Euripides and in Racine were but the objectification of human passions; yet their diminution can only increase her own responsibility for her character. In Racine's play two elements brought down the queen: the gods, against whose caprice no mortal can prevail, and the sly counsels of her nurse Oenone, who fills her ears with the politic advantage, first of declaring her passion to Hippolytus, then, after her husband's return, of denouncing his son as her seducer. Reduce the power of the supernatural element, then should not a queen be strong enough to resist the evil counsels of a servant?

A further alteration of Lowell's is cognate with the first. He shifts the center of our sympathy away from the feckless queen undone by her lust. In his *Phaedra* it is Hippolytus whose plight is more pitiable and terrifying. When first seen declaring his love for Aricie, the rightful heiress to Athens whom his father Theseus has condemned to live a virgin and beget no children, Hippolytus seems, like her, a touching figure of innocence. These young lovers, like Romeo and Juliet, are the promise of the world, their love frustrated by the cruel and arbitrary injustice that authority, the old order, has visited upon them. Once Phaedra has succumbed to Oenone's arguments justifying her illicit desires, true love is doomed. In this classical plot of the stepmother who lusts for her husband's son, Lowell found a paradigm for themes that have run through his own work: innocence entrapped in a fallen world, rebellion against the corrupt stasis of authority, and the anguish of familial relationships. In *Phaedra,* thanks to what he calls the "justness" of Racine's "rhythm and logic," he found treated with a "hard electric rage" the tangled allegiances which he had so complexly tried to dramatize in "The Mills of the Kavanaghs," "The Death of the Sheriff," and elsewhere. The resulting play is written in a forceful iambic couplet modeled on Dryden and Pope, a Gothic version of their Augustan style. Having shrivelled the extenuating role of the gods, Lowell produces a more exacerbated tragedy than Racine's. His Phaedra is herself responsible for her own fall, and together with the impetuous Theseus, the inflexible father, brings disaster to all in Athens. In this sense Lowell's is the more Christian treatment of the theme.

The Old Glory is Lowell's free adaptation of tales by Hawthorne and Melville into a triptych of one-act verse plays. Lowell is as bold with these classics of American fiction as he was in *Imitations* with those of European poetry. He no more intends faithfully to dramatize his originals (as did Louis Coxe with *Billy Budd*) than he meant to be as faithful to Racine as Richard Wilbur was to Molière. Instead, Lowell borrows the characters and conflicts—and sometimes even the language—of his sources in order to refashion them in his own version of what contemporary America inherits from its own past. He has added new characters, new language, and reinterpreted the conflicts to do this. With unerring accuracy he chose from the literature in which Melville found "the power of blackness" those tales that gave symbolic form to three of the most significant moments of rebellion in our history: severance of the State from the Established Church, separation of the Colonies from the Crown, and the mutiny of Negro slaves against their masters. His title, *Old Glory,* suggest what Lowell intends to hold his three plays together. In each there is a flag of rebellion. Endecott rips the Red Cross from the English standard. The colonials in "My Kinsman, Major Molineux" conspire beneath their defiant banner, the rattlesnake flag inscribed "Don't Tread on Me." In "Benito Cereno," the Spanish ensign appears as a barber's bib when the slave Babu holds a razor to his captain's throat. But these flags of rebellion do not really unify the three parts of *The Old Glory,* nor are the plays equally successful. "Benito Cereno" is a proven masterpiece, having run for a year after its première at the American Place Theatre; it has been shown across the country on television, and Jonathan Miller, its director, plans a London production in the spring of 1967. "My Kinsman, Major Molineux" ran for a few weeks but was dropped from the bill at the American Place. Staged as a series of Hogarthian tableaux, its characters stock figures from Restoration Comedy, it seemed to me a static piece which diminishes the subtlety and force of Hawthorne's story without compensating for these losses in other ways. The published text is the weakest of the three plays. But "Endecott and the Red Cross," the first part of *The Old Glory,* which was thought too long and unwieldy for the stage, is a brilliant piece of writing. I am not willing to relegate it to that dusty shelf of unread and unacted plays marked "closet drama," for I agree with Philip Toynbee's judgment that in *The Old Glory* Lowell has devised the strongest dramatic verse since Yeats's plays. "Endecott and the Red Cross" is sinewed by this style.

In his adaptation of Hawthorne, Lowell seems to have approached his source in the spirit proposed by Q.D. Leavis, who found in Hawthorne's tales the outlines of a ritual drama of colonial history analogous to that in Shakespeare's history plays. To understand how Lowell has bent those borrowings, we may consider Hawthorne's own criticism of the Puritan past from which he, like Lowell, was descended. Both look back to ancestors who had wrought God's will in blood to make the wilderness of New England into the Promised Land. From Lowell's point of view, Hawthorne anticipates his own judgment of the Puritans with a justice at once poetic and true. When we read Hawthorne on his own terms, however, we see that his judgments are always ambiguous, even duplicitous. He recognizes that the Puritans, stained as they were by guilt for sins of pride and misdirected piety, were also rebels against a tyrannical king and a persecuting church. That their own rebellion led them to become tyrants themselves is the ironical crux of Hawthorne's view of colonial history. Our libertarian institutions are born of revolt against authority, but that rebellion contains the seeds of its own dark future. Hawthorne was fully sensible of the nineteenth century's faith in progress, yet he inherited much from the eighteenth century, with its love of balance. He posed against his condemnation of the Puritans his faith in equality and reason, which they so contradictorily embodied. Lowell's treatment of Hawthorne's materials always emphasizes the dark side and irons out the balanced ambiguities with which Hawthorne had hedged his judgments of the past, for Lowell is more a man of the uncompromising seventeenth century as well as of the anguished twentieth. His own experience makes him reject even the equivocal faith in progress and equality with which Hawthorne balanced his view of the iniquitous past.

Lowell's first play combines characters and conflicts from Hawthorne's "Endicott and the Red Cross" and "The Maypole of Merry Mount." In Hawthorne's latter tale, "Jollity and gloom were contending for an empire." Those for gloom were Endicott and the Puritans; those for jollity, a band of Royalists and Anglicans who, under Thomas Morton, has established a post at Merry Mount near Boston where they traded whiskey and guns to the Indians for furs. With great subtlety Hawthorne built upon this historical foundation. As I have shown in *Form and Fable in American Fiction,* the party of Merry Mount represents both the cultural and the psychological survival of paganism. In fact the revellers are conducting a ritual marriage of the Lord and Lady of the May. In his typically ambiguous way Hawthorne makes this fertility rite both frivolous and serious, for the young couple are really in love. Their pagan celebration is also their wedding, conducted by a renegade priest named Blackstone to whom Hawthorne gives the attributes of Bacchus. Endicott's iron-clad troops attack the irresponsibles of Merry Mount, but, curiously, after meting out punishments to the revellers in their animal costumes, Endicott himself completes the marriage ceremony which Blackstone had begun. Thus, Hawthorne's symbols seem to say, true love has its beginnings in an Eden of hedonistic joy, but to survive in our unhappy world it must be brought under the discipline of human law. His lovers cross from the unfallen world in which their love began to the Heaven toward which Hawthorne sees them wending at the tale's end. But they must live meanwhile in our world, under the rule of Endicott.

In Hawthorne's other tale of Endicott, we learn how, rather than submit to "the idolatrous forms of English Episcopacy," the Puritan ripped St. George's cross from the English flag. It was Roger Williams who brought him the letter from Governor Winthrop announcing the arrival of a Royal Governor General; to Williams' milder counsel Endicott is deaf. As he strikes the Red Cross, he is seen surrounded by the victims of his own intolerance—a Wanton Gospeller in the stocks, an adultress with her gold-and-scarlet letter on her breast. Hawthorne's Endicott is all glowering rage and rebellion; only by inference are we led to reflect that the flag he has disfigured in the name of piety now lacks Spenser's symbol of Holinesse.

Lowell's play economically combines these two tales and expands them, but with his rather than Hawthorne's criticism of the Puritans. He omits Roger Williams, subordinates the love of Edgar and Edith, and develops the character of Endicott, changing Hawthorne's spelling of the name. Borrowing Racine's technique, he gives his major figure a confidant who at the same time represents one side of that person's character. Now Endecott's alter ego is Elder Palfrey, a vengeful zealot to whom Lowell assigns some of the opinions Hawthorne gave to Endicott himself. Lowell's Endecott is more complex, more reflective that Hawthorne's, though to be sure in the tale the iron governor had a heart touched by the young lovers. Lowell builds much on this suggestion; further, he gives his Puritan a soliloquy in which he struggles against his knowledge of the need to extirpate humane values in the exercise of power. When Endecott and Elder Palfrey speak it is as though the two strands of Puritanism, baleful piety and worthy pride, are in a public dialogue. The soldier Endecott tells his dream:

> I began to see that men are twisted,
> that bearing with diseases is the body's business. . . .
> . . . .
>
> The whole world sees itself as fuel for a system.
> The Catholic Church, Calvin's church.
> The State Church of England, the State Church of Germany,
> divine right kings, imitation Roman republics of fanatics—
> A hundred flags and all made of cloth:
> he who is not with me is against me.

Endecott's dream continues: he dreams he was Elder Palfrey, preaching from Palfrey's pulpit—

> I saw the people of Boston and Salem
> coming before me, one by one:
> Winthrops, Dudleys, Williamses, Welds and Peterses.
> I was sending them off to be burned. . .
> These people burned like birch logs. . . .

And then, in a passage perhaps suggested by Hawthorne's sketch, "Earth's Holocaust," everything in the world is burned save himself. God appears in this dream as an obscenely senile old man who "looked like a dirty old Italian Pope." The dream's apotheosis is Endecott's realization of the choices before him:

> I now understand statecraft:
> a statesman can either work with merciless efficiency,
> and leave a desert,
> or he can work in a hit and miss fashion,
> and leave a cess-pool.

Seeing the young couple, Endecott was stirred to think of the young wife he had buried years before in England. She had loved the May dances and village frolics there, and so had he. His first impulse toward the revellers at Merry Mount was human, mollifying Palfrey's zealous punishments. But now Endecott realizes what "statecraft" demands of him. Caught between the "merciless efficiency" of Archbishop Laud and the King and Morton's corruption, Endecott must turn ruthless himself. He puts behind him all humane instinct and becomes a statesman. His rhetoric converts his followers from loyalty for England to revolt for New England. As his sword cuts the Red Cross he cries, "No flag shall stand between us and our God!" Blackstone protests, "This is treason and blasphemy!" And Endecott, now free from the established order of the Old World, commits his first act as a free agent: "Sergeant, tie up Mr. Blackstone!"

> Then go to the ice-house and release the Indians.
> Take them out in a field and shoot them!
> Sergeant, when our men are finished with the Indians,
> they can start burning down the houses of Merry Mount. . . .
> Tomorrow, we will burn the Indian village.

And so Governor Endecott, having torn down the flag of law and restraint in the name of freedom, becomes a despot in God's service. He has already dreamed of such a God.

Hawthorne himself did not scruple to make "a sort of allegory" from "the grave pages of our New England annalists." Lowell has been as free again with Hawthorne. Whether or not "Endecott and the Red Cross" may have too much speech, not enough gesture, for the stage, it is a deeply felt interpretation of America's Original Sin in political terms. The language is spare, the rhythm varied, achieving eloquence when necessary, but only then.

The other two stories Lowell has made into plays offer difficulties as well as boons to the dramatist. In each a character, intended to be a typical American, confronts a situation in which, despite his native wit and manly independence, he cannot distinguish good from evil or truth from illusion. In both "My Kinsman, Major Molineux" and "Benito Cereno" the essential action is interior, in the consciousness of the principal character. Neither Robin Molineux nor Captain Delano is actually an interesting person, since both are defined by their limitations, their failures to see what the reader sees or suspect what the reader suspects. Although there is conversation in both tales the main burden of the narrative is held by the omniscient author recounting the thoughts of his bumbling hero. To overcome this undramatizable circumstance Lowell has again followed the convention used by Racine and Molière and provided both Robin and Delano with companions to whom they can speak and so externalize what psychological development is possible for them. Tobin's companion is a little brother, Delano's a young bosun. In one case the device of a *ficelle* limits the play to a rigid rendering of a story marked by its divided sympathies; in the other, the like device succeeds dramatically as a brilliant illumination of character.

In Lowell's "Benito Cereno," the historical circumstance is every bit as relevant to our own situation as it was when Melville wrote the tale just before the Civil War. Lowell's only drastic change is in the ending, a change designed to shock us into realization of his theme. In an interview in 1964 Lowell said of this play, "My theme might be summed up in this paradox: we Americans might save the world or blow it up; perhaps we should do neither." This was not quite the theme in Melville's "Benito Cereno," but Lowell's theme has been grafted on to Melville's study of the naive American character bewildered by its blundering confrontation with unimaginable evil. This tale of the American captain who offers help to the Spanish commander of a seemingly plague-ridden slave ship is a masterpiece in the literature of rebellion. "Benito Cereno" is America's black mystery play. It is hard to say who is its most tragic character. Is it Babo, the Promethean slave who commits atrocities to free his people, or is it Don Benito, the suffering scapegoat for his race's guilt? Or is it perhaps Captain Delano, the American who, Melville writes, had "a singularly undistrustful good nature, not liable. . . to indulge in personal alarms, any way involving the imputation of malign evil in man"? Despite his experiencing the malignity of an older civilization and an older savagery than that of his own country, Melville's captain seems as incapable as Hawthorne's Robin of learning from what he has lived through. At the end he reassures Don Benito, "You are saved, you are saved: what has cast such a shadow upon you?" Delano cannot understand Benito's reply, "The negro."

Lowell, once asked by an English critic what effect his being an American had upon his work, replied in terms he drew from *Moby-Dick:*

> If I have an image for [America], it would be. . . the fanatical idealist who brings the world down in ruins through some sort of simplicity of mind. I believe that's in our character and in my own personal character. . .

In the event, it is Amasa Delano rather than Ahab who proved the perfect protagonist for Lowell's most powerful play about the American character. In the play, as in Melville, we follow the captain aboard the Spanish ship; we gradually realize that Benito Cereno is in fact the captive of his obsequious Negro servant. We see that Delano, in his hearty innocence and bluff good faith in human nature, is not getting any of the signals that Don Benito and the few surviving Spaniards are trying to give him. In Melville's tale, he learns the truth only when pulling away from the *San Dominick* in his long boat; then the frantic Spaniard leaps into his boat, and Babo follows, trying to murder Don Benito. Here Melville's tale breaks off and offers depositions from Babo's trial in Lima; for his fiction was not stranger than fact.

Lowell's play is set aboard the *San Dominick* and is faithful to Melville's version until the end. Lowell has marvelously dramatized both the dangerous innocence of Captain Delano and the atmosphere of brooding evil into which he has so unknowingly thrust himself. Here, too, Lowell uses to good advantage the Racinesque technique of providing his main character with a confidant. Delano's bosun, Mr. Perkins, is Lowell's invention. Perkins is more than a mere interlocutor for Delano; in the two men together Lowell manages to suggest the twin strands of the traditional New England character already run to seed—those his forebear James Russell Lowell pointed to in describing Emerson as a "Plotinus-Montaigne." Captain Delano is a hearty bon vivant, a self-styled man of the world, smug ("America is wherever her flag flies"), his bonhomie concealing his moral blindness from himself. Perkins has the more austere New England character, as Delano makes him admit:

> DELANO: You don't believe in slavery or Spaniards or smoking or long cruises or monks or Mr. Jefferson! You are a Puritan, all faith and fire.
>
> PERKINS: Yes, Sir.
>
> DELANO: God save America from Americans!

Delano then peers through his glass to get a closer look at the *San Domingo,* unaware of the double edge of his last remark.

In Lowell's play, while Delano is in the Spanish captain's cabin, oblivious that Babu shaving Cereno is holding the razor to the captive master's throat, Perkins meanwhile prowls the decks with his eyes open. It is the prudent Puritan who sends back to their ship for men with muskets and bayonets, for he has found a skull and crossbones flag, and seen the giant Negro king Atufal without his chains. What finally does alert Captain Delano to Don Benito's perhaps not telling the full truth is not any of the veiled and sinister goings-on, but the Spaniard's cavalier attitude toward repaying the Americans for their provender and supplies.

From this point on Lowell extrapolates from Melville's tale. The changes bring onstage in nightmarish succession one violent horror after another. Taunted by Delano's condescension, Babu commands his blacks and they surround the American, hatchets upraised. In a frightening scene Lowell dramatizes the Negroes' hatred of the white man as they chant, "Freedom! Freedom! Freedom!" Now Babu forces Benito Cereno to walk upon the flag of Spain, and to kiss the skull of his partner

Don Aranda, the cruel master whom the blacks have murdered. Then Perkins must kiss Don Aranda's skull, and then must Captain Delano. But Delano has a pistol in his pocket, and he threatens Babu. The Negro is undeterred:

> You can stand there like a block of wood
> As long as you want to, Yankee Master.
> You will drop asleep, then we will tie you up,
> And make you sail us back to Africa.

Lowell has perfected and sharpened Melville's metaphor for the technological helplessness of the Negro. Here they stand: the exhausted Spaniard in his courtly decadence; the Negro defiant but helpless in his freedom without the American's scientific seamanship; and the American, at last beginning to comprehend the evil in which he has so blithely become entangled. And here Lowell leaves Melville's script completely behind him. In the tale, as in the real Captain Delano's journal, Babo was brought to Lima and executed after the civil formalities of a trial. But in the play the stage is rocked by gunfire. The American sailors mow down all the Negroes but Babu. Perkins and Delano still think that Atufal, bacause he looked like a king, was the leader, and Babu, bacause he seemed Don Benito's valet, a servant. But Babu cries, "I was the King. Babu, not Atufal." He picks up a sceptre and glass ball—"This is the earth. This is the arm of the angry God"—and smashes the ball. Perkins pleads for his surrender ("We want to save someone"), Don Benito is still further amazed by the Americans ("My God, how little these people understand!"), and Babu, raising a white handkerchief, pleads, "Yankee Master understand me. The future is with us." Delano replies, "This is your future," then fires all six bullets into Babu.

This is a terrifying and shocking finale. To one who knows his Melville it seems at first the desecration of a classic; but on reflection one can see that Lowell's ending is both just and consistent with the situation and the character of Delano. The captain's incapacity to imagine evil leads directly to his total reliance upon force to cope with it. He had, in a moment of doubt (it was Benito Cereno, not Babu, he thought sinister), mused to himself, "Who could want to murder Amasa Delano? / My conscience is clean. God is good." To retain his faith in his own Election and in God's goodness, Babu must be recognized as an enemy of God as well as of Amasa. This looks back with all consistency to Governor Endecott's way of dealing with dissenters, Royalists, and revellers. But to what does it look forward? No longer to the Civil War, as did Melville, writing in 1857; but surely to the extremities of the Black Nationalists, the anarchic hatred in the riots in Watts and elsewhere, and the white backlash. Lowell offers no panacea for the holocaust at his final curtain, no solution save that of tragedy; clarification through purgation by terror and pity. Melville's tale remains a classic and inviolable; Lowell's play does not replace it, but has already made a high niche for itself among the small number of effective tragedies written for the American theatre.

In *Near the Ocean,* Lowell suggests, there are implied connections between the Rome of his translations—"the greatness and horror of her Empire"—and the America of his own poems. In these Roman translations a whole culture is arraigned in its relations to time, to nature, to God, and to man. Here Caesar claims not only what is Caesar's. This implicit image of America perhaps will prove more useful in Lowell's own poems than was that of Melville's blind idealist.

There is a grave, poignant melancholy in Lowell's Rome. The Horatian odes begin with "Spring," celebrating natural delight, lamenting the transitoriness of man's life and of all his satisfactions. The ethos of Rome exalts war and a brave death; but these odes describe defeat, cowardice, disaster ("Serving under Brutus"); and death is but a liberator from disgrace ("Cleopatra"). Juvenal's satire, "The Vanity of Human Wishes," displays, as on a stylized mural, man's subjection to lust, to mortality, to time and the inexorable extinction of all joy in an empire where "Success is worshipped as a god." We leap from the pagan Roman Empire to the Holy Empire of Rome, and in Dante's Brunetto Latini find the secular poet as tragic hero. (Lowell first quoted this canto in his poem to Santayana, but Ser Brunetto may also prefigure Pound.) His version, in open-rhymed tercets, has a fluid formality of style, more like Eliot's fire-watcher passage than like anyone else's Dante, and far indeed from the Ezratic distortions of *Imitations.* The four Spanish sonnets measure man against "those brilliant hours that wore away our days, / our days that ate into eternity."

When Lowell was writing one of the poems in *Life Studies,* he later told Alvarez, he tried to use Marvell's four-foot couplet; but "the meter just seemed to prevent any honesty on the subject." Yet in *Near the Ocean* it is Marvell's stanza of four couplets, using assonance and interior rhyme, that provides a beautifully balanced means for fusing Lowell's feeling with his thought. The syntax is natural and the formal design retains those virtues Lowell praised in Williams—"changes of tone, atmosphere and speed." These qualities were present in Marvell too, for in "The Garden" the stanza moves with the mind that withdraws from its "uncessant labours" into the solitude of "a green thought in a green shade"; and that shade is cast by the tree of life, not merely by the tree of knowledge.

This is the stanza used in the three principal poems in the first half of his new book: "Waking early Sunday Morning," "Fourth of July in Castine," and the title poem. All are assured of high place in Lowell's canon. The title of the first invites comparison with Stevens, as its stanza does with Marvell. Lowell's poem begins where "Sunday Morning" ended, with the repetitive plenitude of nature. But the leap of the salmon, "alive enough to spawn and die," is no consolation here, for the first line pleads, "Oh to break loose" *like* the salmon. Indifferent to time, the salmon and other creatures re-awaken in the speaker of the poem "unpolluted joy / and criminal leisure of a boy." Our workaday life also goes on indifferent to time, for inanimate objects are "serene in their neutrality." Unlike the spirit, wood remains darkened but unstained by time. With deceptive lightness these stanzas move toward the fortitude of the homeless but not hopeless spirit. "Better. . . lost with the Faithful at Church—/ anywhere, but somewhere else!" Yet the Church is mere mechanical formalism, like its "new electric bells." Although its hymns preserve the "Bible chopped and crucified," at least "they gave darkness some control, / and left a loophole for the soul." In the first printing of this poem the next stanza moved into the theme of "Dejection: an Ode"—"When I look into my heart / I discover none of the great / subjects: death, friendship, love and hate—/ only old china doorknobs, sad, / slight, useless things to calm the mad." The present text, however, erases this concern with the exhaustion of imagination (the poet-as-hero theme of *Imitations*). The new stanza returns to a still greater subject than those listed:

> When will we see Him face to face?
> Each day, He shines through darker glass. . . .

—an ambiguous comfort. But among "His vanishing emblems" appear the "white spire and flag—/ pole sticking out above the fog / like old white china doorknobs. . . . " Lowell is still wrestling with the angel that hammerlocked his youth, but now in middle age neither rhetoric nor theme is as agonized as in "Black Rock." The darkening world conforms to God no more now than then; but if its "slight, useless things" appear as doorknobs atop flagpoles and steeples, what doors might these handles of our state and church open but the gates of heaven? The poem, however, does not end with this hope, for the world's attention is fixed rather on "top-heavy Goliath in full armor." Even "a new diminuendo"—an easy peace?—may bring "no true / tenderness, only restlessness, / excess, the hunger for success. . . while we listen to the bells. . . . "

Here is the confluence of Lowell's Rome and his America: worlds without grace, where success is worshipped by those who, like Ser Brunetto, run in the wrong race. In a highly developed pagan culture the fecundity of nature is always felt as a source of melancholy (*vide* Lucretius, a Roman not in Lowell's pantheon), since nature's continuation emphasizes man's short date. Now Lowell repeats the images and phrases with which his poem began, invoking fish, animal, and youthful pleasures in a scene that leaps unexpectedly but assuredly from the personal to a larger context:

> O to break loose. All life's grandeur
> is something with a girl in summer. . .
> elated as the President
> girdled by his establishment
> this Sunday morning, free to chaff
> his own thoughts with his bear-cuffed staff,
> swimming nude, unbuttoned, sick
> of his ghost-written rhetoric!

Among these sensual and pagan images, LBJ appears as one of the Caesars at his bath. The image of the bear recurs a few lines down—"No weekends for the gods now. . . earth licks its open sores. . . . " In such a de-faithed world of war, assassination, "Only man thinning out his kind," there is no consolation against "the blind / swipe of the pruner and his knife / busy about the tree of life. . . . " The poem ends with the stanza, "Pity the planet, all joy gone," quoted at the beginning of this essay. In it, man concludes the pruner's work.

The other poems in *Near the Ocean* speak with like inventiveness and authority though they embody themes less wide in range. "Fourth of July in Castine" treats a Yeatsian subject which Lowell has long made his own and domesticated to New England "in Calvinism's ebb"—the dynastic house, both the family and its dwelling. The title poem is a beautifully unpredictable, yet integrated and controlled, handling of the loyalties of love. "Near the Ocean" subdues the gorgon's head with a poise Lowell has hitherto not come near achieving. Other poems portray the violence simmering in the New York streets; and there is a tribute to Theodore Roethke.

Each book of Lowell's has won him new laurels on which he has never been content to rest. His creative energy seems ever-renewing, and his poetic means have changed with the changes in his vision. His work thus far is the most authoritative and compelling body of verse by any living poet in English save Auden. In *Near the Ocean* Lowell seems well into a new phase. The ravaging tensions of his youth have been outlasted and subsumed in poetry less fractious than in *Lord Weary's Castle,* less determinedly experimental than in *Life Studies,* yet ribbed with conceptual power and rippling with the virtues of style at which he aimed in *Pheadra*—"a certain dignity, speed, and flare." Lowell's poems begin in suffering, not, like Frost's, in delight, although like those they end in wisdom. It is Lowell's continuing triumph to have turned both suffering and wisdom into that delight which is achieved only by those few poets who have mastered experience through their art.

AFTERWORD

A few months after the above essay appeared, a colleague, meeting me in the hall, asked, "When did you write all those lines in Lowell's 'Endecott and the Red Cross'? They're not in my copy of the play." I looked at the paperback he held in hand, and sure enough, hardly one of the passages I'd quoted remained in the play. I had copied them with my usual scrupulous care from the hardbound first edition of *The Old Glory* (1965), a text the author would seem to have renounced, for in the list of his publications which faces the title page of his latest work, he lists the play this way: *The Old Glory (revised edition).* The changes, in the third Noonday paperback edition of 1967, do not affect the pagination, so the unwary reader might not realize that the text has been rewritten. Particularly between pages 31 and 34, the key scene presenting Endecott's dream now has lines other than those quoted in my essay.

Lowell has made Endecott more reflective, less volatile, his imagery not so violent. His attack on the Roman Church is toned down, he now omits such condemnations of human nature as the line, "I began to see that men are twisted." No longer does he say, "The whole world sees itself as fuel for a system. . . . / divine right kings, imitation Roman republics of fanatics / . . . . he who is not with me is against me." In his apocalyptic dream Endecott no longer names the actual families of Boston whom he sends off to be burnt, nor does he tell us that "These people burned like birch logs." The outline of the dream is still the same but the language and reference is much more generalized than before. Perhaps most revelatory of the changes is the last revision in the scene. In place of the lines quoted above, "I now understood statecraft. . . ," we now find,

> I was hitting men with an axe—
> It was a warped American axe: it hit askew.

ELDER PALFREY:
Kneel!

ENDECOTT:
I couldn't kill them.
Our flag was knocking and hacking in the air.
I was trying to nail them to the Red Cross.

ELDER PALFREY:
Let us pray. [*They kneel.*]

This version eliminated Endecott's rather desperate wisdom. He no longer says "a statesman can either work with merciless efficiency / and leave a desert, / or he can work in a hit and miss fashion, / and leave a cess-pool." Saying this, Endecott had placed himself in a self-destructive dilemma; since statecraft is what he *must* exercise, he seemed to be acknowledging that nothing he could do would be right. The new text rather tells us that the exercise of power has tempered his religious zeal—we have seen him mollifying Palfrey's savage punishments—and that his native weapon ("a warped American axe") will not do violence to men who serve the king's flag. He must win them away from their loyalty to the flag of the Red Cross. These new images are more consonant than the old with the theme and language of the rest of the play, although the ensuing action still dramatizes the truth of Endecott's now-deleted self-realization.

An obvious dramatic device which I somehow failed to mention is the parallelism in the play between the two sets of adversaries. If Endecott, representing Puritan statecraft, has his religious persona in the fanatical Palfrey, so too does Thomas Morton have his, the Anglican priest Blackstone. Lowell has quite altered the character of Blackstone from the Bacchus-like renegade priest in Hawthorne's "May-Pole of Merry Mount" (he appears in this same guise also in Conrad Aiken's historical poem, *The Kid*). Lowell's Blackstone is an elegant courtier, a very high-church ecclesiast, fastidious to the point of parody, quite out of his element in the rude society of Morton's band of sensualists and their Indian consorts. Morton is developed in the play as representing the cavalier type, shrewd, cynical, debonair. However little these Lowell characters may resemble their historical originals, they complement each other well and serve to represent the uneasy alliance between Royalism and expediency, between Episcopacy and worldly indulgence. (Both Anglican and Puritan parties are accused by Morton of being in the new world solely for trade and gain.) The main action of course is the testing of wills and strength between these two pairs of antagonists, none of whom is comfortable with the ally God has given him.

My hope that "Endecott and the Red Cross" be rescued from its fate as an unproduced drama was fulfilled in the spring of 1968. John Hancock directed a production at the American Place Theatre in which the most effective performances were John Harkin's Thomas Morton and Kenneth Haigh's Governor Endecott. Lowell further revised the script—I haven't seen the prompt book but recall a lengthy and static prologue involving the Indians, who had figured in a minor way among Morton's minions. There seemed two reasons for building up the Narragansett column of the cast: one was to present an obvious analogue to the way Endecott's successors are dealing with another dark-skinned people in Viet Nam, the other was to provide further opportunities for alternating speeches with masques. Lowell seems very partial in these plays to masques; not, I find, a very effective way for furthering what should be the central interest in a play, the action. Thus in "Benito Cereno" the stage is stilled in a trance-like hush while Babu leads his obsequious blacks through a mimed performance around the mainmast, ostensibly to amuse their visitor, Captain Delano. In "Endecott" there is a similar masque, performed joyously at the start of the play, and, after Endecott spoils the sport at Merry Mount, put on again for the last time, at his ironic direction. The Indian stage business with which the play opened was yet another such masque. It didn't much enliven the play. The central action remains the scene between Endecott and Palfrey. A reader might think this scene—in which the action is in the language, in the images, not the gestures—would be very hard to stage. But here the actors were at their best.

Lowell's next project after *The Old Glory* was his adaptations of Aeschylus' *Prometheus Bound,* produced by the Yale Drama School and printed in the *New York Review* (July 13, 1967).[2] Perhaps it was the poetic license Lowell gave himself in *Prometheus* which brought to a boil the simmering of that tetchy guardian of literary morality, John Simon, for in the winter 1967-1968 issue of *Hudson Review* he abused Lowell in a twenty-page article, "Abuse of Privilege: Lowell as Translator." This excerpt typifies Mr. Simon's tone and the range of his objections:

> Does a translator—even if he calls himself by another name, such as "imitator," supposed to set himself beyond the reach of criticism—have the right to change the entire mood, intention, import of a poem? Of a serious poem by a genuine poet? At what point does an act of "imitation" become an immoral act?

2 The play has just been issued as a book by Farrar, Straus & Giroux.

Lowell's alleged crimes are further compounded on the stage, as in *Prometheus Bound*, where the director recreates what the adaptor has already misinterpreted. Not having myself witnessed the perpetration of these offenses at New Haven, I must forebear to discuss the production. But there are other questions of motive which Mr. Simon cannot leave unraised, nor I unrebutted:

> By adapting a celebrated poem or play, or by "dislocating" the play one is directing, one cashes in on the original's prestige while also exhibiting one's prowess in the alterations; at the same time, one can always blame the foreignness or intractability of the original for one's failures. Second, one uses this as a surrogate for whatever creativity one finds oneself lacking. A poet runs out of poetry of his own, so he must make it out of someone else's, rather like the fly that lays its egg in the living body of a certain caterpillar for the larvae to feed on. . . .

Mr. Simon is at no loss to show the violence done to Rilke or Rimbaud by Lowell's imitations, or how un-Aeschylean is Lowell's *Prometheus.* By accusing the adaptor of both parasitism and immorality, however, this critic reveals his own ignorance of the creative process, a realization of which may be inferred from a dispassionate consideration of the great translations and imitations made in any earlier period of literature. For many of the translators of "serious poems by genuine poets" who have proposed to give us the genius of their originals have in fact been imitators, whether admittedly or not. Would Simon accuse Chaucer of the sins with which he taxes Lowell for having been both so bold and so free with Boccaccio? Or would Dryden earn the same derision for his adaptations of Chaucer? Anyone reading a characteristic passage from the Homers of, say,

Chapman, Pope, Bryant, Butcher, and Lattimore will readily recognize in each the typical features not so much of Greek epic poetry but the assumptions of their respective periods regarding versification, sublimity, heroic diction, and the proprieties of poetry. Are these poets all vandals desecrating the sacred body of a higher literature, or parasites who have fed upon the living tissue of the past to conceal the exhaustion of their own creative energies?

Apart from such general objections to Simon's simplistic view of poetic work, whether original or adapted, is his inability to understand what Lowell is trying to do. When Lowell says, in his brief preface to *Prometheus Bound,* that "Nothing is modernized. . . . Yet I think my own concerns and those of the times seep in," Simon of course is outraged by the sheer egotism of the assertion. If we ask whether the same might not have been true for Shelley, Simon would doubtless answer that Lowell is no Shelley. It's obvious that I'm among those commentators who take their cuffings from this commentator for having *encouraged* Lowell in the error of his ways. (Mr. Simon characteristically assumes that poets write to please their reviewers.) I may not think Lowell Shelley, but I praise him for being Lowell, without feeling obliged to approve everything he has written. I admire his creative energy, equally his own in his adaptations as in his "original" poems. The lines between imitation and creativity, between originality and adaptation, are not in fact separated by the chasm which Simon would throw down between them. A poet must feed on the past, absorb it, digest it, use it, renew it. Whether one man's sensibility is the viable medium through which "the concerns. . . of the times" seep in along with his own concerns depends, of course, upon the nature of both sets of concerns. It will be inferred that Robert Lowell's concerns may in the end best be apprehended as deeply personal and that his excursions into the literature of other times and tongues may be searches for paradigms and parallels to those personal concerns.

For instance, it might be claimed that Lowell has distorted New England history in order to exorcise personal ghosts. The Puritan commonwealth, which the Puritans themselves imagined as a new Israel, Lowell renders as riddled with hyprocrisy, avarice, and the other seven deadlies. This judgment comes not from a historian's assessment of period documents; it reflects a private war of a descendant of Puritans against his own fathers. But—I believe fortunately—it also reflects a truth about the Puritans which they themselves were incapable of admitting and which their historians are not much inclined to stress. It dramatizes the response to a restrictive past of a nation, and particularly to a section of that nation, which has had uncomfortably to live with the inheritance of both the Puritan's sense of man's fallen nature and of their own election to Grace. This is our Manifest Destiny, and no son of the Puritans since Hawthorne has shown it to us as clearly as has Robert Lowell.

Once again, with *Notebook 1967-68,* Lowell has devised a new phase in his own work, at once a departure from and a continuation of everything he's written hitherto. Here are nearly 250 unrhymed sonnet-length poems, by turns metered and as free as prose. "Even with this license, I fear I have failed to avoid the themes and giganticism of the sonnet," Lowell says in a brief prose "Afterthought." Most of these poems don't succumb to the swell-and-squeeze rhythm of the sonnet, eight lines swell, six squeeze; rather like they inhale and exhale, constrict and resolve more frequently, less predictably, by processes and in rhythms of their own.

The *Notebook* poems show how well Lowell has absorbed his own experience as poet. He uses the referential framework of the changing seasons, from the summer of one year through the summer of the next, but although there are references to and poems about public events (the "pacification of Columbia," the Democratic convention in Chicago, the Spock trial, the assassination of Robert Kennedy) and public figures (Senator McCarthy, Norman Mailer, a dozen poets living or recently dead), and to Lowell's travels during the year (summers in Maine, trips to Mexico, Brazil, and Israel, the burdens of life in New York City), the external events and references are but a series of points touched by the jagged trajectory of the poet's imagination, continually backsliding, sidewinding, deepdiving into his remembered own past, into history, into his readings which have become part of his past. Everything is turned into poetry, swallowed by the poet's ravenous need. His experiences, loves, conversations, dreams, advocacies, nightmares, broodings on history and the present, all are fused in the synergizing rhythms of the same yet ever-changing stanza. The movement of the verse is rational and intuitive by turns, the mind making unexpected leaps of association, the pressure upon the reader that of the verse, the pressure of the verse that of time, the poet at fifty breathing hard to write easy, working everything into his poems while the past pours through him as the present slips away.

There's a heroic *largesse* in the achievement, the now-easy, long-earned familiarity of the poet with his magniloquent images of power and corruption, his life's divagating course now purified of the trivial and revealed as a thrust toward an understanding of the center of his own time. All his experiences lend and tend to this: marriage, fatherhood, friendship, the inner life of a humane and deeply troubled man, a poet who from adolescence moved familiarly among the great figures of modern writing, in middle age still mindful of the justified impatience of the young, yet mindful of youth's dangerous intolerance of history; a poet who leads the march on the Pentagon and is the companion of a presidential candidate. All this and more comprises the experience which these stanzas are able to use, the sensibility which *Notebook* expresses. Although the references in the poems are sometimes private, the movement of mind occasionally as arcane as unexpected ("I am devoted to rationalism but lean heavily on surrealism"), *Notebook* is anything but hermetic. It is thinking-aloud, to be overheard; the mind as well as the psyche speaking, in a manner much more public in its concerns than was true of confessional verse, Lowell's or anyone else's. The book, for all its openness to the public world, is at the same time intensely personal (as a poet's response to the public world must be). Its personal materials—the poems to his wife and daughter—have a tenderness and an acknowledgment of the flawed fulfillments of human possibility which comprises the one distinctly new tone in Lowell's work, though it has been incipient since the end of *Life Studies.*

In technique, too, *Notebook* is not so much a new departure as may at first appear. Its very stanza has been repeatedly foretold, for who else among contemporary poets has been as faithful to, or as unable to escape from, the sonnet? There are ten sonnets in *Lord Weary's Castle;* one of them—"In the Cage," a tetrameter sonnet—reappears on page 32 of *Notebook.* Along with its breakthroughs into free cadences, *Life Studies* is interspersed with sonnets: "Beyond the Alps"; "Words for Hart Crane" (irregularly rhymed); and "To Speak of the Woe That Is In Marriage" (a sonnet in couplets). *Imitations,* of course, is studded with sonnets, while the versions in *Near the Ocean* from Quevado and Gongora reflect his long mastery of the form.

In his effort to pour his whole life through the funnel of the free sonnet stanza, Lowell reuses some of his earlier work. It is just at this point that *Notebook* seems most vulnerable. It may well be asked whether what has already been expressed in a nearly perfect form intrinsic to the shape of its experience can be improved upon by expanding it to sonnet length and filling in the elisions of the original in phrase or imagery (cf. the Roethke elegy in *Near the Ocean* and *Notebook,* p. 132); or by amputating the second half of so memorable a poem as "Night Sweat," reprinting only the first of the two stanzas from *For the Union Dead* (Notebook, p. 103); or by recasting the 52 lines of "Caligula" into an abrupt fourteen-liner (*Notebook,* p. 104). Such exercises seem willed and arbitrary, but retreads of old snow tires are infrequent among these pages.

The only thing at all like *Notebook* in our poetry is Berryman's *Dream Songs,* which also subordinate a lifetime to the changing repetitions of a single stanza form. But Berryman's persona is a doppelgänger, more nearly as though the id were speaking, and his diction and tone are accordingly different from Lowell's, who speaks more directly in *Notebook.* Berryman's language is much more arch, his speech a confected dialect, though Lowell seems to acknowledge the kinship of their enterprises in one of his last stanzas, "For John Berryman":

> I feel I know what you have worked through, you
> know what I have worked through—these are
> words. . . .
> John we used the language as if we made it.
> Luck threw up the coin, and the plot was swal-
> lowed,
> monster yawning for its mess of pottage.

The "monster" that Lowell's life has fed "its mess of pottage" (in another place he says "one wants words more meat-hooked from the living steer"), the monster has rewarded its keeper. In a stanza titled "Reading Myself" he says, "I memorized tricks to set the river on fire, / somehow never wrote something to go back to." Not so. Certainly not so here, where it seems more than ever likely

> . . . that the perishable work live long
> enough for the sweet-tooth bear to desecrate
> this open book. . . my open coffin.

•

ABOUT ROBERT LOWELL

Robert Lowell's interest in writing poetry took him from Harvard University, where he had spent two years, to Kenyon College, where he studied under John Crowe Ransom. After his graduation from Kenyon in 1940, Lowell worked for a short time with a publisher in New York.

During World War II he served a term in a federal penitentiary, for being a conscientious objector. His first book of poetry was also published during the war—*Land of Unlikeness*—in 1944. In 1947-1948 Mr. Lowell served as poetry consultant to the Library of Congress. He is a frequent lecturer at the State University of Iowa and the Kenyon School of English. He has also taught at the Salzburg Seminar in American Studies in Austria, at Boston University, and at Harvard.

In 1947 Robert Lowell won the Pulitzer prize

in poetry for *Lord Weary's Castle.* He has recently turned to playwriting: *The Old Glory* opened in New York in 1964, and his adaptation of Aeschylus' *Prometheus Bound* was premièred by the Yale School of Drama in 1968. Lowell's latest book is *Notebook 1967-68.*

Mr. Lowell is married to Elizabeth Hardwick, herself a writer.

BOOKS BY ROBERT LOWELL

LAND OF UNLIKENESS
Cummington, Mass.: Cummington, 1944.

LORD WEARY'S CASTLE
New York: Harcourt, Brace, 1946.

POEMS, 1938-1949
London: Faber & Faber, 1950.
London: Faber & Faber, 1960.

THE MILLS OF THE KAVANAGHS
New York: Harcourt, Brace, 1951.
Toronto: McLeod, 1951.

LIFE STUDIES
New York: Farrar, Straus & Cudahy, 1959.
London: Faber & Faber, 1960.
New York: Vintage, 1960. (pb)

IMITATIONS
New York: Farrar, Straus, 1961.
London: Faber & Faber, 1962.
Toronto: Ambassador, 1962.
Toronto: Ambassador, 1962. (pb)
New York: Noonday, 1962. (pb)

LORD WEARY'S CASTLE & THE MILLS OF THE KAVANAGHS
New York: Meridian, 1961. (pb)

PHAEDRA AND FIGARO (Racine's *Phèdre* trans. by Lowell & Beaumarchais's *Le Mariage de Figaro* trans. by Jacques Barzun)

New York: Farrar, Straus, 1961.
Toronto: Ambassador, 1961.

FOR THE UNION DEAD
New York: Farrar, Straus, 1964.
London: Faber & Faber, 1965.
Toronto: Ambassador, 1965.

THE OLD GLORY
New York: Farrar, Straus & Giroux, 1965.
London: Faber & Faber, 1966.
New York: Noonday, 1966. (pb)
New York: Noonday, 1967. (pb) (rev. ed.)

SELECTED POEMS
London: Faber & Faber, 1965. (pb)

NEAR THE OCEAN
New York: Farrar, Straus & Giroux, 1967.
London: Faber & Faber, 1967.

VOYAGE AND OTHER VERSIONS OF POEMS BY BAUDELAIRE
New York: Farrar, Straus & Giroux, 1967.
London: Faber & Faber, 1968.

LIFE STUDIES & FOR THE UNION DEAD
New York: Noonday, 1967.
New York: Noonday, 1967. (pb)

RANDALL JARRELL: NINETEEN-FOURTEEN TO NINETEEN-SIXTY-FIVE (ed. with others)
New York: Noonday, 1968.

PROMETHEUS BOUND
New York: Farrar, Straus & Giroux, 1969.
New York: Noonday, 1969. (pb)

NOTEBOOK 1967-68
New York: Farrar, Straus & Giroux, 1969.
New York: Noonday, 1970. (pb)

The Black Clock:
The Poetic Achievement of Louis MacNeice

by William Jay Smith

Louis MacNeice's last volume of poems, *The Burning Perch,* went to press in January 1963; he died suddenly in September of the same year at the age of 56. Critics since have generally acknowledged that he was a poet of genius, and that much of his finest work was produced in the three years immediately preceding his death. While granting him his place in the front rank among the poets who came to prominence in the thirties—W.H. Auden, Stephen Spender, Cecil Day Lewis—they have had considerable difficulty in assessing the nature of his achievement. On his death, T.S. Eliot commented that he "had the Irishman's unfailing ear for the music of verse." During his lifetime, however, many readers felt that his ear did indeed fail him, that his rhythms were frequently too easy, and his parodies and imitations of jazz lyrics too flat and mechanical in nature to hold one's interest for long. While he had much in common with his contemporaries, he was, in many ways, totally unlike them. His poems are easy to understand on the surface (seemingly far less complicated than those of Auden or Dylan Thomas), but they present deeper, less obvious difficulties. They appear to be the open, easy expression of an engaging and intelligent personality, but basically that personality, and the poems through which it manifests itself, is not easy to grasp.

Stephen Spender, who knew him at Oxford, has spoken of him, as have many of his contemporaries, as one who was brilliant but aloof. "He had a way," Mr. Spender writes, "of leaning back and gazing at one through half-closed eyes which scarcely covered a mocking glance. Secrets he surmised about oneself he did not intend to share, the glance said. . . . That this detachment of MacNeice's was noticeable enough is notorious. A famous occasion at which I happened to be present was when, late in the war, Archibald Clerk-Kerr (later Lord Inverchapel), the British ambassador at Moscow, returning to London for a visit attended a party given by John Lehmann for the young English poets of the thirties and forties. Throughout the party MacNeice, holding a glass in his hand, leaned against a piece of furniture, and gazed around him disdainfully, without addressing a word to anyone. Finally Clerk-Kerr went up to him and told him there was a matter about which he would like to be informed. Did MacNeice come from the northern coast of Ireland? MacNeice acknowledged that he did. 'Ah,' said Clerk-Kerr, 'well that corroborates a legend I heard in my youth that a school of seals had landed on that part of the coast, cohabited with the natives, and produced a special race, half-seal, half-human.' MacNeice did look a bit taken aback, as Clerk-Kerr left the room" (*The New Republic,* January 28, 1967).

MacNeice's friend John Hilton, in an appendix to *The Strings Are False,* an unfinished autobiography now published, speaks of him in similar, if more sympathetic, terms: "On the whole at that time he preferred to study mankind indirectly. He liked—or perhaps this came on a bit later—to read the 'small ads' in the papers. Meeting people face to face he was apt to make too clear that he was treating them—head thrown slightly back, eyes quizzically narrowed—as specimens, bearers of the potentialities of the race, concrete universals perhaps. A remark ventured by the specimen would be visibly rolled around his mental palate and mental ear; and the response if any would be less than wholehearted. He was afraid—as in the *Prayer before Birth*—of being spilled. He did not mind at times appearing sly; and he did not always choose to recognize people he had met before (though his increasing shortsightedness was probably responsible for many imagined offenses of the kind)." I felt when I met MacNeice myself several times in London in the spring of 1948 that he was treating me, through his narrowed eyes, as a specimen of the sort of poet America produced, for whom he appeared to feel only disdain. I discovered from his friends Reggie Smith and Ernest Stahl, whom I saw often, that this was not true. I did not meet him again until a year or so before his death; he came in out of the rain in Greenwich Village to a party at Howard Moss's apartment looking literally like the half-seal that Clerk-Kerr had encountered in London. Soon dry and warmed by liquor, he appeared far more human than I had remembered him, the brilliant and engaging person one expected from his poems.

There is in everything that Louis MacNeice wrote a surface brilliance, an extraordinary verbal dexterity, a poise that shows itself in a command of complicated verse forms. There is a distance maintained, even when he is being most personal, that gives his poetry, at its best, a cold classical power, and, at its worst, the casualness of an uncommitted poetic journalist. MacNeice during his career engaged in many literary pursuits which took him away from the writing of poetry. But he was never deceived, no matter how well he succeeded in journalism, criticism, translation or radio work, that these were anything but diversions from his main course. Of the prose books for which he accepted commissions from publishers during the late thirties he writes: "It flattered me that publishers should ask me to do something unsuitable. The more unsuitable, the more it was a sign of power. Many of us were still reacting overmuch against Art for Art's Sake, against the concept of the solitary pure-minded genius saving his soul in a tower without doors. Our reaction drove us to compete with the Next Man. But once you come up against the Next Man you begin to lose sight of the sky. The Next Man swells to a giant, you find your face buried in his paunch and on his paunch is a watch ticking louder and louder, urging you to hurry, get on with the job—when the job is finished there will always be another. In commercial writing, in 'book-making,' one comes to think of carelessness and speed as virtues." His extensive work for the BBC served to accentuate his desire for the use of direct and colloquial speech, but for the trained classicist that he was, the virtues of harmony and measure were ingrained.

It was important for MacNeice to look at the world from a certain distance in order to view it, and himself as part of it, with honesty and without self-pity. MacNeice was interested in the concrete, as true lyric poets always are: he wanted to get things straight. (He believed that a critic should not speak of poetry in the abstract, but should point out specific qualities, merits in individual poems.) Dr. Johnson was wrong, he remarks at one point, when he said that the poet is not concerned with minute particulars, with "the streaks on the tulip." MacNeice was passionate about particulars; in "Autumn Sequel" he writes:

> Everydayness is good; particular-dayness
> Is better, a holiday thrives on single days.
> Thus Wales with her moodiness, madness, shrewdness, lewdness, feyness,
> Daily demands a different color of praise.

Absorbed in the dailiness of life, he could not tolerate lofty rhetoric, the grand gesture: he was not to be taken in. His last poems in *The Burning Perch* showed that he could "let commonplace be novelty," and that he had the power, with the lightness of his touch and the bite of his wit, to create a lasting resonance.

John Hilton describes a speech that MacNeice made at the Marlborough School in November 1925: "It really was simply astounding; an amazing and magnificent conglomeration of dreams, fables, parables, allegories, theories, quotations from Edward Lear and Edith Sitwell, the sort of thing that you want to howl with laughter at, but are afraid to for fear of missing a word. He spoke in a loud, clear, fast matter-of-fact voice going straight on without a pause from a long story about two ants who fell into a river and went floating down in company with two old sticks and a dead dog, until they met a fish to whom they said 'stuff and nonsense; it's contrary to common sense to swim upstream; we won't believe it' and went on and were drowned in a whirlpool, while the fish swam on upstream until he met St. Francis of Assisi preaching to the fishes and gained eternal happiness." Mr. Hilton concludes, in a letter, that MacNeice was undoubtedly "a great genius," even though he "stands for nonsense."

MacNeice's gift for nonsense was given full play at Oxford. He describes his verbal collaboration at Oxford with his friend Graham Shepard, "not that we had ever heard of Joyce or surrealism or automatic writing; we just liked to play about with words." Their experiments took such forms as this: "Mr. Little Short of Extraordinary was little short of extraordinary. He went to bed with his wife and dislocated his jaw. And that was the Night the Isms came to Auntie. General Useless MacNess was always in a mess. The Boy stood in the Burning Bush. 'What are ye doin' the day?' Quoth the cat. I'm minding my pees and peeing my queues. Oh the Harp that Once and never got over it!" He was especially fond, he said, of parodying hymns: "every little blasphemy a blow for the better Life." He could look at the grotesques who typified Oxford with the eye of a Lewis Carroll: "When I think of Oxford dons I see a *Walspurgisnacht,* a zoo—scraggy-necked baldheads in gown and hood looking like marabou storks, giant turtles reaching for a glass of port with infinitely weary flippers, sad chimpanzees, codfish, washing blown out on a line. Timid with pipes or boisterous with triple chins. Their wit and themselves had been kept too long, the squibs were damp, the cigars were dust, the champagne was flat." The verbal play was a way of keeping his distance.

MacNiece made technical use of nonsense right up to the end. In *The Burning Perch,* the poem "Children's Games," written in 1962, is a playful handling of children's nonsense phrases, but even the simplest one, such as "Keep your fingers crossed when Tom Tiddler's ground is over you," takes on a deeper significance. In "Sports Page" he observes his doppelgänger as a participant in games:

Nostalgia, incantation, escape,
Courts and fields of the Ever Young:
On your Marks! En Garde! Scrum Down! Over!
On the ropes, on the ice, breasting the tape,
Our Doppelgänger is bounced and flung
While the ball squats in the air like a spider
Threading the horizon round the goalposts
And we, though never there, give tongue.
Yet our Doppelgänger rides once more
Over the five-barred gates and flames
In metaphors filched from magic and music
With a new witch broom and a rattling score
And the names we read seem more than names,
Potions or amulets, till we remember
The lines of print are always sidelines
And all our games funeral games.

The "metaphors filched from magic and music" in *The Burning Perch* build up a nightmare world from which there is no escape; and distance—the objectivity of the artist—is of no help. The iceberg is a favorite figure in MacNeice's poetry (he always remembered seeing the Titanic as a child in Belfast on her maiden voyage) but in these later poems he explores the iceberg's underside. The nonsense world of childhood has become the real world, the grotesque figures that could once be laughed at are now omnipresent in a packaged and plastic, dehumanized world:

On the podium in lieu of a man
With fallible hands is ensconced
A metal lobster with built-in tempi;
The deep-sea fishermen in lieu of
Battling with tunny and cod
Are signing their contracts for processing plankton.

On roof after roof the prongs
Are baited with faces, in saltpan and brainpan
The savour is lost, in deep
Freeze after freeze in lieu of a joint
Are piled the shrunken heads of the past
And the offals of unborn children.

In lieu therefore of choice
Thy Will be undone just as flowers

Fugues, vows and hopes are undone
While the weather is packaged and the spacemen
In endless orbit and in lieu of a flag
The orator hangs himself from the flagpost.

The poems depict a world in which "Greyness is all":

But, as it is, we needs must wait
Not for some demon but some fate
Contrived by men and never known
Until the final switch is thrown
To black out all the worlds of men
And demons too but even then
Whether that black will not prove grey
No one may wait around to say.

"Budgie" presents a final grotesque vision of experience:

The budgerigar is baby blue,
Its mirror is rimmed with baby pink,
Its cage is a stage, its perks are props,
Its eyes black pins in a cushionette,
Its tail a needle on a missing disc,
Its voice a small I Am. Beyond
These wires there might be something different—
Galaxy on galaxy, star on star,
Planet on planet, asteroid on asteroid,
Or even those four far walls of the sitting room—
But for all this small blue bundle could bother
Its beak, there is only itself and the universe,
The small blue universe, so *Let me attitudinize,*
Let me attitudinize, let me attitudinize,
For all the world is a stage is a cage
A hermitage a fashion show a crèche an auditorium
Or possibly a space ship. *Earth, can you hear me?*
Blue for Budgie calling Me for Mirror:
Budgie, can you hear me? The long tail oscillates,
The mirror jerks in the weightless cage:
Budgie, can you see me? The radio telescope
Picks up a quite different signal, the human
Race recedes and dwindles, the giant
Reptiles cackle in their graves, the mountain
Gorillas exchange their final messages,
But the budgerigar was not born for nothing,

He stands at his post on the burning perch—
I twitter Am—and peeps like a television
Actor admiring himself in the monitor.

In *The Strings Are False* MacNeice writes about the breakup of his first marriage: "Sometimes in the nights I woke and wondered where we were going, but most of the time I was doped and happy, most of the time except when I thought about time that most of the time is waste but whose is not? When I started again to write poems they were all about time. We had an old record of 'The Blue Room,' one of the most out-and-out jazz sentimentalizations of domestic felicity—far away upstairs but the blue began to suffocate. I wrote a novel which was basically dishonest and ended in a blue room as if that solved everything." After his wife had left him, he writes of not being able to sleep. In a large room with a ten-foot skylight he "felt the skylight encroaching, tried to dodge it; sometimes it was a falling tent and sometimes it was the gap that cannot be closed." In this room he had "two precise visions, both by electric light, both solidly planted in the air about five foot up from the floor. The first was a human eye a yard or so long; the rest of the face was invisible but on both the upper and the under eyelid there were worms instead of eyelashes, transparent worms curling and wriggling. The second vision was of a sky-blue little beast like a jackal but with horns; he sat there pat on the air, his front feet firmly together."

In "Budgie" he confronts the same "sky-blue little beast," the same "small blue bundle," the same suffocating blue of "The Blue Room," but now in broad daylight, close-up and with an honesty that is terrifying. Life, reflecting upon itself, is reduced to a blue and pink baby-like vision, utterly nonsensical; but its nonsense parroting of its own parroting echoes through an expanding universe. "Budgie," in its mad vision and its alliterative and obsessive *b's,* reminds one of "The Hunting of the Snark" by Lewis Carroll: Budgie is a space-age Boojum, and its twittering "I am" comes from every TV screen.

The image of the bird on the burning perch calls to mind also an earlier poem by MacNeice, one of the finest of his war poems, "The Springboard," in which the poet contemplates man, called upon to sacrifice himself:

He never made the dive—not while I watched.
High above London, naked in the night
Perched on a board. I peered up through the bars
Made by his fear and mine but it was more than fright
That kept him crucified among the budding stars.

and concludes:

And yet we know he knows what he must do.
There above London where the gargoyles grin
He will dive like a bomber past the broken steeple,
One man wiping out his own original sin
And, like ten million others, dying for the people.

In "Budgie" the poet again looks through the bars, but sees not a human perched on a board ready to spring, but the "sky-blue beast" on its burning perch, sailing totally without meaning through a meaningless universe while the gargoyles—now real beasts—cackle and grin, and the human race "recedes and dwindles."

MacNeice speaks at one point of the importance that his generation attached to personal relationships. "It is better," he says, agreeing with his friend E.R. Dodds, the editor of both his poems and his unfinished autobiography, "to be like Rilke and capitalize your own loneliness and neuroses, regard Death as the mainspring. Or it is better—if you can do it—to become the servant of an idea. But if you take either of these courses, you have got to commit yourself utterly; if you give yourself to Loneliness or Otherness it must not be a negative thing—a mere avoiding of other troubles, mere sublimation—but it must be positive, an End. Thus people have become monks sometimes in order to avoid the trouble of sex, sometimes out of perverse sexuality, but that is not how people become saints. Not real saints. In spite of analytical researches into the pathology of sainthood, the saint, like the mathematician, has got hold of something positive. And so have the real hero and the real artist."

Beneath the bright and lively surface of his poems death seems to have haunted MacNeice throughout his work. He tells of dreaming of a house that was a skeleton, the walls and floors of which were gone. (He speaks elsewhere of having enjoyed climbing over ruined houses, of fearing blindness, long corridors, and light glancing off a mirror.) The dream ends with a vision of Dr. Mabuse, from the film that he had just seen, with a "great bush of orange-red hair," cackling and leering at him. The war poems of the forties present a panoramic vision of death and destruction, as in the masterful "Brother Fire:"

O delicate walker, babbler, dialectician Fire,
O enemy and image of ourselves,
Did we not on those mornings after the All Clear,
When you were looting shops in elemental joy
And singing as you swarmed up city block and spire,
Echo your thought in ours? 'Destroy! Destroy!'

At the same time he wrote a far more personal poem, "Prayer in Midpassage," which addresses death, in its "fierce impersonality" ("O Thou my monster, Thou my guide"), as the mainspring of his work:

> Take therefore, though Thou disregard,
> This prayer, this hymn, this feckless work,
> O Thou my silence, Thou my song,
> To whom all focal doubts belong
> And but for whom this breath were breath—
> Thou my meaning, Thou my death.

In a later poem "A Hand of Snapshops: The Left-Behind" the poet asks, peering into his glass of stout, a series of riddles:

> Where can you find a fire that burns and gives
> no warmth?
> Where is the tall ship that chose to run on a rock?
> Where are there more fish than ever filled the ocean?
> Where can you find a clock that strikes when it
> has stopped?
>
> Oh, poverty is the fire that burns and gives no warmth.
> My youth is the tall ship that chose to run on a rock.
> Men yet unborn could more than fill the ocean,
> And death is the black clock that strikes when it
> has stopped.

In much of his work his obsession with his past, with memories that "flitter and champ in a dark cupboard," seems to predominate. Often he tries to regain the bright particularity, the sensuous awareness, of childhood; and to do so he uses child-like playful rhythms and metrical devices. With sparkling nonsense and satiric savagery he hacks away at the deadness of language and of life; and many of his poems are verbal triumphs. But often, as he expresses it in the dedicatory poem to his first *Collected Poems* (1948), he "is content if things would image / Themselves in their own dazzle, if the answers came quick and smooth. . . . " It is not until the poems in *The Burning Perch* that he listens with full attention to "the black clock that strikes when it has stopped," and confronts his Loneliness and Otherness head-on. The poems in *The Burning Perch* are more direct and terrifying than any he had written. He goes over the same ground, treating the same subjects and frequently in the same manner, but with greater honesty and intensity. He uses the "same tunes that hang on pegs in the cloakrooms of the mind," but "off the peg seem made to measure now." And in the direct confrontation of loneliness and death, he became, with greater dimension than one would have thought possible, not only a real, but also a great, artist:

THE INTRODUCTION

They were introduced in a grave glade
And she frightened him because she was young
And thus too late. Crawly crawly
Went the twigs above their heads and beneath
The grass beneath their feet the larvae
Split themselves laughing. Crawly crawly
Went the cloud above the treetops reaching
For a sun that lacked the nerve to set
And he frightened her because he was old
And thus too early. Crawly crawly
Went the string quartet that was tuning up
In the back of the mind. You two should have met
Long since, he said, or else not now.
The string quartet in the back of the mind
Was all tuned up with nowhere to go.
They were introduced in a green grave.

ABOUT LOUIS MACNEICE

In 1963 at the age of fifty-six, Louis MacNeice insisted on accompanying the engineers down a hole while recording for a feature program he had written for the BBC. He caught a bad cold which developed into pneumonia. He died of it on September 3, 1963, ending in its prime a career which had begun in the early 1930s when he was one of the leading talents of the brilliant young group which included W. H. Auden, Christopher Isherwood, C. Day Lewis, and Stephen Spender.

MacNeice was born in Dublin of Irish parents on September 12, 1907. He was sent to Marlborough School in England at the age of ten. At Oxford (1926-1930) he read classics and philosophy at Merton College and took a First in "Greats." Until 1936 he was lecturer in classics at the University of Birmingham and lecturer in Greek at Bedford College for Women in the University of London.

He was a visiting lecturer at a number of American colleges and universities. He held other temporary posts in South Africa and India, and in 1950 he was director of the British Institute in Athens.

Beginning in 1940 he worked with some regularity for the BBC until the time of his death.

He was married and divorced, and was the father of a son.

BOOKS BY LOUIS MACNEICE

BLIND FIREWORKS
London: Gollancz, 1929.

ROUNDABOUT WAY
London: Putnam, 1932.
London: Putnam, 1933.

POEMS
London: Faber & Faber, 1935.
New York: Random House, 1937.

OUT OF THE PICTURE, A PLAY IN TWO ACTS
London: Faber & Faber, 1937.
Toronto: Ryerson, 1938.
New York: Harcourt, Brace, 1938.

AGAMEMNON (Aeschylus' *Agamemnon* trans. by MacNeice)
London: Faber & Faber, 1936.
New York: Harcourt, Brace, 1937.
Toronto: Ryerson, 1937.
London: Faber & Faber, 1951.
Toronto: British Book Service, 1951.
New York: Harcourt, Brace, 1951.

LETTERS FROM ICELAND (with W.H. Auden)
New York: Random House, 1937.
London: Faber & Faber, 1937.
Toronto: Ryerson, 1937.

EARTH COMPELS
London: Faber & Faber, 1938.
Toronto: Ryerson, 1938.

I CROSSED THE MINCH
London: Longmans, Green, 1938.
London: Longmans, Green, 1939.

MODERN POETRY, A PERSONAL ESSAY
London: Oxford, 1938.
New York: Oxford, 1939.
London: Oxford, 1969. (pb)

ZOO
London: Michael Joseph, 1938.
Toronto: S.J. Reginald Saunders, 1938.

AUTUMN JOURNAL
New York: Random House, 1939.
London: Faber & Faber, 1939.
Toronto: Ryerson, 1939.

POEMS: 1925-1940
New York: Random House, 1940.

LAST DITCH
Dublin: Cuala, 1940. (reg. & autographed eds.)

SELECTED POEMS
London: Faber & Faber, 1940.
Toronto: Ryerson, 1940.

PLANT AND PHANTOM
London: Faber & Faber, 1941.
Toronto: Ryerson, 1941.

THE POETRY OF WILLIAM BUTLER YEATS
London: Oxford, 1941.
New York: Oxford, 1941.
Toronto: Oxford, 1941.
London: Faber & Faber, 1967.
New York: Oxford, 1969. (pb)

CHRISTOPHER COLUMBUS, A RADIO PLAY
London: Faber & Faber, 1944.
Toronto: Ryerson, 1944.

SPRINGBOARD POEMS 1941-1944
London: Faber & Faber, 1944.
Toronto: Ryerson, 1944.
New York: Random House, 1945.
Toronto: Random House of Canada, 1945.

DARK TOWER AND OTHER RADIO SCRIPTS
London: Faber & Faber, 1947.

HOLES IN THE SKY: POEMS 1944-1947
London: Faber & Faber, 1948.
New York: Random House, 1949.
Toronto: Random House of Canada, 1949.

COLLECTED POEMS, 1925-1948
London: Faber & Faber, 1949.
New York: Oxford, 1963.

FAUST (Goethe's *Faust,* Parts I & II abridged and translated)
London: Faber & Faber, 1951.
Toronto: British Book Service, 1951.

New York: Oxford, 1953.
New York: Oxford, 1954. (pb)
London: Faber & Faber, 1965. (pb)

TEN BURNT OFFERINGS
London: Faber & Faber, 1952.
New York: Oxford, 1953.
Toronto: British Book Service, 1953.

AUTUMN SEQUEL
London: Faber & Faber, 1954.

THE PENNY THAT ROLLED AWAY
New York: Putnam, 1954.
Toronto: Thomas Allen, 1954.
as THE SIXPENCE THAT ROLLED AWAY
London: Faber & Faber, 1956.

VISITATIONS
London: Faber & Faber, 1957.
New York: Oxford, 1958.

EIGHTY-FIVE POEMS
London: Faber & Faber, 1959.
Toronto: British Book Service, 1959.
New York: Oxford, 1961.

SOLSTICES
London: Faber & Faber, 1961.
New York: Oxford, 1961.

THE BURNING PERCH
London: Faber & Faber, 1963.
New York: Oxford, 1963.

ASTROLOGY
New York: Doubleday, 1964.
Toronto: Doubleday, Canada, 1964.
London: W.H. Allen, 1964.

THE MAD ISLANDS: THE ADMINISTRATOR
New York: Oxford, 1964.
London: Faber & Faber, 1964.

SELECTED POEMS (selected by W.H. Auden)
London: Faber & Faber, 1964. (pb)

THE STRINGS ARE FALSE: AN UNFINISHED AUTOBIOGRAPHY
London: Faber & Faber, 1965.
New York: Oxford, 1966.

VARIETIES OF PARABLE
London: Cambridge, 1965.
New York: Cambridge, 1965.

THE COLLECTED POEMS OF LOUIS MACNEICE (ed. by E.R. Dobbs)
London: Faber & Faber, 1967.
New York: Oxford, 1967.

ONE FOR THE GRAVE
London: Faber & Faber, 1968.
New York: Oxford, 1968.

Morris the Magician
A Look at *In Orbit*

by George Garrett

With a gesture, no more, this boy makes old things new.
—In Orbit.

What has to be said first of all is that there are precious few if any novelists alive and working who are as able as Wright Morris to make both sense and art out of the brute, raw, flashing, shifty facts, the material of the American present. Which is what he is up to in *In Orbit.*

Of course many other writers, young and old, talk about doing this a great deal. Like the hucksters of soap, soft drinks, patent medicines, cigarettes, and underwear etc., they talk a great game and let their lives depend on it. Not that it matters very much whether they ever really deliver. At a time when the *image,* almost any image, is more important, even more "real" than any truth it may reveal or deftly conceal, it is only natural that your successful image-maker should be deeply appreciated. He is the fascinating sleight-of-hand magician and, thus, an image of the times himself. The things he can do with a deck of cards are only tricks, but we all know that, don't we? It's curiously reassuring. We know the deck and the names and suits of the cards, and we are comfortable with the game. There are no wild cards to worry about except the inevitable Joker, and we know all about him too. We are ready for him. Shuffle and riffle. Bright tricks in two dimensions. We can admire the learned dexterity. And he, the smiling or poker-faced card sharp, is really just one of us after all. Art-smart!! It is a relief to be reminded that, talent or not, the artist is just another hustler. It is more fun to read about Norman Mailer's antics in the newspapers, to hear what Gore Vidal is saying about the Kennedys, to turn on the television set, *educational* television, and to look at John Updike's extraordinary profile etched against the wind and surf of Cape Cod than it is to read their novels. Even Ginsberg, wrapped in something like a stained bed sheet, banging gongs and muttering the old mumbo jumbo, is finally just one of the boys. Buy the kid a drink, anything he wants. He talks a lot but he talks a pretty good game. He can make you laugh. And, you know?, once in a while he can make you think about different things. We can afford to pay for a little culture these days. The fast-talkers, the hustlers, barkers, the image-makers get what they deserve. Which happens to be a share of the white meat and good gravy, albeit after the grownups have left the table.

Here and now, in this context, ours, it would seem that Wright Morris has practically everything going against him. For one thing he works so hard. Fifteen novels since *My Uncle Dudley* in 1942. That comes perilously close to being, pardon the expression, *prolific.* Which is not a good thing for a serious novelist. What is he trying to prove? What does he want? He doesn't even write journalism or instant history. He has had a few grants, and back in 1957 they gave him the National Book Award for *The Field of Vision.* Of course, as serious as he is, he's never hit it with a real best seller. But even that can be arranged. The publishing houses are full of bright young editors with all kinds of ideas. If it's money he's after, there's money, at least enough for all the good guys, the reliable ones, to have a piece of the action. You do have to be cool, clean, discreet, keep your ear to the ground, and above all be patient, though. Morris won't stand in line. He can't stand still. Take a look at the checklist of his published books. Note how he goes from publisher to publisher. Whatever else that may mean, it's a sure sign of a troublemaker, an agitator. Maybe even a sore loser. And all the time he keeps writing these books. He comes from Nebraska, a rube, and maybe nobody told him the novel is dead and art is for kids.

All that activity is embarrassing. For one thing, it makes it tough on the critics. They have a hard time keeping up anyway. So many books are published every year. Mostly trash, of course, that you can skim or ignore. Even a real *reader* like Granville Hicks can't begin to deal with them all, as he is the first one to admit. The big trouble with Wright Morris is that he keeps writing and changing. You can't get a line on him. He won't stand there and let them put a name tag on his lapel. By now, already, he has worked up a regular *canon,* just like a decently dead writer. And still he keeps on. It's some kind of a compulsion or something, the kind of thing that can ruin a man's reputation.

On top of which the books, all of them, aren't exactly easy reading. He couldn't turn out some light summer reading if his life depended on it. He can be funny, sure. In fact he is one of the funniest writers around. But there is some kind of an edge to all his jokes. He can go for the gag line with the very best of them, and you can't help laughing. Then later on you may get the suspicion that the joke is partly on you, too. Just when you think you have somebody or something to *laugh at,* he comes along and spoils everything by making you wonder, *think* even, why you are laughing. He has the same problem with his plots and characters. Things start out comfortably enough, even though he likes to play around with time and point of view and won't put it all down *straight,* and he can be as neatly and tightly schematic as you please. Then just when you settle down to relax and let it all happen the way it usually does, he has to get cute. Blink a couple of times, rub your eyes, and next thing you know you can't tell the good guys from the bad ones. Morris is no *New Yorker* writer. It is like he wanted to disturb the peace.

Think of it. What a thing, to step out into the light and bow politely, holding an ordinary deck of cards, riffling and shuffling and then all of a sudden for no reason at all the cards turn into marvelous brilliant birds flying off and away in every which direction. That's not a trick. There is no trick to it. It is purely and simply magic.

Which is why so many people, professed readers of good books, haven't read much Wright Morris. And which is why the critics, for the most part, have chosen to ignore him. It is ever so much easier to write about the mythopoeic world of, say, Reynolds Price.

And there are many other things going against him as well. For example, there is the fact that even though his novels are individual and separate, they are also built upon each other, as intricately and subtly related in their own way as Faulkner's. In one sense more so. In *After Alienation: American Novels in Mid-Century* Marcus Klein points this out, indicates how it works up through *Cause for Wonder* (1963). Sometimes it is an explicit relationship of place or character in directly linked novels like *The Field of Vision* and *Ceremony in Lone Tree.* Sometimes there is a variation, another *version* of place, character, or event, and in this sense all the books and stories become complex variations. The result is that the books keep getting better. The more you read and follow the design, the better, richer they get. Very self-conscious, someone might say. Besides which he is a frankly *literary* writer. He not only admits to having read a book or so and, when it suits him, alludes to same, but also he uses his reading in an odd allusive way to give more dimension to the story at hand. It's all right, of course, to use the old standards—the classics and the myths, the Bible, Shakespeare etc.—but what about a modern writer who uses *The Sun Also Rises* or *The Great Gatsby* or *Finnegans Wake* quite openly as grist for his mill. He is not often exotic and esoteric in the functional use of this device. The books and stories he echoes and uses are, after all, all books and stories that we have read, or anyway ones we are supposed to have read.

Not that he sees those books exactly as everyone else does. Not that he reads and criticizes by consensus. Back in 1958 he decided to do some talking himself, and he put together a book of criticism—*The Territory Ahead.* It seems to have baffled a good number of people. Instead of the conventional and acceptable pitch about how tough it is to stand in the huge shadow of the Masters, he seemed to go out of his way to point out their flaws, faults, and failures as he saw them. He dealt with a good many writers, principally with Thoreau, Whitman, Melville, Twain, James, Hemingway, Wolfe, Fitzgerald and Faulkner, and these artists were treated as intelligent, sentient, dedicated, and responsible men. They got full credit and with it full responsibility. He did not concern himself much with the role and function of the critic, except to demonstrate it gracefully. He did not address himself directly to the critics. He spoke more to that probably extinct breed—the intelligent reader. He did not even use the usual jargon of contemporary criticism, let alone the respectable conventions of manner and method. He used his own language and words, words which, in fact, show up in his fiction, so that *The Territory Ahead* has to be taken as part of his whole body of work too.

Those who troubled to read *The Territory Ahead* seemed to get two or three notions out of it. Morris seemed to be against a kind of backward looking and dreaming that, he said, has possessed American writers from the beginning, a characteristic he incorporated under the label of Nostalgia. He also seemed to indicate that there has been a little too much unrefined, unprocessed experience, "raw material," and not enough art and technique in the American novel. And he was obviously annoyed by the prevalence of clichés. Aren't we all? Find a writer or critic who is willing to come on strong in favor of bigger and better clichés. Like Calvin Coolidge's preacher, they are all against the cliché.

What people missed in *The Territory Ahead* is quite a lot. One of these days a clever young critic on the make or the ascendancy will glance back at that book and notice the *prophetic* quality. He will see how well it predicts and describes the direction that much American fiction has indeed taken in the past decade. Somebody also may notice that the book is really about a kind of *balance*, about holding opposites in your hands at the same time. That he isn't just against something as natural as the urge and need for Nostalgia, but that he doesn't see any future or virtue in an *art* based solely on doing what comes naturally. Someone will observe that he isn't just *against* the cliché in the abstract, in general. He wants something else. He wants to know what the big and little clichés are, to identify and name them, and finally to *use* them, to transform them into something else by means of intelligence and imagination. An alchemy of the cliché. It may be seen that he is not attacking the past, but instead is talking about the present and the future in the sure and certain hope that both exist too and matter. But above all Morris pleads a case for an art of the deeply involved imagination, for intelligence, technique and conceptual power as absolutely essential to any truly living imagination. What he is against are all the easy ways out, all the artistic cop-outs. Just when practically everybody, assured of certain certainties, was ready to settle down and wait for the death of the novel, just when many a working novelist found himself almost enjoying the genteel pleasures of twilight and demise, along came Wright Morris saying that we have only just begun, demanding more, not less, of every artist. Considered this way, *The Territory Ahead* is a literary offense, a book of hard sayings.

Other things that seem to have hurt Wright Morris' chances? (Never mind, for the moment, that his bold assault on the dwarf and giant clichés of our life and art has led to the exposure of the heart of phonus balonus in much that is dear. Many a sacred cow has been shown to be a creature of plywood, plastic, and epoxy. Never mind, for the moment, that much of what Morris has to show and tell must surely annoy all kinds of people, especially the professional *sages* of the times, who put their hats over their hearts every time a cliché marches by.) A big fault, Morris won't stay put in any *decade.* Starting out when he did, he is supposed to be a Writer of the Forties. Maybe, looking back, we could allow him a slot in the fifties. But the sixties? By continuing to create, by writing here and now at the peak of his energy and power, Morris thumbs his nose at one of the most sacrosanct and convenient clichés of contemporary literary history—the Decade. You would think that, if nothing else, the normal wear and tear, the adversity, the relative public neglect and indifference to all that he has done, would have slowed him down a little.

And then there is the undeniable fact that he has so much talent, such great and various gifts. He has a superb ear, none better. It is exact, right, and surprising. He has a trained eye. Which is not surprising, for he is a first-rate photographer and in two books, *The Inhabitants* (1946) and *The Home Place* (1948), he used his photographs integrally with the text. As a photographer he knows, no doubt, the frustrations of that art, so well expressed by Cartier-Bresson in *The Decisive Moment:* "We photographers deal in things which are continually vanishing, and when they have vanished, there is no contrivance on earth which can make them come back again. We cannot develop and print a memory." Except, of course, in a novel. Morris has always shown a rich and various power of close observation, a memory for detail. His fiction is full of *things,* not just the names, but the look, feel, and texture of them. The surface is dazzling. In view of which his emphasis in *The Territory Ahead* on the necessity of overcoming the tyranny of raw material and memory is important. Unlike the imagemaker, he is not trying to disguise a weakness. He is trying to train and control a powerful strength.

Using that strength and his talent, he could easily have gone a long, long way, maybe a much easier way, and nobody would have noticed the difference. But Morris has other things he can do very well, too. He can create characters of all kinds, shapes and descriptions, young and old, men and women, lots of them; and having created them he can keep them alive and kicking. He stays with his characters, letting them have time and space to grow, change, become until finally the best of them are suddenly all there, as solid and three-dimensional as bronze figures. And like great sculpture they are finally and forever mysterious. They appear first of all as people do in life (and art), veiled in familiar and gauzy clichés. Morris gets the music going, and they start to dance and peel the veils away and down to skin and bones. When the striptease is over, we see human nakedness, but it is a nakedness infinitely more mysterious and beautiful than any veiled figure. Only a very few of our writers have ever been able to create characters like that. It is commonplace, easy enough, and often just right for the modern reader to have a character stripped in scorn and exposed in shame. Morris has great compassion for his characters. He gets it without permitting himself or the reader one faint whiff of sentimentality. Which may be defined as the bogus gesture, the cold comfort, of allowing the reader to try on a character's ill-fitting shoes for size. He gets it, too, by being a master of every aspect of *point of view.* Which really means that no matter who is telling the story or how he is telling it, you don't cheat. When you are with a character that's where you are.

A lot of writers can write pretty well. Fewer by far, but still a fair number, live long enough and learn enough to be able to create some real characters. And then there are a very, very few, the great ones, who have taken one more step. They take story or plot, or whatever you please to call the *fable* of fiction, and they make it mean something in and of itself. Not say something. It is easy enough to say things and write messages. De Mille (or was it Sam Goldwyn, Sr.?) was right. Western Union is the medium for messages. To mean something is something else.

The structure of a fiction becomes a world, a meaningful and deeply mysterious pattern, and in that sense it can become, however small and broken by comparison, a creation mirroring the Creation. Morris has come this far. He does it in the individual book. He has done it and is doing it, intricately, when you consider the design of his whole work. Of course this has great risks too. In general this abstract and probably arbitrary scheme of a writer's development—from words to characters to the pattern—can be attended by a diminishing of interest in (and thus ability with) the primary stages. The earlier qualities are refined away, and we expect this to happen, believing, as we do, that growth is as much loss as gain. Somehow (by magic again?) Wright Morris has managed to keep all three qualities alive at once, in suspension, in near perfect balance. And this puts him up at the very top where the air is thin and where a man and his work can be judged by the highest standards we know of, past or present. When he writes a book and it is published we who profess and call ourselves readers had better read it.

"After some time she said, 'You ever feel you're in a friggin movie? You ever stand up in a movie and tell the friggin hero which way to run?'
'That's right, Daughter, and this is the movie.'
'The friggin moonlight made me think of it,' she said. And that was all."
—Ceremony in Lone Tree

The brute, flashing, shifty facts of the American present. Told mostly, except for brief memories and recollection here and there, in the present tense. And working fast, in a brief span of condensed time, the time of a day, as in the larger and more expansive novel which immediately precedes this one—*One Day. One Day* dealt with a day in the nutty California community of Escondido, a wild and woolly day for the restless natives, a day on which, almost as a by the way, the president of the United States was killed in Dallas, Texas. *One Day* is a tough book, because, since Morris wrote it, he doesn't have to and won't remind the reader of the national pathos of that day. He can and does take for granted the elegiac mode. He sticks to his characters, their zany, absurd, boloxed up personal tragi-comedy. He is fearless even of the cliché reactions to the assassination, and he is fearless of satirizing the clichés of the human means toward worthy goals, such as Civil Rights. *One Day* and *In Orbit* are very closely related, in general and in details. *In Orbit* tells of one memorable day in the town of Pickett, Indiana. It's the day when a twister roared through town raising all kinds of hell. It is also the day on which a kind of human tornado, Jubal Gainer, wearing a crash helmet and a J.S. Bach sweatshirt, came barrelling in from Olney County on a stolen Suzuki and ran out of gas. He hits town, it *seems,* like the twister, like a plague. He is involved in a rape (of sorts), an assault (of an odd kind), an ambiguous robbery and stabbing, a brief "reign of terror," and before he can get out of town and on his way to nowhere in particular again, he and the twister meet and he takes a ride on the wind. All the principal characters, an odd and entertaining bunch, survive, and in a curious way get what they deserve or wish for. In what happens and in the way it is told, the main line of the story is comic, then. People get clobbered by the twister, all right. There is plenty of damage. But not Jubal or the principals. Not anybody we *know.* They have their own wounds and troubles, but they are still alive, living with them, at the end. As the distant murder in *One Day* can be taken for granted, so also the twister, no joke, can be *assumed,* but not forgotten.

If Marcus Klein is right—and I am not at all sure he is, or, better, that it is all as neat and schematic as he makes it—the arrival of Morris on the *present* scene was "signaled by *Love Among the Cannibals*" (1957). He can cite the authority of the author in any case, Morris' statement in a published interview (Sam Bluefarb, "Point of View: An Interview with Wright Morris, July, 1958," *Accent,* XIX, Winter, 1959). There Morris said: "The *Cannibals* is the first book in which the past does not exist. We begin with the present, we live in the present, and it is an effort to come to terms with the present, in terms of only the present." True enough for that swinging story of two Hollywood song writers and their girl friends; except that, even there, there is an implied past. From then on the main interest and surface of the stories may be the present, but always Morris is careful to give his places and his people a past which is at least present to them. It can be extensive in a large novel like *One Day,* or it can be beautifully sketched without interruption of the forward rush of a tight story like *In Orbit.* There are as many pasts as there are people, characters, and places. And in just the same way there are as many varied *present* times. But all those become part of two not distinct, but related histories, layers of time, the history of the land, America, and the cumulative history of the work of Wright Morris. The day of the twister, the day when Jubal Gainer, looking like some kind of a spaceman and taken for one, too, by those who have the luck to encounter him, hits Pickett, Indiana, also the day in which the Beatles movie *Help!* is playing, is the day when an historic elm (a lone tree) is cut down:

> Through the window, shaded by an awning, he observes the day's major event: the felling of an historic campus elm. Small fry stand in a circle anxious to be hit by falling branches. A rising wind sways the branch supporting the man with the saw. This elm is special. It is known to have been there when the Indians scalped the first settlers, hardy stubborn men who worked like slaves to deprive their children of all simple pleasures, and most reasons to live.

The American past is there and except for Jubal and the chance of the twister, the cutting down of the elm would very likely have to be "the day's major event."

The past of Wright Morris' novels, the cumulative family history of his work, is very much present in the present of this book. It is also very complicated to talk about in detail, like trying to explain a joke to a humorless inquisitor. But it can be suggested with examples. *Item:* in *One Day* Alec Cartwright, a free-swinging, freedom-riding chick who opens the events of the day by leaving her mulatto baby in the Arrivals slot at the animal pound, wears a Brahms sweatshirt. Jubal Gainer wears Bach, alike but different, as Kashperl, who runs the army surplus store in Pickett, is quick to note: "Best-sellers all, but here in Pickett, Brahms edges Bach, thanks to his beard." Evelina Cartwright, Alec's mother, loves and pampers cats. So does Charlotte Hatfield, the faculty wife, in *In Orbit.* That biracial baby: well, Jubal Gainer *appears* to be an odd mixture of races, thanks to a cigar butt and stove paint job done on him by an erstwhile buddy.

> The helmet framed in the window seems to have no face. An amber visor screens the eyes, out of the shadow a nose slowly emerges. Is it of pewter? The color is fading around the wide mouth. It is like nothing Haffner has ever seen, but it does not go beyond what he has often imagined. A white man emerging from a black man, or the two in one. A man who makes the most, or is it the least, of a color-fast situation. Better yet, a man whose colors, madras-style, are guaranteed to bleed. Haffner can only laugh: he laughs in the boy's dark two-toned face.

They are trying to *save* redwoods in the Escondido of *One Day* with the SPARE THAT TREE CLUB; they are cutting down the campus elm in *In Orbit.* People imagine headlines to cover events in both books:

> (a) *One Day:*
> INFANT LEFT AT POUND
> Prankster Suspected
>
> (b) *In Orbit:*
> VISITING SPACEMAN
> ASSAULTS
> HOLLY STOHRMEYER

When an ice machine goes berserk in *One Day* and Evelina Cartwright's car rolls away down a hill, Evelina races after it, calling the car to come back. Here is Haffner of *In Orbit:* "Not infrequently Haffner will forget about the handbrake and the car will idle down the street, Haffner trailing, calling aloud *Here! Here!* as if to some unleased pet." After all the disasters of the day in Escondido, the Fuzz, represented by Sheriff

McNamara, is mostly worried about *what else* is going to happen. The Fuzz in Pickett appears in the form of Sheriff Cantrill. "He doesn't smile. It is clear that the events of the day are beginning to weigh on Sheriff Cantrill. Particularly the events that have not yet occurred." There are dozens of such parallels between the two books. They are not accidental.

If *One Day* and *In Orbit* are close kin, we have to recognize that, exactly in the same way, *One Day* and *In Orbit* incorporate a variety of bits and pieces from all of Morris' work so far. Again some simple examples will have to do. Italy and Greece (*What a Way to Go,* 1962) are important to a greater or lesser extent, used or alluded to in both novels. So is Austria (*Cause for Wonder,* 1963). So is the Mexico of several past novels, evoked at considerable length in *One Day,* swiftly handled in *In Orbit* during an inventory of the extraordinary contents of Haffner's pockets, at the top: "The first item proves to be a snuffbox made of horn, stamped *Hecho en Mexico.*" Alan and Charlotte Hatfield recall with nostalgia, and in a way reminiscent of *Love Among the Cannibals,* the beaches of the west coast. And so it goes. It can be a matter of vocabulary. Characters keep thinking *what next?,* which was not only a recurring question but also a song title in *Love Among the Cannibals.* The movies and movie stars, the way people are *like* some movie star, the way events are *just like the movies,* are significant *motifs* in these novels. "Key" words, sparingly used, leap off the pages in *In Orbit.* Example: "Avery speaks eagerly but a little hoarsely: the disaster has aroused his *nostalgia*" (italics mine). And isn't Jubal's crash helmet very much the same as that of young Lee Roy Momeyer in *Ceremony in Lone Tree?* Miscellaneous and random examples. They could be multiplied many times. The point is quite simply that they are functional in a very special way. They do more than just "link" the works of Wright Morris together. They allude to and evoke the *past* of those works, to the extent that the reader is familiar with them. But turn it around another way. They give a sense of all the novels progressing forward, too, building to the latest. Which in this case is *In Orbit. In Orbit* will no doubt dissolve into the next book, carrying the whole evolution forward again.

What is happening, in a sense, and we can sense it happening, is a grand and total *design,* complex and organic, built upon "real" history and literary history and the history and experience of his own work. It is, by now, a very large design, and it is more a gesture of honest self-appraisal than bravado when Morris suddenly and briefly alludes to *Finnegans Wake* (discussed brilliantly in *The Territory Ahead*) near the end of *In Orbit.* This grand design is like other ambitious literary designs of the past, yet different. He uses all the conventions and methods we know of to keep his work together as a whole, but the effect is completely his own. His hand of cards is once and for all his own. It hasn't been dealt before, and the same hand will never be dealt out exactly again.

What he seeks lies just beyond the flickering, rain-screened beam of the car lights, the twilight zone that is neither light nor dark. In this light some things are seen at their best. Such light as they have they seem to give out.

—*In Orbit*

In *In Orbit,* in and of itself, the relationships between events, people, and things are as close and complex, as similar and different, as the suggested quality inherent in all of Morris' work. The words are there, the always interesting and well-realized characters are there, but the *design* is crucially important and superbly achieved. Every *thing* comes to work for the design. For as widely different and separate as the characters are, and quite unbeknownst to each other, they keep seeing and feeling and experiencing the same things, and not just in "fact" but in imagination. They make the same metaphors and similes, same and different. They live through the same weather, one and all. Their separation from each other, the fragmentary character of their individual lives, is heightened by a virtuoso exercise in rapidly shifting point of view. The principal characters all see different things and reflect upon them and are forever unable, it would seem, to communicate these things and reflections to each other. Yet they all *share* a common experience, in general and in close detail. All things, all events, become symbols then, by a process of cumulative association. One thinks, for analogy, of Malcolm Lowry's *Under the Volcano.* And then one realizes that Morris has achieved a similar effect in a very short novel.

There is a difference. He carries it a step beyond; he wants something else. Lowry did it in terms of a single tortured consciousness known in depth. Morris does the same thing using half a dozen points of view, all seen briefly, swiftly. Ordinarily, and we all know it, this method is used to demonstrate what we cannot know. The cliché of the method is that the reports of many witnesses establish that there is no design, no "truth." Yet each of these witnesses does in fact and within the context and confines of his or her very specific limitations, faults, and hangups, see the same thing without knowing it. Who knows it, then? The reader does. The reader has all the pieces. The reader is therefore privileged to be aware of the outlines of the design, though the Design it reflects, the Creation, remains enigmatic, beyond simple answers. It is a glimpse of the working out of that ineffable Design in time, a flashing view of what was once called Providence. Chance is terribly urgent, but Chance (like Dame Fortune of old) is part of the Design. When all things come together, as they do, we the readers discover that the characters are not so different as they dream they are and they wish to be. In a profound sense, in spite of rape, stabbing, violence, and a terrible twister, *In Orbit* is a human comedy. A black comedy? Not quite. It's more like the boy, Jubal Gainer himself, with his madras face. He didn't *mean* anything. But—"As luck would have it"—fleeing the draft, his past, lunging into an unknown future on a stolen motorcycle, he happened to hit the town of Pickett and to run out of gas, happened to run into enough eccentrics and mischief to last a man a lifetime, happened to get lifted into literal orbit by a twister he didn't see coming from behind him, and in the end is back on the road, gassed up, and rolling. . . well, *somewhere.* Looking much as he did before; described in fact in the same terms and with the same analogies. With a difference.

> On his chest J.S. Bach dries in a manner that enlarges his forehead, curves his lips in a smile. Is that for what looms up ahead, or lies behind? This boy is like a diver who has gone too deep and too long without air. If the army is no place for a growing boy, neither is the world. . . . There is no place to hide. But perhaps the important detail escapes you. He is in motion. Now you see him, now you don't. If you pin him down in time he is lost in space. Somewhere between where he is from and where he is going he wheels in an unpredictable orbit. He is as free, and as captive, as the wind in his face.

Morris has created, with elegant precision, control, and condensation, a comedy of doom and destiny. The wounds of comedy are real enough, but laughter helps to ease the pain. Nobody we have around could have done this book. It took a lifetime and twenty-five years of professional writing to do it. *In Orbit* makes the image-makers look like what they are—bush league. It makes the novel seem brand new again. It ought to make those who are trying to write novels and those who are trying to read them happy. Like Jubal we've got something to look forward to. Unlike Jubal we know that whatever it is it will be good. Meanwhile here in *In Orbit* we have as much of the magic, as much of the joy of art as we could ask for.

AFTERWORD

Following *In Orbit* came an extraordinary book by Wright Morris—*A Bill of Rites, A Bill of Wrongs, A Bill of Goods.* Fifteen closely-related essays on the perplexities and absurdity of the here and now, put together, *constructed* as Morris at the peak of his powers puts a novel together, the same devices, large and small, working in consort together to create a cumulative effect; the same dazzling ability to keep mixed and complex feelings alive, by the power of intelligence and the eloquence of art; the same result of savage honesty, of open-minded energy.

It is a remarkable book, demanding of the reader not cleverness, but care; not selling yet another bill of goods, but daring the reader to test his own fragile certainties in a trial by ordeal.

It is rather common these days for poets and novelists to turn their sensible attention to the areas, the manner and matter, once reserved for "non-fiction." At worst they produce inferior journalism. Or, perhaps, the grand and frozen gestures of the sage descending from the mountain top to tell us all. And those few who have managed some degree of excellence seem to have done so at the expense of their other work, which, weighed against the separate achievement, seems somehow shabby and inadequate.

This is not the case with Wright Morris. Just as with *The Territory Ahead, A Bill of Rites* has a place in the whole of his work, grows naturally out of his work in fiction. All is changed and altered slightly; for being an artist and involved in the energy and change which we name Creation, he will not stand still this side of *rigor mortis.* All is changed, yet nothing, neither the matter nor its essential energy is lost.

All of which adds up to something so extraordinary that we ought to celebrate. In his new book Morris has demonstrated (again) that a man, an artist, can intelligently, rigorously deal with the mixed feelings of a shattered time without settling for the simplistic, without accepting self-division as inevitable, without joining the chorus of salesmen and telling lies in the name of the presumed truth. His achievement here, as in the sum of his novels, seems to me unique, yet at the same time exemplary.

It is ironic, but not surprising that this new book received, relatively, very little attention from reviewers and that, when reviewed, it offended and confused them. The more subtle and clever were, of course, proportionately the more annoyed.

The new book is important in and of itself, a true report and record of the times. In a larger sense it is an important addition to the lifetime labors of a great writer. The final twist, the best irony, is that it *cannot* be ignored.

My essay on *In Orbit* was inadequate from the start. A slight appreciation of something wonderful. It is a pleasure to admit that, though. Faced for once with the real thing, the rare thing, the critic has the privilege of standing at attention, offering a salute, and, for once, meaning it.

At the moment of this writing (November 1968) there has just appeared a beautiful book by Morris in the genre he has named "Photo-Text"—*God's Country and My People* (Harper & Row). Returning to the method he earlier used in *The Inhabitants* and *The Home Place,* but on a grander scale and with the advantage of an elegant format and reproduction, he has combined his own photographs and text to present a coherent aesthetic experience.

As one might expect, Morris understands as well as any man alive the proper relation of the word to the photographic image, that is the *dif-*

ference between the two. He does not subordinate text to image as, for example, by making text mere expository caption or comment on the presented photograph. Nor is the photograph used to "illustrate" the text. Rather, separate and equal, they relate to and react to each other in such a way that the sum of the two is more than its parts. The cumulative effect of this living relationship, this wedding of distinct expressive forms, is that once the reader-observer's imagination, awakened, has become engaged, it is impossible any more to imagine the one without the other.

This is, then *multi-art,* not mere "multi-media," and a natural, seemingly inevitable outgrowth of his whole lifetime of work, directly related to all his work.

Though a marvelously-executed print, almost an abstraction of roots and dry soil (it almost *might* be a contoured aerial view from a receding moon-bound rocket), has the last word, the last *words,* even out of context, form an impeccable conclusion: "Our talent is still for dreaming, and our recurrent dream is flight: a few hours away the luminous fueling stop of the moon. House or ark, sea or plain, shimmering mirages or figures of earth, God's country is still a fiction inhabited by people with a love for the facts."

Facts and fiction, taken together until the two become one. And the name of that one is art.

ABOUT WRIGHT MORRIS

Wright Morris spent the first ten years of his life in "whistle stops along the Platte Valley." His books, he believes, are apt to bear the stamp of "an object made on the plains." Although he is not a regional writer, the characteristics of this area of the country have conditioned what he sees and how he expresses himself. Hence the arrangement of a minimum number of words for the maximum effect which is so typical of his style.

In commenting on his approach to literature and symbology, Morris has said: "Objects, what few there are on the plains, acquire a dense symbolical significance, and certain simple artifacts have a functional and classic purity. The windmill, the single plow, and the grain elevator are both signs and symbols at the same time. They speak for themselves. They would rather talk than be talked about. The man who loves these things, whether he knows it or not, is a photographer" (*Twentieth Century Authors,* First Supplement, p. 692). Morris knows what he speaks about: his prose has a photographic clarity, and he has also successfully experimented with the art of photography. A number of his books include photographs.

Morris has held Guggenheim fellowships on three occasions—in 1942, 1946, and 1954. He won the National Book Award for *The Field of Vision* (1957). In 1960 he was awarded the National Institute Grant in Literature and later received a second grant from the Rockefeller Foundation.

He has lectured at Haverford, Sarah Lawrence, Swarthmore, and other colleges and universities. Morris is currently a member of the faculty of San Francisco State College where he lectures on the novel and teaches creative writing.

BOOKS BY WRIGHT MORRIS

MY UNCLE DUDLEY
New York: Harcourt, Brace, 1942.
Toronto: McLeod, 1942.

THE MAN WHO WAS THERE
New York: Scribner's, 1945.
Toronto: S.J. Reginald Saunders, 1945.

INHABITANTS
New York: Scribner's, 1946.

HOME PLACE
New York: Scribner's, 1948.
Toronto: S.J. Reginald Saunders, 1948.
Lincoln: University of Nebraska, 1968. (pb)

THE WORLD IN THE ATTIC
New York: Scribner's, 1949.
Toronto: S.J. Reginald Saunders, 1949.

MAN AND BOY
New York: Knopf, 1951.
London: Gollancz, 1952.
Toronto: McClelland, 1952.

THE WORK OF LOVE
New York: Knopf, 1952.
Toronto: McClelland, 1952.

THE DEEP SLEEP
New York: Scribner's, 1953.
Toronto: S.J. Reginald Saunders, 1953.
London: Eyre & Spottiswoode, 1954.

THE HUGE SEASON
New York: Viking, 1954.
London: Secker & Warburg, 1955.
New York: Pyramid, 1969. (pb)

THE FIELD OF VISION
New York: Harcourt, Brace, 1956.
New York: New American Library, 1957. (pb)
Toronto: McLeod, 1956.
London: Weidenfeld & Nicolson, 1957.

LOVE AMONG THE CANNIBALS
New York: Harcourt, Brace, 1957.
London: Weidenfeld & Nicolson, 1958.
Toronto: Longmans, Green, 1958.
New York: New American Library, 1958. (pb)

THE TERRITORY AHEAD
New York: Harcourt, Brace, 1958.

Toronto: Longmans, Green, 1958.
New York: Atheneum, 1963. (pb)
Toronto: McClelland, 1963. (pb)
Gloucester, Mass.: Peter Smith, 1964.

CEREMONY IN LONE TREE
New York: Atheneum, 1960.
London: Weidenfeld & Nicolson, 1961.
New York: New American Library, 1961. (pb)

THE MISSISSIPPI RIVER READER (ed.)
New York: Doubleday-Anchor, 1962. (pb)

WHAT A WAY TO GO
New York: Atheneum, 1962.
Toronto: McClelland, 1962.

CAUSE FOR WONDER
New York: Atheneum, 1963.
Toronto: McClelland, 1963.

ONE DAY
New York: Atheneum, 1965.

IN ORBIT
New York: New American Library, 1967.
New York: Ballantine, 1968. (pb)

A BILL OF RITES, A BILL OF WRONGS, A BILL OF GOODS
New York: New American Library, 1968.

GOD'S COUNTRY AND MY PEOPLE
New York: Harper & Row, 1968.

WRIGHT MORRIS: A READER
New York: Harper & Row, 1970.

Toward an Existential Realism: The Novels of Colin Wilson

by R.H.W. Dillard

We fight not for ourselves but for growth, growth that goes on forever. To-morrow, whether we live or die, growth will conquer through us. That is the law of the spirit for evermore.

—H.G. Wells, The Food of the Gods

There is no need to recount the literary career of Colin Wilson. It follows an all too familiar pattern and unfortunately has a great many counterparts: the encomiums of praise and delight upon the publication of a writer's first book and the quick critical turnabout when a second book is released. The exceptions are few today, and the damage is severe. A young writer has fame thrust upon him and snatched away before he has assimilated it and adjusted to it; too many writers never recover from the shock. And if a writer keeps working, his readers still suffer, for once he has been dismissed by the critical press, his later books are seldom even mentioned; he becomes an invisible man. Like Melville, he may be "discovered" much later, but only after he has been lost to his contemporaries who simply have no way of knowing what he is doing and writing.

Colin Wilson's example is, of course, more exaggerated than most. His first book, *The Outsider,* published in 1956 when he was twenty-four, was an amazing critical and popular success. One critic wrote that "Not since Lord Byron woke up one morning and found himself famous has an English writer met with such spontaneous and universal acclaim." When his second book, *Religion and the Rebel,* appeared the following year, it was as universally condemned. The eighteen books which followed over the last ten years have received a small and varied response, but on the whole they have been more ignored than attacked or praised. To the great majority of the reading public, Colin Wilson has become, at thirty-five, a finished man, remembered only for his early success and not for his work which has continued beyond that success and despite its attendant critical reverse.

The publication in England of Wilson's seventh novel, *The Mind Parasites,* last spring roused, however, a revival of critical interest. Hilary Corke announced in *The Listener* that it was time the literary world stopped ignoring Colin Wilson, and Robert Nye, in *The Guardian,* called Wilson "one of the most earnest and interesting writers of his generation." In this country *The Mind Parasites* was published in July by Arkham House, the small publishing house in Sauk City, Wisconsin, founded by August Derleth to print the works of H.P. Lovecraft and other books in the Lovecraft tradition. Since the tiny advertising budget of such a small firm and the force of critical inertia will probably preclude much serious mention of the novel in the American press, I should like here to greet its appearance and to discuss Wilson's novels and his development as a novelist of independence and real ability.

Of course Colin Wilson thinks of himself primarily as a philosopher, and the bulk of his writing has been critical and philosophical, from *The Outsider* to his most recent *Introduction to the New Existentialism*, although his "Outsider Cycle" (*The Outsider, Religion and the Rebel, The Age of Defeat, The Strength to Dream, The Origins of the Sexual Impulse, Beyond the Outsider*) is a sustained attempt to define a new synthesis of evolutionary humanism and phenomenological existentialism, he is no systematic philosopher. He is rather a man thinking through his ideas in print, a philosopher who feels, to use Emerson's description of the wise writer, "that the ends of study and composition are best answered by announcing undiscovered regions of thought, and so communicating, through hope, new activity to the torpid spirit."

Like Emerson, he sees man as "a god in ruins" who must only be awakened in order to fulfill his godly potential, but because he is "Anglo-Saxon and empirical" by nature and heritage, his is a more specifically rational philosophy than Emerson's, depending more upon the analytical faculty than creative intuition. By phenomenological analysis, he argues, man can capture and extend moments of vision (like Nietzsche's on the hilltop in the storm or the mystic's vision of unity with God), can expand human consciousness, and can chart "a geography" of "the world of the inner mind." As he fulfills his own identity, he will also find himself part of a larger identity, life itself; he will be able to attune himself fully "to purpose and evolution." Perhaps the clearest statement of his aims is this brief account in the *Introduction to the New Existentialism:*

> The "new existentialism" accepts man's experience of his inner freedom as basic and irreducible. Our lives consist of a clash between two visions: our vision of this inner freedom, and our vision of contingency; our intuition of freedom and power, and our everyday feeling of limitation and boredom. The problem cannot be reduced to simpler terms. The "new existentialism" concentrates the full battery of phenomenological analysis upon the everyday sense of contingency, upon the problem of "life-devaluation." This analysis helps to reveal how the spirit of freedom is trapped and de-

stroyed; it uncovers the complexities and safety devices in which freedom dissipates itself. It suggests mental disciplines through which this waste of freedom can be averted.

His is an attempt to satisfy man's absolute need for religion with a rational understanding of his own nature. His method is one of synthesis, a bringing together of science and art, of reason and imagination. He is striving to reach a new synthesis of the ideas of William James, Husserl, Wittgenstein and Whitehead on the one hand, and Blake, Dostoevski, Wells, and Shaw on the other. It is a bold attempt, and it is not my place to evaluate it here. What does interest and concern me is that more and more, like his direct literary forebears Wells and Shaw, he has discovered the limitations of exposition and is turning to art rather than philosophy to shape and transmit his ideas and belief—a shift similar to his earlier turning from science to philosophy. He has recognized, as he puts it in the postscript to the new edition of *The Outsider,* that "There are things that can be said in a work of fiction that are unsayable in a work of philosophy," and although he has by no means abandoned his philosophical writing, he has turned strongly to fiction (and drama) to bring his ideas artistically alive.

"What I would like to do," Wilson said in a preface to one of his novels, "—what I feel it will one day be possible to do—is to write a white dwarf of a book, a book that is so dense that it can be read fifty times. Not a book of ideas, in the sense that my *Outsider* is a book of ideas, but a book that deals with life with the same directness that we are compelled to live it." His novels show him to be searching for a form, a proper metaphor, a true hero to give his ideas the directness of life. And the direction of his search has been toward more imaginative and artificial means which convey truth by effect more than by statement, by art more than by philosophy. Of his seven novels, the first three use the traditional form and methods of psychological realism, the fourth breaks out of those strictures by exploiting the freedom of the diary form, and the three most recent use openly artificial popular forms (detective and science fiction) to develop metaphoric and parabolic novels of vital imagination, of what Wilson calls "existential realism."

The creation of a hero has progressed as steadily as the search for a proper form. The thesis of *The Outsider* is "that religion begins with the stimulus which heroism supplies to the imagination," so that the hero is essential to the religious intensity necessary to evolutionary purposiveness. He is a hero detached by the condition of a complex and possibly dying civilization from the social and political problems of that civilization. As a part of an evolutionary vanguard, he must strive for essential power and disregard temporal power; he serves a saintly function by awakening us to our true selves by persuasion and example. He is a personification of the vision of inner freedom, of human possibility as Wilson describes it in the *Introduction to the New Existentialism:*

> He has glimpses of a joy that is beyond anything possible to the born coward: the ecstasy of power and freedom. He knows about the miseries and insecurities of human existence, about weakness and contingency. But he does not believe in them, since he is certain that freedom is an absolute power. He knows that man is only subject to pain and misery insofar as he allows himself to be dominated by the coward, and that most human misfortune is another name for stupidity and self-pity. Consequently, he is inclined to suspect that even death may be a disguised form of suicide, and that human contingency will prove to be an illusion in the light of ultimate freedom. In short, he is totally the optimist and the adventurer; he cannot believe that human reason, powered by the human will to freedom, can ever encounter insurmountable obstacles.

The hero is any man who can see the "exit" from the human dilemma, and "is capable of making the choice that the insight demands." To create such a hero, to make him artistically plausible, requires a newer and more imaginatively flexible art than that afforded by ordinary realism, so that properly the development of the hero progresses along with Wilson's search for a form; he takes on substance from novel to novel as Wilson searches for metaphors strong enough on which to build heroic novels. All of the novels are concerned with the same basic theme, an awakening and activating of the slumbering god in man, so that to some degree they are repetitive, but they are better seen as variations and developments of a theme, each one growing out of the preceding ones. Together they reveal the steady growth of Wilson's talent and his progressive creation of a viable hero for an existential realism.

Ritual in the Dark (1960), *Adrift in Soho* (1961), and *The World of Violence* (1963; in America: *The Violent World of Hugh Greene*), Colin Wilson's first three novels, are all novels of initiation, of a young man's first painful encounters with experience and reality, and of the heightened awareness he gains from that initiation. They are concerned with the birth, the first real awakening of the hero to his evolutionary purpose. As in most religious initiation rites, the subject of the ritual is primarily passive, acted upon by the experience which will ultimately allow him to act himself in experience. Missing, however, is the wise older man who traditionally guides the youth through the initiation, for Wilson's hero is alone, existentially isolated, able to seek advice from his elders but forced finally and always to discover and decide for himself. The three young initiates in these novels are all thinkers, budding philosophers to whom learning is in great part living; they are involved in understanding, while the more fully developed heroes of the later novels are involved in transforming understanding into action, idea into being.

Gerard Sorme, in *Ritual in the Dark,* is a young man possessed of an incubating vision, but he is not sure of himself so that his moments of vision are matched by feelings of vastation and utter meaninglessness. "There was a futility about physical existence that frightened him," but, as Wilson was to describe it later, he "sits in his room and hurls his mind at the problem of the *negative nature of freedom.*" Gerard is an outsider, a man who has instinctively rejected everyday reality, "feeling that it is somehow boring and unsatisfying, like a hypnotized man eating sawdust under the belief that it is eggs and bacon." He is an outsider with a growing subjectivity, a developing harmony with the life force itself, and his initiation consists primarily of his confrontation with another outsider who is being destroyed by his sense of alienation and frustration. In *Religion and the Rebel,* Wilson described the novel, then in progress, as one "about two Outsiders, one based on Nietzsche, and the other on Jack the Ripper." Gerard, like the young Nietzsche, is on the brink of transforming his alienation into creative awareness; Austin Nunne, like Jack the Ripper, is releasing his frustration in a brutal series of sex murders. Nunne succumbs to and is destroyed by "the insanity of the age," the life-negating despair which convinces modern man too often of the loss of his freedom, while Gerard transcends his sense of limitation, develops an active subjectivity while he makes the living world around him truly his, and expands his consciousness and vision to accept the complexity of experience and being (a continuing epiphany akin to Wordsworth's mystical moment on Westminster Bridge).

The confrontation is a dramatic one, for it takes place in the last weeks of Nunne's freedom and the terror resulting from his fear of that freedom. At first, Gerard sees Nunne as a fellow spirit, a rebel against the pervasive futility of ordinary life, and this belief continues even after Gerard discovers that Nunne is the Whitechapel murderer. But stimulated by his sexual affairs (*loving,* but not really *love* affairs) with Caroline, a young drama student, and her aunt Gertrude, Gerard gains a human insight into and feeling for Nunne and at the same time a sense of superiority to him, for Nunne is not truly a rebel against disorder and meaninglessness, but only a victim of his own belief in disorder and his inability to impose meaning upon experience. But Gerard remains detached despite his new understanding, for he expresses that new vision not by decisive action but by a passive acceptance, a refusal to despair. He has learned from Nunne's failure, but he has not taken part in correcting the wrongs caused by that failure nor the wrongs that gave rise to it. But he has made the first step; he has not given in to complexity, but has rather decided to be of complexity; he does not choose between Gertrude and Caroline but maintains his involvement with both:

> In spite of his tiredness, he felt a curious sense of certainty, of order. It was as if he could see inside himself and watch processes that had been invisible before. There was no longer a desire for simplicity; an accumulation of self-knowledge had made it less important. . . . A curious elation stirred in him, an acceptance of complexity. He stared at his face in the mirror, saying aloud: What do you do now, you stupid old bastard? He grinned at himself, and twitched his nose like a rabbit.

Adrift in Soho picks up the lightness and comic spirit of Gerard's mime in the mirror. In it Harry Preston is initiated into free life and complexity by the bohemians of Soho whose careless lives attract Harry away from the problems of life and ultimately release him again to those problems but with the strength and desire to solve them. He rejects the bohemian way ("For better or worse I am a bourgeois"), but he gains from his experience an insight into himself which frees him for a life larger than the self, an understanding that the future is an extension of his belief in himself, that the future flows from within. He realizes that "there is no such thing as future success. It is either there all the time, or it is non-existent."

The novel is slighter than *Ritual in the Dark,* but it does develop the moral understanding a step further, pressing acceptance toward affirmation:

> It was true that the only thing wrong with the world is human beings. But perhaps one day there would be a new type of human being who would understand that time is the same thing as eternity, that life is a million times more desirable than any man ever realized; that there is no such thing as evil, because the only reality is the power house, the dynamo that drives the world.

Although Harry finds an artist, Ricky Prelati, who approaches the "new type of human being," his real victory is, like Gerard's, the gaining of an insight into possibility, a glimpse of the dynamo. He manages, also, to move beyond acceptance to choice, even if his choice is one of rejection. That rejection is a necessary second step toward action and vocation.

If the dynamo that he sees is essentially Shaw's life force, the idea of the new man is very much H.G. Wells's, as he stated it in such novels as *The Food of the Gods, In the Days of the Comet, Men Like Gods, The Croquet Player,* and *Star Begotten.* It is appropriate, then, that Wilson's third novel, *The World of Violence,* which carries the hero a step closer to the new man, should sound very much in its first half like one of Wells's social novels (*Tono-Bungay* or *The New Machiavelli*). The tone is serious and comic at once, a wry Wellsian tone which is both warmly human and curiously detached and objective. The novel even comes complete with a set of eccentric uncles, each of whom has a distorted but true glimpse of the nature of things and all of whom influence young Hugh Greene in an intellectual and human way:

> My grandfather had died of delirium tremens at the age of forty, and there is a tradition in the family that his uncle. . . was either Jack the Ripper or Peter the Painter (the leader of the Sidney Street Gang). My father's Uncle Sam (of whom I shall write later) was definitely peculiar, but had a talent for making money, so that the family never tried to have him certified. But Uncle Nick had once spent a year in a mental home, after he declared that he was a bird and jumped off the roof.

Springing from a background of madness and violence, however comic it may have been, Hugh Greene, the narrator of the novel and a young mathematical prodigy, becomes obsessed early with violence and the search for pure truth in chaos. Mathematics offers him an intellectual escape from the external violence and chaos, but it cannot free him from the fact of his own human inner darkness. His obsession and the frustration he feels in being able to do nothing about the way things are lead him into a Nietzschean belief in the will to power beyond good and evil, and also into an adolescent attempt to combat senseless violence with a murderous but seemingly purposeful violence of his own. His narrow escape in a scrape with a gang of Teddy boys which ends with his shooting one of his assailants, and his first sexual experiences, and his meeting with a half-witted sex criminal and murderer (modelled after Charley Peace), startle him out of his obsession and enable him to understand the lesson of his mad Uncle Sam who locked himself permanently away in a dark attic in order to "treat directly with God in behalf of my fellow human insects." He learns that to fight violence with more senseless violence is to surrender the real fight with the real problems inherent in and beyond violence, those of man's evolution and his sleeping consciousness. Like Gerard and Harry, he transcends his early intuitions and attitudes in a discovery of vocation, a conviction that he, too, like his Uncle Sam, should take up man's struggle in the presence of God. His way is to aid in the evolution of a new science of man in the universe by thinking and by writing such books as *The Structure of Language* and *Mathematics and Phenomenological Analysis.* Hugh carries the hero from acceptance through new conviction to action, but his action is of description and understanding rather than doing and being. His is still a transitional stage in the development of the hero and the new man.

All three of these novels, then, develop a single initiatory metaphor of human awakening similar to one of Emerson's in "Self-Reliance," a fable "of the sot who was picked up dead-drunk in the street, carried to the duke's house, washed and dressed and laid in the duke's bed, and, on his waking, treated with all obsequious ceremony like the duke, and assured that he had been insane," which "symbolizes so well the state of man, who is in this world a sort of sot, but now and then wakes up, exercises his reason and finds himself a true prince." But the success of the novels rests in great part not on the metaphor but on the details of the narrative, the bits and pieces of color and flavor which are essential to realistic fiction. Wilson's purpose suffers, as he recognized, by the limitations of traditional realism, which suffices as the tool for fashioning novels of awakening but is useless, with its dependence on the present and the known, for the creation of metaphors for the shape of things to come, the world of action beyond the awakening.

Man Without a Shadow (1963; in America: *The Sex Diary of Gerard Sorme*) is Wilson's first attempt to break out of the fetters of realism. Using the form of the philosophical diary and the sex novel, he found the freedom to present his understanding of the life force in an elemental form. "The sexual urge," he has written elsewhere, "particularly in its purer forms, seems to reveal an underlying purpose. In the light of sex, we can occasionally glimpse the purpose of history." Gerard Sorme, already "awake" and trying to shape vision into experience, meditates in his sex diary on the insights gained from sexual experience on his vocation of overcoming the temptations of freedom and disciplining himself for the task of beginning to map the unexplored inner mind. Caradoc Cunningham, a sex magician modelled after Aleister Crowley, is Gerard's foil in this novel. Both have discovered the revelatory orgasmic power leading through and beyond sex, but Cunningham is prey to his own weakness and an over-awareness of society; he is concerned with surfaces. Gerard, on the contrary, finds meaning beyond society ("I am evolution made conscious," he says at one point) and uses the sexual power for his own ends; he is concerned with essentials.

The novel is one of Wilson's most interesting, for the ideas are at the surface, and the sexual intensity drives them along. Gerard settles in, at the end of the novel, to his vocation (and his new wife, an example of his ability to exercise choice which he lacked with Gertrude and Caroline), but, like Hugh Greene, his vocation is primarily intellectual and descriptive. He is the author of *The Methods and Techniques of Self-Deception,* not the new hero who must act in the world without self-deception. He is a transitional hero, as his diary is a transitional novel, for in his three most recent novels Wilson moves into new forms which plunge their heroes from thought into action, from understanding into being. The new active heroes and the more imaginative modes of fiction all reflect Colin Wilson's own determination to carry his beliefs into action, to move from philosophy and criticism to art. Or, as he put it in an essay in *Eagle and Earwig,* "intellectual discussion becomes a bore; only some form of action can redeem the existential thinker. And the only form of action that is meaningful is creative." The three novels, *Necessary Doubt* (1964), *The Glass Cage* (1966), and *The Mind Parasites* (1967), two detective novels and a science fiction novel, are his most imaginative, and they carry his hero from awakening into purposive and creative action. They are, to my mind, his best novels.

The title, *Necessary Doubt,* of Wilson's fifth novel is borrowed from the theology of Paul Tillich, and the central character is an aging existential theologian, Karl Zweig. He has become a television personality in England (on a show called "Ask the Experts"), although he is still an active thinker after thirty years of writing, but both his Christianity and his existentialism have failed him, have led him "to feel stoical about my life—to accept defeat as inevitable." By a series of coincidences, he finds himself involved with a motley set of associates in a private manhunt to stop one of his former pupils (the son of an old friend and associate) from continuing a series of murders of old men which he has apparently accomplished by means of a new habit-destroying drug and powerful hypnotic suggestion.

The stimulus and tension of the chase along with the sexual tension and desire which he feels and satisfies with Natasha Gardner, the wife of one of his colleagues in the manhunt, shatter Zweig's complacency and prepare the way for a new awakening. As events progress, Gustav Neumann, the quarry in the hunt, appears to him less and less a murderer and more and more a genuine "new man," working on the fringes of legality and morality to discover for the human race a means to new and higher conditions of consciousness. Neumann, cornered but not desperate, explains to him how the drug, neurocaine, was of his father's making and how, after his father's death, he has continued to experiment with it to discover its capabilities and proper uses. The drug destroys habits of thought and frees the brain from its fetters, but it gives its user "a sensation of existing in a desert of freedom" which is destructive to a mind weak in will and belief. The old men were, then, victims of themselves rather than of Neumann.

Reawakened to a new youth of insight, Zweig turns from his life's career as a theologian, which he recognizes has always been a shield to protect him from the necessity of acting, and joins Neumann in his quest for a method of freeing the mind from its purely physical limitations to a new consciousness and vitality. As he explains it, "You remember what Gustav said as he went out: 'I need your help.' His way can provide the vision, but what good is vision without a purpose? A man needs a lifetime of discipline to make use of such a vision." Age and youth, reason and imagination, purpose and vision, all are united in heroic action as detective and "murderer" break together the conventions of a limited consciousness in order to free that consciousness to its own future. The novel is a metaphor for thought's freeing itself by necessary doubt to creative belief, an artistic rendering of an "unsayable" moment of truth.

The Glass Cage is also a detective novel and a reworking and development of the basic situation of *Ritual in the Dark*. In it Damon Reade, a Blake scholar and recluse, is initiated and awakened by his love for a young girl and his need for human communion, and, like a medieval knight, he puts his love (and his new awareness) to the test in action; he goes to London from his home in the Lake District to solve a series of brutal sex murders which have involved the scrawling of quotations from Blake on walls by the bodies. Where Zweig was a man of reason, Reade is, like John Cowper Powys to whose memory the novel is dedicated, an instinctive nature mystic, and his success as a detective (and as a hero) is a product of a fusion of vision and reason, of ratiocination and imagination like that of Poe's Dupin.

The murderer in *The Glass Cage,* George Sundheim, is, like Austin Nunne and Carodoc Cunningham, a distortion of the new man; modelled after Rasputin, he is a man of enormous congenital energy and gargantuan appetites, who is so afraid (and, as it turns out, for no reason) of inheriting madness that he has crippled his mind and become a victim of his imagination and energy rather than their master. Damon Reade tracks Sundheim through the urban world which he abhors, solves the crimes, and, like Inspector Barlach in Friedrich Dürrenmatt's *The Judge and his Hangman,* manipulates events so that justice is served in the best and most humane manner, tempered by his understanding of the true nature of the "evil" being punished. The reclusive mystic acts in the human world on the strength of his vision, and Damon Reade becomes himself a hero, being and doing, no superman but a real man. The serpent who changes his skin in an ordeal of pain and illness to be born anew (Sundheim's pet boa constrictor for which Reade assumes responsibility at the end of the novel) is at the center of the novel's metaphoric structure, appropriately the emblem of evil become the emblem of change and the promise of the future.

Written at the suggestion of August Derleth, *The Mind Parasites* moves further from realism and is built upon a most effective and comprehensive metaphor. Wilson outlined it earlier in the *Introduction to the New Existentialism:*

> To express the problem in science-fiction terms: it would seem that there is some mysterious agency that wishes to hold men back, to prevent them from gaining full use of their powers. It is as if men contained an invisible parasite, whose job is to keep man unaware of his freedom. Blake called this parasite "the spectre." In certain moments of vitality and inspiration, the spectre releases his hold, and man is suddenly dazzlingly aware of what he could do with his life, his freedom. . . . On the other hand, if man can become fully conscious of the enemy and turn the full battery of his attention on it, the problem of "alienation from the source of power, meaning and purpose," and a new phase of evolution will have begun, the phase of the truly human. . . .

The novel is both Volume III of the *Cambridge History of the Nuclear Age* (2014) and the new gospel of Gilbert Austin, an archeologist, who, in communion with a handful of colleagues, defeats the mind parasites and sets man on the next leg of his evolutionary journey, only to "vanish in such a way that the human race could never be certain of his death." The novel both parodies and develops the manner and situation of H.P. Lovecraft's *The Shadow Out of Time,* and uses the full panoply of science fiction devices—rockets and space travel, ESP, telekinesis and even a "neutron dater" lifted from John Taine's *Before the Dawn.* With good humor (one of the characters did "a term on Wilson and Husserl" at college) and a real imaginative force, Wilson combines the familiar pieces of science fiction in a new way to form his own myth, a metaphor for his own vision of human destiny. His heroes commune to become a larger self; from the new perspective, they are able to view other men both as apes and as brothers; they form an evolutionary vanguard for the future and leave the account of their victory (the gospel according to Gilbert Austin) behind to guide their fellow men in taking the evolutionary leap. In some ways less emotionally powerful than *Necessary Doubt* or *The Glass Cage, The Mind Parasites* nevertheless is the fullest picture of the new hero as he can be and an apocalyptic parable of Wilson's insight into the nature of things. It and those other two most recent novels are meaningful examples of an imaginative and transforming art, an existential realism.

The novels of Colin Wilson are, then, a developing and growing artistic expression of the serpent's statement in Shaw's *Back to Methuselah* that "every dream could be willed into creation by those strong enough to believe in it." He has used literary forms as he has needed them to create love and life from the crude materials of sex, violence, and death, and, as he says in the preface to *The Mind Parasites,* speaking of his use of detective and science fiction, "In every case, it has been my aim to raise the form to a level of intellectual seriousness not usually found in the *genre,* but never to lose sight of the need to entertain." He has succeeded in that purpose, and his novel in progress, *The Black Room,* a spy novel and therefore less cosmic than *The Mind Parasites,* will, as the excerpts published recently in *The Minnesota Review* indicate, also make effective and meaningful use of a popular form.

Wilson once said that "a good novel can't be faked," for it can only show "what it is actually like *to be* the writer." If doing and being are somehow one, his novels, with their developing manner and matter, their movement toward a viable existential realism of inner as well as outer truth, show Colin Wilson to be a young man of real vision who has never ceased to grow and whose promise, for that reason, outshadows even his present achievement.

AFTERWORD

In re-examining my essay on Colin Wilson's novels, I realize that I should have noted more specifically the close relationship between Wilson's novels and his books of philosophy. For example, *Ritual in the Dark* is a fictional approach to the matter of *The Outsider, Man Without a Shadow* to *The Origins of the Sexual Impulse,* and *The Glass Cage* to *Beyond the Outsider* and *Rasputin and the Fall of the Romanovs.* But other than that confession I shall allow the essay to stand as it is. I shall, however, add a statement about the work Wilson is doing now as an indication of the directions of his growth.

Colin Wilson is living in Cornwall in pastoral quiet but by no means fallow ease. A & P Phoenix is due to produce his play, *Strindberg,* off-Broadway soon, and Random House is to publish it. Paramount holds an option to make a film of his novel, *The Glass Cage,* and he has written a screenplay of *Ritual in the Dark,* the production of which is now in progress. He has been working on a number of critical, philosophical and psychological books: a new book on George Bernard Shaw; a critical study, *The Strange Genius of David Lindsay,* which he is writing with E.M. Visiak; an essay, *Poetry and Mysticism,* which he is writing for Lawrence Ferlinghetti and which will be published in England along with other essays on poetry; a history of the occult which he is preparing for Random House; a sequel to his *Encyclopaedia of Murder* to be called *Casebook of Murder;* a book on phenomenology to be written in collaboration with Henry Winthrop of the University of South Florida; a textbook of psychology "from Mill to Maslow"; a small book on the psychology of Abraham Maslow; a book on his own psychology to be called *The Self Image;* and the publication of his autobiography, *Voyage to a Beginning.*

He has also been working on three novels, and he is completely rewriting his spy novel, *The Black Room,* and continuing to work on a large novel, *Lulu,* which he has been planning for years. Wilson wrote a short novel, "Return of the Lloigor," for August Derleth, which led him to write a new fantasy novel akin to *The Mind Parasites.* He was inspired by George Bernard Shaw's preface to *Back to Methuselah,* especially Shaw's comments about the nature of that play and about a literature of the future:

> I exploit the eternal interest of the philosopher's stone which enables men to live for ever. I am not, I hope, under more illusion than is humanly inevitable as to the crudity of this my beginning of a Bible of Creative Evolution. I am doing the best that I can at my age. My powers are waning; but so much the better for those who found me unbearably brilliant in my prime. It is my hope that a hundred apter and more elegant parables by younger hands will soon leave mine as far behind as the religious pictures of the fifteenth century left behind the first attempts of the early Christians at iconography.

Wilson's novel, *The Philosopher's Stone,* is a conscious attempt to take up Shaw's challenge and to write a new fable of longevity, a new book in the "Bible of Creative Evolution." The novel is, in many ways, like H.G. Wells's *Star Begotten,* but it is more like Wilson's own *Necessary Doubt* and *The Mind Parasites* (which is, as I noted, "the new gospel of Gilbert Austin"), a parabolic extension of the thinking and the artistic thrust of those novels.

Wilson has, then, continued to grow in the ways which I expected and in some new ones. His interest in psychology was certainly present in his "Outsider Cycle" and in the novels, but it is taking a more tangible form than I could have predicted. As a novelist, he is continuing to test new forms, to make a new kind of fabulous novel which can bear the weight of idea which he demands of art. I continue to believe that his promise outshadows even his present achievement.

ABOUT COLIN WILSON

Colin Wilson was born June 26, 1931, in Leicester, England, the first-born of Arthur and Anetta (Jones) Wilson.

He started reading science fiction at the age of eleven and then moved on to psychiatry, philosophy, and the sciences. At thirteen, he defended Albert Einstein against an English mathematician in a paper and next wrote a book attempting to summarize all the scientific knowledge of the world. Wilson "could no more help writing than a dog with fleas can help scratching," he wrote in the introduction to Sidney Campion's *The World of Colin Wilson* (Muller, 1962). "Until I was fourteen I intended to be a scientist and had a great admiration for Einstein. My ambition was to develop the atomic bomb and when this was done in 1945, I lost interest in science. However, I had also been writing since I was nine. . . and admiration for Shaw decided me to be a writer."

His record in school was only ordinary, however, and when he failed the tests to move on, his formal schooling was ended at the age of sixteen. He left Leicester's Gateway Secondary Technical School and went to work for a hometown firm, Cranbourne Products, Ltd., where his job was weighing wool. He went back to his school as a laboratory assistant, was fired, and spent 1948-1949 as a civil servant in Britain's internal revenue department, then served as an airman in the Royal Air Force from 1949-1950.

Between 1950 and 1956, when *The Outsider* was published, he worked as a ditchdigger, laborer, farm worker, in a laundry, and in a coffeehouse. He spent the winter of 1950-1951 in Paris and Strasbourg. After settling in London in 1951, he joined the London Anarchist Group and the Syndicalist Workers Federation of North London, but soon quit. In 1954 he began what would become *Ritual in the Dark* (published 1960).

When *The Outsider* was published and his reputation was made, Phillip Toynbee in the *Observer* of May 27, 1956, called it "an exhaustive and luminously intelligent study of a representative theme of our time. . . a real contribution to an understanding of our present predicament."

Then his stock went down among the critics, and there were some personal complications. "This reached a climax in February, 1957, when his future father-in-law, mistaking Wilson's blood-curdling notes for *Ritual in the Dark* for a private diary, threatened to horsewhip him" (*Current Biography*, 1963).

He was writer-in-residence at Hollins College, Virginia, for the school year 1966-1967 and then went to the University of Washington at Seattle.

Wilson was married to Pamela Joy Stewart in 1960. They have one daughter, Sally Elizabeth, and a son, John Damon. He has a son, Roderick Gerard, by a previous marriage, to Dorothy Betty Troop in 1951.

Immensely productive and hard-working, he has gone steadily forward working hard without regard to the ups and downs of the "literary stockmarket." Wilson's avowed ambition is "to finish as the greatest writer European civilization has produced."

"Although I would not consider myself an 'engaged' writer," he has said, "I am presently opposed to capital punishment. Am also for total disarmament, but not for Britain alone abandoning the bomb... am not and never have been an 'Angry Young Man.' I consider my life work that of a philosopher, and my purpose, to create a new and *optimistic* existentialism, a deliberate breakway from Sartre and Heidegger, in the tradition of British empiricism and Husserl's phenomenology."

BOOKS BY COLIN WILSON

THE OUTSIDER
London: Gollancz, 1956.
Boston: Houghton, Mifflin, 1956.
New York: Dell, 1967. (pb)

RELIGION AND THE REBEL
London: Gollancz, 1957.
Boston: Houghton, Mifflin, 1957.
Toronto: Bond Street, 1957.

THE AGE OF DEFEAT
London: Gollancz, 1959.
as THE STATURE OF MAN
Boston: Houghton, Mifflin, 1957.
Toronto: Doubleday, 1959.

RITUAL IN THE DARK
London: Gollancz, 1960.
Boston: Houghton, Mifflin, 1960.
Toronto: Doubleday, 1960.
New York: Popular Library, 1961. (pb)

ENCYCLOPAEDIA OF MURDER (with Pat Pitman)
London: Arthur Barker, 1961.
Toronto: McClelland, 1961.
New York: Putnam, 1962.
London: Pan, 1964. (pb)

ADRIFT IN SOHO
London: Gollancz, 1961.
Boston: Houghton, Mifflin, 1961.
Toronto: Doubleday, 1961.
London: Pan, 1965. (pb)

THE STRENGTH TO DREAM
London: Gollancz, 1962.
Boston: Houghton, Mifflin, 1962.
Toronto: Doubleday, 1962.

THE WORLD OF VIOLENCE
London: Gollancz, 1963.
Toronto: Doubleday, 1963.
London: Pan, 1965. (pb)
as THE VIOLENT WORLD OF HUGH GREENE
Boston: Houghton, Mifflin, 1963.

THE ORIGINS OF THE SEXUAL IMPULSE
London: Arthur Barker, 1963.
New York: Putnam, 1963.
London: Panther, 1966. (pb)

MAN WITHOUT A SHADOW
London: Arthur Barker, 1963.
London: Pan, 1966. (pb)
as THE SEX DIARY OF GERARD SORME
New York: Dial, 1963.
New York: Pocket Books, 1964. (pb)

NECESSARY DOUBT
London: Arthur Barker, 1964.
New York: Simon & Schuster, 1964.
Toronto: Ryerson, 1964.
New York: Pocket Books, 1966. (pb)

RASPUTIN AND THE FALL OF THE ROMANOVS
London: Arthur Barker, 1964.
New York: Farrar, Straus, 1964.
London: Panther, 1966. (pb)
New York: Citadel Press, 1967. (pb)

THE BRANDY OF THE DAMNED
London: John Baker, 1964.
Revised edition:
CHORDS AND DISCORDS
New York: Crown, 1966.

COLIN WILSON ON MUSIC
London: Pan, 1967. (pb)

BEYOND THE OUTSIDER
London: Arthur Barker, 1965.
Boston: Houghton, Mifflin, 1965.
London: Pan, 1966. (pb)

EAGLE AND EARWIG
London: John Baker, 1965.
Toronto: Nelson, Foster & Scott, 1965.

SEX AND THE INTELLIGENT TEENAGER
London: Arrow, 1966. (pb)
New York: Pyramid, 1969. (pb)

THE GLASS CAGE
London: Arthur Barker, 1966.
New York: Random House, 1967.

INTRODUCTION TO THE NEW EXISTENTIALISM
London: Hutchinson, 1966.
Toronto: Nelson, Foster & Scott, 1966.
Boston: Houghton, Mifflin, 1967.

THE MIND PARASITES
London: Arthur Barker, 1967.
Sauk City, Wis.: Arkham House, 1967.
New York: Bantam, 1968. (pb)

VOYAGE TO A BEGINNING
New York: Crown, 1969
London: C & A Woolf, 1969.

THE PHILOSOPHER'S STONE
London: Arthur Barker, 1969.

BERNARD SHAW: A REASSESSMENT
London: Hutchinson, 1969.
New York: Atheneum, 1969.

POETRY AND MYSTICISM
San Francisco: City Lights, 1969. (pb)

A CASEBOOK OF MURDER
New York: Cowles, 1970.

THE KILLER
London: New English Library, 1970.
as LINGARD
New York: Crown, 1970.

THE GOD OF THE LABYRINTH
London: Rupert Hart-Davis, 1970.

L'AMOUR: THE WAYS OF LOVE (with Piero Rimaldi)
New York: Crown, 1970.

William Styron and Human Bondage: *The Confessions of Nat Turner*

by Louis D. Rubin, Jr.

"If this is true, from my soul I pity you. . . "

—Judge Cobb, sentencing Nat Turner.

This time Styron was off to a good start. "A wonderfully evocative portrait of a gifted, proud, long-suppressed human being. . . "—Alfred Kazin in *Book World.* "The most profound fictional treatment of slavery in our literature. . . "—C. Vann Woodward in *The New Republic.* "One of those novels that is an act of revelation to a whole society. . . "—Raymond A. Sokolov in *Newsweek.* "A first-rate novel, the best that William Styron has produced and the best by an American writer that has appeared in some years. . . "—Philip Rahv in the *New York Review of Books.* There were a few dissents, to be sure, but it was clear that *The Confessions of Nat Turner* was making its way from the outset.

In that respect it was in startling contrast to *Set This House on Fire,* which when it appeared in 1960, was jumped upon by almost everybody. That novel had the misfortune to be the long-awaited second novel by a man whose first book was a tremendous success. In the nine years that followed *Lie Down in Darkness* (a novella, *The Long March,* didn't really count), the critics grew tired of waiting. Almost everyone had predicted great things for William Styron, and the longer it took for him to produce a second big book, the more exasperated everyone became. So that when Styron finally managed to complete his second novel, its publication was almost certain to be anti-climactic. In addition, *Set This House On Fire* was very long, it was filled with much soul-torment, and there was no neat tragic pattern such as characterized Styron's first novel. Thus when *Set This House On Fire* finally appeared, all the journalistic reviewers began scolding at once. Supposedly the new book was windblown, self-indulgent, sentimental, bathetic, over-written, and so on—the chorus of castigation rose to an impressive decibel volume. Only a corporal's guard of reviewers dared to disagree, to insist that while *Set This House On Fire* wasn't a flawless novel, it was nevertheless a very impressive accomplishment, a moving work of fiction, in every way worthy of if not superior to *Lie Down In Darkness,* so that its author need in no way feel that he had failed to live up to his notices.

During the seven years between *Set This House On Fire* and Styron's new novel, however, critical opinion has pretty much come around to the viewpoint that Styron's second book was a quite respectable performance. Once the reviewers in the critical quarterlies, who are notably unswayed by journalistic reviews, began writing about the book, the initial verdict was reversed. Critical essays and chapters of books appeared which treated *Set This House On Fire* as a work which, though flawed in parts, contains some of the better writing of our time. For example, a good critic, Frederick J. Hoffman, has this to say about *Set This House On Fire* in his recent book *The Art of Southern Fiction:* "Styron's most recent novel sets the imagination agoing, in the expectation of an American literature of existentialism. . . . But it is perhaps best not to name it that, for fear of weighing it down with labels and classifications. The important fact is that Styron has used his talents mightily and to a good effect in this novel."

Set This House On Fire is the story of Cass Kinsolving, an artist unable to paint. A World War II veteran, married and living in Europe, he must undergo a terrifying stay in the lower depths before he can win his way back to sanity and creativity. The leading characters, very unlike most southern fictional folk, engage in long, probing psychological analyses of their inner souls. There are no Negroes (though there is a memory of them), no First Families going to seed, no church services, no bloodguilt of generations, no oversexed southern matrons. It is thoroughly, completely modern, even cosmopolitan. Cass Kinsolving is a man in bondage; in Paris, Rome and Sambuco he lives in an alcoholic daze, tortured by his inability to paint, drinking, wandering about, pitying himself, doing everything except confronting his talent. He had sought to find a form for his art outside of himself; he could not put up with his creative limitations, and he looked to the society and people surrounding him for what could only be found within himself: the remorseless requirement of discovering how to love and be loved, and so to create. Only through violence and tragedy could he win his way through to self-respect, and attain an equilibrium with the world that enables him to function effectively.

All very odd and strange, this sort of thing: Styron wasn't supposed to write that kind of a novel. What also perplexed many reviewers was that this process and this outcome were not presented ironically or obliquely; there wasn't the self-conscious distrust of high rhetoric and ultimate judgment that characterizes much "existential" fiction today. The language was unabashedly resounding and rhetorical. And because it was the kind of book it was, the form of the story was restless, groping, searching, and not at all neat and tidy.

The difficulties inherent in any attempt to use the high style to deal with contemporary life are of course obvious. Our sense of irony is too strong to permit it to function without severe qualification. Faulkner, for all his greatness, could never successfully handle an intelligent modern man learning how to cope with contemporary urban society: his Gavin Stevens is among his less convincing characterizations. Robert Penn Warren managed it in *All The King's Men,* but to do so he had to filter the rhetoric through a wisecracking, hard-boiled type of narrator who could protect his more sounding declarations from irony by getting there first himself. Few other contemporaries even dare to try it; they fear, and with reason, that they will come out of it talking like the later prose of Carl Sandburg.

Styron's attempt, in *Set This House On Fire,* was not completely successful either. There is a shift of character focus in the novel, to the effect that part of the true explanation for Cass Kinsolving's plight lies not in his own past experience but in that of his friend Peter Leverett. This isn't ultimately fatal; such is Styron's artistry that we accord Kinsolving the right to feel and think as he does, in defiance of the strict logic of plot. The main thing is that *Set This House On Fire* works; one way or another, it adds up. There are moments when Cass's believability seems to be in jeopardy, but each time Styron comes through.

Styron, Hoffman remarks, "moved away (in *Set This House On Fire*) from the special moral dimensions of the southerner looking at portraits of colonels, or addressing himself to the landscape of his youth, or to the special qualities of feudal vengeance or pride. . . he has assumed a larger risk, moved into a more competitive field, entered a tradition of psychological and moral analysis that has been occupied by Kierkegaard, Mann, Sartre, and Camus before him." So concluded many another critic after reading *Set This House On Fire,* though usually without Hoffman's ability to perceive that in so doing, Styron had written an excellent novel. Yet the implication, voiced by numerous other critics as well, that in *Set This House On Fire* Styron had ceased to be a "southern writer," in the way that Faulkner, Warren, Wolfe, Welty, Lytle, and so forth had been southern writers, was unwarranted, I think. For the so-called "southern quality" in modern American fiction is not at bottom a matter of subject matter or theme, so much as of attitude; it is a way of looking at the nature of human experience, and it includes the assumption that to maintain order and stability the individual must be part of a social community, yet that the ultimate authority that underlies his conduct is not social but moral. It is, in short, a religious attitude, though most often it does not involve the dogmas of revealed religion. This attitude, not the presence of the particular institutions and events that customarily embody the attitude, is what has enabled the work of the better southern novelists to seem so "meaningful" in our time. It is precisely this attitude, too, that has made possible and believable the use of the full, unstinted high rhetorical mode that so marks much of the work of Faulkner, Warren, Wolfe, and others. We will not buy rhetoric unless we believe in the absolutes that justify it, and the southern writers do believe in them. In many ways Styron's second novel represents a kind of examination into the soundness of such a view, ending in a confirmation. Cass Kinsolving's emotions and ideals are examined and tested in the furnace experience of Paris and Sambuco, and are finally pronounced sound. Whereupon Cass may come home.

He comes back, however, not to the community in which he grew up, but to another place, where he is ready to install himself—another southern community, but one without historical and social links with his own past. It had been necessary for him to leave the scene of his past behind him, to travel to another continent and there ratify the individual and social worth of those attitudes and ideals, independently of their institutions and for himself, in order to make them *his,* and not merely something automatically bequeathed to him.

Thus for Styron, *Set This House On Fire* represented a clearing away as it were of the debris of the southern fictional texture—all the accustomed artifacts of setting, history, community that have for several generations provided the experience out of which southern fiction has been created. But the underlying attitude toward the nature of human experience in time remains, and far from representing any kind of abdication of what has come to be recognized as the southern literary mode, *Set This House on Fire* is an extension, perhaps the only possible extension, of that mode into a new day and a different kind of experience.

Toward the close of the novel Cass Kinsolving hears his family stirring about the house in the morning light, and thinks as follows: "I didn't know what it was but there they were sort of strutting face to face and soundlessly clapping their hands together, like Papageno and Papagena, or something even more sweet, paradisiac, as if they were children not really of this earth but of some other, delectable morning before time and history." As if there could be any possible doubt of the literary mode out of which that style of rhetoric comes!

It might offend Negroes that I as a white man have presumed to intrude on the consciousness of a Negro.

—William Styron, interview in *Book World.*

Which brings us, seven years later, to *The Confessions of Nat Turner.* This time the scene is again the South—the Commonwealth of Virginia, scarcely more than an hour's ride by automobile from the very city in which Peyton Loftis, Peter Leverett, and William Styron were born and grew up. Furthermore, *The Confessions of Nat Turner* is an historical novel, based squarely on the single most complex and pervasive theme of all southern history, the presence and role of the Negro. The central character and narrator is a preacher, whose thoughts and deeds are based on Biblical admonition and whose language is charged with Scriptural rhetoric. So that Styron would seem to have come full circle—starting out with Peyton Loftis from Port Warwick in Tidewater Virginia, then north to New York City; then eastward across the ocean to Paris and Italy with Cass Kinsolving, and at length back home to the South. Now it is tidewater Virginia once more, the year is 1831, and there is the selfsame Black Shadow that has darkened the pages of southern literature from the romances of William Gilmore Simms on through to Mark Twain, George Washington Cable and Thomas Nelson Page, and more recently William Faulkner, Robert Penn Warren, and every other southern writer of the twentieth century so far.

But there is a difference. The story is told both by and *about* a Negro. Styron has sought to put himself into the mind and heart of a slave preacher who in August of 1831 led a bloody insurrection in Southampton County, Virginia. No southern writer has ever really done this sort of thing before with much success. The faithful Negro retainers who relate in such ornate dialect Thomas Nelson Page's idylls of Virginia plantation life Befo' De War were stereotypes, designed to exhibit the graciousness and romance of ante-bellum society. Joel Chandler Harris' Uncle Remus was also a delightful old darky, but he knew his place, and his creator was careful most of the time to keep to the surface of things. Even Faulkner, who Ralph Ellison says has written more accurately and truly about the Negro than any other writer living or dead, black or white, shows us not the Negro so much as the white man learning to see the Negro—learning to see him more sharply and honestly than ever before.

Styron goes further. He is satisfied with nothing else than to try to *become* Nat Turner. Now it seems to me that, from the standpoint of the developing cultural history of the South, this very attempt is important of itself. In the years after 1865, writers such as Page and Harris created

Negro narrators to tell their stories under the naive belief that this was a comparatively easy thing to do, since their notion of what it was like to be a Negro was itself something quite simple. Their Negro was the "Old Time Darky," faithful, true, obedient, whose every thought and allegiance was for Massa (sometimes spelled Marster, sometimes Mars', occasionally Maussa). A Thomas Nelson Page was confident that he understood the Negro; it never occurred to him that he might not. The great southern novelists of the 1920s, 1930s, and 1940s—Faulkner, Warren, Wolfe, the others—made no such easy assumptions; rather, they focused upon the difficulty, the impossibility even, of the white man knowing what Negroes really thought and felt. This recognition that the complaisant pastoral figure that a Thomas Nelson Page could so naively accept as a "true" representation of the Negro was in fact a vast oversimplification, symbolized a long step forward in the white South's willingness to accord the Negro full human status. Now comes a fine novel by a leading southern writer of the post-World War II generation, essaying to portray the innermost thoughts of a Negro, and doing so without very much self-consciousness. One cannot help but see this as emblematic of an important social breakthrough. For the point about Styron's characterization of Nat Turner is that Nat's existence as a Negro is not seen as making him in any recognizable way importantly "different" from what a white man might be in similar circumstances. Nat Turner comes eventually to hate all white men; but this emotion is not portrayed as an inherent racial characteristic. Rather, it is a response, a desperate and tragic one, to the social inhumanity of human slavery. A Negro as seen by William Styron is in no important or essential way different from a white man. Social conditions, not heredity and biology, set him apart. The walls of separateness are man-made.

Nobody, of course, knows "who" the real Nat Turner was. Except for a twenty-page "confession" dictated to a white lawyer and read before the trial court as evidence, there is little to go on. Not much additional information is to be found in the only book written about the Nat Turner Insurrection, William Sidney Drewry's *The Southampton Insurrection,* published in 1900 by a long-since defunct publishing house dedicated to defending the Confederate Heritage and racial segregation.

That Styron's Nat Turner is surely not the "real" Nat Turner is indisputable—in the sense that every human being is a unique personality, so that nobody could possibly reconstruct anything resembling the real Nat Turner without abundant evidence. In any event, *The Confessions of Nat Turner,* as the southern historian C. Vann Woodward says, is "not inconsistent with anything historians know" and is "informed by a respect for history, a sure feeling for the period, and a deep and precise sense of place and time." This seems to me likewise indisputable.

Yet at least one other southern historian, and a good one, has told me that he felt that Styron had committed a grievous historical mistake, in that he makes Nat Turner, a slave preacher on a southside Virginia plantation thirty years before the Civil War, think and talk exactly like a modern Black Power advocate; Styron's Nat Turner, he believes, sounds not like a slave, but like Stokely Carmichael. This is a severe criticism. Though I think it is not true, I confess that there are certain moments in Styron's novel in which one gets something of this feeling. Nat's reiterated insistence on the need of all Negroes to strike the Happy Darky pose when dealing with whites—"I replied in tones ingratiating, ministerial—the accommodating comic nigger"—tends to make the reader uncomfortably aware on such occasions of the author laboring to present the "Negro point of view." Doubtless Virginia slaves learned to do exactly what Nat says, but Nat's self-conscious theorizing about it would seem somewhat anachronistic. Similarly there are several passages in which Nat and other slaves talk at some length about the "smell" of white people—we glimpse the author waxing ironic about certain often-echoed white shibboleths. (Cf. Thomas Jefferson, in the *Notes on the State of Virginia:* "They secrete less by the kidneys, and more by the glands of the body, which gives them a very strong and disagreeable odor"—as if there were bathrooms available for the slaves at Monticello!)

But these instances are relatively few, and are unimportant. So also the argument that by making Nat Turner into a much more intellectual and reflective person, possessing a much more complex vocabulary than the real-life Nat Turner could probably have had, Styron violates the historicity of the situation. This seems to me to overlook the fact that Nat Turner could never have been a "representative" Negro slave of the 1830s. A "representative" slave could not possibly have led the Nat Turner Insurrection. Furthermore, it is not required or fitting that Styron's Nat Turner be "representative," "typical"; on the contrary, he *must* be an exaggeration. His thoughts, his emotions, his language must be plausible only to the extent that the reader must feel a slave preacher in southside Virginia in the year 1831, given the admitted uniqueness of Nat Turner's situation, could conceivably have thought and felt and spoken as he does. Besides, what is really involved here is the reader-writer relationship; for after all, is not the reader already engaged, by the mere fact of reading the book, in an "illogical" activity, inasmuch as he is being asked to imagine that what he is reading is the thoughts and words of a long-dead Negro preacher about whom almost nothing whatever is known? To echo Johnson, surely he that imagines this may imagine more. What matters is that Negro slaves (and Negro freedmen) *did* have to play roles in order to deal with the whites, and Nat's awareness of the role differs from that of most Negro slaves only in that it is made conscious and articulate. The truth is that Styron's Nat Turner is nothing more and nothing less than a tragic protagonist, and we ask representativeness and typicality of such a character no more than we ask that Sophocles show representative and typical Greeks of ancient Thebes in the *Oedipus Rex.*

"To a mind like mine, restless, inquisitive and observant, there was nothing that I saw or heard to which my attention was not directed."

—Nat Turner, "Confession" (1831)

The Confessions of Nat Turner is told in the first person present. The language purports to be that of Nat, but not as spoken to anyone. Nat is thinking, "explaining" himself—to the reader, to "posterity," to himself. Though in point of strict logic this is quite impossible, it is an acceptable literary convention, much as the Shakespearean soliloquy is a literary convention.

The use of Nat as narrator affords Styron several advantages for telling his story. First of all, since Nat is a preacher, and deeply immersed in the language and style of the King James Bible, we will accept from him a high rhetorical style which we might otherwise not permit, especially from a Negro slave in ante-bellum Virginia. More importantly, we soon become aware that when Nat actually talks, whether to whites or Negroes, his language is much more idiomatic and colloquial. The reader's awareness of the difference in language and voice, of the contrast between the manner in which Nat thinks or remembers and the way that he talks, is essential to the form and meaning of the novel. For not only must Nat, despite his learning, continue to play the role of humble, barely-literate slave before his betters, but the very fact of his intelligence and learning serves to isolate him all the more. The whites, no matter how sympathetic (and some *are* quite sympathetic), must by reason of time and place inevitably view Nat as an inferior, a freak—a slave, less than human, a bond-servant, one who surprisingly can read and write, but is still an inferior creature.

This of course is the true horror of slavery for Nat. He is considered less than a Man, and open, human contact with the whites is utterly forbidden him. The result is loneliness and rage. He comes to *hate* the whites because they have placed him and kept him in this position, and his rage is most keen at those times when he is being most patronized. For those whites who are kindest to him—in particular the girl Margaret Whitehead—inevitably do most to reinforce his consciousness of his inferior status, since they believe they are *not* patronizing him while still expecting him to remain safely in his place. In her romantic, naive way Margaret Whitehead means only the best for Nat, and genuinely likes and admires him, yet she fails utterly to comprehend the nature of his position and cannot for a moment grasp what torture is involved for him. In part her good intentions are only an aspect of her sentimentality; in being "frank," she condescends. Yet she *does* mean well; she does, in her own way, even love Nat, and before he dies he comes to realize that.

The contrast between what Nat thinks and can think, and what he must say and appear to be to whites whether of good intentions or bad, enforces the sense of isolation and loneliness that characterizes Nat's life. With the slaves, he does not have to pretend in the same way; in their company he can be himself as he cannot with white people. But his fellow bondsmen, being without his literacy and intelligence, cannot communicate with him either, especially after he has conceived his plan for a revolt and must bend every effort to manipulate and direct them toward his ends. Not even Hark, his closest friend and his chief lieutenant in the insurrection he organizes, can understand or imagine what Nat is thinking or feeling. Thus Nat Turner as depicted by Styron is cut off from whites and blacks alike, and the violence of his protest is his insurrection.

There is still another advantage in Styron's use of Nat as narrator. In the very contrast between the complex, subtle diction of Nat's thoughts, and the verbally crude language he must use to express himself aloud, there evolves a tension which grows more and more acute as the narrative develops and as Nat increasingly comes to comprehend the nature of his enforced isolation. The gulf between Nat's private self and his role in time and place builds up toward a point at which language itself will no longer suffice to provide order. There must then be the explosion of action, whereby language and deed are unified through violence—and the tragedy is accomplished.

Why did Nat Turner stage his insurrection? This, after all, is the question that Styron sets out to answer by writing his novel. Because slavery was evil, and for a slave capable of a high degree of thought and feeling, intolerable—yes. Because Nat in particular had been promised his freedom by his first owner, only to be betrayed into renewed and hopeless bondage—yes. These are the topical answers. But because William Styron is the fine novelist that he is, they are not the full or even the most important answers.

Nat Turner, a human being, rebels because he is deprived by his society of the right to love and be loved. I do not mean by this merely that Nat rebels because he is denied sexual fulfillment, though he is (save for one youthful homosexual experience Styron's Nat Turner is an ascetic, thereby providing psychological grounding for his messianic religious visions). The question is larger than that. Nat cannot love—physically or spiritually. The world he inhabits is such that at best he can expect from whites only pity, and at worst outright hatred, while from his fellow slaves he can expect only inarticulate admiration at best, and at worst envy and contempt. Thus he cannot *give* himself to anyone. No one wants him for what he is. For everyone, white and black, friend and foe, he must play a role. For his first owner, who educated him, he is a noble experiment, an object of benevolence, a salve to the slave-holding conscience. For Margaret Whitehead he is a sympathetic auditor to whom she can pour out her girlish fancies and exhibit her broad-mindedness. For his last owner he is a clever, valuable mechanic, a source of financial profit. For his fellow slaves he is a leader, one who can plan and organize their revenge. Even to his fellow conspirator Hark, who does indeed love and admire him, he cannot be fully himself, for Hark's imagination and intelligence are too limited to enable him to share Nat's innermost thoughts. Denied, therefore, the right to give himself, to love, Nat can only hate, and the result is destruction.

What good, the interrogating lawyer asks Nat, did his insurrection accomplish? The lawyer answers his own question:

> "Here's what it got you, Reverend, if you'll pardon the crudity. It got you a pissy-assed record of total futility, the likes of which are hard to equal. Threescore white people slain in random butchery, yet the white people firmly holdin' the reins. Seventeen niggers hung, including you and old Hark there, nevermore to see the light of day. A dozen or more other nigger boys shipped out of an amiable way of life to Alabama, where you can bet your bottom dollar that in five years the whole pack of 'em will be dead of work and fever. . . . "

"One hundred and thirty-one innocent niggers both slave and free cut down by the mob that roamed Southampton for a solid week, searching vengeance," the lawyer continues. And finally, the Nat Turner Insurrection will mean much more harshly repressive laws for the slaves:

> ". . . when the legislature convenes in December they're goin' to pass laws that make the ones *extant* look like rules for a Sunday School picnic. They goin' to lock up the niggers in a black cellar and throw away the key." He paused, and I could sense him leaning close to me. "*Abolition,*" he said in a voice like a whisper. "Reverend, single-handed you done more with your Christianity to assure the defeat of abolition than all the meddlin' and pryin' Quakers that ever set foot in Virginia put together. I reckon you didn't figure on that either?"
>
> "No," I said, looking into his eyes, "if that be true. No."

There was and is no Happy Ending for the Nat Turner Insurrection. Styron knew this, and his novel shows it. It did not bring Negro slavery one whit closer to an end; if anything it retarded progress. The harsh Black Codes enacted throughout most of the South in the decades before the Civil War were due at least in part to the fear of servile revolt that the Nat Turner Insurrection had triggered.

This attempt to separate truth from fiction has been exceedingly difficult, owing to the numerous misrepresentations and exaggerations which have grown up about the subject.

—Drewry, *The Southampton Insurrection.*

In staging his insurrection Nat Turner believed that he was doing the Lord's bidding, as it had been revealed to him in a series of supernatural visions. Styron was careful to give these moments of revelation a solid psychological basis: they come always after Nat has gone without food for several days, and is weak and feverish. Yet *The Confessions of Nat Turner* is not primarily a psychological study. The limits of Nat's personality are not defined by the science of abnormal psychology. He represents, and is, the strong man in bondage, a human caught in a situation not originally of his making but ultimately requiring his total commitment. Faced with evil, Nat cannot hide from it, but his appalling attempt to right matters only brings defeat and greater suffering. In other words, it is a tragic situation, and the resolution of it is tragedy.

The specific events of Nat Turner's life which impelled him toward the Southampton insurrection are unknown. As novelist, Styron had therefore to give him a history, and it was the task of his creative imagination to make the personal history contain the meaning forced upon the subject by history. Thus Styron represents Nat during his youth as having been favored and set apart by his owner, and imbued with much hope and optimism. When instead of being freed he is sold into renewed bondage, Nat's sense of personal rage and helplessness forces him to take account of the wretched lot of his less-gifted fellow slaves, for whom he had once felt contempt and disdain. It is at this stage in his life that the conviction of religious mission comes upon him (in which respect Styron departs from the 1831 "Confession," for Nat Turner says there that from his childhood onward he had felt himself "intended for some great purpose"). Nat then begins mapping out his plan to lead an insurrection. The growth of the spirit of rebellion in Nat is charted by Styron with calculated deliberateness; the calm, carefully chosen language with which Nat tells his story only serves to intensify the sense of impending crisis and explosion.

In *The Southampton Insurrection* Drewry repeatedly expresses astonishment over the fact that Nat Turner himself had been treated with kindness by his owner, and had stated as much in his "Confession." Drewry insists that not only Nat but almost all the slaves in ante-bellum Virginia were kindly treated. This is proved, he declares, by the fact that so few slaves joined Turner. Most remained loyal to their owners, and some distinguished themselves by their bravery in defending their white families against the insurgents. Thus the only explanation Drewry can suggest for the insurrection is that Abolitionist propaganda had inflamed the mind of Nat Turner, already crazed by a fanatical belief in his supernaturally prophetic destiny.

The true explanation, as is obvious, is that it was precisely *because* Nat Turner himself was treated well and had so distinguished himself in education and intelligence that he was prompted to lead his revolt; as Styron shows, his superior attainments and status only made more clear to him the hopelessness of servile bondage. Thus nothing could so madden Nat as the occasional expression of pity on the part of a white man or woman. In one of the finest episodes in the novel, Styron depicts Nat's sensations upon seeing a Northern-born wife of a planter break down and weep at the sight of a particularly wretched and abject Negro. This unusual passage cannot be satisfactorily excerpted; suffice it to say that it is a masterful portrayal of complex emotions of hate, lust, love, and shame contending within a man's heart. "I was filled with somber feelings that I was unable to banish," Nat remarks afterward, "deeply troubled that it was not a white person's abuse or scorn or even indifference which could ignite in me this murderous hatred but his pity, maybe even his tenderest moment of charity."

The point is that in this and numerous other instances, *The Confessions of Nat Turner* is a very *wise* book. Styron's understanding of his material is most impressive. When one thinks about it, the possibilities for melodrama and easy pathos inherent in the subject matter of this novel are very broad. What a less gifted novelist might have produced, one shudders to think. Styron, for example, barely mentions the period of ten weeks that actually elapsed between the suppression of the insurrection and the capture of Nat Turner, during which Nat himself hid out in the woods and fields. Another novelist might have attempted to make this episode the occasion for a long, pseudo-philosophical meditation by Nat on the meaning of what has happened. But Styron lets Nat's thoughts about what he has done arise in the actual retelling of the story—in, that is, his confession—so that by the time the actual insurrection itself takes place, what it means has been convincingly anticipated and prepared for us. The events of the insurrection, therefore, bloody as they are, are not merely horrible; they are the motivated, terribly meaningful violence climaxing an intolerable situation.

One could make many other observations about William Styron's new novel. Most of them have already been made or will soon be; publication of the novel is obviously one of the more noteworthy literary events of recent years. Its importance lies simply in the fact that a dedicated and talented American novelist has written a book dealing with one of the most fateful and pressing concerns of our country's history, one that is by no means fully resolved. The topical relevance of this book is obvious—so much so that one need not comment on it.

This observation should be made, however: at a time when many influential critics have been saying that the day of the novel is done, Styron has produced a first-rate work of fiction while working very much within the traditional novel form. By bringing his intelligence and imagination to bear upon an important and deeply human situation, he has reinvigorated the form, and shown that it is still quite alive. He has thus given the lie to all those tired critics who have been going about lamenting the death of the novel, and proclaiming the superior merits of this or that substitute. It is time, therefore, that we cease bewailing the passing of the demigods of an earlier generation, and recognize the fact that with such writers as William Stryon, Saul Bellow, and John Barth regularly producing prose fiction for us, we have no occasion for complaint. A novel as good as Styron's can hold its own in any company.

AFTERWORD

The best thing I can do to indicate what has happened to William Styron since my piece on *The Confessions of Nat Turner* last fall is to append a review that I wrote for *The Washington Sunday Star* for September 1, 1968, under the title "The Literary Attacks on Styron's *Nat Turner.*" [3]

Those of us who, last fall, read, admired William Styron's *The Confessions of Nat Turner,* and said so in print, have subsequently been treated to as odd a literary—or, more properly, a cultural and sociological—phenomenon as has recently existed in American letters.

For Styron's *Nat Turner* got good reviews at first—and not by journeyman reviewers alone, but by such respected literary critics and historians as Philip Rahv, C. Vann Woodward, Alfred Kazin, and others. What Styron was especially praised for was the way in which he, a white man, had been able to get so thoroughly into the personality of a Negro slave of the 1820s and 1830s, so that without stereotype or condescension he made a believable tragic hero out of the leader of the Nat Turner rebellion of 1831.

It soon developed, however, that Styron wasn't going to be let off so easily. Led by the historian Herbert Aptheker, a chorus of advanced reviewers began jumping on Styron's book, and soon various Negro intellectuals joined in, until by the late winter of 1967-1968 Styron's supposedly antiracist novel was being condemned as an insult to the memory of Nat Turner, an embodiment of traditional white stereotypes of the Negro, a flagrant perversion of history, and—I quote from the introduction

3 *William Styron's Nat Turner: Ten Black Writers Respond.* Edited by John Henrik Clarke. Boston: The Beacon Press (1968). $4.95.

to the volume under review here—a "deliberate" attempt to distort the true character of Nat Turner because of the author's "reaction to the racial climate that has prevailed in the United States in the last fifteen years."

This book, a collection of attacks on Styron and his novel by ten Negro writers, will surely go down in literary history as one of the most curious documents ever compiled. It reminds me, in miniature, of nothing so much as the barrage of novels produced by Southerners during the 1850s in answer to the "lies" and "distortions" of Harriet Beecher Stowe's *Uncle Tom's Cabin.* And, I might add, the present-day refutations are just about as relevant as the antebellum models.

The question that comes to mind upon reading these essays is, Why? What is it that has prompted so many Negro critics—and these ten essayists are not the only or even the best objectors to the novel—to rise in anger at Styron's novel? Is it because, as several of the essayists say, Styron has demeaned a great man, portrayed an authentic Negro hero as a neurotic, and so forth?

I don't think so, really. The novel that I read and admired last fall made an obscure, little-chronicled Negro slave preacher into a tragic hero of great stature, and made the remorseless, irresistible current of events that led him toward bloody rebellion into the tragic drama of a strong man caught up in the demands of an intolerable social and moral situation. How anyone can see Styron as degrading or stereotyping Nat Turner is still quite unaccountable to me.

Is it because Negro writers resent the fact that Styron, a white man and a Virginian to boot, produced the first really important literary work about a Negro slave insurrectionist? There is a little of this feeling in these essays, though several of the contributors go to some pains to deny it: as for example when John A. Williams begins by saying that "since I do not believe that the right to describe or portray or in other ways delineate the lives of black people in American society is the private domain of Negro writers, I cannot fault Styron's intent," and then concludes with the remark that "black writers, it appears, have lost the race, if ever there was one, to air the truth. The likes of Styron are already past the finish line."

Yet I do not feel that the fact that Styron, and not Ralph Ellison or James Baldwin, wrote *The Confessions of Nat Turner* is what is behind the current furore. Just now the prevailing attitude is that white writers are not supposed to be able to understand how a Negro—any Negro, rich or poor, intelligent or stupid, intellectual or non-intellectual—thinks and feels, but I feel that there were ways that Styron might have written his book and portrayed Nat Turner that would have won him the admiration, however grudging, of almost all Negro critics.

The real trouble with Styron's novel, in the eyes of Negro critics, is not that it is a racist document, I think, but paradoxically that it isn't racist enough. In other words, Styron did things with the characterization of a Negro slave preacher and revolutionary that no one who was a racist could or would have done, and which he could do only because he did not himself even consider the possibility that most of the racist shibboleths and dogmas were to be taken seriously.

In his novel, for example, Styron makes Nat Turner a celibate, who desires several white women, one of whom in her naive and sentimental way actually returns his love. To Styron's critics this is an example of racist thinking: it supposedly embodies the racist doctrine that all Negro males secretly want to rape white women.

What Styron was instead trying to show was that in setting Nat Turner apart from his fellow slaves, making him into something special, encouraging him to think of himself as not only better than but different from his less-favored brethren, white racist antebellum society was in effect robbing Nat Turner of his virility. It was setting up an artificial barrier between Nat and his own race. It was placing him in an impossible situation, in which he was permitted to exist on the fringes of the dominant white society but without being allowed to enter it fully, and at the same time so isolating him from the enslaved black society that he could find no membership and fulfillment there either. This, Styron was saying, was what slavery (and, by implication, racism of any sort) does. The whiteness of Nat Turner's imagined lovers is a measure of the distortion that slavery (and racism) produced in him.

Styron's depiction of Nat Turner's sexual fantasies in this way, then, constitutes not racism, but an attack upon racism, and exists because he considered the whole folklore about all Negroes inherently desiring white women so absurd that it was impossible to take it seriously. But the difficulty is that Styron's Negro critics do take it seriously—seriously enough to fear that any suggestion that Nat Turner, or any Negro leader, might desire a white woman is the repetition of a dangerous racist shibboleth.

Most of the criticism of Styron's treatment of Nat Turner in this collection of essays is of this order, and based on these assumptions. At one point, for instance, Styron depicts a free Negro starving in a time of drought. Because he isn't anyone's "property," he is allowed to starve. Styron's critics object that this is an example of the old racial dogma that slavery had its good side, and that Negroes were really better off as slaves than as free men. What Styron was showing instead was that in a society that was based on race, and which considered men worthy of being kept as chattels because their skin was dark, mere political freedom could mean little. Again, an attack on racism, not a defense of slavery, and one based on the assumption that there could obviously be no truth in the notion that anybody was really better off as a slave. Apparently, however, to the Negro critics of his book the claim that Negroes were inferior creatures who were better off protected and cared for like animals is all too serious to be ignored. It must be refuted.

And that is what is at the heart of the whole business. The ten Negro intellectuals who object to Styron's portrayal of Nat Turner in his novel don't want racial absurdities ignored. They want them refuted, and they want Nat Turner, or any other Negro chosen for the hero of a novel, designed specifically as a refutation of the various racial clichés and shibboleths and stereotypes.

Styron might have produced such a novel. There have been such; some are singled out for praise in the course of these essays. But they are inferior works of fiction, in part because their authors thought it more important to present their characters as Negro heroes than as tragic protagonists. Styron didn't want his protagonist to be an exemplary Negro; he wanted him to be a great man. It is my belief that when the smoke of controversy blows away and important fiction about a Negro slave leader can be read as fiction and not as either pro- or anti-Negro propaganda, the best critics both white and Negro will recognize how fine a characterization, and how great a man, William Styron's Nat Turner is.

ABOUT WILLIAM STYRON

While taking officer candidate courses at Duke University in the early years of World War II, William Styron also studied creative writing under William Blackburn, who encouraged him and published one of his stories in an anthology of student writing at Duke. At the end of the war, Styron returned to Duke and was awarded his B.A. in 1947.

In the spring of 1947 he obtained a job as an editor at Whittlesey House in New York. However, he was fired at the end of six months and took a writing course under Hiram Haydn at the New School for Social Research in his new-found spare time.

After the successful publication of his first novel, *Lie Down in Darkness,* Styron journeyed to Paris. Here he was befriended by George Plimpton, Donald Hall, and other founders of the *Paris Review,* for which he wrote the credo. Receiving a grant from the American Academy of Arts and Letters, he spent several months in Italy before returning to the United States in 1953.

Styron favors the "bit-by-bit" process of writing, sometimes completing only three pages a day, which he revises before moving on. In his study is a quotation by Flaubert: "Be regular and orderly in your life, like a good bourgeois, so that you may be violent and original in your work."

BOOKS BY WILLIAM STYRON

LIE DOWN IN DARKNESS

New York: Bobbs-Merrill, 1951.
London: Hamish Hamilton, 1952.
Toronto: McClelland & Stewart, 1952.
New York: New American Library, 1952. (pb)
New York: Viking-Compass, 1957. (pb)
New York: Modern Library, 1964.

THE LONG MARCH
New York: Bobbs-Merrill, 1951.
New York: Modern Library, 1956. (pb)
London: Hamish Hamilton, 1962.
New York: Vintage, 1962. (pb)
New York: Random House, 1968.
New York: Random House, 1968. (pb)

SET THIS HOUSE ON FIRE
New York: Random House, 1960.
London: Hamish Hamilton, 1961.
New York: New American Library, 1961. (pb)

CONFESSIONS OF NAT TURNER
New York: Random House, 1967.
New York: New American Library, 1968. (pb)
London: Jonathan Cape, 1968.

LT

My Silk Purse and Yours: *Making It,* Starring Norman Podhoretz

by George Garrett

I desire that all men should see me in my simple, natural, and ordinary fashion, without straining or artifice: for it is myself that I portray.

—Montaigne.

Norman Podhoretz's *Making It* is a fascinating piece of work. Candid as he can be, he lifts the long Victorian skirts of that lady sometimes called the Bitch Goddess of Success and once upon a time known as Dame Fortune. He sneaks more than a peek. Framing his anatomy of ambition and the American lust for success in the form of an autobiography, Podhoretz seeks to make his story an *exemplum* of the gospel he preaches. It is a story of and for here and now; and only Norman Podhoretz could have done it. If it raises more questions than it answers, that is the purpose: to make us admit those questions exist, to meet them without shame, and to grope with him for answers.

> *A highly readable account of one young man's search for his identity. Recommended for adult readers.*

Not many girls enjoy posing in the nude and it must be admitted that cooperation is mostly for the purpose of earning fees.

—André de Dienes, *Best Nudes.*

Mr. Norman Podhoretz
c/o Random House Inc.
457 Madison Avenue
New York, N.Y., 10022

Please Forward if Necessary

Dear Norman,

Hope this reaches you all right. Mail service these days leaves something to be desired. And you never can tell about publishers. Here today and merged with Dow Chemical or something tomorrow.

I enclose blurb from the *Hollins Critic.* Not that you need it. Your book seems to be getting attention in the right places and mostly they are good reviews. Except maybe that one in *Life* where John Aldridge came on laughing and scratching and slipped you a mickey in a cup of good cheer. But you know old John. He's still trying to top Daniel Defoe's *The Shortest Way With Dissenters.*

So anyhow you are getting reviews. Sure they are riddled with reservations, but they add up to praise in the end which is better than the end of a boot. And, ironically, this is a tribute to the kind of power you have learned to live with as the editor of *Commentary.* Of course people in power have to put up with a certain amount of flattery, even if it's only the dubious flattery of being taken at face value. But it's like saluting officers which they taught you in basic training. Now that you're an officer, too, don't sweat, you've got it made. The time to worry is when they stop saluting. When that happens, it won't be subtle. You'll know.

Not that I am making a big deal about this review in a humble organ of limited circulation and modest means. I am not in favor of humility or false modesty any more than you are. The meek are the real secret troublemakers. All they want to do is inherit the earth. But, let's face it, this is the provinces, the sticks, the boondocks. Far from the bright amazing center of culture you write about, the pleasures of court life, masques and masks. Take it for what it is, then, a "get well" message from the remote reaches of the Empire (o far from the Empire City!). At least maybe you'll be amused. And if, between parties sometimes, you get hung up in idle or in pensive mood, remember what the hangman says when he slips the noose over somebody's head—"Wear it in good health."

You may be wondering. Maybe you have even asked yourself: "What's with this crank whom I have never met coming on with a big, fat, cheerful 'Dear Norman'?" I am glad you asked that question, Norman. It is true you don't know me from the Man in the Moon. And I don't know you from Jason Epstein or even Jason Podhoretz, a minor comic character in a novel called *The Exhibitionist.* Of course, I have read some of your work. And even way out here I have "heard things." But I never pay attention to malicious gossip. I could argue, if I felt hostile, that as a self-confessed celebrity, you have got about the same right to privacy as, say, The Playmate of the Month. But don't get me wrong. My reason for the unwarranted familiarity is that it seems like the thing to do in a literary way. It seems fitting and proper, decorum as it were, to call you Norman in response to the experience of reading your life story. Not that I really feel I know you any better than I did when I picked up the book, admired the prestigious jacket, good cloth binding and paper (excellent production job), and the photograph on the back. But I feel like I *ought* to know you better. Sort of a poor man's Categorical Imperative. . . . But there is a more relevant reason. It is a literary allusion. You like to play with literary allusions too. I can tell from your book. So maybe it is a bad habit and tends to stunt intellectual growth, but we both had the same kind of liberal arts education and can't help ourselves. Anyway, years ago I ran across an article by Diana Trilling. I recall it began with "Dear Norman" too. Man, was I out of it! I was half way through before I figured out it wasn't Norman Vincent Peale.

So it is with a glow of nostalgia that I am bold to address you by your first name. Please, sir, do not misconstrue it as an attempt to pretend to a familiarity it is not my privilege to possess. Be big about it and don't let it bug you. At least I didn't call you "Norm."

Best wishes. Have to run now. Have to write a review of *Making It.* Say, if you want to read some really recent books I recommend: *Feel Free* by David Slavitt, *Killing Time* by Thomas Berger, and one you should take a good look at—*A Bill of Rites, A Bill of Wrongs, A Bill of Goods* by Wright Morris.

Yours truly,

George

P.S. Is it true that Bennett Cerf thinks he is the Alfred Knopf of publishing?

They had always known that I would turn out to be another Clifton Fadiman.
—*Making It.*

Making It is described by its publisher as "a confessional case history." In one place the author says it is "in a way, a letter," and in another he says that it is "a frank, Mailer-like bid for literary distinction, fame, and money all in one package. . . . " All these descriptions are helpful in defining the qualities of this book. It is a confession in the form of a case history, with some of the ease of the epistolary style. The confessional quality is adroitly established by a series of allusions to St. Augustine. This, too, purports to be a story of conversion. The realm of confessional literature, from the Epistles of St. Paul to such recent examples as Norman Mailer's works and George Plimpton's *Paper Lion,* is explicitly alluded to and used functionally in mock-heroic works. The book is addressed to several groups of readers: one personal to the author and beyond critical scrutiny; one semi-personal, the named and unnamed figures of the New York Literary Scene whom the author designates as The Family, the real wheeler-dealers, shakers and movers of the intellectual *Milieu* to which the author belongs; and last, the larger group, you and me, Reader, to whom the book must be addressed if the author is going to get all the fame and money he says he is after. He wants distinction, too, though whether anyone can give him that is debatable. He seems to feel distinction is the inevitable handmaiden of the other two, tripping along like Charity with Faith and Hope. He also seems to feel that power in America exists as a result of the coupling of fame and money. No question about that, I suppose, unless one starts wondering if power can be conferred at all in the same way fame or wealth can be inherited, stolen, earned, or received. In any case, the book is simultaneously addressed to several audiences. Since the apparent form of the book is non-fiction, this presents some artistic difficulty for the author. Consider the problem of exposition. Members of the elite, The Family, can be expected to know most of the details of their own history and, as well, the author's part in it. He runs the risk of boring them to distraction, a risk he compensates for by offering his original interpretation of the meaning of The Family and its history. No doubt this is of considerable interest to that group. And he even makes it interesting to us who have no knowledge upon which to evaluate the merit of his notions. The passages concerning The Family offer some of the most energetic writing in this book. Added to the author's enthusiasm for the subject is the explicit sincerity of his belief. He cares about them and he shows this. Therefore the larger audience is invited to care too, insofar as they can care about the narrator.

In autobiography there is always a problem of the credibility of the chief witness for the defense—the author. When matters of truth and innocence, fact and guilt are involved, the reader necessarily arms himself with a device for which Hemingway had another name, here called the divining rod of skepticism. Unlike Norman Mailer in *Advertisements For Myself,* the author does not include representative examples of his literary work. Perhaps he assumes a widespread awareness of them, but this is unlikely, for it would indicate a very advanced stage of self-delusion. Maybe he decided this rhetorical risk was less than the danger of losing the attention of The Family. But I am inclined to credit him with the bold intent of "making it," this book, all on his own and by its own merits. Nevertheless we still have the problem of the "credibility gap." In fiction the reader is free to believe, disbelieve, and to suspend disbelief. This freedom, acknowledged, becomes a strength for the novelist. But in non-fiction we are less free. We can take it or leave it. Thus autobiography starts at a disadvantage, because no man, be he ever so loathesome and evil, is not without some self-esteem. Even Crabby Appleton, the villain of *Tom Terrific,* enjoys the cackling self-deception that he is the meanest man in the world and "rotten to the core." But this hyperbolic estimate is not fully shared either by Tom or by Mighty Manfred, The Wonder Dog, despite Crabby's assaults upon their sense of justice and fair play. Meaning that all confession is assumed to be a statement by the author of his own case in the light that pleases him most. We automatically mark that this book is not the work of an elder who can prop his weary shanks upon the pillows of a lifetime's reputation. This young man still has a lot to lose. He is most vulnerable by his own admission. And he asserts that he cares a great deal about being a winner. The Family, though depleted and dwindling in power, is still alive and kicking. His own admiration for that group and pride of belonging would incline one to doubt that he would risk their wrath while he retained a measure of sanity. He has plenty of reasons for being untrustworthy.

Slum child, filthy little slum child, so beautiful a mind and so vulgar a personality, so exquisite in sensibility and so coarse in manner.

—*Making It.*

This book does not exist in abstraction from literary tradition or the scene which it proposes to celebrate by paradoxical encomium. I asked the best critic of American literature I know of, William R. Robinson, to give me a one paragraph statement on the background of American autobiographical writing. Robinson is able to take a dare, and here is what he wrote:

> Mythic autobiography, the major indigenous narrative form in American literature, originates in the Puritan diaries, where divine intent regarding an individual's spiritual destiny is sought amid the obscure omens of personal events within the physical world. Melville generalized this focus upon the juncture where the divine manifests itself through nature into a theory of art when he asserted that art is a meeting and mating of opposites. But this theory and such inside narratives as *Billy Budd* and *Moby Dick* issuing from it had been preceded by Emerson's Transcendental version of the Puritans' symbolic drama within the single, separate person; and they were later philosophically justified by William James's vigorous defense of the 'I', the interior life, as the only place where we can find real fact in the making. As James saw it, then, the American imagination grabs

> hold at the precise moment where the transformational event takes place, which occurs from the inside out, so its truth can only be observed there, inside, while, miraculously, existence erupts from being. It bears witness to and exemplifies creation, the individuating process whereby, having gathered its powers at its source, purified of whatever would weigh it down, whether matter, guilt, or egotism, the imagination leaps free. Thus, whether practiced by Cotton Mather, Thoreau, Whitman, Hemingway, Henry Miller, or William Carlos Williams, to mention only the established literary figures, this form affirms as the supreme value for man the individual liberated from necessity and free to act joyfully and for good in the world. Without a doubt, and vigorously, it celebrates fact in the making.

The tradition of "mythic autobiography" persists. But in the present situation all the forms of non-fiction thrive while the novel keeps on dying and dying like the lead soprano in certain Italian operas. From *In Cold Blood* to Paul Holmes's *The Candy Murder Case: The Explosive Story The Newspapers and T.V. Couldn't Tell;* from *Paper Lion* by George Plimpton to *My Own Story: The Truth About Modelling* by Jean Shrimpton; and not to forget that the more successful works of fiction in our time base much of their appeal upon "authenticity." For example, there is much in common between *The Exhibitionist* and *The Confessions of Nat Turner,* both best-sellers. In terms of popular appeal, both are blessed with the illusion of authenticity. In one we are led to imagine that we are privy to the inside story of Jane Fonda. In the other we are encouraged to think we are getting the lowdown on the Walter Mitty dreams of James Baldwin. The essential difference in the two books lies in the fact that some people enjoy the titillation of "bondage" stories and violence while others prefer simple sex; that some prefer to escape the problems of the present by blaming them on the past (thus sharing their problems with the dead, practicing, as it were, intellectual necrophilia) while others escape from their own hangups by reading about movie stars who have hangups too.

In short the literary situation could not be better for *Making It.* The distinctions between fiction and non-fiction have become meaningless. It is possible that nobody can distinguish between truth and fiction any more and nobody cares. In which case this autobiography with its large credibility gap is well-timed. I prefer, however, to take a more charitable view of both the author and the public. I am a Democrat and cautiously egalitarian. Even though Norman Podhoretz makes a shattering assault against any possible equality among men, I like to imagine that the public is not so stupid as it allows its manipulators and managers to assume. If we ever let them know that we know the score and have been keeping it all along, our leaders might become subtle and dangerous instead of being merely mischievous. It is possible that the public has simply recognized that the *only* mode of our times is fiction. From Walter Cronkite to Walter Lippman, from Norman Vincent Peale to Norman Podhoretz, all are equally purveyors of entertainment, more or less entertaining.

Therefore, *Making It* is, in truth, a modern novel and should be treated as such. When it is treated as a work of fiction, it becomes a more interesting book. And it is spared from the greatest danger that besets the author of his first confession. As Henry Sutton puts it: "The confessional pretends to candor but generally misses the mark: X confesses to pederasty and Y to treachery and deceit, and we forgive them these sins, and easily; what we cannot forgive—X, Y, or anyone—is the sin of boring us." By examining *Making It* as fiction we at least mitigate the circumstances of *ennui.*

I was supposed to be endowed with exceptional intelligence, and yet it took me hours to learn how to lace up my new combat boots efficiently, it took me days to learn how to reassemble my rifle in the required time, and I never learned how to adjust a gas mask properly. What was my kind of intelligence worth then?

—Making It.

Making It brings together a number of kinds of fiction. Basically a classic example of the *bildungsroman* of the nineteenth century, it includes such diverse contemporary types as the Jewish novel, the college novel, the army novel, the American-in-Europe novel, with lesser elements from the novel of espionage, the *roman à clef,* the works of Horatio Alger, to name only a few. It is then extremely *literary,* which is perfectly in keeping with the concerns of the protagonist. There is clever use of the conventions of the Pornographic novel; for the protagonist asserts that the hunger for success has replaced sex as "the dirty little secret," and by imagery and analogy he keeps this notion continually present in the story. Not that the protagonist *sublimates* his sexual energies. He refers to any number of girls, in passing, with whom he has enjoyed some intimacy. He mentions a wife and children too, though most often in the Baconian sense as "hostages to Fortune." There is one girl who stands out from the faceless crowd of others, an English girl whom we learn is blond. The protagonist admits that he loved her for a time. Otherwise, however, love does not enter into this story at all.

The protagonist, now a successful literary critic, remembers his life and adds some commentary to show its meaning. He tells how he grew up in Brooklyn, went to school and got along fine until a teacher, Mrs. K., whose unpleasant motives he now understands, pushed and prodded him towards "achievement." She wanted him to go to Harvard, but he went to Columbia (while simultaneously studying in the Jewish and traditional Seminary College), and then to Clare College, Cambridge. Blessed with the benefits and cursed with the deficiencies of the best in liberal arts education, and having acquired some good "connections" through such of his teachers as Lionel Trilling and the irascible F.R. Leavis, he set out to be a critic. He was beginning to make his mark when he got caught in the Draft. Basic Training was a horrible shock, but he managed to survive and wound up with a soft berth overseas. Once he got back, though, things moved along swiftly. He made a name for himself, writing things for *Commentary, The New Yorker,* and other magazines. After some ups and downs he finally made it as editor of *Commentary.* Along the line he was taken in, almost formally, by The Family. As the book ends he has got it made and is glad of it.

The life described, while enviably tranquil, would hardly seem of interest to anyone except the protagonist himself. He never has much trouble and never fails to get what he wants. Probably the nearest thing to a crisis (excepting Basic Training which he sees as a *trauma*) came when he wrote a sassy review of *The Adventures of Augie March* by Saul Bellow. This could have caused him real trouble, but, ironically, it served to his advantage. It was his key to membership in The Family who, it turns out, were just waiting around for someone to give Bellow a bad time. In short, *outwardly,* there are no problems and no suspense unless you happen to be the protagonist. And at the same time he is remembering all this, in comfort and security, he knows how it will all turn out anyway.

Yet it is not a simple and straightforward Success Story because the protagonist is not a simple man. Inwardly it is a story of turmoil and a series of "conversions." Simplified, his dilemma is: what to do with his success? His own background rendered him more or less unable to aspire to the things of this world. Overcoming inhibition, he went on to get an excellent education and to win prizes, awards, and the first and best fruits of it. Only to discover that the principles cherished by the liberal arts rendered him unfit to do anything in the world and especially rendered him unable to enjoy the ends of ambition when they came to him; for both success and ambition were suspect, particularly in terms of the egalitarian ideals that the society paid lip service to. Through some soul searching he finally came to an adjustment, realizing that riches, fame, and power are not in and of themselves bad and that everyone else is "doing it" and "making it" anyway, no matter how piously they otherwise pretend. And, as a critic, he was able to turn his own discipline to work for him, to come to an understanding as to why this conflict in his own mind, a *typical* American conflict as he sees it, came to be there. The epiphany for which he had prepared himself came when he went to a conference of Big Shots at a place named Paradise Island by its wealthy owner. Symbolically, *it*, too, had been converted from its original status and name—Hog Island. There the protagonist saw and felt, helped by good rum and the pleasant surroundings, the true meaning of The Good Life. And he saw that it was good. And he resolved never again to be ashamed of wanting it, any more than he would be ashamed of his sex drives. The understanding which he reached, concerning the egalitarian ideology and its consequent negative view of success, has broad implications. It is more than the hypocrisy of the living. It is a deliberate confidence trick, fine print in the complex social contract of the U.S.A., designed by the WASPS to keep the post-Civil War immigrants and their descendants at a decent distance from the banquet table. Now, however, thanks to him and others, the word is out, the con game is exposed. Thus the protagonist can hope his story may serve to inspire others. In this sense there is conflict in the story and some narrative suspense. A suspense not ending with the book, for the protagonist having committed himself to his goals, becoming as the Elizabethans would have said "a child of Fortune," is ripe and ready for whatever the future may bring. Since Dame Fortune is reputed to be fickle, that could be anything. The possibility is left open for further adventures as he rides the Wheel of Fortune up or down.

But *Making It* is more subtle than that. There is another level to be considered. And this requires some examination of the first-person narrator. We must consider whether he may not very well be an example of that figure who haunts the pages of contemporary fiction—the Anti-Hero.

As the protagonist sees himself, his gifts are intellectual. There is no indication that he has the slightest doubt concerning his intellectual accomplishments. This makes him a very positive character. Of course it is "in character" that he would not bother to demonstrate the rock-foundations of his certainty. Nevertheless, there are certain clues. Evidently trusting in the power of redundancy, the protagonist *tells us* over and again that he is an exceptionally smart fellow. And to doubters and shruggers he can point to certain accomplishments which have won him applause. And from time to time he offers us some examples, in synoptic form, of his critical judgment at work. Unfortunately these are not always dazzling examples of mental acrobatics; indeed, as presented here, they are uniformly unimpressive. Sometimes we are given examples of his reasoning powers. Not even the most sympathetic reader will be as pleased by these examples as the protagonist is. His views of history, the arts, modern life, etc. are a string of clichés, largely derived from the authority of rather well-known popular books, brilliant, if at all, only in the way that the signals formed by ships' flags are brilliant to behold. In this sense, there is a redeeming thread of humor running through the whole book, though the protagonist himself is nothing if not serious minded.

Led on by these clues we begin to notice that the protagonist has other serious flaws. One of these is that practically everything in the story is *abstract* to him. Even his physical descriptions of things and places, which are all too rare, are clearly out of books, perfunctory and lifeless. The protagonist is presented as immune to all sensuous affective experience in life as well as in the arts. He would appear to have experienced little or nothing of the joyous dance of the five senses and, it would *seem,* doesn't know what he is missing. Always (perhaps a true seminarian, despite his "conversion") when faced with a new experience, he cites the authority of books. And when he feels that the books did not prepare him for an experience, he blames the books. There is a touching innocence here, for it never occurs to him that he may have read the wrong books, or that he could have read them without understanding or imaginative engagement. A superior example: He notes that while waiting for his Draft Notice to arrive ("Greetings, Norman!"), he busied himself preparing the now-celebrated Bellow review. One of the books he read was *Dangling Man.* Which, though he offers no evidence of knowing this, *is about a man waiting to get drafted.* In one ear and out the other? Not quite. . . . In another place he offers some observations upon the limbo of waiting to be called. Anyone familiar with *Dangling Man* will see where his "original" observations came from. With few exceptions all the books he mentions are widely known, indicating nothing special about his reading habits as compared with anyone else's. In fact, on the evidence he gives us, it would be impossible to conclude he is "well read" at all. Perhaps this is merely a rhetorical device; he alludes to those things he can be sure his reader will know. On the other hand it may be a wonderful sort of *style.* One thinks (to be bookish) of Jay Gatsby who never descended to the vulgarity of cutting the pages of his elegantly bound sets of books.

Beyond that, with the exception of a very few who have briefly captured his admiration, people are merely names when they are named at all. There are some golden names all right, and well-dropped; but the protagonist will allow them no life. They are objects to him. Even his parents are given short shrift, and the death of his father serves mainly as an occasion for him to defend continuing on at the Seminary, not out of belief, but out of a deathbed promise which he eventually breaks in any case. Girls are just "girls"; sex is just "sex." He shows an ability to analyze the motives of others, almost always to their disadvantage; and he is especially sharp in perceiving the dark and unpleasant motives of his "friends" and any who have done him a good turn. Conversely, when subjecting his own motives to scrutiny he is willing to ascribe the best and most favorable interpretation. Though he subjects himself to rack and thumbscrew, he always comes out smelling like a rose. He is, in fact, without awareness of the point of view of other human beings. The sentimental attribution of motives is, after all, a very different thing than consideration of another's point of view.

This becomes downright peculiar when we consider his endorsement of the uses of power. Power is predicated on self-interest and depends upon the exquisite awareness of the self-interest of others. Power cannot afford to be sentimental. It becomes unstable, dangerous, and ceases to be power at all. It becomes evident that he means *privilege* when he speaks of power. And there is a startling irony in his drive for fame and all that the Elizabethans called "honor." As the protagonist presents himself, he has no concept of honor whatsoever, a lack which would seem to preclude the possibility of achieving any kind of stable fame. He is at great pains to prove that he is a phoney and so is everyone else around him. Phoneys in a Barnum and Bailey world. But, paradoxically, there is no relief from self-doubt here. Instead of rejoicing in the Brotherhood of Phoneys or the Phoneyhood of All Mankind, he still feels somehow "different" from, *alienated* (to use his word) from everyone else.

And though he is a writer and writes with some perception about the mysterious process of writing, he opts for only one *kind* of writing, the product of pure and simple inspiration. Just as "research" and scholarship are pejorative terms and, in his view, inhibitions to intellectual excellence, so labor and skill in writing are contemptible to him. He mentions *skill* in opposition to "authority." "Authority in writing need not be accompanied by consummate skill or any other virtue of craft or mind, for like the personal self-confidence of which it is the literary reflection, it is a quality in its own irreducible right, and one that always elicits an immediate response—just as a certain diffidence of tone and hesitancy of manner account for the puzzling failure of many otherwise superior writers to attract the attention they merit." The way I understand this is that the protagonist comes out for invoking the Muses and winging it.

Which is great unless, like the protagonist, you want to be a *professional.* Because a professional can't afford "writer's block" or he is out of business. Like Bart Starr, he has to play in bandages. But our hero, here in *Making It,* suffers long and hard, he says, from writing blocks. He sees this book, his confession, as a big breakthrough. Well, it has its ups and downs, but the Muses conned him if they let him think it swings. As for *authority,* well the protagonist has got the words, but he can't carry the tune in a galvanized bucket.

All this adds up to an extremely unreliable narrator. Who can neither be trusted nor trust himself. And thus it brings immediately into question his bigger assertions. Like the fact that he ever had any experience of "conversion" at all. What I see is that at every stage he hedges his bet, by leaving himself as a hostage behind. Therefore there are many of him—a boy in Brooklyn, a Seminarian ("sermons" is a word he uses again and again), a Student still hoping that Trilling or Leavis or Hadas or please *somebody* will give him A+; a poor, bewildered, uncomfortable Draftee being yelled at by a mean old Sergeant, a Cambridge gentleman, sipping tea while his Gyp builds up the fire, etc., etc. The book, intended to exorcise all his ghosts, in fact invokes and summons them.

In any case, we have a protagonist who knows neither himself nor the world, who seems crippled in feeling, vulnerable in pride and arrogance, able only to love himself, and *that* in moderation. Almost blissfully unaware, you might say, maybe able to be *happy* because his self-deception is almost total.

Even in this, the covert level of his character, we are not yet near the naked truth of him. The protagonist gives every indication of seeing himself in this same unflattering steel glass. And, like a patient under analysis, reveals most by that which he tries to conceal. He is, then, desperately, urgently insecure. He wants to feel joy, but cannot. He wants to be able to love and to be loved, but he cannot because he despises himself and feels unworthy of love. He wants to be a poet, his long lost childhood dream, and is unable to convince himself that he has any right or "authority," and has managed to stifle the poet by creating insurmountable frustrations. He says he wants fame, power, wealth, and, even, social position. But it is painfully clear he does not want these because he is deeply terrified of responsibilities and dangers. Truly powerful men love danger. And they love to gamble. Even as the protagonist commits himself to Fortune at the end, he tries to hedge his bet, in full, certain and sad knowledge that Dame Fortune is always most cruel to those lovers who mock her by this transparent device.

I will get Peter Quince to write a ballad of this dream: it shall be called Bottom's Dream because it hath no bottom.

—*A Midsummer Night's Dream* (IV, ii).

What does all this have to do with the real live Norman Podhoretz in person? It is not only possible, but necessary, to distinguish between the character of the man in the book, which can be known, and that of the man who wrote it, which cannot. We make this distinction with no difficulty in the works of Henry Miller, never really crediting the author with the sexual exploits of the character, Henry Miller. Podhoretz asks us to do the same thing. The result of this divorce is to make for a much more interesting and praiseworthy book. For, without denying the literal sense of the book, one is directed to consider the *sentence,* in the Chaucerian use of that term. The medieval literary critics, taking their model from St. Augustine (just as Podhoretz does), were extremely sophisticated. They recognized that all literary work has meaning, its own form of *allegoria.* Their basic three-level reading of a work is helpful here. The first two levels of the character of the protagonist are so contradictory as to approach *enigma.* Enigma, as a figure, indicates that the meaning of the work is outside of literal interpretation. Thus, though *Making It* appears to be a simple-minded *fabliau,* it is more complex and more fabulous. The "real" Norman Podhoretz, the author of the book, has created an allegory of pilgrimage. But it is a *false* pilgrimage. The protagonist arrives at what is clearly Babylon and is fooled by the "Welcome to Jerusalem" signs. There he is, up to his knees in the Slough of Despond and trying to make the best of it because all the maps say this is The Delectable Mountain. In his innocence he wants to believe and to do right. Innocence is the key to the character. He is the bumbling *naif* of great satire. Echoes of *Candide, Rasselas, Joseph Andrews,* etc.

The meaning is then clear: "Take a perfectly ordinary innocent guy, a guy like me (or you, hypocrite reader) and let him believe in the ideals of the society and do his best to live by them, and look where he ends up—*Nowhere!* And look what he becomes—either a figure of fun or a pathetic Frankenstein monster."

Put it this way. In selling Norman Podhoretz a sow's ear and letting him think it is a genuine silk purse, the society conned him. Just as Huntington Hartford tried to con the suckers by calling Hog Island a Paradise. It is a shell game, ladies and gentlemen, and (he's so right) you can't win even at the charity bazaar booths run by art, religion, education, etc. The whole society is one big seamless garment. And the goals of all, by definition, look exactly like sugar lumps, but turn to bitter ashes on the tongue. Even the man who is lucky enough to find out before it is too late that he is supposed to be a winner and that it is "all right" to win, even *he,* laurels of victory on his brow, is revealed to be another loser. Either a pathetic bum of the month or a clown in cap and bells. Take your pick. Nobody wins. There are only alternative ways of losing.

Unless...

Unless a man can learn this and has the courage and ability to play both roles at the same time. To clown it up (like the Fool in *Lear*) or to put on sackcloth and ashes and then, amazing, begin to dance for joy in memory of Isaiah's truth, that the oil of joy is for mourning.

As a child Norman Podhoretz dreamed of being a poet. The protagonist tells us he failed. Perhaps the real Podhoretz succeeds, though. For the truth of this book, disguised as it is from the protagonist, is poetic, a statement of the eternal paradox of man's goals in the only world he knows for sure, the one he lives in and will die in. As the protagonist of *Making It* is always saying, if he had not come along, we'd have had to invent him.

And so we just did.

ABOUT NORMAN PODHORETZ

Born in Brooklyn in 1930 to poor Eastern-European Jewish parents, Norman Podhoretz has worked his way into the intellectual upper-middle class of New York City; he is a controversial personality who has been called "the most brilliant young critic of our day."

Mr. Podhoretz spent what he has described in his newest, autobiographical book, *Making It,* a happy and successful childhood, during which time he became a budding poet. While making A-plus grades at Columbia University, his ambitions for a career turned from poetry to literary criticism, and he pursued his interest during the three years he spent at Cambridge's Clare College on a Fulbright Scholarship. Following his stay in England, Podhoretz turned down a graduate fellowship from Harvard in order to become a New York literary intellectual.

Between 1953 and 1955 he completed his military service in the army; prior to and following his service, he worked for the magazine *Commentary.* For a brief time Mr. Podhoretz left *Commentary* to become a free-lance writer, but he returned as editor of the magazine in 1960 at age thirty.

Besides a collection of critical essays, *Doings and Undoings,* published in 1964, Mr. Podhoretz has written since the early fifties over a hundred or more critical essays and book reviews, which have appeared in numerous magazines including *Partisan Review, Commentary,* the *New Yorker, Esquire* and *Harper's. Making It* is an account of his struggle to achieve success in the inner group of New York's literary circle. Mr. Podhoretz is married and has four children.

BOOKS BY NORMAN PODHORETZ

DOINGS AND UNDOINGS: THE FIFTIES AND AFTER IN AMERICAN WRITING
New York: Farrar, Straus, 1964.
New York: Noonday, 1964. (pb)

THE COMMENTARY READER
New York: Atheneum, 1966.
London: Hart-Davis, 1968.
Toronto: McClelland & Stewart, 1968.

MAKING IT
New York: Random House, 1967.
London: Jonathan Cape, 1968.

Genius of the Shore: The Poetry of Howard Nemerov

by Julia Randall

Standing and thinking on the shore of the wide world has long been a favorite situation of the poet. With sand between his toes (the atoms of Democritus? Heaven in a grain?), he gazes out to the swaying unsyllabled sea, and back toward his rocky, babel-tongued city. Birds and stars wheel over him; pods and shards, fishbones and bugs turn up under his feet. Clearly, it is all a Great Writing, in which the poet on the shore is a character attempting to read the sentence in which he appears.

Once, writes Nemerov, villainous William of Occam exploded the dream that we could confidently assign the authorship of the Great Writing. And yet science, social science, and philosophy go on confidently assigning. "Nature," they cry; "Man," they cry; "God," they cry—physics in one tongue, theology in another. What Occam in fact pointed out was that what a thing is in itself in no way depends on how we think of it. But it is by thought embodied in language, and by language embodied in institution, that we construct the civilization in which we live, the human world which so often appears to be simply the Self writ large. The poet's job, strangely enough, is to 'unwrite' by going back to the beginning; to make such speech as we have faithful to 'things as they are' rather than to our arrangements of them; to make language live by confronting things with the 'innocent' mind of an Adam, by naming them to themselves afresh through the powers of that mind which is somehow continuous with them. Nemerov is not alone in observing how many of our languages are dead. Since the medieval synthesis

> It's taken that long for the mind
> To waken, yawn, and stretch, to see
> With opened eyes, emptied of speech
> The real world where the spelling mind
> Imposes with its grammar book
> Unreal relations on the blue
> Swallows.

Nemerov, then, does not seek to impose a vision upon the world so much as to listen to what it says. He works in closer relationship with literal meaning than is presently fashionable; consequently his worst fault (he says so himself) is sententiousness, but his corresponding virtue is a clarity whose object is not to diminish the mystery of the world but to allow it to appear without the interposition of a peculiar individuality, or of fancy-work or arabesque. He is, as much as any modern can be, a romantic poet; he is a religious poet without religion; a prophet, especially in the polemical and ironic mode, without portfolio. When he writes about history, as Stanley Hyman has said, his theme is "history from the point of view of the losers." Thus when he wants to write about Moses, he does so from the point of view of Pharaoh after the Red Sea debacle; and instead of writing about Perseus, he presents the nitwitted predecessors of that hero, who approached Medusa without a mirror and were turned to stone. To judge by his later poems, being turned to stone is the least agreeable and most probable fate for human beings and their institutions together.

Nemerov's experience of the Great Society is the common one, and his cry the same cry that has been ringing in our ears since at least Dover Beach. His poems begin in the personal pain of the 1940 war, and move through the shock of specifically modern history to the consideration of human history generally, backward to the Fall and forward again through its repetitions. "Succession" pictures history as a furnished room whose former tenant, a priest, has departed nobody knows where. The apartment does not record his stay. The present occupant has

> no further wish to follow him
> Where he has gone, for now the room awaits
> The thud of your belongings and your name—
> How easily it will encompass them!
> Behind the door the sycophantic glass
> Already will reflect you in a frame
> That memorizes nothing but its place.

Indifference and rigidity characterize the room; complacency or confusion, the roomers. Any red-blooded American boy can buy a passport to the war, a subway ticket to suburbia, even an access to the Academy of Fine Ideas. He can make like Ike, Santa Claus, Don Juan, Professor Publish, or any number of free-trial examples (and if not satisfied in twenty years, double your hypocrisy back). The monuments of his aching intellect resemble the stark angularities of Steinberg, and the poet can only serve as wry guide to such ruins, which include, for instance, New York, the "frozen city"; the statues in the public gardens; the stacks of the university library; the pulpit; the motel; the segregated cemetery; the packaged meat in the supermarket; the loyalty oath; the Indian-head nickel, and so on. The dead goosefish leers up at lovers on the beach, and the poet reviews his youth:

Accumulating all those years
The blue annuities of silence some called
Wisdom, I heard sunstorms and exploding stars,
The legions screaming in the German wood—
Old violence petrifying where it stood.

The recording artist of this happy scene is the camera, whose "incisive blade" takes "frozen sections": "maybe a shot of Lenin tombed in glass." For the camera "makes the constant claim that reality is visible," whereas "language asserts it to be secret, invisible, a product of relations rather than things." But if we look before, we see Lot's wife pillared on the plain, and if we look after we see—but like Saul at Endor we forget what we have seen, which was probably the ghost of Norbert Wiener.

Nevertheless, if there are no capital Heroes, there are, as there have always been, Hangers-On to the pain and the puzzle. "The point of faith," reiterated in several poems, "is that you sweat it out," you *continue*. In one metaphysical poem, the heart is a voracious vacuum cleaner:

The Vacuum

The house is so quiet now
The vacuum cleaner sulks in the corner closet,
Its bag limp as a stopped lung, its mouth
Grinning into the floor, maybe at my
Slovenly life, my dog-dead youth.

I've lived this way long enough,
But when my old woman died her soul
Went into that vacuum cleaner, and I can't bear
To see the bag swell like a belly, eating the dust
And the woolen mice, and begin to howl

Because there is old filth everywhere
She used to crawl, in the corner and under the stair.
I know now how life is cheap as dirt,
And still the hungry, angry heart
Hangs on and howls, biting at air.

It hangs on and howls in a stubborn contradiction to the Pleasure Principle:

There, toward the end, when the left-handed wish
Is satisfied as it is given up, when the hero
Endures his cancer and more obstinately than ever
Grins at the consolations of religion as at a child's
Frightened pretensions, and when his great courage
Becomes a wish to die, there appears, so obscurely,
Pathetically, out of the wounded torment and the play,
A something primitive and appealing, and still dangerous,
That crawls on bleeding hands and knees over the floor
Toward him, and whispers as if to confess: *again, again.*

What all this amounts to, I suppose, is that salt blood still beats inside the frozen skull: salt blood we inherit, the freezer we inhabit. Or to put it another way, freezing is an illusion, a trick of the temporal camera, a phase of the land which claims us but not of the sea which makes prior claims. In a clarifying poem from *Mirrors and Windows,* the poet stands "where the railroad bridge / Divides the river from the estuary," deciding that he has fallen from the "symboled world" into the great silence of "reality." A loon's cry shatters that silence:

I thought I understood what that cry meant,
That its contempt was for the form of things,
Their doctrines, which decayed—the nouns of stone
And adjectives of glass—not for the verb
Which surged in power properly eternal
Against the seawall of the solid world,
Battering and undermining what it built,

And whose respeaking was the poet's act,
Only and always, in whatever time
Stripped by uncertainty, despair, and ruin,
Time readying to die, unable to die
But damned to life again, and the loon's cry.
And now the sun was sunken in the sea,
The full moon high, and stars began to shine.

The "verb's" properly eternal urge to creation and destruction seems to be echoed in the bleeding hero's confession: *again.* The loon's cry recalls the poet to his job of celebrating the single force. Perhaps, after all, there is a coherence in the voices of things.

It is tempting to mythologize the history of Howard Nemerov somewhat as follows. Hero tramps through rocky wastes, stout Cortez in reverse, having heard tell of mermaids singing (he improvises a song for them in the manner of his grandfather the Pioneer), of a lake isle Innisfree (a song in the manner of the indomitable peasantry), and of a colony at Key West where they have ideas of order (he practices orders). And indeed his songs are the magic which carry him, undaunted but not undinted, through the perennial dangers of pilgrimage.

In place of pain why should I see
The sunlight on the bleeding wound?
Or hear the wounded man's outcry
Bless the Creation with bright sound?
I stretch myself on joy as on a rack
And bear the hunch of glory on my back.

On first looking into Nemerov's hunch, we perceive among other things the family Bible, the collected works of St. Augustine, Shakespeare, and William Blake, plus what appears to be a *Prelude* in brown wraps. In 1948, arrived at a port called Bennington, Hero has his first view of the sea, recognizes his mission, and attended by winged tutelaries does *not* start building an ark or an empire. Instead he paces the beach, one ear landward and one ear seaward, and you will find him there to this day.

This would, of course, be a poem more true than history. At about the time he went to live in Vermont, Nemerov had outgrown his immediate influences and had found his own spare and flexible tongue. And his theory of poetry, later embodied in the *Poetry and Fiction* essays, was developing out of his own practice and his scrupulous and open-minded attention to literature past and present.

Peter Meinke, in his helpful monograph on the poet (University of Minnesota Pamphlets on American Writers), sees Nemerov as, from the beginning, a deeply divided man, as evidenced in "the tensions between his romantic and realistic visions, his belief and unbelief, his heart and mind; and in his alternating production of poetry and prose." I think this is true, and that it is as apparent in the later volumes as in the earlier—perhaps even more so, for the divisions between the serious and the funny (which Nemerov claims are one) come clearer. Two tones of voice, less distinct in the early work, become apparent. One is the ironic flourish: e.g., at the expense of Santa Claus, the "annual savior of the economy," who "speaks in the parables of dollar signs: / Suffer the little children to come to Him." The other is a quiet, insistent, but immensely versatile voice, one which can speak songs, sonnets, and sestinas, but perhaps speaks best the loose blank-verse well exemplified in two short plays, *Endor* and *Cain* (in *The Next Room of the Dream*), and in many quotations included in this essay.

Nemerov's fiction (with which I am not here concerned) is basically comic. The curious self-analytical volume, *Journal of the Fictive Life,* discusses his personal and professional tensions in Freudian terms, but the goose-chase gets nowhere (well, hardly anywhere): "The net of association, for a responsive intelligence, is endless and endlessly intricate; moreover it never will reach a fundamental or anagogical reading that might simplify and make sense of all the others." But the upshot of the *Journal* is that if psychology cannot arrive at anagoge, poetry may. Poetry may somehow recognize the *substance* of things under the disguises of culture and personality: "the thought comes to me that the predicaments of my most characteristic and intimate imagery strangely belong to Shakespeare too, who resolved them by the magical poetry of his Last Plays. May it happen to me also one day that the statue shall move and speak, the drowned child be found, and the unearthly music sing to me." Individuality is a form which we must suffer. But it contains a secret power to get beyond itself, to be purified (Joyce would say) out of personal existence. The mortal man continues, as in the conclusion to the *Journal,* in the birth of his son; the poet continues in the larger spirit of his poems.

It seems to me that Nemerov's "progress" consists in a solution to the predicament of his imagery. Bugs, birds, trees, and running water have been there from the start; death, war, and the city are there still, but they are less disturbing for being more acutely seen, distanced, separated out. Movement and light permeate *The Blue Swallows,* as the title indicates. And it is far and away the most significant and least recognized volume of poems of the sixties. Via deep doubts, deep self-questionings, painful recognitions, and sere embracings Nemerov emerges on the shore between two worlds whose relation is the subject of his most serious and most moving poetry. He joins there a ghost whose composite face reminds us now of Shelley, now of Coleridge, now of Jeremiah, now of Arnold or Roethke. It is a handsome face that literature fathers-forth. But literature is only the formal cause, as the well-to-do Jewish parents were the efficient one. The final cause is neither man's invention nor his own power:

> The aim of the poet is to write poems. Poems are arrangements of language which illuminate a connection between the inside and outside of things. The durability of poems, as objects made out of language which will be around for some time because people experience this illumination and therefore like reading them, results from the clarity, force, and coherence with which this connection is made, and not from anything else however laudable, like the holding of strong opinions, or the feeling of strong emotions, or the naming of beautiful objects. Because of the oddly intimate relations obtaining between the inside and the outside of things, the poetic art is always with us, and does not decay with the decay of systems of philosophy and religion, or fall out of fashion with the sets of names habitually given, over more or less long periods of time, to the relations between the inside of things and the outside. With all the reverence poets have for tradition, poetry is always capable of reaching its beginning again. Its tradition, ideally, has to do with reaching the beginning, so that, of many young poets who begin with literature, a few old ones may end up with nature.

"Wo ist zu diesem Innen / ein Aussen?" cries Rilke like a blind man. And Coleridge:

> In looking at objects of Nature while I am thinking, as at yonder moon dim-glimmering through the dewy window-pane, I seem rather to be seeking, as it were asking for a symbolical language for something within me that already and forever exists.

And Nemerov:

> I look not so much at nature as I listen to what it says. This is a mystery, at least in the sense that I cannot explain it—why should a phrase come to you out of the ground and seem to be exactly right? But the mystery appears to me as the poet's proper relation with things, a relation in which language, that accumulated wisdom and folly in which the living and the dead speak simultaneously, is a full partner and not merely a stenographer.

It is odd that we have to learn a language in which to talk to our central selves, and that the artist should be our naive tutor; that the eyes turned into the skull are blind until thought illuminates the objects inside as the sun illuminates those outside. But it is by its likeness to natural or objective form that we recognize psychic or subjective form, through the medium of the living art-form.

> The way a word does when
> It senses on one side
> A thing and on the other
> A thought; like sunlight
> On marble, or burnished wood,
> That seems to be coming from
> Within the surface and
> To be one substance with it—
> That is one way of doing
> One's being in a world
> Whose being is both thought
> And thing, where neither thing
> Not thought will do alone
> Till either answers other.

In *Creative Intuition in Art and Poetry* Jacques Maritain writes:

> The poet does not know himself in the light of his own essence. Since man perceives himself only through a repercussion of his knowledge of the world of things, and remains empty to himself if he does not fill himself with the universe, the poet knows himself only on condition that things resound in him, and that in him, at a single wakening, they and he come forth together out of sleep. In other words, the primary requirement of poetry, which is the obscure knowing, by the poet, of his own subjectivity, is inseparable from, is one with another requirement—the grasping, by the poet, of the objective reality of the outer and inner world; not by means of concepts and conceptual knowledge, but by means of an obscure knowledge... through affective union.

That art is an objectification of invisible life in terms of the visible and sensible world, that it is the essential means to self-awareness not of individual life (I am Jane Doe of 1842 Williamson Road) but of common human life (I am Adam, I am Hamlet), and that such awareness of life "in widest commonalty spread" is the best agent of sympathy and hence of disinterested action—all this Romanticism made apparent. Nemerov, conscious of the potentiality of romantic or pseudo-romantic attitudes for self-delusion, and wondering if he is not sometimes their dupe, is shy of claiming a moral role for poetry. Only occasionally, as in his lines to Lu Chi, does he glance openly at the effect of a purified dialect on the tribe:

Neither action nor thought,
Only the concentration of our speech
In fineness and in strength (your axe again),
Till it can carry, in those other minds,
A nobler action and a purer thought.

He does claim, however, poetry's power to bear new parts of a world up to consciousness out of an unmindful "sleep of causes." One of his figures is the chessboard or tennis court: the room of our dream defined by the traditional rules, the "nouns of stone and adjectives of glass." "The existence of tennis courts is also a guarantee of the existence of undefined spaces that are not tennis courts, and where tennis playing is unthinkable. The object of exploration is to find what is unthinkable in those immensities." The object of exploration, Eliot claims, is to arrive where we started. Nemerov too implies that the out-of-court immensities may be our being's heart and home; that the poet, if we attend him, may guide us there. But he is often in doubt. If we started in the neat Commerical Gardens, then

it is right that we return
To exit where we started, nothing in our hands.

He is certain that wherever we started, it will not be knowledge we carry off in the end. The art-form which imitates not our appearance (the camera does that) but our living relations, is not a means to conceptual knowledge; it is a light which illuminates wider and wider areas of our obscure experience, the next and next room of the single dream.

To watch water, to watch running water
Is to know a secret, seeing the twisted rope
Of runnels on the hillside, the small freshets
Leaping and limping down the tilted field
In April's light, the green, grave and opaque
Swirl in the millpond where the current slides
To be combed and carded silver at the fall;
It is a secret. Or it is not to know
The secret, but to have it in your keeping,
A locked box, Bluebeard's room, the deathless thing
Which it is death to open. Knowing the secret,
Keeping the secret—herringbones of light
Ebbing on beaches, the huge artillery
Of tides—it is not knowing, it is not keeping,
But being the secret hidden from yourself.

The secret which we are is the same as the secret in the seed, in the sea, in the word. Nothing belongs to the self alone, although thought belongs to the human mind alone. And thought, like its parent nature, is fiercely generative, both of what it sees as good and of what it sees as evil.

Great pain was in the world before we came.
The shriek had learned to answer to the claw
Before we came; the gasp, the sigh, the groan,
Did not need our invention. But all these
Immediacies refused to signify
Till in the morning of the mental sun
One moment shuddered under stress and broke
Irreparably into before and after,
Inventing patience, panic, doubt, despair,
And with a single thrust producing thought
Beyond the possible, building the vaults
Of debt and the high citadels of guilt,
The segregating walls of obligation,
All that imposing masonry of time
Secretly rooted at the earth's cracked hearth,
In the Vishnu schist and the Bright Angel shale,
But up aspiring past the visible sky.

Great pain was (and is) in the world; great loveliness, too. Happiness is "helpless" before the fall of the white waters (of time) which bear away "this filth" (of personal and communal history). Nemerov can watch the spring freshets and speak of the literal rising of the dead. He can break a stick and find "nothing that was not wood, nothing / That was not God." The stick can figure equally well the tree of Eden or of Calvary, the forest tree brought down by the vine, the family tree or its sexual organ, Aaron's rod, Daphne's wrist, and so on in an endless string of ambiguities which keeps fraying out and away "since Adam's fall / Unraveled all." The poet makes his knot and holds it up to our attention. But he can't knot water. He can only tell us

A new thing: even the water
Flowing away beneath those birds
Will fail to reflect their flying forms,
And the eyes that see become as stones
Whence never tears shall fall again.

Meanwhile, at least, the poet "by arts contemplative" finds and names reality again. Like Conrad's Marlow ("my favorite person in fiction"), he is enamoured of simple facts but finds the world unavoidably symbolic. Writing of Nabokov, Nemerov says

> His subject is always the inner insanity and how it may oddly match or fail to match the outer absurdity, and this problem he sees as susceptible only of *artistic* solutions. He may well be the accountant of the universe... but he is not its moral accountant, and his double entries seek only the exact balance between inside and outside, self and world, in a realm to which morality stands but as a dubious, Euclidean convenience; that balance is what in the arts is conventionally called *truth*.

In his excellent book, *The Lyrical Novel,* Ralph Freedman writes: "Equating the subject and object of awareness with the 'inner' and the 'outer,' Virginia Woolf suggests that both are included in a single whole." And Woolf herself writes of Conrad: "one must be possessed of the double vision; one must be at once inside and out. To praise... silence, one must possess a voice." So, according to Nemerov,

> ... the work of art is religious in nature, not because it beautifies an ugly world or pretends that a naughty world is a nice one—for these things especially art does not do—but because it shows of its own nature that things drawn within the sacred circle of its forms are transfigured, illuminated by an inward radiance which amounts to goodness because it amounts to Being itself. In the life conferred by art, Iago and Desdemona, Edmund and Cordelia, the damned and the blessed, equally achieve immortality by their relation with the creating intelligence which sustains them. The art work is not responsible for saying that things in reality are so, but rather for revealing what this world says to candid vision. It is thus that we delight in tragedies whose actions in life would merely appall us. And it is thus that art, by its illusions, achieves a human analogy to the resolution of that famous question of theodicy—the relation of an Omnipotent Benevolence to evil—which the theologians, bound to the fixed forms of things, have for centuries struggled with, intemperately and in vain. And it is thus that art, by vision and not by dogma, patiently and repeatedly offers the substance of things hoped for, the evidence of things unseen.

These are high claims, and easily misread. But we cannot misread two necessary qualities of the poet: openness and the double vision, qualities which Howard Nemerov possesses to a high degree. Look inward, look outward, and speak of what you have seen. But finally, perhaps,

poems are not
The point. Finding again the world,
That is the point, where loveliness
Adorns intelligible things
Because the mind's eye lit the sun.

ABOUT HOWARD NEMEROV

It has been said that Howard Nemerov's writings reflect three major influences in his life—childhood in the city, violence in the war, and the world of nature. Born in New York City in 1920, he was graduated from Harvard University in 1941, where he had won the Bowdoin Prize Essayist award a year earlier.

After serving as an instructor at Hamilton College in New York from 1946 to 1948, Mr. Nemerov joined the faculty in literature at Bennington College in 1948, and remained until 1966 when he became a member of the faculty at Brandeis University.

He received a Kenyon Review fellowship in 1955 for *The Homecoming Game*, which was later converted by Howard Lindsay and Russel Crouse into the play *Tall Story*. Awarded an Institute of Arts and Letters grant in 1961, Nemerov also received a citation and award from the Brandeis Art Awards in 1963. He was elected a member of the National Institute of Arts and Letters in 1965.

BOOKS BY HOWARD NEMEROV

THE IMAGE AND THE LAW
New York: Henry Holt, 1947.
Toronto: Oxford, 1947.

THE MELODRAMATISTS
New York: Random House, 1949.
Toronto: Random House, 1949.

GUIDE TO THE RUINS
New York: Random House, 1950.

FEDERIGO, OR, THE POWER OF LOVE
Boston: Little, Brown, 1954.
Toronto: McClelland, 1954.
London: Victor Gollancz, 1955.

THE SALT GARDEN
Boston: Little, Brown, 1955.

THE HOMECOMING GAME
New York: Simon and Schuster, 1957.
London: Victor Gollancz, 1958.

MIRRORS AND WINDOWS: POEMS
Chicago: University of Chicago Press, 1958.

A COMMODITY OF DREAMS
New York: Simon and Schuster, 1959.
London: Secker & Warburg, 1960.

NEW & SELECTED POEMS
Chicago: University of Chicago Press, 1960.
Chicago: University of Chicago Press, 1963. (pb)

THE NEXT ROOM OF THE DREAM
Chicago: University of Chicago Press, 1962.
Chicago: University of Chicago Press, 1962. (pb)

POETRY AND FICTION: ESSAYS
New Brunswick, N.J.: Rutgers University Press, 1963.

JOURNAL OF THE FICTIVE LIFE
New Brunswick, N.J.: Rutgers University Press, 1965.

A SEQUENCE OF SEVEN
Hollins College, Va.: Tinker Press, 1967. (pb)

THE BLUE SWALLOWS
Chicago: University of Chicago Press, 1967.

INDEX TO THE HOLLINS CRITIC

Volume I, 1964

Number 1, February. "Hard Times and the Noble Savage: J.P. Donleavy's *A Singular Man*" by John Rees Moore. Poets: John Alexander Allen and Daniel Hoffman.

Number 2, April. "John Cheever and the Charms of Innocence: The Craft of *The Wapshot Scandal*" by George Garrett. Poets: Theodore Hirschfield and Howard Nemerov.

Number 3, June. "The Long Chronicle of Guilt: William Golding's *The Spire*" by Walter Sullivan. Poet: Elliot Coleman.

Number 4, October. "Hunting a Master Image: The Poetry of Richard Eberhart" by Daniel Hoffman. Poet: Richard Eberhart.

Number 5, December. "The Search for Lost Innocence: Karl Shapiro's *The Bourgeois Poet*" by Louis D. Rubin, Jr. Poets: Vassar Miller and Jean Farley.

Volume II, 1965

Number 1, February. "That Old Triangle: A Memory of Brendan Behan" by Benedict Kiely. Poet: Julia Randall.

Number 2, April. "To Do Right in a Bad World: Saul Bellow's *Herzog*" by George Garrett. Poet: Charles Edward Eaton.

Number 3, June. "A Fear of Dying: Norman Mailer's *An American Dream*" by Brom Weber. Poets: Daniel Hoffman and John Alexander Allen.

Number 4, September. "Flannery O'Connor, Sin, and Grace: *Everything That Rises*

Must Converge" by Walter Sullivan. Poets: R.H.W. Dillard, George Garrett, and Daniel Hoffman.

Number 5, December. "An Embarrassment of Riches: Baldwin's *Going to Meet the Man* " by John Rees Moore. Poets: Bruce Berlind and John Alexander Allen.

Volume III, 1966

Number 1, February. "Crime and Punishment in Kansas: Truman Capote's *In Cold Blood* " by George Garrett. Poets Margaret Leigh Ferguson and Louis Coxe.

Number 2, April. Poetry Issue: "The Twelve And The One: A Parable" by Howard Nemerov. "Now Yeats Has Gone: Three Irish Poets" by John Rees Moore. "King Lear, Act Five, Scene Two, Proustified and Moncrieffed" by Howard Nemerov. Poets: Robert Hazel, Roy Basler, Jane Gentry, William Jay Smith, and Julia Randall.

Number 3, June. "Not Text, But Texture: The Novels of Vladimir Nabokov" by R.H.W. Dillard. Poet: Jane Gentry.

Number 4, October. "'Mithridates, he died old': Black Humor and Kurt Vonnegut, Jr." by Robert Scholes. Poet: C.G. Hanzlicek.

Number 5, December. "Ripeness Was Not All: John Barth's *Giles Goat-Boy*" by Benedict Kiely. Poets: Alan Stephens and Rose Styron.

Volume IV, 1967

Number 1, February. "Robert Lowell's *Near the Ocean*: The Greatness and Horror of Empire" by Daniel Hoffman. Poet: Stanley Poss.

Number 2, April. "The Black Clock: The Poetic Achievement of Louis MacNeice" by William Jay Smith. Poets: Charles Edward Eaton, Carl Bode, and Bink Noll.

Number 3, June. "Morris The Magician: A Look at *In Orbit*" by George Garrett. Poet: Julia Randall.

Number 4, October. "Toward An Existential Realism: The Novels of Colin Wilson" by R.H.W. Dillard. Poet: John Alexander Allen.

Number 5, December. "William Styron and Human Bondage: *The Confessions of Nat Turner*" by Louis D. Rubin, Jr. Poet: Daniel Hoffman.

Volume V, 1968

Number 1, February. "My Silk Purse and Yours: *Making It,* Starring Norman Podhoretz" by George Garrett. Poets: Virginia Moore, Marion Montgomery, Vassar Miller, Charles Edward Eaton, and Jim Seay.

Number 2, April. "American Wandering Minstrel: Peter S. Beagle and 'The Last Unicorn'" by Benedict Kiely. Poets: David R. Slavitt, John Alexander Allen, John Pauker, and Valery Nash.

Number 3, June. "The Gift of Tongues: W.S. Merwin's Poems and Translations" by Daniel Hoffman. Poet: R.H.W. Dillard.

Number 4, October. "Thomas Kinsella's Nightwalker: A Phoenix in the Dark" by John Rees Moore. Poets: Charles Edward Eaton and Margaret Gibson.

Number 5, December. "Beyond Nihilism: The Fiction of George P. Elliott" by Blanche H. Gelfant. Poet: Brewster Ghiselin.

Volume VI, 1969

Number 1, February. "Swimming in Sharkwater: The Poetry of Samuel Hazo" by R.H.W. Dillard. Poets: George Calvert Kinnear, Henry Taylor, and Rosanne Coggeshall.

Number 2, April. "Death Without Tears: Anthony Burgess and the Dissolution of the West" by Walter Sullivan. Poets: Stephen Mooney and Robert Bagg.

Number 3, June. "Genuis Of The Shore: The Poetry of Howard Nemerov" by Julia Randall. Poets: none.

Special Issue, July. "Two World Taken As They Come: Richard Wilbur's *Walking to Sleep*" by Henry Taylor. Poets: Richard Wilbur, Bruce Berlind, Christine Costigan, Robert Bonazzi, Brewster Ghiselin, Marion Montgomery, and Judith Moffett.

Number 4, October. "Ringing the Bell: William Harrison's *In a Wild Sanctuary*" by George Garrett. Poets: Charles Edward Eaton, Carl Bode, and Marion Montgomery.

Number 5, December. "The Orgastic Fiction of John Fowles" by Robert Scholes. Poets: John Alexander Allen and Annie Dillard.

THE HOLLINS CRITIC POETS

John Alexander Allen / *February 1964, June 1965, December 1965, October 1967, April 1968, December 1969*
Robert Bagg / *April 1969*
Roy Basler / *April 1966*
Bruce Berlind / *December 1965, July 1969*
Carl Bode / *April 1967, October 1969*
Robert Bonazzi / *July 1969*
Rosanne Coggeshall / *February 1969*
Elliot Coleman / *June 1964*
Christine Costigan / *July 1969*
Louis Coxe / *February 1966*
Annie Dillard / *December 1969*
R.H.W. Dillard / *September 1965, June 1968*
Charles Edward Eaton / *April 1965, April 1967, February 1968, October 1968, October 1969*
Richard Eberhart / *October 1964*
Jean Farley / *December 1964*
George Garrett / *September 1965*
Jane Gentry / *April 1966, June 1966*
Brewster Ghiselin / *December 1968, July 1969*
Margaret Ferguson Gibson / *February 1966, October 1968*
C.G. Hanzlicek / *October 1966*
Robert Hazel / *April 1966*
Theodore Hirschfield / *April 1964*
Daniel Hoffman / *February 1964, June 1965, September 1965, December 1967*
George Calvert Kinnear / *February 1969*
Vassar Miller / *December 1964, February 1968*
Judith Moffett / *July 1969*
Marion Montgomery / *February 1968, July 1969, October 1969*
Stephen Mooney / *April 1969*

Virginia Moore / *February 1968*
Valery Nash / *April 1968*
Howard Nemerov / *April 1964*
Bink Noll / *April 1967*
John Pauker / *April 1968*
Stanley Poss / *February 1967*
Julia Randall / *February 1965, April 1966, June 1967*
Jim Seay / *February 1968*
David R. Slavitt / *April 1968*
William Jay Smith / *April 1966*
Alan Stephens / *December 1966*
Rose Styron / *December 1966*
Henry Taylor / *February 1969*
Richard Wilbur / *July 1969*

SUBJECT INDEX TO THE HOLLINS CRITIC

BIBLIOGRAPHIES OF *THE HOLLINS CRITIC* AUTHORS

BOOKS BY PETER S. BEAGLE

A FINE PLACE AND PRIVATE PLACE
New York: Viking, 1960.
New York: Dell, 1963. (pb)
London: Frederick Muller, 1961.
London: Corgi, 1963.
Toronto: S.J. Reginald Saunders, 1963. (pb)
New York: Ballantine, 1969. (pb)

I SEE BY MY OUTFIT
New York: Viking, 1965.
New York: Ballantine, 1969. (pb)

THE LAST UNICORN
New York: Viking, 1968.
Toronto: Macmillan, 1968.
London: Bodley Head, 1968.
New York: Ballantine, 1969. (pb)

BOOKS BY SAUL BELLOW

DANGLING MAN
New York: Vanguard, 1944.
London: Lehmann, 1946.
New York: Meridian, 1960. (pb)
Middlesex: Penguin, 1963. (pb)
New York: New American Library, 1965. (pb)

THE VICTIM
New York: Vanguard, 1947.
London: Lehmann, 1948.
New York: Viking, 1956. (pb)
Toronto: Macmillan, 1956.

THE ADVENTURES OF AUGIE MARCH
New York: Viking, 1953.
London: Weidenfeld & Nicolson, 1954.
New York: Popular Library, 1954. (pb)
London: Weidenfeld & Nicolson, 1958.
Toronto: Macmillan, 1956.

New York: Viking, 1960. (pb)
New York: Premier, 1965. (pb)
New York: Crest, 1965. (pb)

SEIZE THE DAY
New York: Viking, 1956.
Toronto: Macmillan, 1956.
London: Weidenfeld & Nicolson, 1957.
The short novel alone:
New York: Viking, 1961. (pb)
New York: Premier, 1965. (pb)

HENDERSON THE RAIN KING
New York: Viking, 1959.
London: Weidenfeld & Nicolson, 1959.
Toronto: Macmillan, 1959.
New York: Viking, 1960. (pb)
New York: Crest, 1965. (pb)

HERZOG
New York: Viking, 1964.
Toronto: Macmillan, 1964.
London: Weidenfeld & Nicolson, 1964.
New York: Crest, 1965. (pb)
New York: Viking, 1967. (pb)
Toronto: Macmillan, 1967. (pb)

THE LAST ANALYSIS
New York: Viking, 1965.
New York: Viking, 1966. (pb)
London: Weidenfeld & Nicolson, 1966.
London: Weidenfeld & Nicolson, 1966. (pb)
Toronto: Macmillan, 1966.
Toronto: Macmillan, 1966. (pb)

MOSBY'S MEMOIRS AND OTHER STORIES
New York: Viking, 1968.
London: Weidenfeld & Nicolson, 1969.
New York: Crest, 1969. (pb)

MR. SAMMLER'S PLANET
New York: Viking, 1970.
London: Weidenfeld &-Nicolson, 1970.

BOOKS BY ANTHONY BURGESS

TIME FOR A TIGER
London: Heinemann, 1956.

THE ENEMY IN THE BLANKET
London: Heinemann, 1958.
London: Heinemann, 1968.

BEDS IN THE EAST
London: Heinemann, 1959.
London: Heinemann, 1968.

THE RIGHT TO AN ANSWER
London: Heinemann, 1960.
New York: W.W. Norton, 1962.
New York: Ballantine, n.d.

THE DOCTOR IS SICK
London: Heinemann, 1960.
New York: W.W. Norton, 1966.
New York: Ballantine, n.d. (pb)

DEVIL OF A STATE
London: Heinemann, 1961.
New York: W.W. Norton, 1962.
New York: Ballantine, n.d. (pb)

THE WORM AND THE RING
London: Heinemann, 1961.

A CLOCKWORK ORANGE
London: Heinemann, 1962.
New York: W.W. Norton, 1963. (pb)
New York: Ballantine, n.d. (pb)
London: Pan, 1964. (pb)

THE WANTING SEED
London: Heinemann, 1962.
New York: W.W. Norton, 1963.
New York: Ballantine, n.d. (pb)

HONEY FOR THE BEARS
London: Heinemann, 1963.
London: Pan, n.d. (pb)

New York: W.W. Norton, 1964.
New York: Ballantine, n.d. (pb)

THE NOVEL TODAY
London: Longmans, Green, 1963.

NOVEL NOW
New York: W.W. Norton, 1967.

INSIDE MR. ENDERBY (pseud. Joseph Kell)
London: Heinemann, 1963.
Harmondsworth: Penguin, n.d. (pb)

LANGUAGE MADE PLAIN
London: English Universities Press, 1964.
New York: Thomas Y. Crowell, 1965.

NOTHING LIKE THE SUN
London: Heinemann, 1964.
Harmondsworth: Penguin, n.d. (pb)
New York: W.W. Norton, 1964.
New York: Ballantine, n.d. (pb)

MALAYAN TRILOGY
London: Pan, 1964. (pb)

ONE HAND CLAPPING
London: Peter Davies, 1964.

EVE OF ST. VENUS
London: Sidgwick & Jackson, 1964.

HERE COMES EVERYBODY (an introduction to Joyce)
London: Faber & Faber, 1965.

RE JOYCE
New York: W.W. Norton, 1968. (pb)
New York: Ballantine, 1968. (pb)

A VISION OF BATTLEMENTS
London: Sidgwick & Jackson, 1965.
New York: W.W. Norton, 1966.
New York: Ballantine, 1967. (pb)

TREMOR OF INTENT
London: Heinemann, 1966.
New York: W.W. Norton, 1966.
New York: W.W. Norton, n.d. (pb)
New York: Ballantine, 1967. (pb)

THE LONG DAY WANES
New York: W.W. Norton, 1966.
New York: Ballantine, 1967. (pb)

ENDERBY
New York: W.W. Norton, 1968.

New York: Ballantine, 1970. (pb)

A CLOCKWORK ORANGE & HONEY FOR THE BEARS
New York: Modern Library, 1968.

URGENT COPY
New York: W.W. Norton, 1969.

SHAKESPEARE
New York: Knopf, 1970.

JOURNAL OF THE PLAGUE YEAR by Daniel Defoe (ed.)
Baltimore: Penguin, 1966. (pb)
Harmondsworth: Penguin, 1966. (pb)

A SHORTER FINNEGANS WAKE (ed.)
London: Faber & Faber, 1966.

BOOKS BY TRUMAN CAPOTE

OTHER VOICES, OTHER ROOMS
New York: Random House, 1948.
Toronto: Random House, 1948.
London: Heinemann, 1948.
New York: New American Library, n.d. (pb)
New York: Vintage, n.d. (pb)
New York: Modern Library, 1955. (pb)
Toronto: Modern Library, n.d. (pb)
New York: Random House, 1968.
London: Heinemann, 1968.

A TREE OF NIGHT AND OTHER STORIES
New York: Random House, 1949.
Toronto: Random House, 1949.
London: Heinemann, 1950.

LOCAL COLOR
New York: Random House, 1950.
London: Heinemann, 1955.

THE GRASS HARP
New York: Random House, 1951.
Toronto: Random House, 1951.
London: Heinemann, 1952.
New York: Random House, 1952. (play)

THE GRASS HARP, AND A TREE OF NIGHT AND OTHER STORIES
New York: New American Library, n.d. (pb)

THE MUSES ARE HEARD
New York: Random House, 1956.
Toronto: Random House, 1956.
London: Heinemann, 1957.
New York: Modern Library, n.d. (pb)
New York: Vintage, n.d. (pb)

BREAKFAST AT TIFFANY'S
New York: Random House, 1958.
Toronto: Random House, 1955.
London: Hamish Hamilton, 1958.
New York: New American Library, n.d. (pb)

OBSERVATIONS (with Richard Avedon)
New York: Simon and Schuster, 1959.
London: Weidenfeld & Nicolson, 1959.

SELECTED WRITINGS
New York: Random House, 1963.
Toronto: Random House, 1963.
London: Hamish Hamilton, 1963.
New York: Modern Library, n.d. (pb)
Toronto: Modern Library, n.d. (pb)

IN COLD BLOOD
New York: Random House, 1966.

New York: Modern Library, 1968.

A CHRISTMAS MEMORY
New York: Random House, 1966. (reg. & autographed)

THE THANKSGIVING VISITOR
New York: Random House, 1968.
London: Hamish Hamilton, 1969.

HOUSE OF FLOWERS (with Harold Arlen)
New York: Random House, 1968.

TRILOGY: AN EXPERIMENT IN MULTI-MEDIA (with others)
New York: Macmillan, 1969.

BOOKS BY GEORGE P. ELLIOTT

PARKTILDEN VILLAGE
Boston: Beacon, 1958.
Toronto: S.J. Reginald Saunders, 1958.
Louisville, Ky.: Arlington, 1958.

FEVER AND CHILLS
Iowa City: Stone Wall, 1961.

AMONG THE DANGS
New York: Holt, Rinehart & Winston, 1961.
London: Secker & Warburg, 1962.
Philadelphia: J.B. Lippincott, 1963. (pb)
Toronto: McClelland, 1963. (pb)
New York: Viking, 1966. (pb)
Toronto: Macmillan, 1966. (pb)

DAVID KNUDSEN
New York: Random House, 1962.
Toronto: Random House, 1962.

A PIECE OF LETTUCE
New York: Random House, 1964.
Toronto: Random House, 1962.

IN THE WORLD
New York: Viking, 1965.
Toronto: Macmillan, 1965.

FROM THE BERKELEY HILLS
New York: Harper & Row, 1968.
New York: Harper & Row, 1969.

AN HOUR OF LAST THINGS
New York: Harper & Row, 1968.

FIFTEEN MODERN AMERICAN POETS (ed.)
New York: Holt, Rinehart & Winston, 1956. (pb)
New York: Holt, Rinehart & Winston, 1962. (pb)
New York: Peter Smith, n.d.

TYPES OF PROSE FICTION (ed)
New York: Random House, 1964.

BOOKS BY JOHN FOWLES

THE COLLECTOR
Boston: Little, Brown, 1963.
New York: Dell, 1963. (pb)
New York: Dell, 1969. (pb)

THE ARIOSTOS: A SELF-PORTRAIT IN IDEAS
Boston: Little, Brown, 1964.
New York: New American Library (rev. ed.), 1970. (pb)

THE MAGUS
Boston: Little, Brown, 1965.
London: Jonathan Cape, 1966.
New York: Dell, 1967. (pb)

THE FRENCH LIEUTENENT'S WOMAN
Boston: Little, Brown, 1969.
London: Jonathan Cape, 1969.

BOOKS BY WILLIAM HARRISON

THE THEOLOGIAN
New York: Harper & Row, 1965.

IN A WILD SANCTUARY
New York: William Morrow, 1969.

New York: New American Library, 1970. (pb)

BOOKS BY SAMUEL HAZO

DISCOVERY
New York: Sheed and Ward, 1959. (pb)

THE QUIET WARS
New York: Sheed and Ward, 1962. (pb)

HART CRANE: AN INTRODUCTION AND INTERPRETATION
New York: Barnes and Noble, 1963.
New York: Holt, Rinehart & Winston, 1963.

THE CHRISTIAN INTELLECTUAL (ed.)
Pittsburgh: Duquesne University Press, 1963.
Louvain, Belgium: Editions E. Nauwelaerts, 1963.

A SELECTION OF CONTEMPORARY RELIGIOUS POETRY (ed.)
New York: Paulist Press, 1963. (pb)

LISTEN WITH THE EYE (with photographs by James P. Blair)
Pittsburgh: University of Pittsburgh Press, 1964. (pb)

MY SONS IN GOD
Pittsburgh: University of Pittsburgh Press, 1965.

BLOOD RIGHTS
Pittsburgh: University of Pittsburgh Press, 1968.
Pittsburgh: University of Pittsburgh Press, 1968. (pb)

BOOKS BY THOMAS KINSELLA

THE BREASTPLATE OF SAINT PATRICK
Dublin: Dolmen, 1954. (pb)

33 TRIADS
Dublin: Dolmen, 1955. (pb)

THE SONS OF USNECH
Dublin: Dolmen, 1955.

THE DEATH OF A QUEEN
Dublin: Dolmen, 1956. (pb)

POEMS
Dublin: Dolmen, 1956.

ANOTHER SEPTEMBER
Dublin: Dolmen, 1958. (pb)
Philadelphia: Dufour, 1958.

MORALITIES
Dublin: Dolmen, 1960.

POEMS AND TRANSLATIONS
New York: Atheneum, 1961.
New York: Atheneum, 1961. (pb)

DOWNSTREAM
Dublin: Dolmen, 1962.
Philadelphia: Dufour, 1962.

WORMWOOD
Dublin: Dolmen, 1966.
Philadelphia: Dufour, 1966.

NIGHTWALKER
Dublin: Dolmen, 1967.

NIGHTWALKER AND OTHER POEMS
Dublin: Dolmen, 1967.
New York: Knopf, 1968.

SIX IRISH POETS (a selection ed. by Robin Skelton)
London: Oxford, 1962.

POEMS BY THOMAS KINSELLA, DOUGLAS LIVINGSTON, AND ANNE SEXTON
London: Oxford, 1968. (pb)

BOOKS BY NORMAN MAILER

THE NAKED AND THE DEAD
New York: Rinehart, 1948.
Toronto: Clarke, Irwin, 1948.
London: Wingate, 1949.
New York: New American Library, 1951. (pb)
London: Wingate, 1952.
New York: Grosset & Dunlap, 1956.
Toronto: McLeod, 1956.
New York: Modern Library, 1961.
Toronto: Random House, 1961.

BARBARY SHORE
New York: Rinehart, 1951.
London: Jonathan Cape, 1952.
Toronto: Clarke, Irwin, 1952.
New York: New American Library, 1953. (pb)
New York: Grosset & Dunlap, 1963. (pb)
New York: New American Library, 1968. (pb)

THE DEER PARK
New York: Putnam, 1955.
Toronto: Allen, 1955.
London: Wingate, 1957.
Toronto: Allen, 1957.
New York: New American Library, 1957. (pb)

THE MAN WHO STUDIED YOGA IN "NEW SHORT NOVELS II"
New York: Ballantine, 1956.
New York: Ballantine, 1956. (pb)

THE WHITE NEGRO
San Francisco: City Light Books, 1959. (pb)

ADVERTISEMENTS FOR MYSELF
New York: Putnam, 1959.
Toronto: Longmans, Green, 1959.
London: Deutsch, 1961.
New York: New American Library, 1961. (pb)

DEATHS FOR THE LADIES, AND OTHER DISASTERS
New York: Putnam, 1962.

New York: Putnam, 1962. (pb)
Toronto: Longmans, Green, 1962. (pb)
London: Deutsch, 1962.

THE PRESIDENTIAL PAPERS
New York: Putnam, 1963.
New York: Bantam, 1964. (pb)

AN AMERICAN DREAM
New York: Dial, 1965.
Toronto: S.J. Reginald Saunders, 1966.
London: Deutsch, 1966.
New York: Dell, 1966. (pb)

CANNIBALS AND CHRISTIANS
New York: Dial, 1966.
London: Deutsch, 1967.
Toronto: S.J. Reginald Saunders, 1967.
New York: Dell, 1967. (pb)

THE DEER PARK (play)
New York: Dial, 1967.
Toronto: S.J. Reginald Saunders, 1967.
New York: Dell, 1967. (pb)

THE SHORT FICTION OF NORMAN MAILER
New York: Dell, 1967. (pb)

WHY ARE WE IN VIETNAM?
New York: Putnam, 1967.
Ontario: Longmans, Green, 1967.
New York: Putnam-Berkley, 1968. (pb)

THE IDOL AND THE OCTOPUS
New York: Dell, 1968. (pb)

THE ARMIES OF THE NIGHT
New York: New American Library, 1968.
New York: New American Library, 1968. (pb)
London: Weidenfeld & Nicolson, 1969.

MIAMI AND THE SEIGE OF CHICAGO
New York: New American Library, 1968. (pb)
London: Weidenfeld & Nicolson, 1968.

BOOKS BY WILLIAM S. MERWIN

A MASK FOR JANUS
New Haven: Yale University Press, 1952.
London: Oxford, 1952.

THE DANCING BEARS
New Haven: Yale University Press, 1954.
Ontario: Burn and MacEachern, 1954.

GREEN WITH BEASTS
New York: Knopf, 1956.
London: Hart-Davis, 1956.
Toronto: British Book Service, 1956.

THE DRUNK IN THE FURNACE
New York: Macmillan, 1960. (pb)
London: Hart-Davis, 1960.
Toronto: British Book Service, 1960.

THE MOVING TARGET
New York: Atheneum, 1963.
New York: Atheneum, 1963. (pb)
London: Hart-Davis, 1967.
Toronto: McClelland, 1963.
Toronto: McClelland, 1963. (pb)

THE LICE
New York: Atheneum, 1967.
New York: Atheneum, 1967. (pb)

THE CARRIER OF LADDERS
New York: Atheneum, 1970. (pb)

THE MINER'S PALE CHILDREN
New York: Atheneum, 1970

TRANSLATIONS:

POEMA DEL CID (English verse trans. by Merwin)
New York: Las Americas, 1960.
New York: Las Americas, 1960. (pb)
as *POEM OF THE CID*
Ontario: J.M. Dent, 1960.
New York: New American Library, 1962.

IN MEDIEVAL EPICS
New York: Modern Library, 1963.
Toronto: Random House, 1963.

SOME SPANISH BALLADS
New York: Abelard-Schuman, 1961.
as *SPANISH BALLADS*
New York: Doubleday, 1961. (pb)

THE SATIRES OF PERSIUS
Bloomington: Indiana University Press, 1961.

THE LIFE OF LAZARILLO DE TORMES, HIS FORTUNES AND ADVERSITIES
New York: Doubleday, 1962. (pb)
as *LIFE OF LAZARILLO DE TORMES, HIS FORTUNES AND ADVERSITIES*
Magnolia, Mass.: Peter Smith, 1964.

"THE SONG OF ROLAND" (in medieval epics)
New York: Modern Library, 1963.
Toronto: Random House, 1963.

SELECTED TRANSLATIONS 1948-1968
New York: Atheneum, 1968. (pb)

BOOKS BY KARL SHAPIRO

POEMS
Baltimore: Waverly, 1935.

FIVE YOUNG AMERICAN POETS, Second Series (Paul Goodman, Jeanne McGahey, Clark Mills, David Schubert, Karl Shapiro)
New York: New Directions, 1941.

THE PLACE OF LOVE
Melbourne, Australia: Crozier, 1942.

PERSON, PLACE AND THING
New York: Reynal and Hitchcock, 1942.
Toronto: McClelland and Stewart, 1942.
London: Secker & Warburg, 1944.

V-LETTER AND OTHER POEMS
New York: Reynal and Hitchcock, 1944.
Toronto: McClelland and Stewart, 1944.
London: Secker & Warburg, 1945.

ESSAY ON RIME
New York: Reynal and Hitchcock, 1945.
Toronto: McClelland and Stewart, 1945.
New York: Random House, 1945.

TRIAL OF A POET AND OTHER POEMS
New York: Reynal and Hitchcock, 1947.
Toronto: McClelland and Stewart, 1947.

ENGLISH PROSODY AND MODERN POETRY
Baltimore: Johns Hopkins, 1948.
London: Oxford, 1948.

BIBLIOGRAPHY OF MODERN PROSODY
Baltimore: Johns Hopkins, 1948.
London: Oxford, 1948.

POEMS, 1940-1953
New York: Random House, 1953.
Toronto: Random House of Canada, 1953.

BEYOND CRTTICISM
Lincoln: University of Nebraska Press, 1953.
as PRIMER FOR POETS
Lincoln: University of Nebraska Press, 1965. (pb)

POEMS OF A JEW
New York: Random House, 1958.

AMERICAN POETRY (ed)
New York: Crowell, 1960.
New York: Crowell, 1960. (pb)

IN DEFENSE OF IGNORANCE
New York: Random House, 1960.
Toronto: Random House of Canada, 1960.
New York: Vintage, 1965. (pb)

START WITH THE SUN: STUDIES IN COSMIC POETRY (with James E. Miller, Jr. & Bernice Slote)
Lincoln: University of Nebraska Press, 1960. (bds & pb)

PROSE KEYS TO MODERN POETRY (ed)
New York: Harper & Row, 1962. (pb)

THE BOURGEOIS POET
New York: Random House, 1964.

PROSODY HANDBOOK (with R.L. Beum)
New York: Harper & Row, 1965.
London: Harper & Row, 1965.
Ontario: Longmans, Green, 1965.

SELECTED POEMS
New York: Random House, 1968.

TO ABOLISH CHILDREN AND OTHER ESSAYS
Chicago: Quadrangle, 1968.

WHITE-HAIRED LOVER
New York: Random House, 1968.

Notes on the Contributors

R.H.W. DILLARD

The criticism, fiction, and poetry of R.H.W. Dillard have appeared in numerous journals and anthologies. He is the co-editor with Louis D. Rubin, Jr., of *The Experience of America* (1969), a book of readings in American cultural and social history. And he is the author of *The Day I Stopped Dreaming About Barbara Steele and Other Poems.* He received the American Academy of Poets prize in 1961. Mr. Dillard was a member of the William Faulkner Foundation Novel Award Committee from 1963 to 1966. He is a governor of the Count Dracula Society and co-author of the screenplay *Frankenstein Meets the Space Monster.* Dillard is married, and he is presently teaching at Hollins College where he is an associate professor of English.

GEORGE GARRETT

George Garrett's literary works are various. Editor and critic, he has also written three novels, four collections of poems, four collections of short stories, two plays, and a number of screenplays. His titles include *Do, Lord, Remember Me; For a Bitter Season;* and *Cold Ground Was My Bed Last Night.* Born in 1929, he has taught at Princeton, Wesleyan, Virginia, Rice, and Hollins. He is the poetry editor of the *Transatlantic Review* (London) and is co-editor of the *Hollins Critic.* Married and the father of three children, he makes his home near Roanoke, Virginia.

DANIEL HOFFMAN

Professor of English at the University of Pennsylvania, Daniel Hoffman has taught at Columbia, Rutgers, Temple, Dijon, and Swarthmore. Born in 1923, he received his A.B. from Columbia College and his A.M. and Ph.D. from Columbia University. He has achieved distinction for his poetry and for his scholarly and critical books. He has also edited a number of anthologies. Mr. Hoffman is the author of *Form and Fable in American Fiction* (1961), *Barbarous Knowledge: Myth in the Poetry of Yeats, Graves, and Muir* (1967), and *The City of Satisfactions* (poems, 1963). His new collection of poetry is *Broken Laws* (1970). Professor Hoffman is married and the father of two children.

BENEDICT KIELY

Born in Northern Ireland in 1919 and educated at University College, Dublin, Benedict Kiely is a novelist, historian, and critic. He is the author of eight novels (the most recent of which are *The Captain with the Whiskers* and *Dogs Enjoy the Morning*), a collection of stories (*Journey to the Seven Streams*), a volume of Irish history (*Counties of Contention*), a life of the Irish writer Carleton (*Poor Scholar*), and a critical study (*Modern Irish Fiction*). His stories appear regularly in the *New Yorker.* He is married and the father of two sons and two daughters.

JOHN REES MOORE

Born in 1918, John Rees Moore received his B.A. from Reed College, his M.A. and Ph.D. from Columbia University. With Louis D. Rubin, Jr., he is the co-editor of *The Idea of an anthologies and in such journals as the Massachusetts Review, Southern Review, Sewanee Review,* and *Kenyon Review.* Mr. Moore is perhaps best known for his writings on Beckett and Yeats; his study of the plays of Yeats, *Masks of Love and Death,* is forthcoming. He is married and the father of two children. Moore is currently a professor at Hollins College.

JULIA RANDALL

Julia Randall was born in Baltimore, Maryland. She received her A.B. from Bennington College and her M.A. from Johns Hopkins University. She taught at Towson College from 1958 to 1962. Miss Randall received the *Sewanee Review* fellowship in poetry in 1958, a National Foundation of Arts and Humanities grant in 1966-1967, and an American Academy of Arts and Letters grant in 1968-1969. Her publications include *The Solstice Tree* (1952), *Mimic August* (1960), *The Puritan Carpenter* (1965), and *Adam's Dream* (1969). She has published poems in various literary magazines and journals. She is an associate professor at Hollins College.

LOUIS D. RUBIN, JR.

Louis D. Rubin, Jr., to whom this book is gratefully dedicated, is at once one of the most prolific and influential men of letters in America today. Novelist, critic, editor, and teacher, he somehow finds time for fishing, golf, and harmonica-playing; and he is a noted railroad buff. Born in 1923. he received degrees from the College of Charleston and Johns Hopkins University. He has taught at Hopkins and Hollins, and he has been professor of English at the University of North Carolina since 1967. In the summer of 1969 he was visiting professor at Harvard University. Mr. Rubin is the author of a number of books—among them are *The Curious Death of the Novel* and *The Teller in the Tale.* He has edited many volumes, of which the most recent are *The Experience of America,* a bibliography of southern literary criticism, and a collection of Beatrice Ravenel's poetry. His critical biography of George Washington Cable has just been published by Pegasus, and he is presently writing a novel—and editing the *Southern Literary Journal* which he founded in 1968 with C. Hugh Holman. Professor Rubin is married and the father of two sons.

ROBERT SCHOLES

Born in 1929, Robert Scholes received his A.B. from Yale, his M.A. and Ph.D. from Cornell. He has taught at the University of Virginia and the University of Iowa. His books include *The Cornell Joyce Collection: A Catalogue; The Workshop of Daedalus; The Nature of Narrative; The Fabulators; Elements of Fiction* (1968); and *Elements of Poetry* (1969). Mr. Scholes has edited or co-edited *Approaches to the Novel, Learners and Discerners,* and the Viking Critical Edition of *Dubliners* (1969); and he has contributed articles and reviews to learned journals and literary quarterlies. His reviews have appeared in the *New York Times Book Review* and the *Saturday Review.* Married, with two children, Professor Scholes teaches at Brown University.

WILLIAM JAY SMITH

William Jay Smith was born in 1918 in Winnfield, Louisiana, and was educated at Washington University (St. Louis), Columbia University, and at Oxford as a Rhodes Scholar. He has served as editorial consultant to Grove Press; and he was a member of the Vermont House of Representatives as a Democrat from 1960 to 1962. Mr. Smith is the editor of a book of translations, *Poems from France* (1967), and he is the author of *Poems, Celebration at Dark, Poems 1947-1957, The Tin Can and Other Poems, Mr. Smith and other Nonsense, New and Selected Poems, The Spectra Hoax* and a dozen books of poems for children. A contributor to *The New Yorker,* the *New Republic,* the *Atlantic,* and other magazines. Mr. Smith has for several years been poetry reviewer for *Harper's.* He is married and has two children. Formerly consultant in poetry at the Library of Congress, he now teaches at Hollins.

WALTER SULLIVAN

Walter Sullivan is the distinguished author of two well-received novels, *Sojourn of a Stranger* (1957) and *The Long, Long Love* (1959). Widely published as a critic in the quarterlies and in anthologies, he reviews fiction regularly for the *Sewanee Review.* Mr. Sullivan has been honored by fellowships from the Ford Foundation and the *Sewanee Review.* He is professor of English at Vanderbilt University where he has taught since 1949. Professor Sullivan is married and has three children.